CW01508155

Hole in my _

The true legend of Mickey Jupp:
The rock'n'roll genius who refused
to be a star

By Mike Wade

Well, ain't that the way it goes
Ain't that the way it goes
I got a hole in my pocket
That ain't the way I lose my dough

Hole in my pocket by Mickey Jupp

First published 2015
This Second Edition 2016
South Wing Books

ISBN 9781506088037

Front cover photo by Mike Wade
Back cover photo by Adrian Boot
Author photo by Penny Wade

For Penny

About the author

Mike Wade is also an Old Rock and Roller from Southend. He played drums in a number of local bands, ending up in Wolfe, who recorded an album and singles for Motown, before spending several years as a session drummer and singer. In this guise he appeared on hundreds of tracks - almost all unheard, made many advertising jingles - all long forgotten, and played live at the country's major venues, right up to several appearances at the Albert Hall - although nobody noticed, other than his mum. Music and photography are his passions, (he took the pictures for the sleeve of Mickey's *Living Legend* album), although advertising has been his "real job" since he reluctantly accepted that music was not to be what he did for a living. While he has started writing many books in the past, this is the first full-length one he has actually completed (or at least if you are reading this, it will be).As someone who participated in more or less the same musical era as Mickey - performing in many of the same places around the same time - he has always thought that it would be worthwhile for someone to chronicle the truth, the whole truth and nothing but the truth about the legend of Mickey Jupp. Since first seeing Mickey lead The Orioles at the Cricketers in the sixties he has been an avid fan of the great man, owning every record he ever released and one or two he didn't, so writing this book has been a labour of love; an opportunity to set down in one place the remarkable story of this important musician's extraordinary talent

2

Contents

Introduction

As the reader will find, one of Mickey Jupp's favourite observations when wryly looking back upon his eventful career is, "that's the story of my life".

But while there have been plenty of articles, sleeve notes, fan sites, reviews - even a couple of TV documentaries - down the years, the whole of that story has so far not emerged; not least because Mickey is a private soul, a man who by his own admission can be "difficult and awkward".

To complicate matters further, there are frequently several versions of some of the key episodes in that story. In such circumstances I have sometimes taken a command decision on which one to go with. In other cases I have presented the reader with alternatives from which to choose. On a couple of occasions I've simply gone with the version that's the most fun.

Look, it was a long time ago and nobody can be sure about exactly what happened that far back. So, those caveats apart, here it actually is: the story of Mickey's life - or almost. This is a book about Mickey Jupp's musical career, rather than his entire life. You won't find detailed stories here of his loves or wives or children or homes. Yet some of these aspects of his life had an important bearing upon his musical journey, too: informing what he wrote and why he wrote it, what he did and why he did it.

The more this book developed, the more I realised that it would be impossible to tell the full story of Mickey's musical adventure without examining some of these key inputs to it: his deep love for the Lake District; his in-built distrust of authority; his ambivalent attitude to fame and fortune; the stresses of recording and performing; the music business context in which it all took place; how a creatively fertile mind like his might actually tick.

Yet I was worried that these diversions, interesting and apposite as they might be, could interrupt the flow of the most important element of all: the full and chronological charting of his remarkable career. That's when I hit upon the idea of alternating chapters.

So the chapters shown in **bold** in the Contents section tell the chronological history of Mickey Jupp's story: what happened, and when. The chapters shown in *italics* in the Contents section are intended to aid the reader's understanding of some of Mickey's biggest influences - hopefully giving a better picture of why things happened the way they did.

If you want only to know when he did what, skip the intervening chapters. If you would like the whole story, read them all.

Either way I hope you enjoy the ride.

Mike Wade

Prologue

It's 1959. A teenage Michael Jupp is listening to "popular" music in one of the only two ways most British kids could back then: if not through the swishing veil of interference that permanently hugged transmissions from exotic, commercial, somehow illicit Radio Luxembourg, then round a mate's house listening to his small collection of discs.

Off his friend Peter Byford's scratchy vinyl comes something the like of which Mickey has never heard before.

The distinctive toffee-coloured sound of the Coasters recordings was created through blending their deep, soulful, black voices with the sharp, white, Jewish wit of their songwriter/producers, Jerry Leiber and Mike Stoller.

Poison Ivy, I'm a Hog for you Baby, Charlie Brown, Little Egypt: all catchy tunes with clever lyrics and great, expressive singing, sharply played and produced.

Something went click in the back of the fifteen year-old's mind.

Twenty years later and it's 1979.

Derek Green, UK head of A&M records, is driving his Roller while auditioning some new songs from one of his latest signings. At thirty-five, Mickey Jupp is already a veteran of many record deals, both leading his band Legend and as a solo performer. His is a talent recognised throughout the music business as exceptional, if so far insufficiently commercial. Green is hoping to change that, having recently signed Mickey to a multi-album contract.

The demo of Jupp's song *She Could Have Been An Army* begins to play on the dashboard cassette deck. Green's passenger, another A&M artist, likes what she hears.

Elkie Brooks decides she might want to put the song on her next album, one due to be produced by none other than Jerry Leiber and Mike Stoller, the brains behind the Coasters and architects of Mickey's original musical awakening.

They, in turn, love his song but despite being seminal songwriters themselves, maybe *because* they are, they seem a little jealous of it. Or perhaps it's just that they wouldn't mind a teeny bit of co-credit, in case it's the hit it sounds like it could just be. (This is the oldest trick in the songwriting book; one from which they themselves had suffered when they were struggling to make it back in the fifties).

For whatever reason, Leiber & Stoller decide to "improve" the song by tinkering with the lyrics. This loses Mickey some of his songwriting royalties but creates a number now officially credited to Jupp-Leiber-Stoller. It's a compliment that's surely got to be worth its weight in gold to Mickey, given it was their music that got him started in the first place.

To this day there are still echoes of Leiber and Stoller's craft in what Mickey does, for he, too, has become expert at writing catchy tunes with clever lyrics, to which he brings his own great piano and guitar playing, and to which he can add his extraordinarily expressive singing.

We ripple-dissolve forward another thirty-odd years to 2013.

The soon-to-be seventy-year-old gent sitting on a pub barstool in the village of Boot is reminiscing over a pint. I have just given him Leiber & Stoller's biography to read (unsurprisingly, never have actually met them, he doesn't figure in it).

It may have been an honour for Mickey to share a co-writing credit with his childhood heroes but it didn't exactly turn out to be worth its weight in gold.

Despite featuring on her album *Live and Learn*, and then being released as a single from it, Mickey's song (now re-titled *He Could Have Been An Army*) was not a hit for Elkie Brooks.

Worse still, it was inexplicably left off 1981's *Pearls*, her "best of" follow up: an album that shifted so many millions it was for many years the UK's biggest selling album by a solo female artist.

Such wafer thin decisions bring about massive change in an artist's fate. As Mickey ruefully pointed out to me, they alter the course of the story of one's life.

During his remarkable career, Mickey Jupp inspired many musicians, from local Southend artists, such as Dr Feelgood and The Kursaal Flyers to, some argue, the whole Pub Rock scene. He helped move Paul Weller to start writing and performing. His albums have been produced by some of the business' top names - the likes of Tony Visconti, 10cc, Francis Rossi, Gary Brooker, Nick Lowe and Mike Vernon. He has been signed to a wide range of major labels including Bell, Vertigo, Arista, Chrysalis, A&M and Stiff.

As well as Elkie Brooks, his songs have been covered by artists as diverse as Ricky Nelson, The Judds, Dave Edmunds, Chris Farlowe, The Searchers and many more – selling, quite literally, in millions. Oh, and he was reputedly John Lennon's favourite British rock and roller.

He has to this day a fervently loyal if modest fan base, both in the UK and on the continent; a group of admirers that eagerly snaps up every re-mastered re-issue of his past work (virtually everything has been), plus the occasional private release of more recent material.

Yet despite this, Mickey does not exactly drive a Ferrari. In fact he often doesn't drive anything. Not since his last car failed its MOT.

He walks instead, taking photographs and making paintings, living a happy if Spartan life amidst the beautiful countryside of his beloved Cumbria. Any lack of luxury has neither dented his dignity nor his fundamental drive to keep on creating.

He hasn't stopped writing and recording for more than half a century, assembling a body of work that most musicians would kill for. Yet, there's precious little to show for it in material terms. A few bob from a pub gig every now and then really matters to his standard of living. How can this be? I asked him over a second pint, and also What a ride it must have been, and Is it true that you were deliberately contrary about everything from refusing flying to gigs to blowing out songwriting sessions with Ry Cooder, and Did you really turn down £100k advance from CBS because all you wanted to do was play rock and roll in Southend, and.........

Despite a widespread reputation for prickly reticence when it comes to telling his story, Mickey grinned wryly and told me a little of it. And then a little more.

Someone needs to write this down, I said.

1 Down At The Doctor's

*In which Mickey arrives on the planet, oblivious to the fact there's a
war going on*

Young Mickey   courtesy Chris East

Now come here sonny,
Ain't gonna do you no harm.
Just gonna shoot some rock and roll in your arm

Down At The Doctor's by Mickey Jupp, single B-side

On the 6th of March 1944, Chuck Berry was already leading his own
band in Cleveland, Ohio. In New Orleans, Fats Domino had been
playing piano for a good ten years. In New York, two clever Jewish
lads, Jerry Leiber and Mike Stoller, were fooling around in high
school, yet to meet.

Not only had Wynonna Judd not yet been born, neither had her
mother, Naomi.

That was the day when, across the ocean in Worthing, Sussex,
in the United Kingdom of Great Britain and Northern Ireland, a
remarkable sound was heard for the first time: Mickey Jupp's full
throated yell.

Michael Graham Jupp did right to raise his voice - Sussex
being a busy, noisy place at that time. After all, there was a war
going on.

A hole had been blown through Worthing's pier to prevent it being used as a landing stage in the event of invasion. Barbed wire was spread across the beach, which for good measure was also mined. Canadian soldiers were stationed in several parts of the town. Worthing was used as an embarkation site on D-Day.

In February 1944, just a month before Mickey's birth, the British Army's 4th Armoured Brigade had turned up with 200 tanks, while the US Army Air Force began the construction of a training centre on a nearby 145-acre site.

So impoverished was the region that the people of Timaru in New Zealand, a town considerably smaller in size than Worthing, kindly donated food parcels to the local population.

As we may gather, life wasn't exactly a barrel of laughs.

During those dark warring times, music was one of the few pleasures readily available to the battered and impoverished British public.

Food was rationed, clothes were rationed, but Glenn Miller, Vera Lynn and Gracie Fields were freely available. They formed a backdrop, some would say a backbone, to the nation's dogged resistance; a struggle now looking like it might finally come good. For victory - celebrated at VE day - was only months away. When it arrived, music was the currency many used to celebrate the end of that terrible, bloody conflict. Along with sex, of course. The two went well together.

But any sign of winning was not evident in Britain for many more years, maybe twenty or thirty. In the interim it continued to be a dour, tough, unyielding life in the UK. Food and clothes remained rationed throughout the early years of our young hero's life. Even sweets, heaven forbid.

However, tough as it was, 1944 was to prove an important year for popular music: not so much in what it delivered at the time, more in the arrival of important future exponents of the art born in the UK that very year.

Alongside the baby Mickey Jupp were born the babies Jimmy Page, Roger Daltrey, Ray Davies, Joe Cocker, Jeff Beck, Richard Branson, Arthur Brown, Jim Capaldi, Dave Edmunds, Keith Emerson, Neil Innes, Denny Laine, Alvin Lee and Tim Rice. (Slightly less happily, perhaps, that year also saw the arrival of Gary Glitter and Jonathan King).

To keep its spirits up while waiting for this array of musical talent to grow up and create some cool sounds, our tired, grey nation had taken to celebrating the smallest of triumphs. Many such eagerly absorbed achievements were hangovers from the war and an era of Empire now slipping away. Air shows became surprisingly popular, with hundreds of thousands attending. These were linked with various attempts on world records, proving that even if we didn't have much wealth on show, we still had a bit of competitive grit it in us.

In 1946, the toddling Mickey Jupp and his still younger brother David may well have heard the alien whine of an early jet-engine, as a Gloster Meteor shot over Worthing day after day at 600mph plus. It was busy honing its performance for an attempt on the world air speed record, which it eventually claimed. In those days Britain still gave good tech. Mickey's family had by now returned to Worthing, having temporarily evacuated themselves back to Mrs. Jupp's parents' house at Egremont, in the Lake District, between the birth of the boys and the end of the war. But despite their Southern location the Jupp brothers continued to enjoy pursuing the joys of country life 'up North' at every opportunity, as Mickey recalled in the snug of Brook house, the cosy Cumbrian pub that has become his local:

"When I first came to the Lakes I would have been about a month old, mother bringing me back to Egremont because the war was on. We lived there until brother David was born, and then moved back to Worthing, lock stock and barrel in 1945. We came back up here as kids, from four or five years old, for holidays at Grandma's house in East Road, Egremont: a place with an outside toilet and an allotment at the back. We loved it, especially playing in the field down by the river which, back in those carefree, and Health & Safety-free days, we were allowed to roam unsupervised, chucking stones, playing football…"

While Mickey and a million other baby-boomer kids got their fun kicking a football around, over in America, Chuck, Fats, Jerry, Mike and millions of other youngsters were discovering the joyous hedonism that growing up in the midst of an unprecedented consumer boom facilitated; an era of plenty ironically part-fuelled by the same industrial war engine that had so impoverished Britain.

For the first time in human history this newly liberated younger generation celebrated by making its own exclusive brand of music. In doing so, it crystallised the fresh concept of the teenager. Carefree, solipsistic, moneyed: they were to be the first ever generation that didn't turn into its parents around the age of twenty-five.

These confident youngsters wrote songs not just about sex, usually thinly disguised as love, but also about getting jobs, throwing parties, owning cars and celebrating their freedom to travel across their vast, varied country. And with a staggering seventy five million babies born in the USA in the twenty years after the war ended, their spending power further pumped the American economy.

In Britain, music played an equally valid, if markedly different role. It masked the dull routine of daily life in our washed out world of post-war deprivation. It gave youngsters a glimmer of hope that as well as enjoying listening and dancing to music, they might even make music, too: and in doing so, edge themselves out of the stifling depression of austerity into a brighter, hopeful, more exciting life.

So we, too, started to write songs about love (sex) and having a good time, if not about acquiring cars, (Austin Westminster lacking the blingy lyrical ring of, say, Cadillac), nor travelling the country (Brits firmly rejecting the vulgar jingoism that made one misty eyed upon hearing one's town or city immortalized in song.)

Later on, despite not a single super-finned dream-machine having been sold in the UK, the mighty Cadillac would become a core icon of Americana and thus to poor little us a richly potent symbol of freedom and plenty. Thus it became a useful lyrical component for writers like Mickey, as he explains:

"I love the word Cadillac. It's not just the imagery: it's the sound of the word, too. Chevrolet is good, as well. I even like to work in the odd Oldsmobile if I can."

No mention of Vauxhall or Humber, I note.

Traditional wisdom has it that all these American musical inputs came to the fore in the UK around the mid-sixties, when a band from Liverpool effortlessly processed and re-packaged the output of just about every musical style of the post-war period - rock and roll, folk, soul, even show tunes - to lead the revolution that changed the game good. For everyone, everywhere, forever.

While this argument is not without merit, it perhaps too easily overlooks other important foundation stages – in particular a slightly earlier era when much of the heavy lifting went into forging popular music; backbreaking toil that made the Beatles' subsequent reinterpretations possible.

To a UK teenager in the 1950s, this initially meant skiffle - a slightly edgier brand of folk music presented to our ears through the enthusiastic efforts of young, adventurous trad jazz musicians who sought a more dynamic sound to add to their repertoires, (mostly to the general dismay of the older, less adventurous jazzers who employed them).

In 1957, as the soft, almost country caress of Nancy Whisky and Chas McDevitt's *Freight Train* gave way at the top of the charts to Lonnie Donegan's more frantic, rocking *Cumberland Gap*, several thousand teenagers, including Hank Marvin and John Lennon, urgently started saving for their first guitar.

Mickey Jupp, just entering his teens, was not yet one of them.

Mickey's Musical Heritage

The Paramounts at The Shades

"As a child I wasn't very much interested in music. Didn't want to take piano lessons, never nagged about getting a guitar", remembers Mickey. "I didn't put my head by the radio under the covers to catch Radio Luxemburg or anything – not until I chanced upon *Poison Ivy* by The Coasters. Then lightning struck. That was the turning point of my life. I bought everything I could retrospectively and so discovered Leiber and Stoller. I became interested in the people who were writing songs, back in the late fifties or early sixties, long before I started writing any myself. I would check the writers – 'Oh, this is written by Leiber and Stoller, I'll have that,' I'd think. The day I heard *I'm a Hog for you Baby* was a very important day for me, musically, even though it was a B-side. In those days you played the B-sides. It would have been nineteen fifty-seven or eight. Chris East and me would go round to our friend Peter Byford's, who had a few records, and there was *Poison Ivy*, with *Hog* on the flip side. It remained my top song until I heard *Money* on the Shades juke box in about sixty-three, and then a few years back I heard a song by Jimmy Martin, a long gone so-called King of Bluegrass, called *20/20 Vision*. The first time I heard that, it shot to my number one slot. There's just something about it – the sound, the lyrics, the playing, the harmonies…"

So how did Mickey come across that obscure and ancient number?

"I was staying down in Southend with a mate who got hold of a cassette that a guy called Keith Smith had made, which had Ricky Nelson's version of my song *Do You Know What I Mean* on it - which I had no idea he had done! Further on the tape was *20/20 Vision*, which I loved immediately. Didn't know who it was until years later, when I got broadband and could find out. Be careful, though, there are two versions of it, one has a verse missing..."

It's interesting that such an old piece of music could turn up relatively recently, yet leapfrog to the top of Mickey's chart. Well, that's because, as he once wrote in a famous lyric, *"I stopped buying records back in 1961."* He explained what he meant by that to Jip Golsteijn of Dutch magazine *De Telegraaf* in June 1980, displaying a viewpoint he holds to this day:

"Musically speaking I never learned anything new after that time. What I did learn in this apprentice period was a great respect for the rock and roll classics. Of course, I sing those classics on stage but I wouldn't think of putting one on an album. It's done already. And done perfectly, otherwise it wouldn't have been a classic. Simple as that. I thought all those English musicians covering classics in the sixties was embarrassing. I couldn't even stand The Beatles and The Stones at first because of that. Only later on, when they did their own thing, did I become fascinated. But not as fascinated as I was by Bobby Bland or Arthur Crudup. To this day, if the set requires a slow song, I'd rather sing *St James Infirmary* than *Pilot* or *Barbara,* though the audience begs often for those two songs of mine."

The classics that Mickey was talking about were, in his eyes, 'the real thing', and that mostly meant records that had been made in the late nineteen fifties. That was his musical era sorted for good: carved in stone, set in concrete, non-negotiable.

How an artist, in fact how anyone, gets hooked on a particular genre of music is unfathomable, yet it happens to most of us, often with the same deep power as falling in love, and frequently lasts longer. With Mickey it was always rock'n'roll, with a side order of the blues.

For Eric Clapton it was the other way round, as he explained to Jenny Boyd in her book of interviews, *It's Not Only Rock'n'Roll*:

"I don't know why I chose to play the blues, or rock and roll. I don't know why it settled on me in the middle of the countryside in England, to be a messenger. I've got no idea. I really don't like to analyse it but maybe I've been handed something to lead on, to carry on in this generation. I often feel a strong sense of responsibility towards that, as if it's something not really to do with me. It's like carrying a torch. It's more powerful than I am and I have to be a servant to it."

Mickey Jupp might not choose to conjure up such a grand vision but as we shall see, his dedication to the cause is equally passionate.

But back in the music-deprived UK world of the fifties and early sixties it had been very hard to find his kind of recorded material to listen to and learn from.

In fact, any sort of popular music was pretty hard to find.

This was way before a Google search could deliver you an artist's profile in seconds, a further click revealing their entire catalogue for downloading or streaming. There was no Internet; there were no personal computers;

there were no portable music players and almost no means of home recording, the closest thing being the bulky, fragile reel-to-reel tape recorders mostly owned by a few better-off, for which read middle-aged, hi-fi enthusiasts.

Nor were there many pop records on the "wireless".

In those pre-pirate radio days, the only BBC radio popular music slot was David Jacobs playing the Top Twenty once a week on the Light Programme. Most of the rest of the Beeb's pop output wasn't only sparse, it was ghastly: live cover versions of pop played by 'square' session men, many of whom considered the material drivel: a short-term fad to be tolerated until "proper music" returned. (There is a wonderful rumour doing the rounds that the BBC Northern Dance Orchestra once attempted a live rendition of Hendrix's *Purple Haze*).

As yet there were no Pirate Radio stations to force the BBC's hand, so Auntie remained comfortably complacent.

Only Radio Luxembourg played lots of pop records - but mostly only snippets rather than the whole three minutes, (back then singles were always three minutes at most). Worse still, the records chosen for transmission were selected not on the basis of sales success or musical merit but rather by which record label paid hard cash for the airtime. The resulting programming was a representation of what the older establishment figures running the labels thought young people might like, or at least be persuaded to purchase.

This cynical marketing job-lot was then broadcast through a whistling mush of interference before reaching one's parents' radiogram. Chances were that Mum and Dad wouldn't want you to hear this "jungle beat music" anyway: garish, rude songs, the words of which they could never "hear properly", (which was sometimes perhaps for the best).

To experience the popular music *you* wanted, in the way it had been designed to be heard, you or a mate had to go and buy the actual record, assuming you had the pocket money to afford it, or find a precious jukebox. If you achieved the latter, you had to hope that some enlightened soul had stocked it with a more adventurous selection of tracks than the all-too-popular Ray Coniff Orchestra instrumentals and Rogers and Hammerstein movie soundtracks that were everywhere at the time. A Walk in the Black Forest, anyone?

(Mickey's first ever-record purchase was actually, although I doubt he will thank me for telling you, Pat Boone's *A Wonderful Time Up There*. While it is on the one hand a white bread sanitized gospel song, it is also a twelve bar, which explains a lot. Around the same time, the young Mr Jupp had great affection for *French Heels*, a Debbie Reynolds B-side that featured both some nice doo-wop backing vocals and some rather clever and, for the time slightly risqué, lyrics: *"All day long in my sloppy jeans I just romp like a pup! But at night I put my french heels on and a teenage girl grows up!"*)

But the really good stuff was hard to find, meaning there was considerable peer group kudos in discovering the byways, even more than the highways, of early rock. Unearthing obscure gems was becoming fashionable: no wonder popular music soon became an obsession for so many young people. Their own specific taste quickly became a key part of their soul, often the prime signifier of their chosen identity. Ironically the way to express their "uniqueness" was to locate other similarly "unique" individuals. And so one would make new friends based upon the music badge they chose to flaunt: the records they displayed, tucked under their arm. That was how Mick Jagger and Keith Richards first got together – Chess records being their common denominator.

Many kids spent virtually all their meagre disposable income on records, although even that level of commitment might mean only being able to buy one single every few weeks. In today's money, a single cost £7 back then and an LP a whopping £30.

At those prices, you might imagine that the artists would be rolling in royalties.

The truth is that it was the record companies, publishers and other middlemen who were minting it: the artists were often as badly off as the poor kids who bought the records, getting little in return for the music they provided, bamboozled by managers and cheated by record labels.

Let's take a look at some of Mickey's favourites and see how they fared.

In 1954 Bobby Bland, having already released several unsuccessful records, joined fellow musician Johnny Ace's revue and re-signed to Duke Records. The label handed Bobby a new contract, which Bobby could not read, and helped him sign his name on it. How sweet. The deal gave Bland just half a cent per record sold, instead of the industry standard of two cents.

In 1956 Bland began touring with Junior Parker in a revue called Blues Consolidated, doubling as Parker's valet and driver, a role he also reportedly fulfilled for B.B. King. Defying this menial lifestyle, Bland's records began to sell, racking up no less than twenty-three Top Ten hits on the Billboard R&B charts.

One can only hope he got to re-negotiate his contract at some later point, although he was never the rich man those sales meant he should have been.

Arthur Crudup was an even more severe case. He recorded with RCA in the late 1940s but stopped recording altogether in the 1950s because of battles over royalties - in particular relating to his song *That's Alright Mama,* with which Elvis Presley had one of his early hits, in July 1954. While the label on Elvis' version credits Arthur as composer, Crudup had to fight until the 1960s to get any royalties, at which time he received an estimated $60,000 in back dues. For some reason this relative fortune didn't last him long – one suspects poor advice and a sudden influx of new buddies may have played a part.

By the mid-1960s, Crudup had returned to Virginia, where he lived in relative poverty as a field labourer, occasionally singing while also supplying moonshine to a number of local drinking establishments to eke out a living.

But not all Mickey's musical heroes were downtrodden black blues singers.

Leiber and Stoller, who as the writing and production force behind The Coasters had got Mickey interested in pop music in the first place, were young and white and Jewish and smart. They pulled off the extraordinary trick of writing rhythm and blues songs for black artists - at that time this was still often referred to as "race music" - despite being posh white kids still in their teens. Their all-time rock standards *Kansas City* and *Hound Dog* were first released by black artists - although both became bigger hits later on when they "crossed over" to a white market, the latter with Elvis Presley, (for whom they later wrote *Jailhouse Rock* and *King Creole*). They subsequently composed, or co-composed (see later!), hundreds of hits including *Stand By Me*, *Love Potion No 9*, *Pearl's a Singer* and *On Broadway*, while also penning classic standards for Peggy Lee, such as *I'm a Woman* and *Is That All There Is?*

But it was their production and writing of The Coasters biggest hits, *Charlie Brown, Searchin', Yakety Yak, Little Egypt* and *Poison Ivy,* (they wrote no less than twenty-four Coasters US hits in all) that, as we have seen, first grabbed Mickey's attention. And, oh, the B-sides: such as Mickey's favourite, *I'm a Hog for you Baby*, a song good enough to be anybody else's A-side.

These songs are melodic, beaty and often rather witty: little playlets about contemporary life in America - complete with spoken sections - always excellently played. Leiber and Stoller managed to maintain their high standards despite the fact that the line-up of The Coasters was a movable feast: the four-man vocal group having got through twenty members down the years, (three dying violent deaths, one at the hands of the band's manager).

The Leiber and Stoller influence runs deep in Mickey, as we shall see. Similar dry observational lyrics and acted-out vocal styling can be heard in songs of his like *My Typewriter, Captain Cool* and *Politics*.

One of the other artists whose music has heavily influenced Mickey – not to mention influencing The Beatles and The Rolling Stones and The Kinks - is King of the Twelve Bar, Pioneer Rock'n'Roller and Master of Difficult Behaviour, Chuck Berry.

Born into a middle class family, young Chuck had experienced little grief about to write the blues until incarcerated for three years for armed robbery. He was an early starter, still being in High School at the time.

His musical break came in May 1955 when he packed in his job at the car factory and travelled to Chicago to seek fame and fortune. There he met blues legend Muddy Waters, who suggested he contact local label owner Leonard Chess. At Chess Records, Chuck was prevailed upon to record not the blues material he thought they would be interested in, but a hybrid style incorporating some country music influences.

In *Maybelline,* his first single, Berry "borrowed" the country song *Ida Red*, re-building its rhythms to create what many consider to be the first true rock and roll song. It went on to sell over a million copies, reaching No. 1 in the R&B chart.

In fact, country had always been a big influence on Chuck, who added its greater rhythmic swing and use of melody to the raw beat of the traditional R&B genre. Chuck never minded borrowing: many of his songs shamelessly referenced his own earlier compositions, to the point where today's covers bands frequently forget which one they are in the process of playing. But he proved less forgiving with others who he felt borrowed from him – frequently suing to get his hands on a share of royalties, even with bands as big as the Beatles.

(Mickey, too, has incorporated that country swing and feel into many of his own compositions. He's even dabbled in purer country from time to time, although he feels this has sometimes gone too far, his music perhaps led astray by the greater country music proclivities of his sometime co-writer Chris East).

By the end of the 1950s, Berry was an established star with a string of hits to his name: rock classics such as *Roll over Beethoven, Sweet Little Sixteen, Johnny B Goode, Memphis* and *Rock 'n Roll Music*. In addition to record sales he was enjoying a lucrative touring career. But in January 1962 he stumbled again; once more serving three years in prison, this time for transporting a 14-year-old girl across state lines, an activity generally related to underage sex, prostitution or both.

After his release, perhaps surprisingly, Berry had several further hits - suggesting a more relaxed attitude to immorality with minors than would be found today. These successes included *No Particular Place to Go, You Never Can Tell* and *Nadine*. By the 1970s the hits had mostly dried up and he made his living as a live performer, reliving past glories with local backup bands of variable quality (one of which even briefly included Mickey's long term collaborator, Chris East – no doubt one of the higher quality ones) and minimal rehearsal.

Chuck's insistence on being paid for these gigs in cash, often jacking up the fee via some last-minute blackmail extraction from the promoter, indicated his generally cavalier attitude to the law of contract, something that in 1979 led to his third jail sentence, this time for for tax evasion.

It would be hard to find a more colourful character than Chuck Berry, a persona reflected in his on-stage showmanship and dryly-amusing compositions about teen life. A good example is his classic, *Memphis. Tennessee.*   While not exactly a novelty number, it switches wording at the end, revealing that it's not a song about Chuck's attempts to make contact with a girlfriend, but rather with his six year-old daughter. This is a lyric trick Mickey often employs, too - a song turning out to be about something other than that which it at first appeared to be.

It's easy to see other parallels between Chuck and Mickey. Rock and roll pioneers, writers of witty songs with a twist, often in 12 bar form, haters of rehearsals and set lists. They are both somewhat prickly to deal with and both men who "fought the law" - although to be fair, Mickey's legal misdemeanours were very small beer compared to Chuck's.

But while Mickey isn't always easy to deal with, Chuck is in a different class of obstreperousness. Frank Mead, who these days is a regular member of Bill Wyman's Rhythm Kings, told me of his ex-Rolling Stone boss' view of the man, born of past experience:

"The Rhythm Kings played with Chuck Berry one night in Hilversum. Bill had always told audiences that '90% of musicians are great people, 10% are not, and Chuck Berry is the whole of that 10%!' Then adding, 'but he writes great songs'. Backstage that night Bill offered to introduce me to the great man. Spotting him backstage Bill pointed at him down the corridor and said 'Hi Chuck'. Chuck Berry replied with some venom, 'Don't you point your finger at me, boy' and walked off in a huff!" Mickey may be brusque sometimes but he is rarely rude like that.

But there's one even bigger difference between Chuck and Mickey. Chuck Berry was/is a showman: a performer who, while always primarily motivated by the money, would entertain an audience, employing stagecraft such as his famous 'duck walk'.

Mickey was never in the slightest like this. He sits, he stands, he sings, he plays, he sometimes makes short announcements. That's it, folks.

There's further difference, this time in Mickey's favour.

Chuck Berry was a one-trick pony, albeit a thoroughbred one, writing songs almost exclusively in a single style. Mickey has always done a lot more than that, exhibiting a versatility that may in part be down to another, less obvious musical influence: a man whose songs helped bring balance to Mickey's writing.

For if the wit came from the Coasters and the rock from Chuck Berry, then the emotion - a key component in Mickey's ability to write moving melodies and heartfelt ballads - must come from Don Gibson.

Gibson is usually labeled a country singer because that's the musical genre within which he has received most recognition, but his remarkable songs are too good to be limited by that descriptor. His song *Sweet Dreams* was one of the earliest Mickey was to sing in his first proper band, the Orioles, becoming the number that band chose to record for their one and only demo disc. Much later on, the Mickey Jupp Big Band would play Don Gibson's *Sea of Heartbreak*, too. Over the years, artists as varied as Ray Charles (*I Can't Stop Loving You*), Mark Knopfler (*Just One Time)* and Neil Young (*Oh, Lonesome Me*) figure among the seven hundred plus covers of Don Gibson's songs. Roy Orbison, no mean composer himself, recorded a whole album of them.

The quality of artists and writers like these heroes of Mickey's can never be in doubt, because so many of the great musicians and bands followed and acknowledged them, from Elvis to the Beatles and the Stones. Artists queued up to cover their songs and were happily influenced by their style and sounds. Some slavishly copied them: the Beach Boys' early hits were painfully thin copies of Chuck Berry songs, for example. (Chuck sued, of course.)

Down the years it has become more fashionable for listeners to prefer some of these more modern interpretations over the originals: for example, the Stones versions of R&B standards are considered 'breakthrough' rather than 'derivative'.

Mickey Jupp is not fashionable, though; never has been, never will be.

He pays his respects to the greats by playing their songs on stage, as closely as he can get to the spirit and sound with which they were first created.

He also helps keep that same musical spirit alive by writing new songs in a similar vein to the oldies: be they rock, country, blues or ballads. Not copies, rather originals inspired by and written in homage.

But Mickey has always been loathe to play too much of his own material on stage.

In particular, he appears to dodge the ballades: those songs that may be more revealing of his inner feelings. Is that modesty, a lack of confidence, or is there a more rational reason: one to do with his views of the best ways of getting through to an audience?

In the era that Mickey most admired, recording techniques were still relatively primitive; the instruments artists played being barely amplified on stage. The purpose of any recording was solely to replicate live performance, so that the buyer could enjoy a reminder of it in his or her home, on his or her even more primitive playing equipment.

These technical constraints shaped the sort of music an artist elected to play. The artist made his performance as easy to hear as possible, through strong songs and powerful arrangements. There were few twiddly bits or layers of instrumentation because the live audience would have been unable to make them out at the gig and, had the recording equipment even managed to capture them, the machine on which the record would eventually be played certainly could not. Rock and Roll is a perfect example of the right type of music for these circumstances: uncomplicated and visceral.

But recording equipment has advanced massively in the past fifty years. It is now capable of capturing any dynamic, from giant tympani to tiny finger cymbal, encouraging artists to go further in the subtlety of what they write and record. This is viable because the equipment on which those recordings are eventually played back in-home is almost as sophisticated as the recording gear – not just top-end hi-fi but even mp3 players, whose compressed signal is partly compensated through the aural intimacy that headphone listening brings. Even today, though, the same magnitude of advance does not hold true on stage.

While stage amplification equipment is far more powerful and offers much greater fidelity than it once did, the venues in which artists play are often the same unsuitable places they always were: dungeons full of sweaty bodies; big high-ceilinged halls where thousands attend; massive stadia that echo and ring.

So even today, the music the artist subtly laid down in the studio may not be as suitable for a live gig as good old rock and roll, a distinction that bands and musicologists are beginning to recognise.

Mickey Jupp has been maintaining this view for over fifty years. Another trait Mickey shares with his heroes is a healthy disregard for whatever peer-group kudos might be conveyed by the nature and brand of the instruments he chooses to play. In fact, Mickey has exhibited a dogged loyalty to some pretty unfashionable gear during his career. This may have something to do with his being principally a piano player. The piano man is frequently forced to accept whatever instrument a venue provides, and so gets used to making do - often making do and mending (pliers come in handy, he tells me).

This no-nonsense attitude seems to have spilled over to his guitar choices, too.

When it comes to choosing their axe, guitarists tend to divide into clear groups, none of which apply to Mickey.

Firstly, there are those who choose their instrument on the basis of how good it *looks*. The fact that for six decades the Fender Stratocaster has been the sexiest looking guitar around is not unconnected to its sales success. Bands like The Shadows and The Beatles coveted one even before they knew what it sounded like, falling in love with the image on an LP sleeve (usually being held by Buddy Holly). Louise Wener of the band Sleeper admits to originally wanting any make of guitar, as long as it was green and looked cool.

Secondly, come those more concerned with how good the guitar *sounds*. Maestro guitarist Mo Witham – much on him later – will happily play Gibson copies rather than Gibsons, if they sound and feel right.

Lately, a third approach has arrived, based upon how *cool* that model and its vintage is perceived to be.

Difficult codes operate in this area: a genuine 1962 Fender is way cooler than a modern one, but if one of those highly regarded original vintage models has ever been re-finished - maybe re-sprayed thirty years ago because it was covered in dings and stains - it immediately loses a substantial part of its value, and cool quotient. Which is a bit odd, given that it doesn't change how the guitar sounds. And surely if you bought a vintage car covered in rust and scratches it would be worth a lot less than a fully restored, repainted one, wouldn't it? Sorry, it's complicated and I'm a drummer.

None of these factors apply, even slightly, to Mickey's choices. In fact it can be hard to work out what does. In the Legend years he played an excellent, if far from trendy, Gretsch Electromatic - until it literally fell apart, (I once unknowingly owned some of the bits). For another long stretch he relied on an obscure Microfrets guitar, which Mo Witham cheerfully declares was "totally unplayable", although Ed Deane reckoned "it had a great dry sound and tone, whatever it was..." (Weirdly, despite the rarity of the Microfrets brand, there are recent publicity shots of Mickey's old Stiff stablemate, Wreckless Eric, with one. It can't be Mickey's old one because that sported a Black and Decker sticker for some reason and now lives in the collection of one of his fans).

As for keyboards, today Mickey uses a venerable Roland MV50 keyboard, despite the fact that it lacks the Wurlitzer and Rhodes electric piano sounds he very much wishes he had access to. When I asked him if he'd ever thought about upgrading this ancient model he replied, "No. But I might now you mention it."

With Mickey, it's always been the music that counted most, then the way it was played, very rarely what it was played on.

From the early days Mickey developed a healthy distrust of overly processed sounds. His deep suspicion of synthesizers and his lifelong dogged resistance to reverberation on vocals was to cause quite a bit of grief down the years - to fellow musicians and producers alike - as we shall see.

But at this point in the narrative, he's yet even to learn to play an instrument.

Better get back to the story, then.

2 School

In which Mickey learns the fundamentals of life: appreciating music and how to play it

Mickey (top) in the Scouts   courtesy John Bobin

Everywhere you go, everywhere you turn, seems to be so much we have to learn, like
Mind the door; keep the country clean
Don't sit too close to the screen
And don't cross the street until the little man is green

School by Mickey Jupp, Juppanese

In 1951, for reasons Mickey can no longer recall, the Jupp family moved to Essex. They were to stay living in various parts of the Southend area for many years, which turned out to be fortuitous for Mickey and for those who love his music.

The young Master Jupp did all his schooling in the area. He was also a cub and a scout, (well with his father Stanley a scout master and his mother Elsie a cub mistress he had little choice).

"I wouldn't say it was a close-knit or emotionally bonded family. I never really got on with my father – he was strict in so many ways, which I think he got from his own father. My brother always got on with my father, so I heard a lot about my grandfather - Dad's father - through my brother. I can only remember seeing him one particular time: a shock of silver hair, smoking like a chimney. Whereas Mum's father was the typical roly-poly, happy-go-lucky granddad."

Friend John Denton remembers the fact that Stanley Jupp – very evidently the source of Mickey's red hair - remained stubbornly unimpressed by Mickey's obvious talents, right through his life. So the early days were never going to be easy.

Long-term Jupp fan and supporter, musician and writer, Will Birch was in the same 3rd Thorpe Bay scout troop, (pictured above) as Mickey. Jupp brother David was his patrol leader. According to an article Will wrote for *Mojo* magazine much later, "the highlight of Scouts, post wide game and British Bulldog, was when Dave Jupp took the lid off the piano to perform his impressive Elvis medley."

Home was a rather less relaxed environment for David and older brother Michael. Having been a naval officer, now working for the local Health Authority, their father was keen on keeping everything ship shape and in its place, including his two sons.

A school friend remembers Mr. Jupp as someone who talked at you rather than to you; and that following his issuing of instructions, the recipient - be it Mickey, his friends or Mrs. Jupp - was expected to carry them out to the letter.

Consequently Mickey's mates didn't pay too many social calls to the Jupp household at 27 Caulfield Road, Shoeburyness, Essex.

As is often the case between siblings, Mickey and brother David didn't always see eye to eye, either. But David's better relationship with his father – Mickey was always closer to his mum – didn't stop the younger Jupp boy being ejected from the family home for good around the age of sixteen. Later on, Mickey himself was to do a flit from the Southend area rather than face the wrath of the family over certain misdemeanours that we shall come to.

However, it wasn't all doom and gloom: there were family treats, too, and the highlight of the year for the brothers Jupp, even as they grew older, was the annual holiday in the Lake District.

Back they went each year, with military precision, to Egremont, a slightly scruffy mining town where Elsie Jupp had grown up. (Interestingly, the mother of another legendary rock and roller came from nearby: Bill Haley's mum, Maude, was born in nearby Ulverston).

During these treasured visits, Mickey developed a deep attachment to this part of the world - one that was to shape his music, indeed his whole life, thereafter.

But while he might have fallen for the Lakes, young Mickey was by no means as obsessed with music, although he did listen to it:

"Dad worked on the clerical side for Southend Health Department - for some reason he'd pick up old radios and stuff like that sometimes. One day he came home with some ancient earphones, which we wired up with one of the old radios. Another time he came home with a bureau into which he fitted a turntable and some remote speakers so we could hear records in other rooms, too. He was a bit of a handyman, I'll give him that – I suspect he picked it up in the Navy. He was also an ace gardener. He was very meticulous about, well, pretty much everything. I would say I've got that from him – can't help it."

Mickey's other great childhood joy was the railway, kicking off a lifelong love affair with real trains as a means of transport and model ones as an absorbing hobby. There was something in particular he liked about them: trains were orderly. They ran where they were supposed to run, on rails, not careering all over the place like cars. Or people.

A model railway was precise, although it could always be taken apart and reassembled in a different configuration; any way that you, the master, decided. Mickey was lucky enough to have a fairly big Tri-ang train set that he could put up in a spare room on a semi-permanent basis.

As for full sized trains, well they ran to a published timetable, at least in theory. You could choose which one to catch, knowing exactly when you should arrive and exactly where you would be stopping along the way. You knew what to expect.

You chose the route and the time, thereby fully controlling what was going to happen. You were the boss.

Mickey seemed to like that.

With little opportunity to be the boss at home, he attempted to rebel a bit at school: the usual secret smoking and losing pocket money in clandestine games of cards. Like most kids he got into trouble for this, and like most kids he got taken advantage of by bigger children happy to relieve a callow junior of a few shillings and blank him afterwards. In response, most victims would either get angry or return to the protection of their own little clique. Mickey's reaction was different: he seemed to withdraw.

"He got a certain light in his eyes," remembers school friend, later music collaborator, Chris East, "and you knew he'd gone off somewhere inside his head, a place of his own where nobody else could reach him." Mickey's father noticed this, too, once telling a friend that from the age of eleven or twelve Mickey would often momentarily lapse into an almost comatose state, before suddenly snapping out of it seconds later.

This behaviour underlined an aspect of Mickey's character that was already in place: he was, relatively speaking, a loner - a soul less demanding of company than many.

Chris East put it rather well, "Even standing in the middle of a queue, somehow Mickey remained alone," he mused.

Such feelings of isolation turn out to be surprisingly common amongst successful musicians. In *It's Not Only Rock and Roll*, Jenny Boyd, sometime wife of Mick Fleetwood and sister-in-law to both George Harrison and Eric Clapton, talked to many famous musicians about this 'affliction'. Here's what the Eagles' Don Henley had to say:

"The older I got, the more different I felt from the other kids. I felt that I didn't really belong in the town where I'd grown up, that the other kids were very different from me. The older I got the more I realized it was alright to be different, that it was, in fact, a good thing."

Singer and radical, Sinead O'Connor, expands that thought when she says:

"I still feel different. I got into trouble all my life for saying things that I thought, expressing myself...I wasn't trying to cause trouble. I'm not aggressive at all, but I'm very emotional."

Michael McDonald, a successful solo artist and former member of both the Doobie Brothers and Steely Dan, has a theory of why this might be:

"I think a lot of creative people are emotionally handicapped in some ways. Therefore the creative process is a thing that developed because of those deficiencies, as a way of dealing with the world around them. That kind of forces them to be observers because people who feel that a lot tend to observe other people."

Now Mickey was about to experience another element of isolation.

Passing the eleven plus exam ensured he would not go to school round the corner, at the secondary modern, but some way away at the grammar school:

"It wasn't that I lost all my mates, because I didn't really have any. But the grammar school was all boys - if I'd gone to the secondary modern, which was mixed, I might not have found getting along with girls as awkward as I did.

In fact I have ever since. I've lacked confidence with them from that day until, well, yesterday," he jokes, sort of.

For now, Mickey had to patiently put up with his social gaucheness. Soon there would be chances to spread his wings a little more: an opportunity by the name of college.

Further education in art is a well-trodden musician's strategy for escaping the outside world, instead retreating inside one's head. It was adopted by artists as varied as Joni Mitchell and Ron Wood, John Cale and Brian Eno, Pete Townshend and Michael Stipe, Eric Clapton and Charlie Watts, even Lady Gaga.

Mickey was good at art and soon got stuck into it. Schoolmate and later band mate Chris East followed him to Southend College of Art, when they were both aged sixteen:

"After two years at school you could do woodwork and metalwork, or art or music. I took art – that was the only thing I felt half way good at," he remembers.

However, Mickey wasn't to complete his college course – most musicians don't - dropping out early. But for Mickey this was not so he could form a band, as The Clash and The Stones did. Rather more mundanely, Mickey left in order to work in a paint and wallpaper shop, owned by a Southend neighbour.

Already Mickey was failing to adhere to the standard musician stereotype, something that was to become clearer and clearer later in life.

Art school was supposed to be what dropouts did, not what they dropped out from, but Mickey's an original. He knew better than to do it by the book.

Anyway, the finer points of educational opportunity are not the concern of this book. The music's the point, or at least it soon will be. But it hadn't yet seemed the point to Mickey, who in his schoolboy years had favoured football over music, both as a pastime and possible route out of the humdrum.

The only clues as to what might actually transpire were the piano lessons Mickey's parents had inflicted upon him as a child. The dreaded piano lessons were a prominent feature of mildly aspirant fifties Britain, where 'culture' remained symbolic of a middle class that few families actually belonged to but many had enthusiastically put their names down for.

Had every unwilling teenager kept at it - instead of ducking out of music lessons at the first available opportunity - there might have been more great music for the rest of us to listen to a few years later. As it was, most of us wriggled out of this tiresome obligation as early as possible – before spending the rest of our lives regretting it.

But as he was to do for all his life, contrarian Mickey bucked the trend: he kept on with the lessons – on and off, anyway:

"I was forced to take piano lessons, like you are. At eight or nine years old I'd walk round to the old lady piano teacher a few streets away. After the first few lessons I was already getting fed up with it. I used to walk back home through a little park and one day I found my mates playing football there. It looked a lot more fun, so my music bag became a goalpost and I joined in. For a while, that was the end of the music lessons."

A few years later, when he was just into his teens, the Jupp family moved to 23, Cleveland Road, Thorpe Bay and Mickey recommenced his musical education.

This time the teacher was a younger woman of about thirty who lived in the next street. And this time he lasted a bit longer, even getting to take a couple of grade exams.

But, as before, he hated the formality of it and the limited type of music it was acceptable to practise, so eventually he packed it in again. But enough had stuck.

By the age of fourteen, a vision of the keyboard was imprinted in his mind; he could find the notes, work out some harmonies. It was a foundation for what was to come. But that musical foundation needed one more stone to be laid before it was firm, and contemporary: the guitar, of course.

Mickey came perilously late to the instrument, and but for a bad cold, might have missed it altogether:

"I had a few days off school sick – not really bad but in bed: bored and sitting up but not allowed out. My mum had bought my Dad a guitar some time before. It was a pretty awful Spanish guitar and, worse still, it had steel strings instead of nylon ones. I asked her to bring it up to me, and the chord book she'd got him.

I'd no idea if it was in tune, but I looked at the way the dots were arranged on the chord chart, the ones that tell you where your fingers have to go, put my fingers to what it said for A and strummed. It worked! I can remember strumming that A to this day. Though I soon learned to play A differently to everyone else, 'cos I found an easier way that let me change chords quicker."

Soon the household was ringing to the sounds of the Jupp Brothers singing the Everly Brothers. Mickey had rapidly fathomed how to play the guitar, just as he'd picked up how to play the piano. However, even today, Mickey will tell you that he "can't really play the piano, or the guitar for that matter."

Oh, to not be able to play instruments like that!

Many years later, in *Long Distance Romancer*, a TV documentary principally about him, Mickey spelled out this remarkable assertion:

"I've found over the years that, apart from being able to go boom chagga, boom chagga (guitar sound), I'm useless. I'm a dead loss on the guitar."

In the same documentary, Dr Feelgood guitar hero Wilko Johnson begs to differ:

"You can't be that good and not know it. I tell you what, he's really good. He's got feel, he's a great guitar player," adding "and he's one of the absolute best singers I've ever heard."

Wilko was even more enthusiastic whe I asked him about Mr. Jupp's playing:

"WHAT a guitar player Juppy is. I've seen him on stage and I've seen him playing upstairs at Chris Steven's Music Centre in his break. Jesus Christ, he's good; I mean good like John Lee Hooker. The feeling he has is amazing – he's completely imbued with it. It's very rare to find a guitarist with that much feeling. I know he says he's no good at it but he's wrong – I'll have to rebuke him for that!"

Ed Deane, another terrific guitarist who was to play and record with Mickey in his later career, feels the same:

"I love Mickey's guitar playing. It was rock'n'roll, as it should be played; Chuck Berry as it should be played. He was always very self-deprecating about his guitar playing but it was just right for what he was doing. I don't think he was thinking about going into jazz fusion!"

Frank Mead, another future collaborator, agrees, stating, "Mickey is a very, very, very good rhythm guitarist."

Perhaps what Mickey was driving at is that he isn't able to play figures or tunes on piano or guitar. To him the instruments are there to drive the music forwards, not embellish it or make it prettier:

"I think I'm a fair rhythm guitarist – I know what not to play, how to avoid the obvious. As a piano player, I have lots of gusto, but I use it as a rhythm instrument – I can't play an actual tune on it".

However one defines it, the technical ability was arriving, albeit without as yet any outlet for testing it on the public. But the inspiration to find that outlet was about to be set in motion. The catalyst was that Coasters music, pumped with the wit, soul and the exotic sounds of Jerry Leiber and Mike Stoller's magical writing and production; an effortless lightness of touch that allowed them, for example, to get a song about venereal disease all over American radio: good old *Poison Ivy*.

Mickey loved that song - but he loved the B-side, *I'm a Hog For You Baby,* even more:

"There was a group of us - me, Chris East, a guy called Ian and Peter Byford at school. It was a non-musical relationship on the whole but Peter had quite a few records because his family was fairly well off. I'd heard *Shakin' All Over* and *Reet Petite* and stuff by then, and while I enjoyed them they didn't have the effect on me that *I'm a Hog For You Baby* did. I immediately wanted to know everything about it, although I'm still not sure what sort of music you'd call it: it wasn't rock'n'roll and it wasn't really R&B. It's...just... the Coasters."

Mickey wasn't the only one to be drawn into a musical career through the brilliance of Messrs. Leiber and Stoller. *I'm a Hog For You Baby* was simultaneously getting young Londoner Ray Davies interested in pop music for the first time and would go on to feature as one of the Kinks earliest demo recordings.

A few years later, Southend band the Paramounts' recording debut was their take on the A-side of that Coasters' record, *Poison Ivy*. They hadn't wanted to record it - singer Gary Brooker objected for he held the Coasters in as high esteem as Mickey, calling their music "sacred stuff" - but they allowed themselves to be persuaded. Their version's modest success - it got to number 35 in the UK charts - indirectly propelled Mickey's career forwards, as we shall see.

The Paramounts were resident band at the Shades, a sea-front music club just a short walk from where the Jupps lived on the Southend/Thorpe Bay border. Brother David found the Shades first – becoming sufficiently involved to soon be officially signing new membership cards on behalf of the club; Mickey would soon follow.

In the meantime, his initial Coasters fixation had enabled Mickey to accidentally discover the delights of the London American record label, on which their recordings were released in the UK. It was an event that was to usher even more inspiration in his newly found musical soul.

The London imprint had been created in the fifties as a home for UK releases of the best material from various American labels to which British Decca owned the domestic licenses

These were major fifties imprints within the USA like Jamie, Imperial, Chess, Dot, Atlantic, Specialty and Sun, as well as some of the early output of Motown. By the sixties additional licensing deals had been made with Big Top, Parrot, Hi, Monument and even Phil Spector's legendary Philles label.

This treasure trove of resource made London American home to the crème de la crème of pop music: almost anything London released was worth listening to.

Like Mickey, the Beatles would make a pilgrimage to the record store – in their case NEMS in Liverpool; for Mickey it was Hodges & Johnson in Southend – and ask to hear the A-side and, importantly, the B-side of each new London American release. If you had the charm to get away with it, (most of us were told to clear off by cynical sales assistants who had rightly deduced we lacked the funds to make a purchase) this was how you discovered hidden gems. These gave you bragging rights before you passed the info on to others in a suitably superior fashion. More importantly, if you had a band, this was how you developed your own distinctive repertoire - at least until your musical rivals caught on and copied what you were up to.

As a result of its diverse origins, the London American label boasted a bewildering array of codes and serial numbers, such as HLU, HLW, HLX, HLK and a stack more. If studied and correctly referenced, these hieroglyphics unlocked the key to which US label was the original source. Further information tucked away on the labels provided you with the names of great songwriters to store away for future reference: Leiber & Stoller, Goffin & King, Barry & Greenwich.

The super-orderly side of Mickey's brain, the one so attracted to the logic of railways and their timetables, soon had the codes cracked and the data filed away. So frequent a visitor was he to their shop, after a while Hodges & Johnson were happy to let him riffle through new stock as it arrived. This was heaven. Mickey was bonding with an era of music he was never to leave behind.

Musically speaking, he dwells in that time to this day, as we can see from Mickey's all-time top ten - one he nominated for me in 2014. (I have added the recording or first release date to make the point about their vintage):

1. *20/20 vision*   Jimmy Martin
November 1954
2. *Money*   Barrett
Strong   August 1959
3. *I'm a Hog for You*   The Coasters
August 1959
4. *Some Other Guy*   Richie Barrett
April 1962
5. *If You Gotta Make a Fool of Somebody*   James Ray
November 1961
6. *Land of 1,000 Dances*   Chris Kenner
October 1962
7. *To Know Him is to Love Him*   The Teddy
Bears   August 1958
8. *Here Comes the Judge*   Pigmeat
Markham   July 1968
9. *Monster Mash*   Bobby Boris
Pickett   January 1962
10. *King Bee*   Slim Harpo
March 1957

Honourable mention: -
I Keep Forgetting   Chuck Jackson
July 1962

He notes "No Chuck, no Elvis!!!! 1, 2 and 3 are absolutely steadfast."

All male artists, one might note, though Mickey enjoys a good female voice as well, if it's sufficiently soulful. He recently set out his favourites in a post:

38

"Just been listening to some stuff on Spotify and I feel somehow prompted to name my all-time favourite lady singers - and so at number 4: Maria Muldaur, number 3: Tina Turner, number 2: Ann Peebles - and at an undisputed number 1: Margie Hendricks."

Margie Hendricks may seem a surprise choice to make the top of Mickey's female vocalist tree. A search of the web shows that she didn't actually get to record that much material. But you only have to listen to a fragment of what she did in order to see why Mickey rates her so highly.

That voice is in many ways a female version of his: the rare and impeccable delivery that can only come from skillful, soulful, scorched, storytelling kind of a singer.

Fame And Fortune

The Jupp Brothers imagine their futures courtesy Mickey Jupp

It's natural for the man on the Clapham omnibus - these days perhaps more likely to be the man in the Honda Civic - to imagine that a career in music or TV or film, is equivalent to not having to have a job at all. More like, as Mark Knopfler once wrote, *"Money for nothing and the chicks are free"*.

Compared to tarring the roads this is probably true. But compared to most people's actual jobs, it isn't. For music is at best just another job and at worst only half a job.

Anyone who's been in a band will tell you - at length if you let them - about the terrible privations that attend the business of plugging in a guitar and knocking out a few songs on stage.

There are sleepless nights in scuzzy nylon-sheeted B&Bs, perilous drives through fog and snow, vans that break down and have to be pushed, roadies who break down and have to be sacked, manky motorway pies at midnight, empty fag packets and beer cans at dawn, endless waits while technicians get the sound right (studio) or the light right (video), band members who plot against one another, girlfriends who resent certain band members, girlfriends who resent other band members' girlfriends, producers who have their own agenda, booking agents who can't put an agenda together, managers with only idiotic ideas and - at the heart of it all - writers and band leaders who run out of any ideas at the crucial moment.

For reference, you will find most of this in the film *Spinal Tap*: a fictional "rockumentary" so unerringly accurate that many a viewer has mistaken it for fact. All bands are mandated to watch *Spinal Tap* on their tour bus, (when their fame has been of sufficient magnitude to allow them to afford one, that is.)

In fairness, being in a band is also brilliant fun. In a band you are the four musketeers, or the five (or in one case with Mickey, the ten). It's you lot against the world: a sort of morally justifiable gang mentality that is largely non-violent, at least towards the outside world. You inhabit your very own cool clique, even if to start with you you don't have enough cash to afford food.

So what. If it works out like you feel sure it could, by this time next year you'll all be millionaires, Rodney.

If it doesn't, you'll have your memories, maybe a few records to prompt them and a whole bunch of stories with which to bore your friends, partners, offspring and their offspring: "Yes, it's true – Grandpa's band really did open for King Crimson at the Rainbow...." (in my case, The Crazy World of Arthur Brown at the Cricketers Inn).

Of course, your band might be rubbish. Some would-be players may turn out to be tone deaf or insufficiently coordinated to do different things with each hand at the same time, (for drummers read each hand and each foot). However, as with an actor possessing an unconquerable stammer, the system tends to weed them out fairly early on.

But what if your little band of brothers contains one or two, shall we say, marginal players? This might be called the Pete Best Syndrome, and here things become more difficult.

Very few bands have the good fortune to be made up of classmates, neighbours or siblings who all happen to be brilliant musicians. It is a source of constant amazement to me that all of U2 came from the same class at school. Or that John and Paul and George all bumped into each other as kids in the same small part of Liverpool. Or, that the Bee Gees were real brothers who were all truly talented, including another brother who never even got in the band.

In the main, though, bands are fragile and unstable: they form, break, merge and absorb like amoebae. Pete Frame has prepared several excellent books of *Rock Family Trees*, (there's even a specific Southend tree in existence), that plot this ebb and flow, laying out in devilishly complex interlocking diagrams the constantly evolving dynamic of a set of inter-related bands.

As a rule, young men form bands in the first place because they like music, for something to do with their mates, to impress girls by standing out from the pack and to impress their peers through their musical ability (and their new found ability to impress girls). Not many do it to build a long-term career or through an absolute belief that music will one day make them rich. They may hope it might turn out to be a nice little earner for a while but it would be delusional to bank on it. That isn't how it works. Remember the Beatles gave themselves two years.

Leaving aside the photoshop model-looking, manufactured, one-hit wonders of today's TV "talent" shows (which didn't exist in the era this book covers – talent shows then were on Kid's TV - I should know: my brother Andy's band were once on *Stubby's Silver Star Show*), one simple rule has always applied to making a success in popular music: by and large, if you aren't any good musically then you won't succeed. That seems fair.

Perversely, though, if you are good, even very good, that's no guarantee of success whatsoever.

Ever heard of James Royal? Duffy Power? Steve Ellis? Sharon Tandy?

42

They are just four out of hundreds of brilliant singers, (and they weren't bad lookers, either), who got several chances to succeed in the sixties and seventies but mysteriously never broke through into the big time.

Being bloody good is only base camp for a career in music.

Beyond lies a tangled forest, one populated by a thousand snakes yet boasting only a handful of ladders. That forest isn't called Music; it's called The Music Business. Big difference.

And to make things even more daunting, this is a world where nothing is quite what it appears to be. Here you can even go - as Mickey celebrates in an unreleased song of his - *Up Snakes, Down Ladders*.

Bill Bruford, ex-member of Yes, Genesis and King Crimson, confounds normal expectations of a drummer's intellect when he notes:

"The relationship between talent and popular success is oblique, at best. Popular success is evidence of little more than the talent to be successful. If I have talent will I be successful? I have gold and platinum albums on my walls. Am I talented?" (Rather irritatingly, Bruford was both).

So to recap: to be successful you need lots of talent but you will need lots more:

well-meaning and well-funded, (and ideally not totally dishonest) management; oodles of luck and, most important of all, a totally, endlessly, ruthlessly selfish ego-driven attitude. Roger Waters of Pink Floyd maintains that to be successful, an artist has to have "holes in his ego" so large that he is constantly forced to succeed in order to fill them.

Our would-be star also needs to avoid falling out too early on with band members, management, promoters, record label and roadies, (something Roger Waters, by his own admission, turned out to be not much good at.)

This falling out opportunity grows exponentially as artists become more successful and more confident while simultaneously growing increasingly irritated by the faces, personal habits and musical foibles of fellow musicians and management with whom they are trapped like conjoined siblings, 24/7.

These tensions means that friction can arise through almost anything, from girlfriends who want to get involved with the band (cf The Beatles), to who is going to write the next single (cf The Beatles), to who's going to sing lead on it (cf The Beatles), to who has to sit on the hot, uncomfortable Transit engine cover, without a seatbelt, AGAIN (probably not The Beatles).

Though, in fact in 1961, the year before they struck gold, such rumblings even caused the Beatles nearly to break up several times. And that was long before Yoko turned up.

All this angst and churn is going on continuously, if unseen, in the would-be rock star's personal and musical lives (usually the same thing), rather like the frantic whirling of a swan's legs just below the waterline. For public consumption it may pay an artist to promote a vision of harmony, to cultivate an attitude of uncompromising artistic fortitude. How often does one hear, 'it's all about the music, man. The music comes before anything'. But the truth is it doesn't, not if it's success you're after.

In the real world, if a band has achieved much at all by way of success, their path will most likely have been paved with compromise.

Remember Pete Townshend smashing guitars night after night, as an outlet for his musical frustrations and anger with his band mates? Well, that might have been the reason the first time, but after that it was a gimmick, a way of creating a tough image and exciting an audience. I had been watching the Who since before they started this caper, (when they were still called the High Numbers), and let me assure you they had more than enough talent not to need cheap theatricals, were success based solely on talent. But it isn't.

The Who's shrewd, manipulative management saw the PR potential of the auto-destruction trick and so instructed the band to keep doing it, despite the appalling costs involved. Costs, I recall, that they attempted to mitigate in several interesting ways.

One method consisted of their roadies scuttling around the stage after each gig attempting to locate all the shards of broken Rickenbacker lying around, so that they could painstakingly reconstruct Townshend's guitar for the next night – Pete always being handed the special kamikaze guitar just before the number at the end of the gig at which he was scheduled to destroy it.

Another ploy was the introduction of one particular Marshall speaker cabinet within Townshend's array that bore a Union Jack motif in place of the standard speaker grille. This alerted Pete to the fact that there were no innards behind that flag, so his guitar could penetrate it without the boy wonder wrecking the amp while simultaneously electrocuting himself.

Now Pete Townshend is a very fine musician and a highly intelligent fellow who has gone on record about never having liked participating in this pantomime. But after their false start as the High Numbers, the Who had learned the importance of playing the game - and the great thing about playing the game is that once you have done it long enough to get established, you can stop.

Now you really can go on to make that half a million quid triple album about the planet Zog you'd always dreamed of recording, (or an opera about a deaf, dumb and blind kid).

It's plain to see that the business is full of great artists whose success has been based on making a compromise or ten in the early days:

Did Gordon Sumner want to dye his hair blonde? Did he want to be called Sting?

Did the Beatles fancy ditching their leathers for matching suits and haircuts when Brian Epstein told them to?

Did Ray Davies and the rest of the Kinks love dressing up in hunting gear to play debutantes' balls?

Did ABBA really want to don outfits that made them look like Smurfs from outer space?

Did Gilbert O'Sullivan yearn to adopt a daft name while wearing short trousers and a flat cap on national TV?

Did Mike Batt relish only getting a chance to present his music from inside a Womble suit?

No. But you have to do it, and you have to expect the journalists, other artists and elements of the business itself to batter you while you do it. And then when it's over and you are a star, you can do as you wish.

Frequently this starts by firing, and possibly sueing, the dumb managers who got you your stardom in the first place, (cf Elton John, Gilbert O'Sullivan, Tom Jones, Frankie Goes to Hollywood, etc).

Looking back on his own experiences, Jimi Hendrix's bass player, Noel Redding, had a chillingly succinct piece of advice for those embarking on a rock music career: "Study law. Buy a gun."

But Mickey would never play that game. He wasn't looking to be a star. He wasn't out to fill stadia, packed with thousands chanting his name. He didn't crave such attention, so why put himself through all that pain? Mo Witham, who has been close to him from the beginning right up to today, spells it out:

"Mick hates the business - the way everything works - but the business is the business, it's what you have to do to get on. He doesn't care, he won't ever play ball."

In fact, it goes deeper: Mickey dislikes and deeply distrusts not just the music business system: he hates *any* system, any sort of affiliation or officialdom.

Asked by Chris East why he didn't apply for grants for which he qualified in setting up his gallery in Boot in later life, Mickey said he couldn't be bothered with petty administrative detail. He wasn't looking for any handouts, thank you - even though he could have done with the funds he was legally entitled to claim. He hates the idea of unions, too – although had no choice but eventually join one in order to appear on the BBC, who otherwise wouldn't let him in.

Mickey will simply not play by the rules of the Fame Game. In fact, he's never even bothered to learn them – something that can trip him up from time to time, as renowned songwriter and Mickey's one-time co-manager, Keith Reid, smilingly recalled:

"I remember one point when, through the songs we were publishing for him, he was making some quite good money, some of which we'd told him to put away for taxes but he hadn't. He later blamed us bitterly for the state he'd got himself into with the Inland Revenue, saying, 'If I hadn't earned that money I wouldn't be in this mess now!'"

To succeed today, you pretty much have to surrender to the marketing machine.

They will tell you what to wear and who to write with; they will manage your bank account and your Twitter account for you. Cross them and they will drop you like a hot brick.

The business didn't use to be like this in the fifties and early sixties - the era that spawned the music Mickey loves. Back then, you might have been ripped off on the percentage of royalties that made it through to your bank account but you could still make a living on the strength of your live music, not your promotional strategy.

Thus most musicians were able to present themselves as they actually were, leaving the listener to pay his or her money and make his or her choice, based on the music itself.

OK, Chuck Berry had the duck walk, but that was probably naturally acquired out of innate showmanship, rather than mandated by an adviser.

Roy Orbison wore those dark glasses, but he did have sensitive eyes.

Johnny Cash came across like a fearsome bear of a man, but then he was one.

Jerry Lee Lewis appeared to live on the very fringe of reason, which he then proved by marrying his twelve-year-old cousin.

They were who they were – it was the music you bought, regardless.

There were far fewer promotional opportunites back then, of course: not much TV and no world wide web. As late as the sixties, it was not uncommon to buy records by people whose faces you had never seen – a fact that proved something of an accidental boon to some black acts in the States - in those days their music would have done less well if it had been generally realised they weren't white.

But there's bound to be an exception that proves the rule.

One man, in particular, went on to re-shape all the rules, as Will Birch wisely reminded me:

"If Elvis Presley had looked like Carl Perkins, where would we be? The musical world would look completely different."

It's true. For while Elvis was a musical breath of fresh air - a white boy singing black music - he would never have become the star he did, nor have exerted such enormous influence over youngsters and would-be musicians across the globe, without those extraordinary good looks and his headline-grabbing hip-thrusting antics. (Sam Phillips claimed his legs shook because he was such a nervous performer – this I doubt).

Carl Perkins wrote, amongst many other splendid songs, *Blue Suede Shoes* - with which Elvis had the greater success. Why? Because, unfortunately for Carl, compared to Elvis he looked a bit like one of those shoes.

No wonder MTV later conquered the world by putting pretty faces - and bottoms - ahead of good music. As the years went by, the rules of the old game inverted. The audio-visual world had become more about the visual than the audio; video really had killed the radio star.

But the early pioneers would never be equaled, let alone surpassed.

Here are the thoughts of Sam Phillips – the man who first signed Elvis, Johnny Cash, Carl Perkins, Jerry Lee Lewis and Roy Orbison - on the subject of the founding fathers of blues and rock and roll:

"We've now learned so much from these people we thought were ignorant. When people come back to this music in a hundred years, they will see these were master painters. They may be illiterate. They can't write a book about it. But they can make a song about it and in three verses you'll hear the greatest damn story you ever heard in your life."

Bravo.

3 Making Friends

In which Mickey joins his first band and discovers musical night life

David & Mickey, growing up   courtesy Chris East

Nero played the fiddle, he played it mighty cool
I wonder if he'll play for me if I burn down the school
Don't give me no homework

Homework **by Mickey Jupp, Oxford**

1962 is here and once more there are green shoots appearing in UK popular music after a couple of truly dire years.

In Southend, Mickey has finally agreed to accompany brother Dave to the Shades coffee bar to see outstanding local R&B band the Paramounts. It proves to be a seminal moment.

Will Birch's sleeve notes for Mickey's recent *Kiss Me Quick, Squeeze Me Slow* Repertoire box set capture the effect that the Paramounts, led by 17 year-olds Gary Brooker and Robin Trower, had on Mickey:

"I remember asking Gary about a song they did – *Money* by Barratt Strong. The Coasters were now five years out of date – chronologically at least – and he told me it was on the jukebox upstairs at Shades. That was my introduction to songs like *Mother-in-Law* and *Ooh Poo Pa Do*."

And there were other influences lurking in the dark bowels of that machine, like the great piano-based singer Fats Domino: still inspirational despite being ten years past his zenith. Such timelags always mattered little to Mickey who, far from moving with the times, has always resisted change at all costs. He spelt this out publicly in the words of one of his best-known songs, *Old Rock and Roller*:

> *I'm an old rock and roller and my time has gone*
> *I stopped buying records back in 1961*
> *(But seeing as I'm here, well the show must go on…)*

But like it or not, the fifties had long passed away, replaced by what Mickey considered an inferior musical era. When it comes to the early, pre-Beatles, sixties, history suggests Mickey's lyric wasn't far wrong.

Musicologist Nigel Jones, author of the fine music blog, *Bucket Full of Nails,* maintains that 1961 was the worst year for youth music since the movement had begun, a view that even a cursory glance at the charts for that year supports.

With the rockers gone soft and the beat boom not yet arrived, the best-seller lists were splattered with dross by the likes of Johnny Tillotson (*Poetry in Mo-shun*), Petula Clark (*Sailor* was no doubt big on *Two-way Family Favourites*), Floyd Cramer (pleasant piano-based elevator music), the Temperance Seven (who really were *Driving us Crazy* - despite being produced by the man who was shortly to unleash the Beatles on an unsuspecting world), Shirley Bassey (dads liked her a lot, mums were less sure – not least about their husbands' motives), the Highwaymen (religious folk, nice), Frankie Vaughan (who dug him up?) and, for Christmas, Danny Williams with *Moon River* (the perfect stocking filler).

That's without mentioning Helen Shapiro, a fourteen-year-old schoolgirl in a swingy skirt who sounded like Paul Robeson. She had two number ones.

Much has been made of the later seventies Punk scene being born out of frustration with the grandiose, unengaging music that preceded it, elaborate confections created by bloated, exhibitionist pomp rock bands. Yet this was less the pioneering rebellion it is so often thought to be. It was more of a re-run of what happened at the start of the sixties, when Britain's youth could stand no more show tunes or BBC Home Service crooners hogging turntable and juke box alike. It was the start of a new decade and there was trouble brewing – big time. Fifties skiffle music had taught much of Britain's youth the rudiments of music making. The late fifties had given a taste of what one might aspire to - real rock and roll. The showbiz establishment and their easy listening drivel weren't grabbing it back off us now. Tell you what, we thought - if you won't do it for us, we'll bloody well do it ourselves.

And so the old boys who ran the record business, fundamentally resistant but realising that this new wave of guitars played by spotty youths might be profitable, decided to play along. But they had a cunning plan. Instead of real rebellion, they would create tame clones of their own – pretty of aspect but mild of musical character - who they could easily control and profit from, by foisting them on the dim record-buying kids out there who knew no better.

They took us for mugs but we weren't having it. After an early hit or two we prepared our answer and voted with our pocket money: no thanks, Mark Wynter; no thanks, Craig Douglas.

Instead, up and down the country, and nowhere more actively than in Essex - particularly on the coast at Southend-on-Sea - young hopefuls were forming groups and taking the future into their own hands, or should that be bands.

Mostly, these combos were copycats of the still revered Shadows, with derivative names like The Phantoms (a Southend instrumental combo that contained two future members of Mickey's musical circle – John Bobin and Bob Clouter) or Romford's The Raiders (with this author on drums).

Unable to afford the delicious Fender Stratocasters of their heroes, fledgling Hank Marvins had to go into battle with cheap European copies, typically the Watkins Rapier and the Hofner Galaxie. While instead of the big boys' Vox amps there were Selmers or, lower down the food chain still, home-assembled amps and shed-built speaker cabinets.

Indeed, the Beatles were still using homemade amps when they auditioned for Decca – one of several reasons they failed to get signed. The Kinks, on the other hand, succeeded *because* of their homemade amps, the cones of which Dave Davies had happily slashed with a razor blade, creating the world's first fuzz power chords on *You Really Got Me*.

Soon, many of the local bands wanted to experiment with a small selection of vocal numbers, sandwiched within their mainstay repertoire of twangy instrumentals. But there was a problem: what to actually sing? And quite often: who would be the singer?

The overwhelming influence of the Beatles, with their Motown and Chuck Berry references, was still a year off; the Stones a further year behind that. In the meantime, who wanted to play *Venus in Blue Jeans* at the Youth Club dance?

The solution wasn't in the jeans but it was blue.

It was the blues.

Provided one could get hold of the records in order to learn the chords and words, that is. To get access to the right kind of inspiration, it helped to live in the right place. With its massive docks, Liverpool had a high quotient of visiting Yanks, many of them black at a time when few UK citizens were. These exotic migrants brought favoured records with them, ensuring that the Beatles and their Merseyside contemporaries were well supplied from the outset.

Southend had a pier - famously reaching out into the Thames for over a mile - but no docks. However, it wasn't far from Tilbury, which was a big London trading port back then. From there, Southend R&B music fans such as Tony Wilkinson also could use merchant seamen as couriers to bring back rare US music with them on their UK visits, sometimes even discs sourced to order.

This sideline grew so rapidly that Tony soon became a full-time record dealer. To most local kids, though, such connections were way beyond their horizons. No matter, Southend had two other trump cards: the Odeon and the Shades.

The Southend Odeon was an immovable fixture in the touring schedule of any decent band of the time: the Beatles, the Rolling Stones, the Hollies, the Kinks, the Dave Clark Five and the Uncle Tom Cobbley Six would soon grace the boards of its substantial stage.

Mickey and his mates had already seen the Shadows there. These admirable musicians, all too easily patronised these days for their clean-cut, show-biz ways, were the first inspiration to bandship for most of us. The Shads played the first Fender Stratocaster in the UK, Hank pairing this piece of American exotica with a British Vox amp and an Italian Binson echo chamber, inventing a sound so evocative that it has never gone out of fashion, (just ask Mark Knopfler). The Shadows' pioneering work got Neil Young going in Canada and the Mutton Birds in New Zealand just as much as the Phantoms in Southend and the Raiders in Romford.

But The Shads wore suits and dicky bows, did a little dance step while they played and were as apparently chaste and religious as Cliff, their boss.

Mmmm. That didn't fit our plan.

The same could not be said of proper rock'n'rollers like Chuck Berry or Jerry Lee Lewis. These were bad boys and that was way cooler. Their music was a lot livelier, too.

After Mickey had seen the Shadows he left the gig informed but unmoved.

When he went back to the Odeon to see Chuck Berry, he left illuminated and infatuated. This was the real deal: the songs, the performance, the attitude. The imprint that this event made on Mickey never faded, as anyone who has ever heard his records or seen him play live will testify.

But Chuck Berry wasn't quite the perfect model, either. For all his stagecraft and songcraft, his voice was a little weedy, his sound could be a tad thin, vocal harmony was largely lacking, the songs often too predictable. As Mickey observed, "He didn't have a great voice, but he did know how best to use it."

On Mickey's next visit to the Odeon, any such shortcomings got put right: he saw a double bill of Bo Diddley and the Everly Brothers.

"Bo Diddley just stood there with his square Gretsch and this enormous noise comes out, an absolutely fabulous sound that knocked you over."

Bo's unique sound revolved around playing chords through an amp set to a primitive tremolo position which, combined with an emphasis on the on first beats of the bar rather than rock's preferred "back beat", created an atmospheric, swirling setting for songs of his own like *Mona* and copies of others', such as Buddy Holly's *Not Fade Away*.

These hypnotic, jungly songs went on to become staples of many of the early UK beat and blues bands alike, mainly because they were infectious crowd-pleasers, but also because they featured very few chords - sometimes as few as just the one. Ideal for the learner guitarist.

(The Rolling Stones were heavily influenced by both Bo and Chuck, recording several of their songs in the early years but Mickey has never been a fan of the British band's music, commenting: "I saw them at the Odeon but I wasn't impressed").

Mickey would go on to pay tribute to Bo's sonic power more profoundly by happily absorbing its style into recordings of several of his own songs, stretching over many years, including fan favourites like *Chevrolet* and *Blues On Their Own*.

As for the Everly Brothers, if you can find a musician who's career commenced between 1957 and 1965 who doesn't cite the Everlies as his premier vocal influence, you have probably found yourself a liar.

The brothers sang like angels; even more extraordinarily they sang like one angel with two voices. Blood harmony is as good as it gets - and Don & Phil were as good as blood harmony gets.

On top of that, they played pretty good guitar. And, unusually, they wrote many of their own hits. Extraordinarily, they even went on to produce their own records, including the awesome *Cathy's Clown*. Back in 1960, when that single launched the Warner Brothers record label, *no* artists produced themselves.

The Everly Brothers are acknowledged as having been the template for the Beatles: John and Paul taking the concept of two harmonising, songwriting, joint lead vocalists and giving it a twist by grafting on a full band.

Hard to believe, but no one had put together such a self-contained unit before – in fact it was such a novelty that after signing them George Martin agonized for weeks over whether they should be called John Lennon & the Beatles or Paul McCartney & the Beatles. Everybody had to be 'Somebody and the Somethings'; it was the rule. No, said the Beatles – we are a single unit: a vocal and instrumental band which write its own songs and we don't want session musicians playing our parts on our records or a named leader, thank you very much. The music business scratched its head in bemusement - but not for long.

Mickey's own harmony singing has always been extraordinary – he is able both to hit pitch just right and to copy his own phrasing perfectly, creating a wedge of vocals that wrap around many of his recorded performances. While much of this ability is down to his innate musical talent, he is quick to nominate another reason: practice.

"Practice and more practice. It takes time to work out the right harmonies and phrasing, particularly as I like to use backing vocals as more than just repetition of key parts of the chorus. And when you're overdubbing home demos it's normally the lead vocal that goes on last – so you have to work out the harmony parts very carefully and then sing them, even double them, before there's any lead vocal to work off."

By late 1962, Mickey's key influences were all in place – he had rock grit, blues attitude and country bounce plus a love of melody and harmony. Another bonus was the fact that, unlike a lot of kids, music making would not face any discouragement at home:

"There was no parental anti-feeling about me making music. In fact later on, in 1964, Dad stood guarantor for the HP on my first proper amp, a Selmer Treble and Bass 50. I wanted something with a bit of oomph for the piano to go through."

(The only time young Mickey got into trouble was when he fell behind with the weekly payments – that did cause ructions in the Jupp household.)

The stars were now aligned; it was time to do something about it. Time to see if rather than just listening to music, he might make some himself.

On 2nd December 1962 Mickey alighted from a number 25 bus in Leigh-on-Sea with his new girlfriend, Pat. He had met her at the Youth Club his mother ran:

"When I was eighteen, out of boredom, I'd taken my record player along to be the youth club DJ, sort of. I set it up in a sort of music corner, and anyone who wanted could have a listen. One day Pat brought along some records to play. I found out later that she wanted to get to know me, so that's how we introduced ourselves."

Now it was their first date and Mickey planned to impress his new girlfriend no end by taking her to a rehearsal with the band he'd just joined, the Black Diamonds.

It was a bold move – he hadn't actually played with them yet.

Mickey started out with the Black Diamonds as a guitar player; the keyboard role was yet to come. Neither did Mickey yet sing - Bob Eve did all the vocals, while Angus Staines played bass. Mickey found his role a bit difficult to start with. He'd been learning classical and Spanish guitar pieces, all delicate runs of notes and arpeggios but the band wanted chords – a bit of rhythm, if not yet blues. As there was no piano at the Leigh rehearsal venue, Mickey did his best on the guitar, never thinking about his rusty keyboard skills.

"I vaguely remember playing piano with my brother David at Scouts – he'd play a left hand and I'd do a right hand - but I wasn't really a piano player at that time; I'd taken lessons but ducked out of them. So I didn't take the piano seriously until the Black Diamonds. We used to rehearse sometimes in a big spare room at the front of our house – it had a small billiard table and a piano in there. One day rehearsing, with me on guitar, Angus the bass player said, 'Why don't you try something on the piano?' After that I started practicing again, to the annoyance of the houses in the area."

For his new practice piece Mickey picked something rocky, in every sense: the Jerry Lee Lewis version of *What I Say*. He listened to it carefully over and over again trying to de-construct what was being played.

What's the left hand doing? What's the right hand doing? He could sort of play either, but could he play both at the same time?

"It was like teaching a kid to wink," he recalls, "Both eyes close at the same time at first."

So it was practise, practise, practise, until the hands became uncoupled from one another and new, more flexible pathways opened in the brain - ones that, once there become second nature, stay instinctive for life.

Mickey was learning to be the keyboard player in a band. While his motivation would have been partly musical, it would also surely have been about forming relationships, quietly becoming part of a unit, a comfy cog in the wheel. He was just the keyboard player at this point, part of a brotherhood yet quietly tucked away doing his own thing – no singing, no fronting, no tension.

He didn't know it yet but all this was soon to change.

His talents - instantly recognized by those who heard him - were going to demand it. But a band is a zero sum game: the rise of one member requires the demise of another: a failsafe recipe for big friction ahead.

The problem with bands made up of mates is that, as imbalances in musical abilities emerge, tensions grow between groups of previously inseparable buddies. Guitarists get dropped for better players, often barely known to the group a few weeks previously. The deposed individual may then start a rival band and a feud begins. Other, less confident cast-off players may default to a sort of honorary road manager position, helping hump the gear or drive the van or collect the money from the promoter. (Even the Stones had one of those, once Ian Stewart had been ousted from the band for not looking cool or being confident enough.)

More worrying still, it was by no means unusual for an inferior musician to be welcomed into a band of a higher calibre solely on the strength of his convenient ownership of a PA system or a tidy, only-four-previous-owners, Transit van, rather than his possessing perfect pitch or guitar virtuosity.

Pink Floyd have owned up to this being the case with their line-up in the early days.

The freshly formed Black Diamonds had yet to reach this stage.

Undismayed by inexperience - in the arrogant/innocent way that only teenagers can pull off - they chose not to restrict themselves to rehearsing in a front room as so many would-be groups did. The Black Diamonds soon went out and played real gigs, including the local tennis club. Mickey remembers proudly sporting his first proper guitar at that tennis club gig. It was a Rossetti Lucky Seven. The Lucky Seven was a wonderful artifact of the times. In the sixties Egmond, the Dutch manufacturer of these guitars, was the largest luthier in Europe, though known more for quantity than quality. Their cheapest models had a price tag that was but a tenth of the cost of a comparable model from the premier US guitar manufacturers, Gibson or Fender.

Mickey remembers playing quite a few gigs with the Rossetti, though not much about where they took place. It was a very long time ago, so a bit of vagueness is understandable, but he can remember that his influence in the band was growing:

"By now I played guitar (a bit) and piano (a bit) and sang (very little). Bob did most of the singing – he would sing the pop songs and I would sing the odd r&b or rock'n'roll song".

The Black Diamonds only lasted into 1963, but this brief chapter proved invaluable early experience for Mickey. It also had an effect on those in the band's smallish audiences: kids who needed a bit of local inspiration, however rudimentary, to get their own musical arses into gear. It seems likely to have been this early that a young Wilko Johnson first saw Mickey play, at St Clement's Hall in Leigh-on-Sea. As he later told Will Birch:

"I don't know what the band was called but he was banging away on a piano and there was a sign on the side of it that said 'Count Michael Von Jupp'. The sound wasn't very good but you could see there was something there."

Despite these first steps, the bulk of Mickey's education about life in bands would come from the teeming musical scene going on all around him.

There were scores, probably over a hundred, local groups springing up around Southend and quite a few of them were undeniably accomplished. Bands such as the poppy Monotones, soon to sign to Pye records; the heavier Cops & Robbers, also later signed by Pye; the Whirlwinds, signed to United Artists after changing their name to Force Five; and, above all others, r&b pioneers, the Paramounts.

Unlike their contemporaries the Paramounts were signed to a really big label – EMI's Parlophone, home to those all-conquering Beatles. Also, unlike their contemporaries, they had some hits, albeit minor ones, with American songs like *Poison Ivy* and *Little Bitty Pretty One*.

Most of all, unlike their contemporaries, they had not one but two world-class musician amongst their number, as became evident when they later metamorphosised into Procol Harum, unleashed the twin talents of Gary Brooker and Robin Trower on the world, wrote *Whiter Shade of Pale* and became global rock legends.

Or at least that's how the story goes.

Keith Reid, Procol Harum founder member, lyricist to all their material from *Whiter Shade of P*ale onwards and, eventually, co-publisher and co-manager of Mickey, soon put me right on that one:

"As a lyricist looking for work, I met famous *enfant terrible* producer Guy Stevens, who introduced me to Gary Brooker. The Paramounts were breaking up and Gary was setting out to make a living as a writer, not a performer. I delivered lyrics for Gary to add music to, but we couldn't get anyone else to record the songs, so Guy Stevens prompted us to form a studio band to perform the songs ourselves. Gary was the only Paramount in it at the start - BJ Wilson was going to be on drums but he let us down and stayed with George Bean and the Runners instead. All that business about the Paramounts turning into Procol Harum was rubbish. But after our record of *Whiter Shade of Pale* was a sudden hit – we had a feeling it was going to be from the minute we started rehearsing it - we had to get players in fast to form a real band who could go on TV and make a quick album. So we went to the people we knew best, and they were mostly the Paramounts. They were all delighted to join up, of course, because now we had a big hit record!"

In 2001, at a Southend gig to mark the retirement of original Paramounts drummer and veteran Mickey Jupp associate Mick Brownlee, by-now superstar Gary Brooker reminisced about the first time he met Brownlee, neatly summing up the hurly-burly of those early days.

It happened at a rock contest at Southend's Palace Hotel, where bands competing included The Raiders (Mick Brownlee's then band, not the Romford ones mentioned earlier), The Outlaws (Mick Brownlee's previous band, not the Joe Meek ones), and The Coasters (who Gary was playing with at the time, not the Leiber and Stoller ones). A bloke called Bob Scott pulled Mick out of the Raiders, Gary from the Coasters and introduced Robin Trower to them both. The Paramounts were born.

The home of the Paramounts from the outset was the Shades. It was quite literally home, in that the parents of lead guitarist Robin Trower owned the gaff. Mick Brownlee, then the Paramounts drummer, filled me in on how the club came into being:

"Robin Trower and me were doing up the Penguin Cafe on the seafront, that his Dad, Len, had just bought. We went downstairs and there was this big, big cellar – full of water and crap and dead rats! So we all worked to clear it out, bought a piano for £4 and that's what became the Shades. There was a little stage up there. No booze, just coffee or coke – you got a free one with admission. It was great."

Over and above their talents in the Paramounts, Trower and Brooker had a further formative influence on Southend music: they curated the priceless jukebox at the Shades. It was packed full of interesting stuff you simply couldn't find elsewhere, like Barrett Strong's seminal *Money*, a song that is about to play a pivotal role in Mickey's story.

"It was brilliant, that jukebox", says Mickey today, "it was the best jukebox this side of, well, juke box heaven."

Actually it was the best jukebox this side of Memphis, from where that famous Southend record collector Tony Wilkinson was obtaining many of the records used to stock the not one but two jukeboxes the Shades boasted.

Unsurprisingly, the Shades quickly became the go-to place for aspiring musicians looking for something more credible than the pop fare on offer at The Elms in Leigh – a pub with an impressive dance hall attached, or Thorpe Bay's sprawling Halfway House pub.

"The Shades is one of those places about which the memory gets fonder as time goes by. It was just a coffee bar really, with a weird electronic bowling alley on the side – eventually it became Shulers fish restaurant, now it's a block of flats, I think," Mickey wistfully recalls.

The Shades was unlicensed but so what?

It could boast coffee, cokes, burgers and the blues - all for just a shilling on the door. Mickey's younger brother David became a regular there. Blonde and good-looking, he didn't develop a musical talent as early, or as deeply as Mickey, but he would have been a brilliant guide to the local music scene for his less socially adventurous elder brother.

Soon Mickey joined David on his nights out in Shades and various other Southend clubs and coffee bars; meeting other youngsters who were to play a part in his musical future; getting to know the bigger boys in the music scene, who would help shape his career in just a few years time.

For now, though, he was still very much an apprentice.

The Southend Music Scene In The Sixties

Mickey in the mid-sixties   courtesy John Ricks

Let's face it: Southend is a bit of a music hall joke.

'Sarfend', as it is commonly pronounced, has traditionally been portrayed as the place chirpy cockneys went for whelks and sunburn and a train-ride down Britain's longest pier. There they would find fish and chips, sticks of rock with the word Southend running all the way through and cheap trilbies imploring other revellers to Kiss Me Quick (and Squeeze Me Slow).

Here was everything a typical bloke could possibly want in order to escape from his daily humdrum: beer, paddling, fairground rides and the prospect of a bit of slap and tickle. Like Margate, Clacton and Blackpool, Southend was working class, a bit run-down, essentially vulgar but, to borrow from *The Hitchhiker's Guide to the Galaxy*, mostly harmless.

Originally a bona fide pre-war holiday destination, the arrival of cheap air fares abroad and the spread of UK car ownership had by now reduced Southend to a mere day trip location. So on sunny weekends its population would bulge: visitors filling to overflowing the shops and pubs and cafes, the bowling alleys and roller skating rinks, the amusement arcades and dance halls.

Whereas on a weekday in winter, when the Thames Estuary was steely grey and the wind whipped down the esplanade like shrapnel, you could have the whole place to yourself.

By the fifties Southend was slowly becoming atrophied and looked a candidate to go under altogether by the early sixties. The families who visited were dwindling in number and the amount they spent while there reduced, although that didn't stop the Davies family regularly visiting in 'Betsy', Dad's old, black Vauxhall 12. Years later these trip inspired their son Raymond to write the song *Drivin'* for the Kinks album, *Arthur or the Decline and Fall of the British Empire*.

But then, just in the nick of time, teenagers were invented. Teenagers who no longer had to undergo dreary, life-sapping bouts of National Service. Teenagers who had a job that paid sufficiently for them to be looking to treat themselves. Teenagers who, if only through their parents, could maybe take advantage of new hire-purchase laws to get their hands on the things they wanted, without having to save up for years.

The first thing many of these teenagers aimed to do was get themselves transport – because transport meant independence from the boring older generation.

And where to go once you'd got your wheels? To the seaside, of course.

The kids reveled in Southend's brashness. They valued its difference from the bland towns they lived in all week – the Romfords and Ilfords and Dagenhams; dormitories squatting on the big roads running out of London, fat with council houses and Ford workers. It wasn't far, so they flocked to Southend. If you didn't have a Norton or a Vespa, you could always take the train, for British Railways operated not one but two lines between London and Southend.

However you got there, you could be sure of a Golden Mile of pubs and arcades and the spider at the heart of that web, the Kursaal – in its heyday capable of fitting eight thousand punters in for a single event.

If you actually lived in the area, all this action made it an exciting place to grow up. Sometimes almost too exciting.

In the early sixties, Britain's media became obsessed with two youth cliques that had sprung up: the sharp dressing Mods (think early Small Faces) - often on mirror-laden scooters in parkas - and the biker-styled Rockers (think Gene Vincent) - usually in leather on a big, black Triumph.

Both these tribes liked to roar off to the seaside on sunny summer days to chat, preen, drink, (mostly the beery Rockers), take mild drugs, (Mods were fond of 'purple hearts'), and occasionally fight one another.

While Brighton was Britain's proper punch-up mecca, Southend was not without violent visitations that, although mostly toothless, nevertheless layered additional tawdry swagger onto the town's already seedy reputation.

Eventually, scared of real trouble, the big coffee bars in Southend - the Jacobean and the Capri - had to sort themselves into being either Mod or Rocker establishments - a specialisation that would encourage more loyal custom and discourage internecine tendencies. Along with the ubiquitous Wimpy Bars, like the one at the top of Pier Hill, these 'dry' venues were the places young people gathered. Leaving aside the obvious magnet of the opposite sex, they were attracted by the 'frothy coffee', scrawny burgers, Brown Derbies and Big Benders (don't ask); yet equally important to them were the jukeboxes: exotic machines that offered them a chance to hear music they couldn't get enough of, or sometimes any of, at home.

In order to accommodate these huge temporary influxes of visitors arriving in their cars and pouring off trains, Southend had to have ten times a normal town's ratio of entertainment venues to regular population.

This meant many more places for new bands to get playing experience; obviously in summer to entertain the hordes, yet perversely even more so off-season, when these same venues needed to attract sufficient local punters to at least cover their overheads until next season's payday.

So it was in winter when the many pubs and clubs became effectively rehearsal rooms for local talent - which may account for why the area proved such a rich source of quality rock musicians. As Britain's seventh most densely populated area outside London, Southend had a big population from which bands could form, and so by the height of the mid-sixties scene there were countless local bands working the area every single weekend: in church halls and youth clubs, at community centres, on the seafront, down the football club, up the pier. Mickey fondly remembers that era:

"You could go out any day of the week and have a choice of three or more bands in the various clubs, pubs and church halls where they played. The town was split into the r&b section, in the minority, and the pop section. There were lots of bands and the standard was pretty good."

At clubs like The Studio and The Night Scene, locals could experience visiting bands from London and occasionally even further afield, but the best place to see local musicians playing was undoubtedly the good old Shades.

Having moved to Southend just too late, this author is inconsolable about never having got to visit the club in its heyday, but he knows a man who did. Soon-to-be Legend bassist John Bobin described it well in his memoir *Bark Staving Ronkers,* which he has kindly allowed me to draw upon as source material for this book. Remarkably, he notes that the Shades attracted both Mods and Rockers, without the levels of friction one might have expected, thanks to the high calibre of music on offer, both live and recorded. He writes:

"The Paramounts, veterans of the Southend scene since their formation in 1960, and a band once described as 'the best rock'n'roll band in a rock'n'roll town', played there on Sundays. Their line-up featured Robin Trower (whose window-cleaning Dad owned the place) on guitar and Gary Brooker on keyboard and vocals (whose Dad Harry had led the orchestra at the Palace Hotel for years).

Admission to this weekly feast of blues, r&b and r&r was one shilling and sixpence – seven and a half pence in today's money! In the week, another band played the Shades – Gary Brooker named them the Orioles. They really took off when flame haired Mick Jupp joined, playing the piano like Jerry Lee Lewis, feet and elbows on the keyboard on some occasions."

Note that Mick wasn't to become Mickey for a while yet - and that, at the beginning at least, he was attempting to make some sort of a show on stage, although that didn't extend to what he wore. Unable to afford dedicated stage gear, young Mick went on in his day clothes, something that helped him from attracting unwelcome attention from the clans present, as did his repertoire:

"The Shades was a Mod stronghold and I was a more of a Rocker in my music – but both sides knew to leave me alone. The rockers would say 'that's Mickey Jupp – you don't touch him because he sings rock and roll', while the Mods would say 'that's Mickey Jupp – you don't touch him because he sings R'n'B. So I was safe!"

At the Shades you could also hear the Flowerpots, featuring guitarist John Wilkinson, who later on switched his name around to become Wilko Johnson, founding member and chief songwriter of Dr Feelgood. Around the same time, he switched his guitar style from bluesy to choppy - partly based on the pioneering simultaneous rhythm and lead playing of the Pirates' Mick Green.

He was also heavily influenced by what he saw closer to home, as he recalls:

"They were two very good bands from Southend. One was the Paramounts and the other was Mickey Jupp's band. Mickey Jupp was a great singer, he could sing like Elmore James, fantastic. He had this great guitarist called Mo Witham, who I think is one of the greatest guitarists I have ever seen. He could walk into Nashville and look anyone in the eye, you know, he's that great."

Wilko acknowledged these characters' importance to the development of his own band in an article in *Zig Zag*:

"The Flowerpots were a kind of poor man's version of Legend. Although the band had a couple of very good musicians in it, me and the drummer weren't up to their standards really. In the last days of the band we had a regular gig in Southend where about ten people used to turn up to see us. On a few occasions the only people in there were Mickey Jupp, Mo Witham and Robin Trower, and after a while they would get up and play our instruments, which was all very embarrassing."

From time to time another Southend band, the Phantoms, would play the Shades. Their line-up included bass player Johnny Bobin and drummer Bobby Clouter, both later of the Orioles and Legend. Their lead guitarist, Steve Porter, went on to join Sight & Sound, a local band in which this author was drummer, alongside singer Giff Wright, bass player Dave Stephen and guitarist Paul Dunning, previously with the Monotones: a good example of how interchangeable the local group personnel base was.

The town boasted a wide range of venues at which live bands could be seen and heard (well, at least heard – only seen if you could get down to the front). The London Hotel is long gone and the Pier Hotel now pure accommodation, but the Elms and Halfway House remain, as does the Cricketers, a pub with a dance hall at the back which in more recent days was rather trendily re-named Club Riga.

Dennis Knott, a local window-cleaning mogul, who also owned the previously mentioned Jacobean and Capri coffee bars, promoted gigs at the Cricketers, a take-me-as-you-find-me establishment that skulked at the root of Southend's London Road. Soon Mickey's first proper band, the Orioles, began to play there three or four times a week. Will Birch recalls that if you got there after 8pm, you weren't going to get in, because it would already be packed to bursting with three hundred happy punters, something Mickey imagines would not pass Health & Safety muster today. Sometimes, to make a few bob extra, the band would go on from the Cricketers to play another venue later the same night. Oh, the stamina of youth.

Back at the start, the earliest wave of Southend bands had been led by the Barracudas who, amazingly early, sometimes played twin necked guitars, and the Rockerfellas. Mickey was particularly keen on the latter, as he spells out:

"Before the Paramounts there was The Rockerfellas and they were *it*. Individually not so good; but together as tight as that. They split in 1962. End of part one."

The next generation was to be much thicker on the ground.

The Whirlwinds were a brilliant covers band led by guitarist Bert Pulham - they played at the Halfway House and were resident band at the Elms. Later, they metamorphosed into Force Five, who made five quality singles for United Artists, including the nearly-hit, *Yeah I'm Waiting*.

Much later, after Flower Power arrived, elements of Force Five re-emerged as the Crocheted Doughnut Ring, recording for the trendy Deram label. A single of theirs, *Havana Anna,* went to number two in Japan.

Another member of the Crocheted Doughnut Ring was singer Ricky Mills, previously of local band the Fingers. The Fingers had also included, at various times, Mo Witham, John Bobin and Bob Clouter, all ex-members of the Orioles and future members of Legend (round and round the connections go).

Bizarrely, at one point the Fingers released a single on Polydor – the Ray Davies song *I Go to Sleep* – on which all the instruments were played by rivals Force Five. Unhappy with Force Five's vocal, the record company got the Fingers to re-voice it!

Later on, the Fingers, through local songwriter Geoff Stevens and local producer Peter Eden, were signed to EMI's top Columbia label, (home to Cliff and the Shads), but the band had to face the indignity of having a bunch of session men record the backing tracks for their releases. Eventually they were allowed to record as a band, usually in regular demo sessions at Abbey Road, around the same time as the Beatles were recording there, (and from whose stash of studio kit Mo Witham recalls 'liberating' a few strings and other vital supplies).

The Fingers didn't make it big despite several record releases, one of which has since achieved cult status. This was perhaps unsurprising given that they became famous for turning down the wrong people in the music business, having passed on management and production deals with both Jonathan King and Mickie Most.

Though not a Southend resident, it was while he was regularly playing Southend's Studio Club that Donovan – soon to be a buddy of the Beatles and Dylan – was discovered by the same local producer who had worked with the Fingers. Peter Eden was to be responsible for Donovan's early hits, like *Catch the Wind*, before Mickie Most took over (small world again).

Of the true blue Southend output, the Paramounts did best of all. Having been name checked by the Rolling Stones as "the best R&B group in Britain" after playing on the same bill as them, the Stones even trekked down to Southend to see the band play their Shades residency and sample that legendary juke box. Heck, the Paramounts even had a proper roadie of their own.

They also had a major recording contract, but after some modest hits, sufficient to get them out on the road, the Orioles fortuitously taking over their prime spot at the Shades, the momentum fell away.

The Paramounts soon found themselves in demand only as a somewhat demoralized backing band, ending up recording the instrumental tracks for Duffy Power records, (his excellent version of *Parchman Farm*, for example), and touring Europe behind the likes of Sandie Shaw and Chris Andrews. OK slog for journeyman session players but a bit workaday for a talented bunch of guys.

So in 1967 Gary Brooker re-invented himself as Procol Harum, along with his new lyricist Keith Reid, and they jointly wrote a little tune called *Whiter Shade of Pale*. It went on to sell over ten million copies and become Paul McCartney's favourite song. As we have seen, when it was time to form a proper band, the Paramounts were recruited to fill the gaps, creating the Procol Harum we knew.

The importance of Procol Harum to Mickey Jupp's career cannot be overstated. Every member of that band either played with him, produced him, managed him, published him or arranged strings for his songs at some point in his career. Several did more than one of these things - Keith Reid most notably.

Perhaps the next most successful Southend band in recording terms, despite their unappetising and derivative name, was the Monotones. Led by guitarist Brian Alexander, they played the Elms each week, on the few nights that Force Five didn't. Pye put a lot of effort into supporting the four singles the Monotones issued in 1964 and 1965. Later a revised version of the band joined the Mecca circuit as the Treetops and recorded six singles for Columbia, including a great close harmony version of *California My Way*.

By far the poshest venue in Southend for any band to play was the newly built Cliffs Pavilion, which put on everything from rock concerts to the Sooty show, by way of opera, classical concerts and am dram. It had a high stage, plush curtains and a sound system, none of which could be found in most of the places a local band might play. In actual fact, local bands mostly didn't get to play there, as the Cliffs was the venue of choice for touring artists, having taken over the mantle from the Southend Odeon, which had by now closed. A few of us squeezed in as support acts from time to time, though.

The oddest venue was probably Victor Sylvester's: a dance studio located directly above the old Odeon foyer, where bands like Sight & Sound played for teenagers, on the nights middle-aged couples weren't practicing their cha-cha moves.

Because of its coastal location, Southend was awash, no pun intended, with yacht clubs. While the Mustangs had the Thorpe Bay Yacht Club sewn up, thanks to an appalling act of nepotism (yes, you, Adrian Philpot), Sight & Sound were kings of the sailing scene, regularly playing at the Benfleet, Leigh and Half Way Yacht Clubs as well as being resident at the Alexander Yacht Club just down from the pier, (sadly recently burned to the ground by an arsonist).

Southend's estuary position also put it in the heart of Pirate Radio country. The first British pirate radio station was Radio Caroline, which started broadcasting from a ship further round the Essex coast in 1964. By 1967 ten pirate radio stations were broadcasting to an estimated daily audience of between ten and fifteen million. They played records that the BBC wouldn't, and often featured "charts" that bore less resemblance to sales figures than they did to the 'payola' changing hands between various bands' management and the station owners.

Both Radio City and Radio Essex operated from the World War Two anti-aircraft forts located in the Thames Estuary between Essex and Kent. They used Southend as a land base, often organising station-branded gigs in the town, until the government tightened the law in an attempt to lay siege to them. From time to time this meant that a local band would be pressed into supporting a singing DJ, such as Tony Blackburn. What joy.

One such band was Sounds Around. They were a more thasn competent pop outfit built around the talents of singer and songwriter John Pantry. John - who wrote songs for many artists, not just his own band - went on to become a much sought after sound engineer at IBC Studios in London, where he worked on many hits, including all of the Small Faces and Bee Gees early successes. Top DJ Kenny Everett was a big fan of John's engineering and songwriting skills.

After two singles on Pye Piccadilly, Sounds Around became Peter & the Wolves, thanks to MGM, their new record company's, 'marketing'. They released five singles for them, with a line-up that comprised John plus Nick Ryan on bass, Robin Slater on guitar, Jon Richmond on keyboards and ex-Monotone Gary Nicholls on drums. Towards the end of that run of recordings, Alan Parrish, later of Southend stalwarts the Hamsters, took over on drums.

The band then morphed into Wolfe, releasing two singles and an album for Motown's Rare Earth label. By this point, at the end of the sixties, bassist Nick Ryan had assumed a more prominent role in the band and yet another new drummer - this author - had joined them.

John Pantry then released two solo albums on Philips before converting entirely to Christian music. In this sphere he became a successful artist and leading producer, using as his standard session crew Mo Witham (ex-Legend) on guitar, Nick Ryan (ex-Peter & the Wolves) on bass and Mike Wade (ex-Wolfe) on drums. These days John is a minister who has a regular radio show on Christian radio station, Premier.

(Another band to be found in the area at the time were The Avengers, who, amazingly, continue to play locally today, their line-up virtually unchanged for decades.)

In later, punkier times, local bands like the Shakers - led by Steve Hooker, who would go on to play a role in Mickey's story - and the Bottles kept the Southend flag flying. While many fell by the wayside, other contemporary groups became nurseries significant in providing an early home for musicians who went on to greater success later. For example, The Kursaal Flyers came together from the remnants of sixties bands Saints & Sinners and the later Surly Bird, while Dr Feelgood's sixties roots included the aforementioned Flowerpots, plus the Southside Jug Band and The Fix.

The Feelgoods, The Kursaals, Eddie & the Hot Rods were the bands that formed the third wave of Southend music, following in the footsteps of Procol Harum, née The Paramounts, and Mickey himself, who influenced all of them from their schooldays onwards.

As Graeme Douglas, who has the distinction of having played in both the Kursaals and Eddie & the Hot Rods, notes on his web site:

"Some good things about attending Southend High School were the list of musos that had been, were currently or would go to school there. A list of Southend's finest would definitely include Gary Brooker and Robin Trower (the Paramounts, Procol Harum, Robin Trower Band), Mickey Jupp, John Bobin and Bob Clouter (the Orioles, Legend), Barrie Martin (Eddie & the Blizzards, the Kursaals, the Hamsters), and the King brothers (the Fugitives)."

This generation of bands happily reflected the gritty image bestowed by their blowsy, coolly shabby hometown, as Max Bell summed up in his introduction to an *NME* feature on Mickey in 1975:

"At just gone eleven you board a Fenchurch Street train bound for Southend, supposed home of the sudden R&B revival and a few other things. Five miles out of the East End there are cows in fields chewing beneath the pylons. Sleepy stations en route that have boarded-up waiting rooms and notices proudly proclaiming "closed through vandalism". As the landscape flattens you come to Benfleet (alight here for Canvey Island, Oil City) where smart yachts sprawl like whales on the oozing mud banks of the Thames Estuary, stuck in the spume topped, curdled waste of a low tide. Southend itself boasts a fairly typical combination of Victorian seaside architecture and the messy incongruity of a twentieth century leisure cult gone mad. It's genteel and sordid all at the same time. Along the front lies The Golden Mile, one time summer meeting place for countless holidaymakers and the mods and rockers who couldn't make Clacton. Not much to see now except "the largest pier in the world", the empty fish 'n' chip shops, the odd whelk stall and, of course...the Kursaal. The Kursaal, once upon a time eight acres of fun and noise, rival to Battersea. Now it's a closedown museum of fruit machines, and side shows, gathering dust until it's redeveloped into "the biggest bingo hall in the world" or, more likely, meets with the hammer...That Day Will Come."

More recently, the Southend music scene has produced Busted and The Horrors (well, one out of two ain't bad), as well as rock veterans the Hamsters, who didn't finally hang up their Transit keys until 2013.

The very latest vintage is strong stuff, too. Nothing But Thieves are, at the time of writing, just arriving in the charts, their self-released early work having attracted the interest of Sony.

And in between, Canvey bands the Vicars and the Screaming Ab Dabs became the nursery for a singular singer called Alf, later of Yazoo and today the brilliant solo performer, Alison Moyet.

So where might Mickey's reputation stand amidst the maelstrom of sounds emanating from Southend down the years? The town has thrown up a varied mix of artists who journalist Mark Dutton believes have always in shared common values of "hard work, giving it all, value for money – claiming no difference from their audiences".

74

Pretty high, by all accounts.

Back in April 1978, at the time of the release of Mickey's first compilation for Stiff, Dave Brown wrote the following in *Sounds* magazine:

"There is one figure who stands out from the rest in the tangled web of the Southend scene; a guitarist/keyboards player/singer/songwriter. A man who all the others admit as being a major influence despite the fact that he has only appeared on three now sadly deleted LPs and is today only known by an educated minority. Mickey Jupp is the name."

While as recently as December 2014, *Record Collector* tagged Mickey as "Southend's singular, insular talent."

But in the real-time narrative of the book, Mickey has yet to make a convincing start on building this enviable reputation, so it's time to get back to the story.

4 Good Money

In which Mickey's talent first shines through before it all goes wrong - starting something of a trend

The Orioles   courtesy Dougie Sheldrake

Function to function, gig to gig
I'm gonna be someone, gonna make it big,
I'll have a country house and a Cadillac car
I ain't got 'em yet but I know where they are,
Function to function, gig to gig

Function to Function **by Mickey Jupp & Chris East, X**

"You play a bit of piano, don't you Mick?"

It was one evening at the Shades in 1963 when Robin Trower asked the question of young Mickey Jupp. Trower knew of a band looking for a keyboard player. They were called the Orioles – a name dreamt up for them by Gary Brooker. The Orioles would be a step up from the Black Diamonds – they played real, paying gigs for a start.

Plus they had a novelty: a singing drummer - Tony "Diamond" Arthurs - as their leader.

Alongside him were Adrian 'Ada' Baggerley on bass (veteran of The Electrics, a skiffle group that had once featured a very young Gary Brooker) and Dave Gilman, on guitar. They felt they needed a piano player and Mickey now hoped he could be just the man. Little did he know just how soon he would become, not just the man for the job, but *the man*.

He remembers it as if it were yesterday:

"One of the first rehearsals we had, Tony, who was the leader, asks if anyone else knew any more songs because we only had about ten. I'd come across *Sweet Dreams* by Don Gibson rather strangely. When my Dad's Elizabethan tape recorder was being repaired, it came back to us with a little test tape on it, including *Sweet Dreams* by Don Gibson and Gene Pitney singing *I Want to Love my Life Away*. So we did *Sweet Dreams* and then I remembered *Money,* which I'd heard on the jukebox in the Shades and fallen in love with, so we did that next.

I bluffed my way through those and at the end Tony, said, 'OK, from now on you're the singer'. I was amazed - it had never occurred to me that I might be a lead singer, but that was that, so I was."

Whether or not he had expected to be one, from the outset Mickey had pretty clear ideas about how he needed to sing, as he explained to Will Birch:

"I tried to inject real feeling into *Sweet Dreams* and push myself vocally. I thought if I'm going to be singing regularly, the thing I've got to do, especially with old rock'n'roll songs like Little Richard's, is get them up to as high a pitch as I can reach, so it takes the thin edge off and the voice roughens up. Nobody told me to do that, I just did it and it worked."

After just a couple of rehearsals the Orioles began playing the Shades on Wednesdays, (the Paramounts were playing the prime Sunday night slot), and soon also became the house band at the Cricketers pub.

While they were inspired by the same styles of music as the Paramounts, the Orioles tried not to duplicate songs in their act – partly out of respect and partly, according to Oriole-follower John Denton, because as yet they weren't quite as good as their mentors.

All the same, Will Birch remembers going along one night and being astonished at how much Mickey had developed in a few short years:

"A couple of years after the Scouts, me and my mates started going to the youth club in Shoebury, which Mrs. Jupp also ran, like she had the Cubs. Mick would be there in the corner – he was too old for it and so he looked uncomfortable, sitting in the corner by the record player, playing all these r&b records - which was supercool, by the way. (In fact, he lent me two albums – a Bo Diddley one and the famous *We Sing the Blues* compilation - that I illegally and embarrassingly lent on to John Bobin. I think he's forgotten by now). Then the next thing I know, just a bit further on, he's in the Orioles at the Cricketers. I couldn't believe this voice: the kid who two years before was being surly in the youth club was singing fantastically well, and like an American. They'd do all those standards like *Matchbox* with Mick on piano and then he'd pick up guitar and they'd have three guitars on Eddie Cochran's *Summertime Blues*. Mick would do a sort of duck walk with the mic stand and his personality started to come out – mind you, he did look a bit uncomfortable doing it!"

Mickey was doing his best to entertain, but he only felt able to do such things if the music moved him to. Sometimes he would do the duck walk, sometimes at the piano he would deliberately slip from his stool to the stage, still playing, but there was no hiding the fact that most of the time Mickey was uncomfortable up front, more than uncomfortable in fact:

"The first Orioles gig, the first time we played at the Shades, I didn't even go. Never turned up. I was terrified. I knew that I was going to be the lead singer – no hiding place. I went the week after, but not the first one - Tony the drummer had to keep singing for that one."

Dougie Sheldrake was asked to join the band by Mickey, with whom he had studied at the Southend Municipal Arts College, where he recalls Mickey had already started to show artistic frustrations:

"I was well used to hearing a groan from behind me, followed by a crunching sound, after which a ball of cartridge paper would fly through the air."

Dougie was serious enough about his art to display rather more patience than Mickey and so completed his studies - thus ending up a career designer and typographer. Despite this dedication to a stable career, at the time of his recruitment to the Orioles Dougie splashed out the princely sum of £174 on a brand new Gretsch Tennessean. He also bought a rare and rather flash Binson amplifier, but this investment in gear did not fool him into imagining he would have much clout in the band:

"It was very much Mick's band", Dougie remembers, "with him not just choosing most of the material but also instructing everyone else how to play their parts the way he wanted them played - in other words everything had to be his way."

This, though, shouldn't be taken to mean that Mickey was blind to Dougie's talents. Some years later he was to say, "Dougie Sheldrake joined us and that made all the difference." Rather it was early evidence that he was already a musical autocrat, one who lacked the gene for praising others.

Mickey's directives didn't always mirror the style Dougie himself would have chosen, given his overall preference for a more delicate, less chugging style than Mickey liked, but he knew that was the way it had to be.

In order to balance things up a little, Dougie was allowed to nominate a few numbers for the band to play. He recalls *Suzie Q, My Babe* and an obscure Ben E King B-side being amongst them, but the deal was that whatever he selected he would have to sing them himself.

Mickey only wanted to do what Mickey wanted to do – an attitude he has maintained unswervingly ever since.

And because he had that voice, and so was the undisputed leader by now, he always got the upper hand, something Dougie unquestioningly accepted:

"I'd been a singer in my previous band but my voice isn't that strong, so alongside Mickey's numbers mine probably sounded a bit flat. Mickey favoured Carl Perkins songs like *Matchbox* - we always opened with that one - and blues standards such as *St James Infirmary*. He did them brilliantly, of course."

This line-up recorded as a band demo the very song Mickey had made first choice for his Orioles vocal "audition": Don Gibson's *Sweet Dreams*, backed by a very early Jupp composition, *Baby, Baby*.

Recorded in Denmark Street, just four copies were pressed following the session. Unfortunately, despite the best endeavours of all concerned, no copy has ever surfaced, Dougie having lost his disc in age-old fashion - lending it to a friend and never getting it back. A bit of investigative work, however, uncovered the fact that Mickey had not actually lost his copy – he provided the first evidence of how little his recorded material mattered to him by selling it!

Mike Stowers, an Orioles fan in those early Cricketer's days, who spent a lot of time in the Jacobean coffee bar with Mickey and the band, remembers buying Mickey's copy from him, along with a couple of Fats Domino classics on 78rpm discs, *Blueberry Hill* and *I Wanna Walk You Home*. This copy of The Orioles *Sweet Dreams* was the first record he ever bought – a pretty smart move given that, if he can find it in his New Zealand attic, it will be the only copy in the world.

And what if he can't?

Well, Mickey maintains it wasn't outstanding anyway, especially the B-side, his first foray into songwriting:

"I know *Baby, Baby* was a simple rock and roll song but I can't remember how it went. It was a very early song of mine. There were a couple of mine we did at the Shades. One was called *Wrong*, maybe it came slightly before *Baby, Baby*; anyway it was built around the *Fortune Seller* riff played backwards - it was crap! We only played it a couple of times at the Shades, never at the Cricketers. I remember people saying 'That's good, is that one of yours?' and then me, rather sheepishly, saying, 'Yeh'. Even then I was ashamed," he laughs.

"Another one was called *Big Pete*: *"Big Pete, got big feet"* is all I can remember."

Why Pete?

Maybe it was something to do with Peter Eden, local Svengali, producer and discoverer of Donovan. He had his eye on Mickey, too – and not just as a singer, as Mickey had noticed:

"I wrote songs but never thought much about it. There was this guy Pete Eden, a record producer I knew well, who often said he would be interested to hear what sort of song I would actually write, knowing the music I liked to play."

In *Long Distance Romancer* - the TV documentary Roger Deakin put together many years later about the Southend scene in general and Mickey in particular - Peter Eden explained what it was that so interested him about Mickey's writing:

"He came out of all that influence - the rock and roll, the rhythm and blues sort of era - and he's one of the few people who can *write* songs for that kind of artist today, like Ricky Nelson."

Texan musician and Jupp fan John Garza illustrates this particularly well:

"The way I've tried to explain it to people is that Mickey completes the catalogue of others: you always wanted to hear that one more great Chuck Berry, Fats Domino, Elmore James, or Elvis song - well, listen to Mickey's stuff and your wishes will come true. Yet in the process it becomes very obvious that Mickey is every bit an icon himself. I remember a writer once described a great band as 'something familiar yet something brand new' and that's what Mickey is to me."

Early on, Peter Eden had spotted these qualities in the unpolished, inexperienced Mickey, although it took some time for the writing bug to take hold, as Mickey admits:

"Peter had obviously seen something else in my character; something I hadn't myself, and wondered how it would work. But I didn't do anything seriously until I moved to Bath and used the family Elizabethan tape recorder and my jumbo Levin guitar to start writing songs proper in my bedsit."

But more of this later.

Whether or not Mickey was proud of the early songs he wrote while he was with them, (John Denton has a vague recollection of another called *Mad Lad*) he knew that the Orioles were a more than competent band, even if their demo didn't show them at their best:

"On stage we were pretty good – we could blow away some of the nationally successful bands who occasionally played sets with us. But the studio was an alien environment to us and so our performances lost a lot of our live power."

Once upon a time there was hard evidence of the Orioles in their pomp to back up this assertion, John Denton having taken a reel-to-reel recorder down to the Shades to record a whole show in early 1964. He can remember many of the songs on the tape – *Down the Line, Over You, Suzie Q, Mother in Law, New Orleans, Lipstick Traces*, even a Booker T instrumental, *Aw Mercy* – but he cannot locate the tape, which he fears was blithely over-recorded at a later date. Ouch!

Around this time the Orioles entered a local band competition but only came second, despite a blast of three of their strongest numbers, led by Gary 'US' Bond's *New Orleans*. So vigorous were the band's Cricketers performances that mid-show on 14th July 1964 they brought part of the roof down on the dancers below – so it would be interesting to know who beat them in the contest!

On the other hand, one of the band's proudest moments came when Mickey was not playing with them at all.

A version of the Orioles played a backing gig in a Prittlewell pub, one where the piano stool was commandeered by blues legend Champion Jack Dupree. Mickey wisely sat that one out. But at least one of those who did play that night must have been glad Mickey for once prepared to play second fiddle. According to Southend music journalist and lifetime Jupp supporter, John Howard, "Champion Jack stopped the show, pointed to guitarist Dougie Sheldrake and announced to the audience, 'This is the man!'"

(John Howard's Jupp connections run back a long way. As a boy he had delivered by bicycle the Jupp family groceries to their house in Milton Road. Around that time he was in a skiffle group with Gary Brooker and one-day Oriole, Adrian Baggerley. Later, as a journalist on Southend papers, he was to become Mickey's biggest publicist).

By 1964, Tony Arthurs, the Orioles' original leader and drummer, (generally competent on the kit but prone to speeding up when playing fills), had left and joined another band. The resulting Orioles changed out of all recognition, in the strangest of ways, and not once but twice.

Drummer Bobby Clouter, then playing in a band called Klimax, was first to become a new Oriole.

"We were playing regularly at the Shades and the Cricketers in Westcliff," remembers Mickey, "and one day our drummer said he wasn't going to be able to make the Cricketers gig that night: some pathetic excuse about his wife having a baby. So we were a bit stuck."

Bobby takes up the story:

"I started playing with Mickey first in Orioles Mk 2. The original drummer was Tony Arthurs - he used to play when we went to see them at the Shades. One night he didn't turn up. They knew I was in a band and had a kit so they called my home but I was out. My Dad took the call, loaded my drums into his van, came and found me and took me and my kit down there. I'd seen the Orioles a few times so I reckoned I could handle the songs OK. Of course you're ultra confident at that age - I probably thought I could have stepped into Buddy Rich's Big Band and you'd never notice the difference!"

Bobby Clouter had also been rehearsing with another outfit called Red Green and his Blues Combo - a band that, like so many, practiced assiduously yet never actually played anywhere - along with John Bobin on bass, virtuoso lead guitarist Mo Witham, and a chap called Mark Mills. (Barry Scanling was also involved and, like Zelig, will turn up as a bit player at various points in Mickey's career).

Mo had got the gig with the Red Green mob by turning up one day and, despite his youth and full-time job as a plumber's mate, launching into unheard-of Django Rheinhart numbers as well as blues, rock, jazz and just about anything else short of folk. Everyone could see his raw talent, although few would have predicted that he would end up playing with some of music's finest, from Chris Farlowe and Suzi Quatro to Sir Cliff himself.

Mo explained to me how he got to be so good, so fast:

"I started out playing ukulele in the Tommy Mills Five when I was twelve or thirteen – they wouldn't let me in some of the venues because I was too young for the licensing laws but the band smuggled me in as I was the only one who knew the chords. I had to play standing behind a curtain shouting them out! But I'd never played with anyone who got paid properly before."

Despite his gentle demeanour, Mo was already manifesting signs of a determination to do things his way, having recently turned down a chance to join Lulu and the Luvvers because they insisted he would have to have his tattoos removed. (Ironically, this was something that BBC cameramen had to work around when, years later, Mo played guitar on Top of the Pops for Cliff Richard, who'd had a hit with Southend boy and early Legend guitarist Chris East's song, *My Kinda Life*). By an extraordinary coincidence, (or did Lulu ask all Britain's guitarists?), Orioles guitarist Dougie Sheldrake had also turned down the Luvvers gig. Soon he was to exit the Orioles, too. While Mickey hinted in some early interviews that the reason for his departure was because Dougie was having trouble coping with band pressures, Dougie remembers it differently:

"It was the typical band versus girlfriend choice. My girlfriend's parents moved to Kent, so I wanted to spend more time over that way, which meant leaving the band."

Within months the girlfriend thing had fizzled out, so Dougie had lost both of his loves. After a couple more years he put away the guitar forever, or very nearly. It was a full thirty years before he picked it up again – to play again with Mickey, of course – and is now happily stepping out with three different outfits around the part of Norfolk where he lives.

Wilko Johnson remembers the Orioles' guitarist 'changeover' well:

"I discovered the Orioles because people at school talked about them. So I went along to the Cricketers to see them, found that as well as Mick they had this great guitarist, Dougie Sheldrake, and I thought Wow. Then somebody told me he's suddenly left and they've got this other guy instead - some bloke with swallow tattoos on his hands, and I'm thinking No! So I go along to watch again, only to find the replacement is Mo Witham, and he's even better!"

So that's what happened, then. Or it isn't.

It will become a regular feature in the story of Mickey's life that there are multiple-choice answers to many questions about what occurred and why, including this one. For there's another version of how Dougie departed.

Mo Witham and a bunch of his mates had been regularly going along to see the Orioles play at the Cricketers, which wasn't difficult as they were now playing there several nights a week. One evening a by now familiar problem cropped up, as Mo explains in his version of events:

"Mickey announced early on that his guitarist, Dougie Sheldrake, couldn't make it so the gig was going to have to be called off. I said to him that I knew all his songs and so could stand in if he wanted. He seemed a bit suspicious and asked if I had a guitar. I said yes, I had the same model as Dougie's, actually - a Gretsch Tennessean. That seemed to do it. 'Right he said, anybody got a car?' We found someone with a car, I went home, got my guitar and Fender amp - and I've played with him ever since then, spanning fifty years."

But was there a little more cunning and planning involved in Dougie's ejection than that? There's a third version on offer.

In an interview with Mike Davies in 1978, Mickey admitted, "Dougie liked things too much his own way and we'd had troubles with the drummer", (whom we were also told earlier had jumped rather than been pushed!).

It seems that having started this band business fairly casually, Mickey now wanted to do it properly and wasn't going to settle for anything but the best in what was now very much *his* band.

Few would have argued that he had the talent to support his claim to be leader, but it is hard not to notice that through sheer strength of musical ambition, this particular musical cuckoo seems to have pushed several Orioles from their nest. Like nature, bands can be cruel: they weren't good enough so they had to go.

Mickey revisited his high ambitions for, and clear frustrations with, the early Orioles in an *NME* interview in 1975:

"We weren't good, in fact we were bloody useless; we lacked confidence. We had a guitarist who was amazing at rehearsals but come a gig he couldn't play through nerves. He had a nervous breakdown and left. After that we got a guitarist (Mo) who I knew at Art College and he was good all the time."

Hang on, that's another version. Oh, well.

However it came about, two of the three key members of the Red Green and his Blues Combo had now become members of the Orioles. Only bass player John Bobin remained out of Mickey's band. But not for long, as John explains:

"Ada Baggerley, the Orioles bass player, was going to leave at one time and as I'd deputised for him once or twice before, I got the call to join full time. I had various practices with Mickey in his place at Cleveden Road before Ada decided to stay after all!"

He didn't stay for long, and by the autumn of 1965 the Mark Three line-up of Mickey, Mo, John and Bob - with Barry Scanling on rhythm guitar (then taking over on bass when John subsequently left) - was in place.

The apparent process of evolution that brought all this about was, it can be seen, more a matter of Machiavellian subterfuge, as Mickey confessed in the version he told me most recently. Let's call it version 4b:

"Dougie was always very quiet. He never really left; actually, it was more that I left the Orioles. This other little band with Johnny Bobin, Bob Clouter, Barry Scanling and Mo used to rehearse in the storeroom at Bobin's bookshop in Southend. I sort of joined them in Red Green and his Blues Combo, leaving Dougie and Ada behind. Then we decided to carry on, not under that name but as the Orioles. It was a better band, I think. This was post-Shades: I think it was 1965, but Mo says 1964, which would make it 50 years ago. Either way, by now our gig at the Cricketers, the local rock house, had grown from one night a week to four nights a week. Of course it was all Mods 'n' Rockers then – scooters, clip-ons, parkas, anoraks and all the girls in them blue plastic macs. We played there two years, then I got married."

During this frantic period of shuffling the band and playing flat out all over town, the "new" Orioles had become a star attraction - to many *the* star attraction - of the Southend music scene. Not only did they play the Cricketers several nights a week, on Saturdays they'd often go on to play an extra late night set at the Studio Jazz Club, which had stretched its music policy to include r'n'b in order to attract a new crowd to the venue.

John Bobin remembers being so exhausted while waiting to take part in one late night jam session there that he eventually gave up and went home to bed, causing Robin Trower to temporarily suspend his "raver's badge", (a neat phrase that pops up later in the lyrics to the Legend track *Captain Cool*, although there it's appended to Bob Clouter rather than John!).

The Orioles' rapid rise to the status of local legends had been chaotic but fun, as Mo Witham recollects:

"In the very early days we used to live together in Western Road. Ada, the bass player, lived upstairs, Juppy lived downstairs, me in between. We never had any money, but when you're young you don't care, do you? Everything was so exciting and full of possibilities. We'd come home from a gig and sit up till five in the morning playing cards, get up in the afternoon and go and blag beans on toast out of Laurie at the caff. It was brilliant."

On the downside, Mickey remembers some less socially fulfilling moments:

"Often it was me on my own down the tiny Little Goldmine Café in Southchurch Road for egg and chips. During the day almost everyone else I knew had a job – so I never saw a soul."

At night, the Orioles played an eclectic mix of rock & roll and soulful blues with high energy and tight precision, driven by Mickey's rolling piano style and Mo's syncopated guitar stabs, overlaying John and Bob's rhythmic anchor. There were few if any Jupp originals in the running order and, unusually for local bands at the time, no covers of contemporary hits. It was strictly what Mickey considered to be the real stuff, the same role of honour he sticks by to this day. *My Babe* and *Suzie Q* continued to thunder out, along with the likes of *Got Love If You Want It, Brand New Cadillac, I Wanna Walk You Home* and *Got My Mojo Working*.

Playing arch top semi-acoustic guitars, rather than the solid bodied electrics that were then more fashionable, and featuring a piano at the heart of their sound, the Orioles were excitingly different. They didn't just rock; they rolled, too.

In his memoir *Looking Back At Me*, written with Zoe Howe, Dr Feelgood lynch-pin, Wilko Johnson, remembers being in the crowd at the Cricketers, admiring lead guitarist Mo Witham's playing in particular:

"I used to go there and stand in front of him thinking 'If I could just catch one little lick, I could go home and try it', but I never could."

He was equally impressed with Mickey's voice, as he told Will Birch:

"The ferocity of Jupp's voice…I couldn't understand how he could make that sound. I was a bit intimidated by him. I remember once in a break, I went up to him and asked him if I could buy him a drink. He accepted and I felt, 'Wow, I've bought Mickey Jupp a drink!'"

Wilko expanded his memories of the Orioles at the Cricketers for me:

"Mo Witham remains one of the greatest guitarists I've ever seen, and to have someone like that in the same band as Juppy, whose voice is simply a phenomenon - real power, real soul - was a terrifying thing. They weren't just good, they were up there somewhere, (pointing to the ceiling). I was frightened of Mick when I went to see the Orioles. I thought someone who could sound that mean must be a pretty mean guy! I was just a boy trying to learn to play, seventeen or whatever, but the sound they were making wasn't a boy thing, it was a man thing. I used to watch them like a hawk, trying to work out stuff, but how they made those sounds I do not know. I just used to goggle at them. And the Cricketers, where they played, was an eye-opener, too. It was like the wild west - all spit and sawdust and real fights breaking out. I can remember on more than one occasion bigger bands, like the Swinging Blue Jeans, would appear at the Cricketers. You'd see them watching the Orioles playing the support slot, thinking bloody hell, how do we follow this!"

Talent apart, there were specific reasons for the Orioles' musical character. Using electro-acoustic instruments had always appealed to Mickey's ear - they sounded more real somehow, closer to the fifties music he so admired. In fact, some years later Mickey complained bitterly when John Bobin chose to replace the relatively muddy sound of his old semi-acoustic Epiphone bass with the snappy clarity of a solid-bodied Fender Precision.

At the Cricketers, as at the Shades before, there was a house piano, which made life pretty simple. But for other gigs, in those pre-digital days, the band had to hump a full size upright piano around with them. It would frequently go out of tune, forcing Mickey to carry a pair of pliers with him to try and get it back in tune, not always successfully.

Each night the Orioles finished with the same song: *Rockin' Robin*, perfectly showcasing Mickey's ever strengthening voice: a roaring, cracking, straining instrument of tremendous power. At strategic moments in the chorus of *Rockin' Robin* it was mandatory for the audience to yell the word "*Oriole*".

While that may have been good branding for the band, the chief objective of punters was simply to try to deafen audience members standing nearby. Many of those interviewed for this book have happy, if hoarse, memories of those days – I know I do.

At one Cricketers gig, Will Birch got closer to the action still; a real chance to live out his long-held dream of playing drums with the Orioles. Or was it a nightmare?

"My band, the Tradewinds, once supported them at the Cricketers. I remember Mo saying to me 'Calm down, calm down', because I was trying to be Keith Moon all the time. In '65 or '66, I was sent for by the Orioles' roadie to deputise for Bob Clouter, who'd blown out a gig at the Basildon Locarno. I got up on Bob's drums and played a dreadful 45 minute set, with Mick banging his foot to try and keep me in time."

(Being a modest man, it is likely that Will wasn't as awful as he suggests. In any case, Mickey is always especially critical of drummers and down the years has testily banged his foot at the best of them).

In any case, whatever the band's standard of playing, Mickey's voice would inevitably have saved the day – it always did, always does. As Mo Witham says of Mickey's singing, fifty years on:

"He is incapable of singing a bum note. Even after all this time playing with him, when he wants to he can make the hairs on the back of my neck stand up."

All the same, that extraordinary talent wasn't producing much of a living. Mickey had even sold his little red notebook of the Orioles song lyrics for five quid, plus part of his record collection, in an attempt to make ends meet. The band got the princely sum of £10 a night between them for the Cricketers' gigs. (The Cricketers' house photographer, who prowled the dancefloor taking pictures of happy revelers at a shilling a shot, probably made a better living). The band's fee had to be split between the five members and roadie Mick Bray, plus cover payments on the venerable Bedford Dormobile that carried them around to gigs. There was no proper manager to pay commission to, but that wasn't entirely helpful either as it meant there was nobody concentrating on furthering the band's career.

Despite this omission, people other than happy punters at the Cricketers were beginning to take notice of the Orioles, as John Bobin relates:

"Around that time the Orioles went up to London to play in a club in the West End, as an audition for an agent named Maurice King. The Walker Brothers were in the audience and seemed to enjoy the show, as it would appear did Maurice. As a result Decca got interested. They wanted Mickey to do a recording for them of old standard *Stagger Lee*, (*plus a couple of Little Richard numbers and a new rock and roll composition that Mickey didn't much like – Ed*). They didn't want the Orioles on it, just him: they were going to get session men in to do the backing. We weren't terribly happy about that but didn't want to stand in his way. On the day he was due to be recording it in London, I somehow got a call saying 'Where's Mickey? He's supposed to be here by now for the recording but all the session guys are sitting around here waiting'. I said I didn't know but would try and find out. So I went round to 37 Colman Street where he had his flat and he was fast asleep! I said you're supposed to be in London making a record. He more or less said he couldn't be bothered."

More recently, Mickey explained to me the strange episode of *Stagger Lee* a little more openly:

"The truth is I was being deliberately bolshie. I thought they would come looking for me, the Decca people, but I never heard any more about it."

Mickey also told me that he had been struck by remorse for agreeing to do the recording without the band – another reason he bailed out.

So why didn't he at least tell the studio that he wasn't coming after all? The man who went on to acquire a pretty fearsome reputation for being Mr. Awkward when he wanted to has a surprising answer. He maintains that he can't handle confrontation, despite only being prepared to do things *his* way, something that by definition guarantees conflict.

John Bobin elaborates on that in his memoir, *Bark Staving Ronkers*:

"Mick is legendary for his uncompromising attitude. He can be very charming and I count him as one of my oldest friends. However, he is temperamental and will only do what he wants to, when he wants to. He is quite capable of driving his band members nuts!"

But while Mickey wants to call the shots, he is uncomfortable about confronting those who might stand up to him. If under pressure they choose to jump, fine; but if Mickey is required to shove them over the edge...

This dilemma crop up over and over again throughout his career, as we shall see.

But for now the signs seemed positive for the Orioles. Despite the unfortunate and unconsummated Decca episode, everything seemed to be in place for the band to move up to the next level: a record deal for the Orioles rather than just Mickey, ideally some serious management input and then, who knows what?

Commenting on it years later, Will Birch remembers what a shock it had been that the Orioles weren't getting picked up nationally:

"This rejection of the Orioles was a great mystery to their local fans. Perhaps it was their lack of original material or perhaps it was an early manifestation of Jupp's reluctance to grab a career opportunity by the balls."

Up until this point, it had all been a bit hand to mouth, fun but hit and miss. Roadie Mick Bray's father had sort of become their stand-in manager but although the band played a lot around Essex, it only once got over the river and didn't do much at all in London.

On one occasion the band had been booked to play London's prestigious Flamingo club, so a coach outing was quickly organized to bus the keen Southend fans to the gig but in the end that show never took place.

So while the Orioles had supported a lot of well-known visiting acts at local gigs, including the Hollies, the Tremeloes and Dave Dee, Dozy, Beaky, Mick and Titch, things just weren't happening for them on the national platform. To have a golden career in front of them, they clearly needed more clout behind them.

"We were a good band," says Mo Witham, "but we never recorded - there weren't any demo studios around then, like there were later. And Mickey wasn't touting songs he'd written then – they didn't really arrive until a bit later, on that really nice Legend first album, with those great songs on."

But this was still two years away.

It was clear to many of us who saw them at the time that the Orioles could have made it and should have made it, and maybe even would have made it.

Instead, Mickey shot himself in the foot - not for the first time, and definitely not for the last.

In March 1966 he got sent to prison.

During the Orioles' rise to local fame, Mickey, aged just nineteen, had contrived to get married, have a child and quickly split up with his wife. Pat, the wife in question - the very girl Mickey had taken along to his first Black Diamonds rehearsal - had obtained a court order enforcing maintenance payments for her and Mickey's son, Gary.

"We were married before I was 20 and it was totally my fault the marriage split up. All of a sudden I was in a rock'n'roll band and a teenager hero, so it must have turned my head", Mickey later told journalist Chris Welch.

Everything had started happening a bit too quickly, as Mickey gingerly recalled when re-visiting those times for this book:

"I left home when I was nineteen and married the girl I'd met at the youth club. I'd packed in my job at the wallpaper shop, Interiors of Leigh, in April 1962 - just walked out, which I shouldn't have done even though the manager was a right little so and so. I should have given in my notice and gone through proper channels. I have regretted doing that ever since. After all these years I've begun to realise I wasn't really suited to the music business! Talent-wise I was okay. I had a fair voice and wrote a few songs and gained quite a bit of respect. For a living I was playing in the Orioles. I just fell into it and went along with it because it meant not having to work nine to five, even though in those early days there was no money in it."

Indeed there wasn't. On top of the expenses noted earlier, there was now new equipment to fund, including a 100 watt PA system, bought on the never-never.

In order to afford somewhere to live once he had split up with his wife, Mickey had rented a flat from the owner of the Cricketers pub.

Some say he cunningly arranged for the rent to be deducted from the band's fees each week before they divvied up the gig money, thus ensuring that the rest of the Orioles effectively subsidised Mickey's rent for him!

Even if that were the case, there still wasn't enough left over to make those full maintenance payments the court had obliged him to.

Exhibiting a lack of grip on matters financial and legal that would dog him throughout his career, Mickey solved this tricky dilemma by ignoring it. Inevitably this strategy rapidly failed, as he explains:

"The Orioles finally broke up when I was carted off to Brixton prison one night. The Warrant Officer was very good about it, actually. He knocked on the door of my flat at about 6.30pm, just as I was getting ready to go off to the Cricketers for our gig, and told me I was nicked. I said to him, 'Look, I need a favour – I have to go and tell the band what's happening'. He very kindly agreed to take me to the Cricketers so I could talk to them. He even bought me half a lager when we got there! But I couldn't play of course. I seem to remember I spent that night in the cells at Southend Police station, then off to the nick in the morning. The band got someone else to sing that night."

Unsurprisingly, the rest of the band members recall the dramatic events equally vividly. Being troopers, they played on.

"Geoff Keane was in the audience that night and saw this as his big chance to take over from Mickey as our singer," says Mo Witham, "but he was bloody awful." Nevertheless, many years later Mickey was to return the compliment, in even more dramatic circumstances, as we shall see.

Looking back on those events today, it all seems slightly surreal, as does Mickey's prison sentence, which these days would surely be more lenient for a first offence. Mickey's lifelong friend, and musical collaborator, Chris East, elaborates on the harsher attitudes that prevailed in that wilder era, a time when he had joined up:

"Well, I got caught on the run from the Navy, twice. Once when I was staying at Mickey's place, when they handcuffed me so fast I hadn't even got my trousers on, and then, of course, couldn't! The second time was at the Cricketers while watching the Orioles. I remember they were playing *Slow Down* when the heavy mob arrived and I thought, here we go again!"

By the time Mickey got out of Brixton prison, six weeks later, the momentum had gone out of the Orioles and the band folded. But Mo recalls that the Mickey who came out of clink wasn't quite the same Mickey who went in:

"We used to have problems with Mickey sometimes because he was a bit relaxed about personal hygiene. Some B&Bs we were supposed to be staying in on the road wouldn't let him in 'cos of the smell, so he'd have to sleep in the van. Trouble was in the morning we then had to get in it and drive somewhere. This didn't make him very popular with us but he was the singer and the best thing about the band, so we had to put up with it. The day he came out of Brixton he came to see me, I was staying in my sister's basement flat in Southend. Now when he went in he had long red hair and stubble, wore an old mac and didn't smell good. When he came out, he was in a suit, had a nice haircut, was clean-shaven and smelt all right. It was a real transformation."

Mickey himself recalls that radical change:

"People said I came out of prison looking a damn sight healthier than when I went in! Mind you, the first thing I did was go to the tobacconists outside the nick and buy ten fags; I think they were called Mascot: tiny little cigarettes but a treat after having to roll my own inside."

Chris Stevens, soon to become Mickey's semi-permanent employer at his shop - the Chris Stevens Music Centre also recalls Mickey's pre-prison persona:

"I first came across Mick when I was working at Gilbert's, which was the original Southend music shop. He often came into the shop, although I'm not sure I recall him ever buying anything much. Mick was one of the great unwashed at the time - but all the same I would go to the Cricketers some nights to see the Orioles because they were a pretty impressive bunch of players."

Mickey considers the prison experience to have been ghastly but of value:

"Prison was what you might call a learning curve: I thought 'I don't want to come back here.' It was the longest six weeks of my life. For many years afterwards, I would now and then dream I was in prison and then that I was waking up there. So when I really woke up I couldn't work out where I was! I think everybody should go to prison for six weeks when they are about sixteen years old to find out this is what it's like."

Mickey's smarter look on release perhaps wasn't that surprising when one discovers that he had abandoned any plans to return to music - in fact his intentions were quite the opposite. Despite his obvious abilities as a singer and player, and notwithstanding his growing local hero status, Mickey felt music was no longer a sensible way forward for him, as he told me:

"Music was not high on my list of things to do. I came out and signed on for two weeks: you had to when you left prison. That's the only time I ever sponged off the state in my life, by the way. Straight off I got a job at Keddies Department Store in Southend, who were enlightened enough to take on ex-prisoners.

I worked in the goods area, taking in deliveries of pots and stuff. After a while, in early '67 I think, the ironmongery department decided to open up a gardening section, and for some reason I was picked to run it. Given my art school background, perhaps, they wanted me to set it out, so I scrounged stuff from the display department - fake grass and all that - and put it together."

Unlikely as it may sound to those who don't know him, Mickey has always enjoyed working in retail, having had several spells at it down the years, when musical income alone wouldn't pay the rent. By far his favourite type of retail is ironmongery.

Put him behind a long mahogany counter in charge of hundreds of drawers containing thousands of nails, screws, bolts, hooks, tacks and goodness knows what, and he becomes serenely happy. Fork handles, sir? Not a problem.

Indeed his tiny home today is so neat and orderly that some have called it 'the Stock Room' – a regime where there's a place for everything and everything is in its place. Those retail experiences would also provide inspiration for songs to come - not that Mickey had started writing seriously just yet.

In February 1966, avid Orioles fan Will Birch bumped into Mickey, now band-less, at the Harold Dog coffee bar and talked him into re-forming the Orioles.

"They played one gig at the Studio Club," he remembers, "but the magic had gone. It was a rather embarrassing affair for all concerned: further evidence that you can't re-live the past, because in their day, for really earthy rock and roll they were unbeatable."

Previously, there had earlier been an even more embarrassing Orioles episode in which a new would-be manager - a businessman who owned Southend's Studio Club - briefly took control of the band's fate, starting with a dramatic shift in marketing strategy.

Re-naming the band Jupp's Jesters, (how he got Mickey to agree to that I will never fathom), his masterplan was for them to wear full harlequin outfits on stage - an attempt to establish a more memorable image than the usual shirt and jeans combination. While this gross indignity never actually occurred, the band did go out under this name several times, wearing a compromise outfit of natty, striped blazers!

Anyway, all that was over now.

The Orioles were history.

Mickey Jupp, musician, was history.

But there was still a worm in his brain: for the drive to create will not tolerate submersion for long, whether Mickey liked it or not.

The Creative Drive And The Creative Brain

Clapton admires the Jupp creative brain courtesy Mickey Jupp

It is 6.30am on a sharp April morning in Crete and I am writing this chapter.

I do not have a deadline to meet; I have a brain to obey.

I awoke just after 5am, surfacing unwillingly from a dream about this book, upon which I have been working for the last three weeks solid. My dream had been a variant of the one I have every night, always about this book. On this occasion I dreamt that I had discovered the existence of a new Jupp song, but suspected it was merely an existing one given a different title (just as *Pilot* had first been known as *The Last Time I Saw Your Face*).

On waking, my conscious brain wearily issues the usual instruction to my sub-conscious brain: forget it and go back to sleep for another hour or two. My sub-conscious brain takes no notice; it never does. Instead it starts writing this chapter, without my permission, forcing me to get up, hurriedly brush my teeth and start work.

It happens to be my 65th birthday today, but no matter.

Mickey's song *Mother and Child* is running continuously on a loop somewhere in the back of my mind as it has been for several days. This is an improvement on the previous Jupp song that occupied that slot, *Nashville,* which gets a little cheesy by day three. Soon there will be another.

Creatively I am no Mickey Jupp - more's the pity - but I am, I suppose, what they broadly term "creative". I'm a musician, a photographer, I write. I love all three of these things but that is not why I do them. I do them because I have no choice.

My brain decided for me a long time ago; my creative drive took me over and occupied my soul. This is not meant as a boast.

For creativity is not about simple intelligence. Nor is it about normality, or perfection. People with autism, or its milder sister, Asperger's Syndrome, are unable to control many aspects of their brain and thus behaviour, yet are often extremely creative. They may lack humour, empathy and social skills; they may crave solitude and routine; they may be preoccupied with specific objects or subjects, but they are often excellent artists, too.

Talking Heads' leader David Byrne has diagnosed himself as having a mild form of Asperger's. He points out that anyone who willingly oscillates between jumping on stage to perform in front of hundreds, even thousands, of people he doesn't know, yet spends the rest of the time hiding in his shell, without thinking such a contrast abnormal, must have some slight maladjustment.

His theory is that a withdrawn introvert makes art in public as a way of reaching out and communicating, given the ordinary social chitchat most people utilise for this purpose would be too uncomfortable.

He is not alone in that view. Many artists would rather play in front of ten thousand people than ten: thousands are beyond comprehension, whereas ten people is few enough to take in expressions, be unable to avoid eye contact.

Byrne also references a 1994 article in *The British Journal of Psychiatry* in which Felix Post claimed that more than two thirds of the creative individuals he had studied had mental disorders.

It is sometimes said that proportionately more creative people are left handed, because left handedness indicates right brain dominance (it's a mirror image thing), and the right side of the brain contains more of the zones related to creativity.

American scientist Dr Alan Searleman, from New York's St. Lawrence University, recently studied 1200 research participants, from which he drew the conclusion that left-handed people had higher levels of "fluid" intelligence and enhanced vocabulary skills. He concluded that this might be why more lefties end up in so- called creative professions such as art, writing and music. Searleman also found that left-handers were likely to boast higher IQs and be significantly better at problem solving than their right-handed counterparts. On the flip side, though, they were not so good when it came to remembering things. Bad news if you write long and complicated lyrics for songs you plan to perform live, (Mickey would understand this reference well).

There's something else I find particularly interesting about how the creative brain works. It involves our neural pathways; specifically the way in which some minds can navigate them more laterally than others.

The ability to acquire and process facts and observations - to reason - is different from the ability to put them together in innovative ways. That extra step is the key thing creative people do better. When humans perform intellectual tasks, neuronal networks appear to function in more directed and linear ways. However, when humans perform more creative tasks it is as if the neural pathways plot more meandering and circumlocutory routes. It looks rather like the brain's equivalent of going for a walk or daydreaming – the very physical moments at which we often find good ideas spring to mind.

Thus truly creative people have the freedom to go for a walk in their mind any time they like. The fences are down so they can take any of the millions of tiny pathways that criss-cross their mental landscape. That's how they can come up with novel solutions. Whereas less creative people see big roads that they prefer to stick to, are slightly fearful of straying from. This makes them more set in their ways and less likely to take risks and be original - but it also makes them easier to understand and rub along with, because most other folk are on those same roads.

Many of the more creative people - who take more 'risks' - never really learn the "right way" of doing things, (or how to understand those who do). As a result they often fail, not just creatively but in life. Their businesses, relationships and life plans are more likely to founder. So to survive they need even greater resolve than most do: which can appear to others as evidence of an egotistical, solipsistic or just downright contrary nature.

To paraphrase George Bernard Shaw, "the reasonable man adapts to the world around him, while the unreasonable man expects the world to conform to what he wants – which is why all progress is achieved by unreasonable men." This apparent 'unreasonableness' can make creative people unpopular but they can't help themselves; their behaviour is programmed into them.

Venerated Rolling Stone Keith Richards has long recognised that creativity is a harsh mistress and an irresistible force:

"The drive to create is just something I obey. I hear something and I've got to learn how to play it. Once you know that, then you have no choice. You can't turn it off. This is a one-way tap: once it's on, it's on. You can try and ignore it but it's far more powerful than you are. It's not a controllable thing; it just keeps coming from inside. You're a slave to it in a way."

For those not blessed/cursed with such a creative brain it can be mysterious - virtually impossible - to fathom such a powerful urge.

It's perhaps helpful to picture this condition less as a drive and more as a hunger, whose presence is partly to do with the sort of brain one was born with, partly to do with nurture and partly about what stage of life's emotional journey an individual has reached: how the individual has decided to relate to the things around them and their innate curiosity levels.

Psychologist Abraham Maslow studied this at length, observing how creative people pursue their goals to the detriment of many other aspects of their lives, noting that, "they do not cling to the familiar, nor is their quest for the truth a catastrophic need for certainty, safety, definiteness and order." Maslow's work is most fully expressed in his theory of the Hierarchy of Needs, in which he posits the idea that people are motivated to fulfill basic needs first but then move on to tackling other, more advanced needs.

This hierarchy is most usually displayed as a pyramid made up of several strata: the lowest levels of the pyramid contain the most basic needs, while more complex needs are located further up. The needs at the bottom of the pyramid are basic physical requirements including the need for food, water, sleep and warmth. Once these lower level needs have been met, people can move on to the next level of needs, which are for safety and security. As individuals progress up the pyramid, needs become increasingly psychological and social. So next the need for friendship, love, intimacy and status become important. Further up the pyramid, towards the top, the need for personal esteem and feelings of accomplishment take priority.

The so-called 'Inner Directed' individuals who have reached this highest level are strong, clear-minded and often a bit difficult. They only really respect their own judgment, so the views of those around them become unimportant. Material success is to be eyed suspiciously. Only the creative fulfillment of their talent matters to them. That is the overwhelming urge that must be obeyed, whether or not it leads to material success or peer group adulation.

Does this remind you of anyone?

Mickey Jupp is ambivalent about his own creative awakening:

"I don't really know when my creative urge arrived. I was good at painting – I only got two GCEs: Art and English Grammar, the latter has helped no end in song writing. I went to Art College and painted there but never felt compelled to do much outside of the lessons.

In fact, I left early and got a job because we weren't doing enough of what I call art; we were doing a lot of stuff like typography with loads of Letraset everywhere, designing book covers and that sort of thing."

What he does know is that his creative urge is unlikely ever to go away:

"When you've been creating all your life, it's hard to stop. But what you can do is stop driving yourself as much. You can walk away from something if you want, knowing you don't have to flog yourself."

And what does Mickey do when he walks away from the creative world of his music?

He literally walks some more - into the mountains.

And there he takes photographs. Or paints.

It's that creative imperative in action once again.

5 Cross Country

In which Mickey discovers that as well as playing songs, he can write them

Legend Mk.1   courtesy Russ Cottee

Some fellah told me, son, you can sing
Here's a guitar, learn how to hold the thing
Shake your legs, wiggle your hips
And sign here sonny, don't give me no lip.
If only mother could see me now
Singing in a rock and roll band, taking a bow

If Only Mother **by Mickey Jupp, Juppanese**

In late 1966, a Southend supergroup nearly arrived.

Stuck between the ignominious end of the Paramounts and the immaculate conception of Procol Harum, Robin Trower attempted to put together a fresh band called The Jam, (this was long before the existence of Paul Weller's band The Jam - who were major Jupp admirers, by the way).

Mickey was a big fan of Robin's early guitar playing style – although less so of how it developed, as a quote of his from 1982 spells out:

"Robbie was always and still is one of the great r&b and blues guitar players – blues just drips off his guitar when he feels like it. He's gone on to this Hendrix thing now, which nobody seems to like, but it keeps him happy so fair enough."

At the time, The Jam was a potentially important development in Mickey's becalmed career. He remembers how it came about:

"The Jam was ex-Flowerpots drummer Tommy Berry, Barry Scanling on bass, Robbie Trower on guitar and me playing piano. Wilko Johnson was invited, too, but he was off to college or India or somewhere."

Wilko also remembers getting his invitation:

"One day, Robin Trower came over to Canvey Island and knocked on my door, telling me he's thinking of getting a band together with Juppy, called the Jam, and that he wanted me to play second guitar. As it happens I was just about to go to university so I said that I couldn't, but I wouldn't have joined in any case. The way I play, based on Mick Green, is all about just using just one guitar to do everything, so having two, sometimes even three guitars, simply wouldn't have worked."

It turned out to be not that big a loss for Wilko - the Jam never came to much.

"We didn't do much other than rehearse," Mickey told me, "we did play once or twice at the old London Hotel in Southend High Street, doing BB King stuff like *I Can't Lose* - the riff from which I've often used in various ways on stage since."

(In fact, rather extraordinarily, Mickey accidentally had the rights to *I Can't Lose* by BB King for a while. The PRS/MCPS people, aware he was performing it live and unable to trace the real writer, forwarded Mickey the royalties for a while. When he also started receiving royalties for Elvis Presley's *Big Hunk of Love*, for the same reason, he thought he'd better put them right pretty damn quick).

"In Jam, I did most of the singing because Rob doesn't have the greatest of voices, - sorry, Rob, nothing personal. We didn't sound bad but then Rob got the Procol Harum thing going and I did my fast exit to Bath."

Mickey cleared off to Warminster, then on to Bath after falling out with his employers at Keddies – the detail of which he has always refused to be drawn on. Whatever the reason, he must have been unsure whether or not that was curtains. Surely his musical career would be over for good now he was living miles from all his old band mates.

In actual fact, his musical career was just about to begin all over again, through a chance meeting:

"Somebody I knew vaguely - the brother of a girl I'd been half seeing when I was in the Orioles – well, his mum worked behind the bar at the Cricketers. When I'm down there one night, back in Southend for a visit, she tells me there's a group of blokes in Brentwood looking for a piano player. So I got on a train to Brentwood, and lo and behold it's only the Rockerfellas."

One of the early influences on the youth of Southend, Mickey included, Romford band the Rockerfellas had been the idols of Paramount Robin Trower, helping inspire that young lad to take up music. By now, though, the band was decidedly past the first flush of youth and taking things a bit more steadily. Mickey remembers them fondly:

"They were David Barnes, Joey Jones, Tony Sumner, and, sorry, forget the name of the drummer. I was living in Bath by now and really starting to get on with my song writing, so I'd travel back to play with them at the Essex Arms on Sunday lunchtimes."

Having moved to Bath to make a really fresh start, Mickey quickly got himself another job (in retail, of course), and rented a little bedsit. With no band of his own either to satisfy his creative urges or take up his spare time, Mickey got seriously stuck into songwriting for the first time.

It was his regular Sunday train journey from Bath to the Essex Arms, where he played the Rockerfellas gigs, that inspired him to write *Cross Country*, one of the best known of his early compositions:

One hundred and forty two miles
Cross country just to hold you for a while
One hundred and forty two miles
Cross country just to see you smile…

The journey and the casual gigs with a veteran band were to be the unlikely springboard for Mickey's fist real crack at the big time:

"One day this bloke from Romford, called Dave Watson, comes into our Rockerfellas gig. He's got his own small publishing company, Golden City Music, and says he wants to sign me up – although I hadn't got that much serious writing by then: maybe *Heather on the Hill, City, Doncaster By-Pass* and one or two other things: the first of all being *National Gas*. So I signed up, why not?

His company was affiliated to Carlin; I still get a few bob through that to this day. I think it was just for the publishing, I don't think he managed me, too.

Did I sign anything else? I can't remember."

Back in 1963, Dave Watson had himself been in a band called the Teasers, another member of which was guitarist Dennis Masterton, who figures sporadically but importantly in Mickey's musical story. Dave and Dennis had started writing songs in the hope of having a hit, (once the Beatles had proved wildly successful, everyone was having a go) as Dennis explained to me:

"We took our early efforts up to Denmark Street, where a guy at Campbell Connelly became interested; everyone was mad for new songs. Through this experience Dave got interested in publishing as well as playing and writing."

The publishing deal with Dave Watson didn't promise much financially but it gave Mickey just the impetus he needed to persevere with his song writing:

"I was on my own, no local band. Also pubs and me hadn't really been introduced at the time – I'd played a lot of them but I wasn't much of a drinker. In fact, it was one or two of the builders I met at the builders merchants I was working at who eventually got me into going to the pub from time to time. But basically I was quite a stopping-in sort of a homebody."

Every decent stop-at-home needs a pastime, and writing songs became Mickey's. He had no plans to perform or record them: he just enjoyed putting them together, flexing his creative muscles:

"Writing songs was my hobby – something I could do at home. They were never written with the intention of being something for me to play in a band. On the other hand, it was a serious hobby – something you wanted to keep doing to get better at; it wasn't just a casual whim."

While upping the tempo of his writing, Mickey still played occasionally with the Rockerfellas, at the same time continuing his work at the builder's merchants in Bath, a job he truly loved. Will Birch has a view about this:

"The retail days in Bath were amongst the happiest of his life. Being in that simple, straightforward environment was probably a big relief for him. When you've been used to bashing away trying to get your music accepted, touring and all the rest, doing a mundane job is sort of equivalent to putting on your slippers and relaxing watching television. The pressure's off, it's really quite enjoyable."

Mickey made some new, non-musical friends in Bath, including a fellow retail worker who went by the nickname of Crun, (real name Jim Walter). Somewhat surprisingly, Crun later turned up in a band, too: playing bass for Stackridge - an outfit who, like Mickey, were to be championed by John Peel and, unlike Mickey, produced by George Martin.

(Five years later, in 1971, Legend Mk 2 would perform live on John Peel's seminal BBC radio show. Typically, for contrast Peel blended their session with one by progressive band Soft Machine. Still later, in 1978, Mickey recorded another session for the Peel show, this time as a solo artist, which was broadcast over two separate nights.

Mickey seems to have enjoyed the BBC sessions more than album recording, perhaps because there was less pressure, the whole thing being closer to a live performance:

"We did several recordings for the BBC, often in Lower Regent Street where they had amazingly old equipment - all Bakelite knobs and sweep dials - but they got a great sound. The *Top Gear* stuff with just me and Mo was done in the nearby small theatre in Lower Regent Street.")

But back in Bath, with all this ahead of him, Mickey's recording equipment was considerably more primitive even than this. He had commandeered the family Elizabethan domestic reel-to-reel tape recorder because its basic sound-on-sound function permitted him to overdub himself. This meant he could create basic song demos to send off to publisher Dave Watson in the post. However, publisher Dave knew that these demos would need to be developed further if he was to get a record company interested. Dennis Masterson recalls what happened next:

"It was 1968 and Dave and me and some other mates, including Tony Sumner from the Rockerfellas and Bill Fyfield, later of Legend, were doing an album of our own material for MGM Records. We did piano and trumpet-led instrumentals, calling ourselves the Romford Golden Sunshine Band for the purposes of the record. The stuff sounds a bit cheesy now but it was all right at the time, I suppose. We used to regularly rehearse at a place in Collier Row called the Lawnsway Club. Dave came along one evening and said he'd discovered this amazing bloke called Mickey Jupp. He told us, 'this man has got more talent in his little finger than all you lot put together!' It was true, of course – I'd seen Mick play at the Essex Arms in Brentwood with the Rockerfellas, so I knew he could sing and play. Now it turned out he could write great songs, too."

The Lawnsway Club became the makeshift studio at which more polished demos of Mickey's songs would be recorded, albeit in a still fairly basic fashion. Dennis, who did the actual engineering, winces as he recounts the episode:

"We had done the demos for our MGM album there. It was all very primitive stuff, using old tape machines and splicing tape together with scissors and sellotape, but it was all we had, so we used the same set up to record the demos for Mickey's first album. Mick came down with Chris East, Steve Geere and an original drummer called Ray; but Ray wasn't well and had to drop out early on, so that's when they got Nigel Dunbar in. I think Nigel had played with the Rockerfellas earlier, at a time when Mickey wouldn't have been aware of him because he was too busy in the Orioles.

I did the recording of the songs for Dave's company, Golden City Music, over several sessions. I remember the last one was on a Sunday, when we did *Heather on the Hill* and *Twenty-Carat Rocker:* straight onto a B&O domestic machine I'd borrowed specially. It was better quality than the equipment we'd been using before. Some of the Rockerfellas helped out on *Twenty Carat Rocker*, I seem to recall. Those demo sessions were the first time I'd met Mickey."

Dave Watson, being something of an entrepreneur, then hawked these improved demos around the business, to sudden and surprising effect.

Bell Records was a big player in the USA but had no British outlet of its own, having previously released its product over here under license to other labels. Now they planned to start up their own UK operation and Mickey was to be their very first signing.

He was to make an album that would come out in America (home to all Mickey's musical heroes) as well as being the new label's first UK LP release.

From it they would also take a track to become the label's first UK single release. There would be a promotional campaign of press advertisements and radio plugging to support these two releases, especially on the all-powerful pirate radio stations that had emerged by now.

It was astonishing. Having removed himself some distance from everything that might have helped him obtain a record deal – one he couldn't get when regularly gigging with a widely admired band - Mickey had now landed one, and an important one at that. All he needed was a band to help him record his music, and then play live to promote it.

But a band of his own was the one thing Mickey no longer had. It was time to get one together again.

By now, school friend Chris East had been officially discharged from the Navy, no doubt as a direct result of his frequent attempts to leave it unofficially. He'd busked his way around Europe with not much more than a rucksack and a twelve-string guitar, so by the time he returned to Southend he'd developed a distinctive playing style and a good high-register singing voice.

"Mickey rang me and told me he'd got the chance of doing an album. He reckoned he needed a 12-string player to fill out the sound as it was going to be largely acoustic. I'd never met the others before, I think Dave Watson must have found them."

Indeed he must have, as Mickey claims they weren't known to him either, despite some reports that Mickey himself found them playing in a club in Shenfield. This casual collection of bods became the musical crew charged with making Mickey's first-ever professional recordings. The four met up and went through the Jupp compositions a couple of times prior to any recording. The songs weren't particularly complicated to play, but even so this was hardly the sort of tight gigging rehearsal schedule most bands would have undertaken in the run up to recording their debut album. However, it didn't take many run-throughs to realize that these largely acoustic, folky sounding numbers benefitted from Chris' twelve-string, which added a more poppy jangle to them.

The songs bore early witness to Mickey's unusual lyrical bent, typified by *Doncaster By-Pass*, as Mickey explains:

"I was back living with my parents in Eastwood Old Road and seeing a girlfriend when I wrote it. The tune came to me as I was strolling the mile or so home from her place. I was walking down the Southend Arterial Road, in the cycle track sort of bit to avoid getting run over, humming this bit of a tune. The words that came to me at first were '*my dog is sat howling, at the midnight sky*' - no idea why, they just fitted together, I guess. It was in any case in my mind to write a song about a UK place - rather than Amarillo or wherever, like the Americans always do - and the Doncaster by-pass had been in the news as one of the first motorways in Britain, so I went for that."

(It is interesting to note how in these early days the tune came first and the final lyrics were dropped in after; not the way Mickey was to work later on.)

In *Heather on the Hill*, another composition from this early batch, Mickey was to create the first of many songs inspired by the Lake District: the place he had been besotted with since childhood. The words may be about a landscape but it is as genuine a love song as he ever wrote to any woman.

But it was a while before that love was to be consummated...

Despite Bell Records' talk of big promotional budgets further down the line, relatively little appears to have been invested in the making of the record itself.

Mickey, Chris, Nigel and Steve went into Central Sound, a less than premiership recording facility in Denmark Street, (in fact it was mostly used as a demo studio) where they cut the whole album in one single day, spread over three sessions of three hours each. Later in his career Mickey would work with producers who spent longer than that just getting the drum sound right.

One explanation for the brevity of the recording schedule is that Mickey may have had to pay the studio fees himself; certainly they could have been deducted from his royalties. Dennis Masterton has another theory:

"Dave was a little bit fly – I reckon he may have blagged the studio time for that one; he used to do it for our stuff, too. You know, out of hours work arranged with the engineer on the quiet, to get a low rate for cash...."

(Unfortunately we can't ask Dave himself as sadly he died of a heart attack, aged just forty-two).

Whatever the reason for the unseemly haste, there was little spare time left after the basic tracks had been recorded, so you won't find much overdubbing - bar some backup vocals and the odd dropped-in piano embellishment. The band simply set up and played live, including vocals, with engineer Freddy Winrose getting it down on tape as best he could, given the limited warm-up time. While it's hard to find much evidence of any real production, other than commanding, "roll tape" at the start of each take, the producer's credit went to one Sandy Roberton.

Now Roberton was at heart a folk specialist who had worked with the likes of Steeleye Span and Ian Matthews, going on to manage John Martyn and then, rather improbably, Steely Dan's Walter Becker. As such he may have been a rational choice for Mickey's slightly country-style songs and instrumental line up. What he lacked was the experience - or to be fair, the time – to make the most of the rockier, bluesier side of Mickey's writing. (Undeterred, he is still producing to this day, having taken the helm on Midlake's celebrated 2011 release *Late Night Tales*).

Dennis Masterton, who had originally taped the demos, went along to watch the recording of the finished album:

"I went to the recording of the album proper at Central Sound, with my then girlfriend, now wife. In particular I wanted to see this mighty Ampex eight-track tape machine! Mickey seemed relaxed enough, and well he might have been: the stuff he'd written for the record was blinding. But I recall the producer doing most of the interaction, such as it was, with Chris East. The producer would suggest changes and Chris would respond by saying he didn't think it would make much difference!"

Mickey recalls little of this, although he does have a vague memory relating to the album rehearsals:

"I do remember the Bell album rehearsals and having some quick photos taken there to help publicise some free equipment we'd got from Vox – ridiculous as we looked so unlike a cool band. But I had forgotten that Dennis did the recording of the demos and briefly came to Central."

Everything about the first Legend album appears to have been a rush job, it obviously having been mixed in rather a hurry, too. One piece of evidence for this is the fact that the mono and stereo versions of the track *Shindig* are clearly more than simply different mixes - they are entirely different takes. (The eventual re-release of the album on CD many years later unusually contained both mono and stereo recordings, thanks to the efforts of Lasse Kärrbäck, whose vinyl was used for the re-mastering. As a result the listener can hear this and several other interesting discrepancies between versions).

Given how quickly it was recorded, Legend's Bell album is a surprisingly satisfying piece of work, thanks to some terrific songs, great singing and a homely, gently shambolic vibe that renders the LP comfortable and accessible.

In fact, it feels a bit like the Lovin' Spoonful in places, which can't be bad.

In other places there is some splendid moody piano from Mickey: for example, *Bartender's Blues* and *Come Back Baby*, which could date from almost any later point in his career. Another feature is the excellent, nimble bass playing of Steve Geere, both on Gibson SG bass guitar and acoustic double bass: inventive throughout and cleverly bowed in places (the bass, not Steve).

On the downside, the whole endeavour is littered with playing errors, from missed chord changes to the poor confused drummer at one point stopping entirely, midway through a song, before gathering his bearings and setting off again. Cock-ups of this sort should be left on the editing room floor or made redundant by a subsequent take, not permitted onto the end product for all to hear.

Not to be outdone by player errors, production and engineering have their unfortunate lapses, too, from inconsistencies in reverb levels via crazily compressed piano to some laughably inappropriate sudden fades. (Amazingly, almost every single track on the album is a fade, perhaps suggesting some discomfort within the chronically under-rehearsed band about exactly how the songs ended!)

According to Mickey, the entire thing sounds as if it was recorded "in a barn last thing on a Saturday night." He sums up the whole album as being "very lightweight" having described the overall feel as "acoustic country rock 'n roll", which certainly covers off most angles. But in a way, its very lightness and refusal to be pigeonholed are parts of its charm.

Certainly, don't let the catalogue of shortcomings above put you off listening to a record that showcases just about every style Mickey was to go on to employ during the rest of his career.

Even if they scrimped a bit on recording costs, Bell kept their word on the marketing push, and the album came out to good reviews, as did the single taken from it: *National Gas*, backed with *Heather on the Hill*.

This was plugged well, being played on the radio a great deal, which, unfortunately didn't make it a hit but, as Mickey commented, "I made quite a bit of money from that."

In France the record came out with a picture sleeve, rare for the period. It did not feature a picture of Mickey, though, being entirely typographic. The album sleeve, on the other hand, did have a picture of the band on the back cover, one taken by Mickey's brother David on location in exotic Muffin Hall Road, Barling.

The main shot, the one on the front cover, is an absolute mystery: a negative inversion of an unknown man or woman on a beach, with a mysterious object in front of them.

Nobody has a clue who he or she might be or why he or she is there except, presumably, the art director at Bell. Mickey's only comment on it was, "I think it's supposed to be a towel, but it looks like a gigantic turd. It was done in America."

Whatever the reasons for this ghastly aberration, it started an unfortunate trend:

Mickey, or his advisers, have studiously kept him off virtually all his album covers ever since – not a strategy likely to improve his chances of achieving fame.

In fact, taken as a whole, Mickey can boast a gallery of some of the worst album covers any artist can have had inflicted upon them and their fans.

As we shall see, this is but one symptom of the broader ways in which Mickey's record companies were repeatedly clueless as to how best to present the man they were investing their money and hopes in.

What's rather more Mickey's own fault must be the consistently unappealing nature of his album titles: if not consisting simply of the word 'Legend', which has happened three times, most are snippets of lyrics randomly drawn from a song from somewhere on the album - often conveying an indistinct or downright misleading impression of the album as a whole.

For example, guess where *Oxford* was recorded? Wrong.

But for now, at least, Mickey was safe from that criticism. His first album was called *Legend*, after his "band's" name. Fair enough.

Any self-respecting record company marketing man, even one who sanctioned a sleeve as bad as the Bell one, will tell you that what was wanted now was a big national tour. That would be the best way to give the public a chance to hear more of Mickey's songs and listen to his great voice.

Legend started off by playing one gig, on a boat on the River Thames, in Staines. It was a private show, for some music publishers, possibly involving a wedding.

Great.

"We couldn't do any gigs. We weren't prepared for it", remembered Mickey, looking back on the episode some years later, as leader of a different Legend. "We had no equipment, no PA, we looked wrong – still do to some extent."

So instead of touring to support the album, the band broke up.

A masterstroke.

Unsurprisingly, record sales were not great. As a result, copies of the Bell *Legend* album today are rare, and originals, especially of the mono version, change hands for steep prices – more than a £100 for a mint copy.

But although his first LP hadn't sold too well, for the first time Mickey experienced the great benefit of being a writer, a musician who was no longer merely a performer of cover versions. Now others could cover *his* songs.

In November 1969, an artist called Conroy Cannon – a pseudonym for the Rockerfellas' original piano player Tony Sumner – did just that. He released a single on Atlantic Records, no less, with *Good Boy*, a Jupp composition from the Bell album, on its B-side. How did it get there?

Well, the producer of that single was none other than Mickey's publisher, Dave Watson. So why then wasn't it the A-side, you may wonder?

Well, not only was Dave Watson also the producer of the A-side, *My Bunny*, he was also the writer of that song – and was no doubt pre-disposed to his own composition getting any glory that was to be had. (Though, let the record show that Mickey doubts that this was the naked self-interest it might at first seem, insisting instead that, "Dave was always a gentleman.")

There was a further Dave Watson/Mickey Jupp/Central Sound recording that never saw the light of day, perhaps for the best:

"We went back afterwards for another session. Dave got a group of people together to do a version of *Oh Happy Day* and I got roped in to do that. I gave up in the end: I just didn't care for the song, even though one of my early favourite albums - a 1962 LP called *Black Nativity* - was of similar material. The track *Rise Up Shepherd and Follow* gives me shivers when I think about it right now."

In the end, Dave Watson's invaluable contribution to the development of Mickey's career never made him wealthy: his final income from the arrangement with Mickey was £500 he was paid to buy him out of his publishing/management deal. The money for this came out of the advance paid by a different record label to a different band called Legend, operating in a different musical genre, represented by a different manager – but despite all that, an outfit about to release an album with the same title as the first one.

Let that be a warning to the reader that this story is going to get very complicated.

Some years later, in 1972, Tremolos singer Chip Hawkes produced a version of Mickey's first 45, *National Gas,* for the Symbols, an Essex close-harmony band that had been around forever but never quite made it. Mickey's composition was one of two tracks in competition for a single release on CBS. While the band preferred *National Gas*, CBS unfortunately chose to put out the other one, so the Symbols' version of Mickey's song never saw the light of day. (It would be most interesting to hear, if anyone has an old acetate lying around).

On reflection, the launch of Bell Records, courtesy of Mickey, may not have been auspicious, but the company went on to do rather well. The label that Legend kicked into life was later to bring us the likes of David Cassidy, Gary Glitter and the Bay City Rollers.

Thanks, Mickey.

However, some time after this golden teenybopper era, times got tough again. Bell was folded into a newly amalgamated label called Arista, which found great success with the likes of Barry Manilow and Whitney Houston.

They also went on to sign another great talent.... yes, you've guessed it, Mickey Jupp.

But there's a lot more story to go before we get to that....

The *Legend* Bell Album

Melody Maker reviewed it on 8ᵗʰ March 1969, noting "… nice noises … like a cross between Country Joe, Fairport and Spoonful."

Record Collector magazine wasn't around for the original release but did review the CD re-release, in which they observe:

"Enjoyable though it is, it's easy to see why the album, (accurately summed up as "nice" by Jupp in the excellent sleeve note) didn't set the world on fire in '69. Despite the contemporaneous blues boom, Legend's laidback, almost rustic sound seems more at home, (especially in its more rock'n'roll moments), in the early 60s beat scene than in the revolutionary atmosphere of its time. That said there is a lot to enjoy here. Jupp's excellent piano playing and both his and Chris East's fine singing enhance the songs' bluesy charm."

Probably fair comment.

National Gas kicks off the album and was to become the single, too.

Mickey sings this catchy, folky, jaunty shuffle in a softish voice, Chris East harmonizing behind him. One of the things Mickey has always admired about Chris is his ability to develop harmonies on the spot. Guitars chime nicely over a suitably boomy upright bass and some strangely emasculated drums – no cymbals and virtually no bass drum can be detected - the beat intimated by a cross-stick snare. It's catchy stuff, no doubt about it, although the stereo mix is quite absurd, Mickey's vocal panned hard to one side as if he were standing in the wings

Heather on the Hill comes up next, quite dreamy and toppy, almost a little bit hippy trippy. The guitars jangle over drums, which pitter-patter distantly as if overspill from a Buddy Holly or Joe Meek recording going on in another room. What is staggering is the amount of reverb on Mickey's voice, making him sound as if he's singing in a deep ravine somewhere up in the Lakes, or possibly actually submerged in a lake. Two backing voices on the "lah lahs" hold the piece together as it is subjected to a sudden, brutal fade – quite the opposite of the slow one the song so evidently needs.

On the excellent *Tombstone* things get a bit heavier and bluesier, with a full drum kit in evidence and Mickey's vocal double tracked for extra oomph.

Come Back Baby could date from just about any point in Mickey's career, from way back then to right now. It's a piano blues; just a nicely recorded piano and Mickey's voice being all that's required.

City is an early song that could well have been a beat-boom pop single, complete with slightly disturbing bowed bass intro, sounding a little like somebody blowing down a vacuum cleaner tube. While the lyrics are hard to quite fathom, (is he leaving her in the city or for the city?), what would always have stopped it succeeding are the floppy drums, the track having to be driven instead by some good, firm upright bass playing.

Good Boy is an out and out guitar-based pop song, sung in a sort of Everly Brothers double-tracked style. Out of nowhere roars in a hugely limited, (in terms of engineering, not performance), piano solo. These piano bits continue on the fade. "*I was a bad boy, baby, but I'm a good boy now*", Mickey sings. Is he confessing his earlier sins or is it just a theme he likes? Decades later he will claim to be have been a *Naughty Boy*, but never to have committed any crimes.

Groovette is a rather unnecessary instrumental interlude, forefather of twins on the Legend *Moonshine* album. A strange thing to do when recording time was limited; unless it was just a warm up they chucked in as a filler to make up the numbers.

Wouldn't You has some terrific chords, shown off by excellent counterpoint between Chris' 12-string and Mickey's 6-string guitars. It features a subtle bowed bass part, a double tracked lead vocal and an intricate harmony pattern more often found in the work of American bands like the Association (no, really). It's one of Mickey's favourites from the album, despite a clanging bum bass note "where Steve misses the strings and hits the bridge!"

Doncaster By-Pass is a chiming, folky, gem with the sort of "sit up and beg" feel found in many of John Sebastian's best songs. It's a bit of a novelty number, but its terrific feel, swung along once again by a fine bass part, gives it a fresh, naive appeal.

20 Carat Rocker is a splendid, er, rocker which, but for the lack of an electric guitar, would have slotted perfectly onto the subsequent Legend albums. There's a full drum kit in there, a pounding piano, multi-Jupp voices and a touch of doo-wop. In another bizarre production decision this track, which unlike most on the album actually ends for once, is faded while it does so!

Bartender's Blues is a piano-based slow blues, sung brilliantly by Mickey in a fashion that sounds almost black in its phrasing and intensity. (In 2000, Procol Harum released a live concert CD from 1992, *One More Time*. At the beginning of their song *Whisky Train*, Gary Brooker sings and plays a few bars from *Bartender's Blues* in homage).

It's back to the band for *Good Money* - a swinger of a pop song, classy and catchy. The 12-string chimes beautifully over an admirable bass line that includes both picked and bowed sections plus some more clippy cloppy drums, while Mickey and Chris harmonise their way to the inevitable fade.

Finally comes S*hindig*, or at least on some pressings, (it was present on the UK pressings but excluded from the US ones due to copyright concerns, given *Shindig* was also the name of a popular, long-running US TV pop music show). This is a hefty, good-time number with an Elvis-like slapback sound to it.

All in all, it's a pretty good first effort. Not for the band – they weren't really one and didn't much sound like one – but as a strong marker of Mickey's vocal and songwriting prowess.

The sadness is that it could have been so much better. If there had been a more realistic recording schedule, which of course means budget, permitting extra takes, some drop-ins to fix errors and rather more intelligent overdubbing, it would have been much improved.

But even given the time constraints, it would still have benefitted from being put together with a tiny bit more care and attention.

It's true that Mickey, the band and the manager were inexperienced, the producer was really a folkie, the studio was division two. But the Beatles first album was made in about the same amount of time.

Now I'm not comparing the two in their entirety: the Beatles being a fully rehearsed, tight band, who were effectively recording their established live act, most of which consisted of other people's songs. What I am comparing is the production quality.

With *Please, Please Me*, George Martin showed what it is possible to achieve in a one-day album recording session. Sure, Abbey Road is a finer recording studio than Central Sound, so it might have the sonic edge, but that doesn't justify the slapdash production and engineering of *Legend*.

That *Legend* was anything other than an unmitigated disaster proved the power of Mickey's songs and his remarkable voice. True, not many people ended up hearing it - but those who did liked what they heard.

6 I'm In Control

In which Mickey finally hits the big time, well, the semi-big time

Legend Mk 2   courtesy John Bobin

I've been here so long, I'm sick of this old town
I ain't getting younger and it's time I got around
I wanna go some places, I ain't seen before
When I turn that corner, momma, you won't see me no more

Cheque Book by Mickey Jupp, Legend 'Red Boot'

After the break-up of Legend Mk 1, and in the absence of sufficient royalties to fund any sort of a living, Mickey had quit the music business for a second time, returning to Bath and the rather more financially solid world of builders' supplies. Six months or so later, that man Trower was onto him again, as Mickey remembers:

"I got a short letter from Robin Trower saying "call me collect". He'd obviously picked up this phrase while in the US with Procol Harum, the mega star band the Paramounts had by now turned into. I didn't actually know what it meant, but I found out and called him up."

It transpired that Procol Harum bassist David Knights had decided to leave the band to go into management and Robin had suggested Mickey as a suitable candidate for him to take on. As Mickey accepts, "if it hadn't been for David Knights, Legend would never have existed."

One of the strongest testaments to the power of Mickey's talent is the way in which successful musicians, with quite enough on their plates already, have repeatedly found time to give him a leg up. They have always understood that any lack of commercial success was not related to a lack of ability. Few of them doubted that Mickey would one day make the big breakthrough and become a well-known and widely respected musician. It was not a matter of if; it was just a matter of when.

However, despite so many people's belief in his God-given talents, in image terms Mickey was some way off the finished article, as Bob Clouter reminisces:

"Loads of people have tried to tamper with Mickey's image, as it were. Even to get him to have one at all. David Knights was a very smart individual, always well turned out and super cool. He tried to point him at a haircut. But Mickey's nearly always cut his own. 'Why should I pay someone else?', he used to say."

In fact, Mickey's objections to having an image created around him were rather more profound, as he recently confessed to me. "I always felt stupid if I dressed up. I felt awkward, thinking this is silly, this isn't me".

Image or no image, Mickey was once more going to need a band within which to operate. Ideally, a band that this time could stick together for more than one gig.

Since the sudden demise of the Orioles, the rest of the band – Mo Witham, John Bobin and Bob Clouter – had formed a new outfit, the Fingers, with front man Ricky Mills and keyboard player Alan Beecham.

Signed to Columbia records and produced by fellow Southender Peter Eden, (who apart from spotting Mickey's talents early on had also been responsible for discovering Donovan and producing early hits like *Catch the Wind*), they released a few singles before falling apart.

It was unfortunate that this excellent harmony band was so heavily manipulated by their advisers, who seemed unwilling to let them be a true band, more session singers. Their single of Ray Davies' *I Go to Sleep* had inexplicably consisted of their vocals dubbed over an old Force Five backing track, while the backing on the Fingers release of *I'll Take You Where the Music's Playing* was provided entirely by session men.

Writer Geoff Stephens, another Southend boy, had also got involved in providing material for the Fingers. Having written songs as good as *The Crying Game* for Dave Berry and as naff as *Winchester Cathedral* for The New Vaudeville Band, he furnished the Fingers with a true stinker called *Shirl*. This record is one that, once heard, will never be forgotten, but for all the wrong reasons. Mercifully it was released under the pseudonym Daddy Lindberg, which spared the Fingers' blushes. Actually, things could have been even worse for the band.

After *Westminster Cathedral* became a hit - credited to the New Vaudeville Band but actually recorded by a bunch of session musicians - Stevens suggested that the Fingers morphed into a 'real' New Vaudeville Band to go on tour. They wisely declined, although the guys who did agree got to spend a very enjoyable few years playing right across America. What the Fingers did instead was... grind to a halt.

Like Mickey after the first Legend album, Mo, John and Bob modestly if regretfully assumed that their allotted fifteen minutes of semi-fame were well and truly up. So cue a return to 'proper jobs', getting wives, producing children and generally establishing normal, if less adventurous, lives. It had been fun but it was a youthful episode, history not to be repeated, finito.

They were wrong. Everything was about to change.

David Knights might have been new to management but he hadn't wasted any time getting to work. Without even a band within which to house Mickey's talents, Knights had secured the Bath retail worker a two-album deal with Vertigo, the trendiest, most progressive record label in the giant Phonogram organization.

But Mickey knew that band was going to be needed:

"I valued a band because - although I felt a bit more like the leader - I wanted people to play and do what I needed done, more like the James Brown kind of thing, where I would be in control - you had to have these fellows. You need your band."

This time it had to be red-hot. It was going to be a new, improved, rocking Legend, and Mickey knew just where to go to find its members.

He went straight back to the Orioles.

He spelled out the demands he had made to his management in an *NME* interview with Max Bell in October 1975:

"I said I've got to have Mo Witham on guitar and little Bob Clouter on drums, 'cos I'd always been with them in The Orioles and I was getting a little older and a little fussier. Anyone round here – Wilko, anyone – will tell you Mo's shit hot. Wilko used to watch him like this (he stares wide eyed and open mouthed)."

In a 2006 article on the blog *bluesinlondon.com* by Rick Webb, Wilko confirmed for the umpteenth time his utmost regard for both Mickey and Mo:

"When I was a little lad learning, there was a great band in Southend called The Orioles, which was Mickey Jupp's band. He was very, very good... but he had this guitar player called Mo Witham and this guy, I think he remains one of the best guitarists I've ever seen, if not *the* best. When the Feelgoods first started I was telling everyone about him, saying, 'this guy's twice as good as me, he's fantastic.'

We went to see them do a kind of revival gig in Southend and Mo came on stage, plugged his guitar in, and did a little twang to test the amplifier. I turned to Lee Brilleaux and said, "I was wrong - he's not twice as good as me - he's ten times as good!"

This is a view that Wilko, a modest man despite his larger than life on-stage persona, has always been keen to broadcast. More recently he told the blog *Zani:* "Mo Witham is one of the best, greatest guitarist I have ever seen – he pisses all over me. The feeling he has got for the guitar is very rare."

He elaborated these thoughts further for when I spoke with him:

"The Feelgoods were four or five years younger than me so they thought I was the bees-knees as a guitar player, which I wasn't. They'd never seen Jupp or Mo but I was always telling them how good they were. So when there was a reunion gig at the Esplanade, I took my band along. When we walked out we were all thinking, 'bloody hell, have we got some work to do!' You see, Mo's got a real understanding of all the scales and the way things work – he can play stuff like Django Reinhardt. He has this touch that's different from anyone else - you can tell it's him playing from just one note. Compared to that I'm just a skiffler - childish compared to him - but it works for me and it can be exciting – it's apparently even influenced a few people, so they say".

Dennis Masterton, long-term associate of Mickey's, chimes in similarly:

"Mo is my hero – always full of musical surprises. I love him. I first met him at the Kings Arms at Chelmsford, where Tony Sumner, Mick Brownlee and me used to play. Mo came down one night and sat in with us - I can't remember why now. Anyway he totally blew us away. So he joined us! We played a regular Tuesday night for a couple of years with him until he joined Suzi Quatro. Even after that he'd come back and play with us from time to time, and Suzi would sometimes sit in, too."

No wonder Mickey was so keen to get Mo out of retirement.

Mo himself told me what happened next:

"One night Mickey came round to my house, where I was living with my wife and child, and says 'I've got a record deal with Vertigo. I've ordered you a guitar and amp, all you've got to do is go and sign for it at Chris Stevens Music Centre'."

John Bobin was subject to similar treatment:

"Mickey asked if I wanted to join Legend as he had a contract, but I said no, so I wasn't on the first single. He phoned me again after they'd recorded it but before the album was done and this time I said yes. It was going to be called the Living Legend of MG Jupp, which thankfully got shortened to Legend!"

Bob Clouter also chose to decline Mickey's offer to join, at least for now:

"They were on at me to join but I didn't have a kit at the time. I was living in Thundersley with my wife Janet and Mick and Mo kept coming round telling me how they'd sorted me out a nice Ludwig kit from Chris Stevens Music Centre but I didn't want to get involved all over again, having just got married."

So Bob held out for a while, which left the band little time to find a replacement drummer.

Dennis Masterton, the man who had recorded the demos for the first Legend album, thought he knew the ideal candidate, though. He suggested a drummer from nearby Hockley, his old band-mate Bill Fyfield.

"Bill Fyfield is one of my oldest friends. He was in my very, very first band at school: I think we were called the Tomahawks or something like that, as well as the Romford Golden Sunshine Band. Dave Watson, outgoing Legend "manager", knew him too, so I suspect it was Dave who would have physically introduced Bill to the new Legend."

Mo recalls Bill's impact on the band:

"Bill was a good drummer – very solid. There's not a better rock and roll drummer around, but he had a thing about losing his hair. It was very thin and he was very sensitive on the subject, so naturally we used to rib him about it. This nearly backfired when he walked out of a sound check at the Revolution one day. He was gone for hours and we were shitting ourselves because it was the night Tony Visconti came to see us about maybe producing our first album."

Hair aside, Bill was indeed a bomb-proof drummer, one who would perfectly underpin the heftier sound Mickey had in mind.

And the sound that Mickey had in mind, for live gigs at least, was not the sound of Mickey Jupp songs being sung – instead it was, as it always had been for him, the sound of good old rock and roll. Whatever record company and personal management might be expecting of their new singer-songwriter, Legend Mark 2 was going to be suspiciously close to Orioles Mark 5 in that respect.

Mickey recalls that the new Legend's first gig was in the Roller Skating Rink at the top of Pier Hill, Southend, on October 6th 1969:

"Me and the guys knew we made a good noise. It was good, I felt good. I wasn't yet thinking this wasn't going to work – that didn't come till later".

Despite going down well - thanks to the quick rehearsal they had slotted in - the intervening years had rendered the team a bit rusty. That even included virtuoso guitarist Mo Witham, who remembers it as a painful time:

"It went really well but it took a long time for me to get my playing back to where it had been, 'cos I hadn't touched a guitar for four years. If you listen closely to my playing on the first single I did with Mick - *Georgia George* - it's absolutely dreadful! The feel is crap, not helped by the fact that the Strat I was playing, the one they'd got me when I joined, was truly awful. It had a neck like a scenic railway. In the end I managed to swap it with a roadie for something a bit less glamorous but more playable."

The same month this Legend Mark Two surfaced, readying itself for the Vertigo deal ahead, Bell released the second 'old school' Legend single on their label!

The band that recorded it was no longer the line up from that Bell-released first Legend album and single – they had long ago split up - but it wasn't the new rocking Legend either: they had yet to record anything, and were in any case contracted to rival label Vertigo.

It was, confusingly (but what in this tale is not?) another, temporary, line up: one owing more to Procol Harum than anything else.

Given the nature of the sound they made it would be hard to call them Legend 1b - which would suggest a sound related to the folksy first incarnation - no, this was more a prequel to the Legend 2 that was waiting in the wings.

Georgia George (Part One) may only have been a 'contractual obligation' single, something to complete the Bell deal, but it is no lightweight. It's an exciting if slightly odd record: the first production by Mickey's long-term advocate, Robin Trower of Procol Harum, (still known as Robbie at the time), once again for Dave Watson's Golden City Productions.

This upbeat stomper positively careers towards the fast fade at the end. It's a Jupp original, but it's also a song that's very much homage to Chuck Berry. Not in terms of ripping anything much off, more because of its subject matter: US musical hero treks through a journey of discovery, laying out the names of various American towns and states along the way. Mr. Berry would surely have approved. Mickey's voice is in fine form and Mo's guitar playing may have been rusty but it's still better than most guitarists would be at their best.

Procol Harum's Keith Reid allegedly makes a unique, surprise musical appearance, playing bass according to some Procol fan web sites.

"I don't know where that story came from but it wasn't true", he laughed when I put it to him. "I was at the session because we had offices in Denmark Street, near where it was recorded, and it was Robin's first attempt at producing a record. I liked the record a lot but didn't really get into Mickey that much until later when we were looking at representing him."

Fellow Procol Harum member BJ Wilson's drums drive the whole thing forward; albeit partly by speeding up throughout the song - a trait particularly notable at each of the rather too frequent drum fills he plays.

Mickey chugs along nicely on guitar in the centre of the storm. There is no piano – in fact, one might have helped round out the sound a bit. And the problem is the sound.

It comes across as if it had been recorded in Mickey's flat on his trusty Elizabethan tape recorder.

The vocals are on the thin side, the guitar a touch too astringent, the bass a bit woolly and the drums, oh, the drums. The snare sounds as though it had been found in a skip and not re-tuned - yet it's mixed suicidally high, dominating the proceedings. As Mickey charitably concedes, "this was Robin's first stab so there's lots of reverb and stuff all over it."

Despite this, perhaps partly because of it, a certain raw energy shines through to pump up what one web site now refers to as a "pub rock psyche classic ", whatever that might be.

The single's commercial prospects were limited by the fact that this was a track that could have been recorded and released at any time in the previous ten years, but there was as yet no niche for music so timeless. Nor was their any publicity to support it, apart from the odd hopeful reference dropped into the small ads for the band's gigs, which at the time were variously credited to Legend, Mickey Jupp's Legend, Mick Jupp's Legend and on one occasion Mike Jupp's Legend.

Paradoxically, *Georgia George* was ahead of its time by being prepared to be behind the times and so didn't bother the charts when released by Bell in

October 1969, a time of slim pickings for any raucous rocker. Number one singles around then including Jane Birkin & Serge Gainsbourg's controversial *Je t'aime*, Bobby Gentry's saccharin *I'll Never Fall In Love Again*, Zager & Evans' faux-profound *In the Year 2525* and the Archies' factory-built *Sugar Sugar*, (actually, Mickey rather admires *Sugar Sugar*). That Christmas, Rolf Harris' ghastly *Two Little Boys* topped the charts.

Maybe Bell should have flipped the single in favour of its B-side, *July*.

A lighter, mellower Jupp original, it featured a beguiling melody sung over Mickey's impeccable three-part harmony - much more in the poppier style of the day.

Early on, the two sides of this single set out in a nutshell a great Jupp conundrum, one that was to continue throughout his career and maybe limit his ability to shift records in big numbers. Put simply, would the real Mickey Jupp please stand up?

Was he the dedicated rock and roller with a voice that could strip paint at twenty paces? Or was he the soulful singer-songwriter, conjurer of exquisite, delicate ballads featuring heartfelt lyrics?

There was no way of knowing then; nor has there been during the subsequent near half century. Mickey has remained resolutely consistent in but one thing - his inconsistency. In fact he's rather proud of it:

"I've never been one to go for a style – it's about what suits the song: this one will be like this, that one will have strings on. If I've got a style it's about the words, there are usually some good lyrics in there. But they always want to put you in a pigeon hole – no one ever knew what to do with Legend because we weren't on this road or that road."

Despite failing to make the charts, the new single served a then unknown purpose. Hotshot producer Tony Visconti, the man who would shortly take the production helm for Bowie's most purple of patches, had heard that pretty B-side, *July*, and liked it. He made enquiries about its writer/singer, got sent some demos, went along to see the band at the gig Bill nearly missed through being taunted about his hair, and as a result signed up to produce the first Legend Vertigo album.

His cunning plan was to slot his production schedule with Legend alongside the singles he was then producing for T Rex and his stints as a playing member of David Bowie's Spiders from Mars. Class, or what?.

It was a great piece of good fortune that, by shuffling his workload in this way, Visconti was able to take on the production of Legend, as Mo Witham confirms:

"I remember that album very fondly because it was so good to work with Tony Visconti. It was only through him that it came out like it did – I don't know anyone else who could have dragged it out of us. It was tough for him. Early on, the band wasn't that good - Mickey wasn't even sure we were good enough to play his songs."

This is a very important insight; and evidence that the musical split personality Mickey's listeners were having to juggle with was affecting him as well. He wanted to play his live rock sets with the band but were they right for performing the most quintessential of Jupp music – his own compositions?

The first Legend Vertigo album, (nicknamed *Red Boot* after the shot on the front sleeve - once again no image of Mickey was visible until you bought it and opened it up), included both rock numbers and ballads. It's considered to be amongst his finest works. It spawned the most cover versions, sold the most copies and garnered the best reviews of the Legend albums.

Contrary as ever, Mickey doesn't much care for it:

"I've never liked all the reverb on it. I could never get a good guitar sound in the studio, either. At the time I wasn't a great musician and it shows. In fact I'm not happy with the sound on that LP at all, actually."

John Bobin recalls this reverb issue well:

"Mickey always has a clear idea of what he wants. On *Red Boot* he said to Tony Visconti, 'I don't want any of that shitty reverb on it, I want it all dry'. So Tony recorded it dry but when it was played back he said, 'It's lifeless, I'm going to ignore him and put effects on', and he did."

Other aspects of the recording process proved equally challenging, as Mo remembers:

"On *Red Boot* we were in Advision and we used to start at 8pm, going through to about 5am, fuelled by a drop or two of whisky. Every day there was a new bottle of whisky waiting for us – I guess David Knights must have got it in for us; he was our manager so I imagine it must have been his job. Every night, when we'd finished work, they had to do 2-track monitor mixes onto Jupp's ancient Elizabethan tape machine, for him to listen back to later. He swore by it. So poor old Eddie Offord, the engineer, had to sit there in the early hours of the morning running off all these copies."

Mo recalls that it hadn't been plain sailing from the very start:

"Before we started to make the record, Tony Visconti invited us all around to his flat. He wanted to get some sort of relationship going with us, mostly with Mickey as the main man. He was a lovely bloke, Tony: really smart and really friendly. He had a lovely flat and a Vespa scooter parked outside that he used to shoot around on. Anyway, we had lots to drink and he got out his records to show us the sort of thing he was into, to make Mickey comfortable. Despite all this kindness, I remember Juppy tried to pull his girlfriend – most embarrassing."

During the actual recording process Visconti mostly kept his cool, but things got too much even for him at one point. The man was a karate black belt and once staged a demonstration high-kick for the band.

"He said, 'I just thought I'd let you know I won't take any shit from you lot,' after he'd missed us by inches", recalls Mo. Visconti had spotted that Mickey was, as he was later to put it, "a little frightening back then: very aggressive and kind of angry."

Undaunted by his relative inexperience in recording, (which up to that point consisted of his own basic home demos, a badly produced album recorded in one day and a not very well produced single recorded even quicker), Mickey was unafraid to express strong views regarding the technical aspects of how the new album ought to be recorded, as he made clear::

"At Advision for the *Red Boot* album I didn't want them to mic Bill Fyfield's kit up at all - just put the mics some distance away. 'Can we try this please, I asked?' Well we did and it sounded absolutely fantastic but they wouldn't do it for the recordings because there was a tiny tad of delay involved."

John Bobin recalls other tensions:

"We were recording *Don't You Never*", (a track recorded with Tony Visconti shortly after the album, specifically to be a single). "It's got a simple piano run down and untypically Mickey just couldn't get it right. He was getting angrier and angrier, so his playing got worse. Tony Visconti sent the rest of us to the pub for a bit and when we got back it was done fine. It was as if Mickey didn't want to screw up in front of us, which was daft because we all knew how brilliant he was."

Mo Witham recalls how they sometimes had to play tricks to get Mickey to make the most of his own songs:

"Tony wanted to put this Moog on the track *Five Years*. The synth belonged to Mike Hugg of Manfred Mann and lived in the studio because it was such an enormous thing. Mick had said No because he didn't hold with modern stuff like synthesizers, but I had a plan to get him to do it, which I told Tony. We agreed that I'd start playing the part, knowing Mick would be bound to take over because he'd reckon he could do it better. It worked a dream: that's exactly what happened: he came over and said, 'What are you doing, you ought to do it like this'. When he did it, it sounded great and Tony got it down on tape. We were really happy about the album – it was the closest we got to thinking it was all going to work out. Mickey was in his world and we were in ours, so we didn't care if he didn't like it - we did!"

The band was getting tighter all the time, as they played more and more gigs at better and better venues. At one club in Oxford Street, Bowie's guitarist Mick Ronson joined Legend on stage for a few numbers, being a friend, colleague and flat mate of Visconti's. Mo remembers being astonished at the action of Ronson's guitar, which, with its super-heavy strings, he found virtually impossible to play; so different were the two guitarists' set-ups.

Less auspicious was a gig Legend played at a smart Hampstead country club, the Haverstock Hill, with the also legendary Billy Fury - now past his prime but still a bankable live draw to a certain type of chicken-in-a-basket punter. Legend were due to open the show and then re-appear later to back Billy on a few of his old hits. Having vaguely rehearsed these in a pub the previous day, on the night of the show Billy decided to swap some of the songs for others that hadn't been rehearsed, resulting in some confusion. Mo, the consummate musical trouper, coped fine - not least because the copious wafts of pot smoke emanating earlier from Mr. Fury's dressing room had alerted him to the fact that the act might get a little, er, loose. But Mickey on piano was less than pleased and under the circumstances felt no obligation to even attempt to play things right - somewhat ironic, given his own lifelong penchant for changing running orders and song keys at will.

Amazingly, despite this shambles, Legend got offered the job of becoming Billy's permanent backing band. They wisely declined. These weren't their sorts of venues; this wasn't their sort of music; there were too many drugs flying around and they were malt and barley boys at heart.

And, most of all, they had an album of their own coming out shortly.

And what an album it was.

Released in January 1971, a little delayed from its original scheduled date of 7th November 1970, *Legend* (aka *Red Boot*) sounds great to just about any ears – well, other than Mickey's.

In fact, producer Tony Visconti is on record as considering it to be one of his personal favourites amongst the many illustrious works he has produced – all the way up to Bowie's final opus, *Blackstar*. On his website he comments in the T Rex section, (don't worry, all will be explained), "Bill and I had worked together when he was the drummer in the group Legend, a superb rock and roll group headed by Mickey Jupp, from Southend". (All the same, when contacted for this book, Visconti needed to download *Red Boot* from iTunes to recall exactly what it was he had so brilliantly brought to life!)

Back in the eighties, the BBC book *The Record Producers* related the *Red Boot* recording experience from Visconti's own, and then more freshly recalled, perspective:

"One album produced by Visconti in 1970 which definitely didn't make it at the time, but which some years later achieved almost mythical status, was the first LP by Southend rock'n'roll band Legend, a group led by Mickey Jupp. This artifact is probably better known as the *Red Boot* album, a reference to its sleeve design.

'That was great, and it was the first time I met Mick Jupp. The group's manager was David Knights, who used to be the bass player in Procol Harum, and we made quite a nice little rock'n'roll album with Legend, although Mick Jupp was a very difficult person to work with. He wanted the authentic sounds of days gone by, and I was torn between doing that and just updating it a bit, and he used to go off into rages and all that, he was very temperamental, but when we got great takes, he was very happy as well, and I quite enjoyed the album overall. I loved some of the tracks, like *Cross Country,* which we recorded twice, although it was quite a hard one to do – like a lot of simple rock'n'roll, there's nothing simple about it, and it's all down to feel and good vibes and the right conditions. But we did record it twice, and in those days, that was big budget, and the version that came out in the end I was quite pleased with."

(By 'recorded it twice', Visconti means that he got the band to overdub a whole second take over the first one, to thicken the sound. Nice in theory, but tough to pull off without the resultant mix sounding unsteady).

More recently Visconti told Will Birch, "Legend were a kick-ass group. They played extremely well in the studio and Mickey wrote some classic rock and roll songs with a bluesy emphasis. I recorded his vocals live and I think those live vocals mostly made it to the record."

While Mickey may have some reservations about it now, he was more complimentary when talking to Mike Davies in an interview in 1978:

"On reflection, Visconti was great, but I didn't seem to be able to get across to him."

Instead Mickey indicated that the source of any problems maybe lay elsewhere:

"We also had troubles with (Eddie) Offord, who engineered it. He had this new console he wanted to play with, while we just wanted to do some basic simple stuff…"

Vertigo kicked things off on November 27th 1970 by releasing *Life*, a non-album track recorded at the same time, as an advance single.

The Vertigo press release issued at the time claimed the label signed the band after their appearance on BBC2's *Disco 2* TV show in March 1970, (this was a sort of *Old Grey Whistle Test* precursor hosted by Tommy Vance in the exciting new colour TV format). The Vertigo story is clearly untrue but was probably deemed more dramatic than reality would have sounded: 'We signed a bloke working in a builders' merchants and some of his friends because his manager used to play in Procol Harum.'

No recording of this rare Legend BBC TV transmission seems to have survived, which is a great pity, not least because it would have been amusing to watch Mickey on a "disco" show! More importantly, though, according to bassist John Bobin, the band actually played the song *Life*, a performance rarity, as well as *Hole In My Pocket* from the soon to be released album. Mickey remembers the recording of the show:

"Slade were on the same show - when they were still skinheads with braces and all that. The various bits were recorded separately and then the show was assembled and broadcast. The night it was shown we were doing a gig in Harlow - I remember we managed to find someone who lived nearby and went there to watch it."

He also remembers what it led to:

"It was on the strength of that TV show that we got the disastrous Italian gig.

I doubt that they could have seen us at The Pheasantry, as Mo thinks, or anywhere else live, because if they had they would have known what sort of band we were. This was something they clearly didn't know, hence the problems we had once they'd seen our first rehearsal in Italy and realised they'd got the wrong type of band for what they wanted."

But this fiasco is still some way off - so patience, gentle reader.

Despite not playing it much, apart from once on TV, Mickey appeared keen on the song *Life* at the time, even if he seems a bit less sure these days:

"It was a big Tom Jones ballad thing", was how he described it to one journalist at the time, "I loved it. Robin Trower told us to put it out – 'great' he says: the maniac!"

On *Life* and the whole of the rest of the *Red Boot* recording sessions, Bill Fyfield turned out to have been an inspired choice as drummer. His performances were particularly good given that, unlike the other band members, he was still trying to hold down a day job, as Mo remembers:

"On the way back from gigs we used to drop Bill off at Bryant & May on the Mile End Road – he was a designer there. Poor sod, he'd played all night and had to work all day – we went home to bed."

(This double life paid-off for Bill in the end: long after his drumming days were over he made a good living as an in-demand illustrator).

Bill would have been stretched by his double shifts, for the band's schedule around this period was busy to say the least. Legend regularly played glamorous clubs like the Revolution, Blaises and the Scotch of St James; "rockers and teds" pub the Northcote Arms in Southall; the bluesy 100 Club in Oxford Street; the jazzy Ronnie Scott's and the decidedly rocky, (musically and, it turned out, financially), Marquee Club in Soho. They were the main act at this legendary Wardour Street venue in a Vertigo-sponsored show on Monday 9th November 1970 and then returned as part of a four-band bill on Sunday 7th March 1971. Alongside gritty venues like these, the band also appeared at the decidedly cut glass Skindles in Maidenhead and the far less elevated yet wonderfully bohemian Eel Pie Island.

Regardless of any tiredness on the drum stool, Tony Visconti quickly noticed Bill Fyfield's solid playing and within a short space of time Bill was getting session work from him on recordings by Ralph McTell, and then T Rex. After Bill did *Hot Love* with them, Marc Bolan joined the Fyfield fan club. Bill's insistent thump had given T Rex just the bedrock they needed; a heavy counterpoint that grounded Bolan's lightly quivering vocals. Tony Visconti recalled this era in his autobiography, *Bowie, Bolan and the Brooklyn Boy:*

"In the autumn of 1970 I had been approached by David Knights, the former bass player with Procol Harum, and asked to produce a group he was managing.

Called Legend, as was their eponymous album, their leader and singer was Mickey Jupp, something of a local hero in Southend. His gutsy voice and earthy writing had been shaped by singing blues and old R and B songs at the top of his lungs in pubs; he nursed his torn vocal chords with whisky. Legend is often referred to as the *Red Boot* album, so called because of a red winkle-picker in flames on the cover. It was another record I made virtually live in the studio. The band was very tight from playing countless pub gigs, but the drummer, Bill Fyfield, was magnificent. Marc, having found a bass player in Steve Currie, wanted to use a proper drummer on the follow up to *Ride a White Swan*. I said, "what about using Bill Fyfield from Legend? He's got the feel of Ringo Starr; even the tom-tom fills kind of spill over slightly into the next beat a la Ringo. Marc agreed and let him play on *Hot Love*; he did a wonderful job. Marc was so impressed he made him an offer he couldn't refuse. 'Bill, why don't you join my band?' With the success of *Ride a White Swan* dangled in front of him, Bill reluctantly left Legend, his long-time friends, to join T.Rex. For Marc, there was only one problem: 'Fyfield lacks rock and roll pizzazz, so from now on you will be – Bill Legend!'"

It's a great story, but not quite how the man himself recollects it. Bill tells of a more mundane re-invention of his surname. He maintains that soon after he joined the band, fans writing to the T Rex fan club didn't know his surname and so wrote to 'Bill (of Legend). Next thing Bill knew the band's management began sending their letters to him as Bill Legend, and so it stuck. "So it wasn't Marc Bolan or Tony Visconti who gave me the name", he maintains. Thanks for setting the record straight, Bill - but the more showbiz story works better, actually.

Whatever the real story, Mickey remembers the specific moment when Bill's 'transfer' occurred:

"We were coming back from a gig one night and stopped off at Watford Gap services, where we bumped into T Rex. We saw Marc talking very earnestly to Bill for a while and then that was it - he was gone. I didn't mind the T Rex stuff, actually - it was simple, direct pop."

So Bill went on to fame, if not fortune - being on wages, of course. Apparently, for the next few years, whenever he returned home to Hockley, the locals assumed him to be on royalties and so easily rich enough to buy a round of drinks for the whole pub! Thereafter, Legend used to take a bit of chalk on the road with them and scribble, 'T Rex Second Eleven were here' on dressing room walls.

Bill had made a sharp exit – eventually luring Legend roadie Pete Walmsley off to join T Rex, too – but it wasn't the first time he'd been offered a chance to jump the Legend ship.

On the first occasion Mickey was also invited, as he ruefully recalls:

"Legend were playing Blaises one night when Dave Edmunds was in the audience and he made it very clear that he wanted me and Billy Fyfield to join a band he was putting together. I said no. I could have done, should have done, 'cos I felt Legend were drifting at the time. It eventually became Rockpile, of course. I could have been in at the start of that".

Not for long, though, methinks, (see later for evidence).

Suddenly short of a drummer and needing to stay on the road to promote their album, Mickey once again turned to his old Orioles band mate, Bob Clouter, who this time weakened and agreed to join.

Legend were now precisely the same line-up as the old Orioles. And six years further on, were playing largely the same material on stage, despite Mickey's growing catalogue of original material. Live, they were the same old standards-based rock band, not an outlet for Mickey's music – which surely wasn't the best way to exploit their strongest card: those great new songs.

Nevertheless, as a result of their rocking live act, and on the strength of their critically well-received album, the band started to go down very well on the student circuit, finding themselves in demand at many of the biggest colleges and universities in the country.

However, Mo remembers promoters finding out the hard way what they were going to get on-stage:

"Just after *Red Boot* was released we played Leeds University, a big bill with Audience and the Idle Race. The social secretary said he'd got our album and loved it, asking if we were going to play all the stuff off it in our set. Mickey said 'Oh we don't do that shit, we only play rock and roll'. I can count on one hand the number of times we played most of those songs off the album, even though our manager kept telling Mickey he needed to."

Despite this insistence on only doing things the way they – well, Mickey - wanted, the band were now gigging hard in clubs, pubs, jubilee halls and halls of residence. From the Diamond Horseshoe Bar at Southend's Pier Head to a Pop Special at the otherwise jazz-only 100 Club, they turned up and gave it their all.

Alongside favourite haunts like The Asylum Club in Basildon and the Blues Loft in High Wycombe came a slew of college gigs at Reading, Wantage, Umist (where they were billed as 'the cabaret'), Barking, Bromley Tech, Ravensbourne College of Art, Queen Elizabeth College, King's College, Brasenose College, Oxford and, more than once, at Leeds University. Most flashy of all was an event at New College, Oxford where Legend played two sets on a bill with the Equals, Alan Bown, the Bonzo Dog Doo Dah Band and, surreally, the Dudley Moore Trio.

Perhaps most heroic of all - and more likely than not most financially rewarding - were appearances at deadly dull Annual Dinner Dances. On more than one occasion the band played venues like the 'Pools United and Stow United Football Club' socials, alongside the likes of comedy 'turns' Chalky White and Mike Reed!

Around this time the band was also getting a fair amount of radio coverage. In Legend's BBC live broadcasts, Mickey walked a fine line between promoting songs off the album and airing his more favoured live fare of classic rock and roll. For the *Radio 1 Club* in February 1971 they played three tracks from the album and three standards, but on *Top Gear* the following month three standards, (*It Hurts Me Too, Further On Up The Road* and *I Can't Lose*), were played versus only one original, (*Don't You Never*). John Peel was impressed, though, recommending it to his listeners as "some good, uncomplicated rockaboogie".

In March Stuart Henry played Legend's version of *Treat Me Nice*, Emperor Rosko played *Cheque Book* and *Don't You Never*, while Johnny Walker aired their songs all week one week, and a further *Top Gear* in June featured *Lorraine Pt 1*. So the UK was getting to hear a fair bit of Legend. But it might have been getting a bit confused, too – by the difference between the music on offer at live gigs and the recordings that were getting released.

This dichotomy is underlined by Legend's inclusion on the one hand in a number of straight-ahead rock and roll revival shows of the time, ('Rockin' at the Roundhouse' with Marty Wilde & Bert Weedon and the 'Camden Rock Festival' with Marty Wilde & Joe Brown), and on the other hand at rock festivals alongside Iron Maiden in Basildon or pop shows, such as one with Marmalade and Tony Blackburn at the Classic cinema, Hendon.

The *Hendon Times* accidentally captured this schizophrenic juxtaposition when it wrote: "Legend will also be there, pitching in. They have recently made a number of television appearances as well as raving in many clubs in the Home Counties".

BBC radio DJ Stuart Colman went to the Roundhouse rock and roll gig never having heard of Legend and came away very impressed, particularly with their piano-based rendition of *Mystery Train*. He told Mickey about his 'conversion' on his radio show, in a much later interview:

"You were the best on the bill - doing it from the heart when the others were just going through the motions."

Mickey agreed, adding, "we were doing it because we really loved it, and it wasn't white man's rock and roll: all of ours was black, except for the odd Jerry Lee Lewis number."

Meanwhile, without the assistance of any gigging at all, a Legend single - Mickey's tortured ballad *Life* - was proceeding up the charts.

But not the UK charts - over in Italy.

Vertigo had released the 45 not just in the UK, but in Italy and Germany, too. While it was probably a touch histrionic for the Teutonic market, the Latins predictably lapped it up. *Life* is an epic production of a dramatic arrangement, full of delicious unexpected chord changes - all driven forward by a vamping piano with John Bobin's excellent bass part roaming all over and under it.

Mickey's vocal is one of his most heartfelt, (though the distinct presence of reverb won't have pleased him). He really acts out the lyric over a massed choir of his own backing vocals. Mo contributes a delicate steel solo that creates a great counterpoint to all the emoting that's going on.

From its chilling, threatening opening guitar figure to Mickey's imploring *'Life, where have you gone?'* in the fade, it's an assault on senses and sentiment.

In the UK it had been briefly reviewed by *Disc & Music Echo*, who commented: "Just like the sort of pumping rock ballad Conway Twitty used to do so well, only here the words actually mean something. Great piano and vocals from leader Jupp."

New Musical Express liked it, too, but with a caveat:

"We've come to expect something different from Vertigo, as we did from Deram in its early days, and this maintains the reputation of the label even though it's a moody and rather sombre piece. The imploring lyric is set to a minor key backing and the whole routine exudes an atmosphere of despair. Extremely well done but likely to leave you deep in the blues!"

On BBC Radio's *What's New*, DJ Gary Taylor called it "an excellent record that deserves to be a small hit", but elsewhere Tony Blackburn faded *Life* down half way through saying, "No that won't be a hit". Now that truly was something to be proud of.

Vertigo owners Phonogram supported the *Life* single through a variety of picture sleeves in Germany and Italy and a tiny ad campaign in the UK. In this strip ad – headlined by the weird catchall banner 'Go For These' - they contrived to bracket Legend's disc together with new releases from Ronnie Corbett, The New Seekers, Frankie Valli and Morecombe & Wise. One would have to say this represents rather random targeting from the Marketing Department.

But despite Phonogram's clumsy promotional efforts, Italy loved Mickey's dramatic song of despair, and it stayed in their national chart for six or seven weeks, rising eventually to number twelve. (The song has since been covered by several Italian acts).

As the *Red Boot* album had not been issued in Italy, the Italian public had no idea of the band's rock and roll inclinations nor, thanks to a complete absence of photographs on the single's picture sleeve, what the band even looked like, (or indeed whether they were a band at all: Mickey could as easily have been a solo artist calling himself Legend). This air of mystery may have been intriguing, but it caused an enormous amount of trouble in the end.

According to some recollections, an Italian booker named Francesco made the trip to the Pheasantry in Chelsea, one of Legend's regular haunts, to give them the once over. (As we learned earlier, Mickey disputes this).

If Francesco had indeed made the trip, he would have seen a band in flux: by now Legend had begun to include a handful of Mickey's songs in the act:

"I was very reticent to sing my songs on stage in the Legend days – I didn't feel confident in them, I'd rather do some blues. We should have done a lot more off the three albums we made. We sometimes did *Hole In My Pocket* or *Cheque Book* but never any of the slow stuff like *Another Guy* or *Writer of Songs*. Now and again we'd do *Lorraine*, but we almost never played *Life*."

However it came about, the Italian duly booked the band for a month's residency in Italy.

But before they could go they had another album to make.

In the interim, in March 1971, Phonogram released a new single, once again produced by Tony Visconti. The sinister, rocking *Don't You Never* was coupled with *Someday,* a pleasant if slightly lightweight - by Mickey's standards - country-style number that had been recorded at the time of the *Red Boot* sessions but left off the album as it was thought to be "weaker" than the other material.

The single came out in the UK and Germany but received little attention. Did it get a release in Italy, where *Life* had been a hit? No.

Well done, Phonogram.

Clearly it was a very different sound to *Life*, but it was a potentially commercial sound all the same, as some reviewers of the time commented. *New Musical Express* opined:

"Anything on Vertigo is worth hearing and this is no exception – though this could certainly not be described as progressive. It's more of a latter-day rocker with a Dave Edmunds feel to the rhythm. And it's laced with some ear-catching and very appealing harmonies. Beaty without being overpowering."

Record Mirror liked it but had doubts, stating, "Quite a powerful piece - group sung, repetitive and heavyish. But it doesn't have that hit feel to it."

Annie Nightingale on BBC called it "heavy", while noting that her colleague Bob Harris was still going on about the Bell-era Legend's *National Gas*!

Don't You Never opens with a bit of guitar interplay to whet the appetite. Some T Rex-like grumbling drums and a thick three-guitar chug are then embellished by delicate flashes of piano from Mr. Jupp. Mickey sounds as if he's getting over a cold but this doesn't impair a strong, rather ominous lead vocal, laid across a fat slab of backing harmonies. The chorus is treated to some Wilko-like staccato guitar stabs (chicken or egg, Mr. Witham?). It's a strong effort to fall on such deaf ears, or in the case of Italy, no ears at all.

Never mind, Vertigo's marketing maestros had another cunning plan.

Also in 1971, they issued a budget priced sampler LP of tracks from a selection of their acts, one of which was Legend. Called *Heads Together: Round One*, we can assume it was not an unqualified success given there was never a *Round Two*.

For reasons too bizarre to fathom, the Legend track the record company chose to feature was not from *Red Boot* or even the *Life* or *Don't You Never* singles. Instead they went with a track that had no band, no rock and no point. *Foxfield Junction* is clearly a demo by Mickey: a lovely, folky number written back in the early days of the original Bell deal. A joint celebration of his beloved Lake District and his beloved railway trains, *Foxfield Junction* idolises a real-life station not far from where Mickey now lives:

"I wrote *Foxfield Junction* in the late sixties – about this little railway station at the beginning of a part of the world I love, where I've been coming since I was a kid. I love railways, stations, trains: a thoroughly civilized way to travel. Got lots of books about them – no, it's not an obsession! Can't remember how or where I did that track, mind you. I know the photo on the front of the album cover with all the various artists on was shot at Plough Lane: Wimbledon Football Club's old ground. The guy with the suit on in it was Hal Carter - he was Billy Fury's manager, who had something to do with the album from what I can remember."

Rolling guitars and layered vocals give this plaintive piece plenty of charm but little could have represented the sound of the band, or their records, less well.

It's tricky to see how anyone at the label thought this might increase sales of the *Red Boot* album. Any punter buying *Red Boot* on the strength of the sampler track would have been mighty surprised at what they found on it. (They would have been much happier with the Bell LP, on which it would have fitted perfectly).

This episode is but one example of the many ways in which Vertigo squandered the talents of Mickey Jupp and Legend. Eventually, the label became famous for such screw-ups with other bands, as we shall see later.

Unfortunately, they hadn't finished mucking things up for Legend quite yet.

Meanwhile, in a parallel universe too distant yet to influence Mickey's life, someone is buying a house - a couple of cottages in fact.

David Jupp has somehow discovered a pair for sale in the Cumbrian village of Boot, just fifteen miles or so from where he and brother Mickey so loved to play as children.

He buys them and moves his wife and family up there, lock, stock and barrel.

Even though Mickey can't yet hear it, a clock starts counting down...

The *Red Boot* Album

By any standards *Red Boot* is a remarkable album. As the great John Peel wrote in his weekly column in *Disc*, also referencing his political grumbles at the time, "…it has been a relief to cower in the darker recesses of the Piggery and listen to such things as the *Legend* LP on Vertigo."

Shot through with the spirit of the fifties, recorded with the bite of seventies technology, played with musical skills honed in the cauldron of the sixties, it is like nothing else from its era.

It is not a rock album, as was the fashionable descriptor of the times; it is a rock and roll album. It achieves this distinction not through atavism – the tribute bands' slavish adoption of throwback playing styles – but rather through Mickey's belief in the validity of this classic musical genre as a home for contemporary compositions.

Although *Melody Maker* carped in February 1971, "quite pleasant and nostalgic but hardly distinctive; an hour after I'd played it I could not recall a single number", in January *Disc & Music Echo* had already put their finger right on it:

"*Legend* takes you completely by surprise. They're a bit difficult to explain: the influence and approach to the songs, all new ones by Mickey Jupp, are without doubt rock and roll influenced, but the influence is so far back as to be country music tinged. It's an enjoyable album of individual sounds which is great fun and we defy anyone to say it's a carbon copy of the heroes of the golden fifties."

As a result, while *Red Boot* sounds great on your hi-fi, (just listen to it on re-mastered CD to relish how well it was engineered), it feels like it most belongs in a travelling fairground. You can imagine it blasting out of distorted metal-coned speakers, while on the dodgem cars lads with oily hands and homemade tattoos flirt with pairs of wide-eyed girls - high on the tang of electricity in the air, giddy with excitement, stocking tops on show.

Guitars stutter and piano clatters, while Mickey croaks and pleads his way through a bunch of timeless songs, all newly written by him, but in forms that constantly echo the past work of his heroes. Way more than derivative, *Red Boot* is an album that actually advances the form it draws upon. That's rare.

Cross Country kicks the whole thing off in fine style: Mo Witham's huge guitar sound usherering in double tracked drums that drive the number forward alongside John Bobin's insistent, melodic bass runs. Mickey's rhythm guitar fills in the gaps, creating a solid yet weaving platform for his playfully sung lead vocal - one that's powerful yet light-hearted, a feel enhanced by the doo-wop backing voices. Phonogram France had the brains to put this out as a single.

Cheque Book lifts the tempo but darkens the mood. It's not a love song, it's a "sod you" song, snarled at parents planning to chuck their wayward son out of the family home, (clearly, there are some autobiographical influences in this lyric).

Mo and Mickey's guitars duel with one another in front of slapping, rolling drums and bass. Mo pulls out a terrific howling solo while Mickey sings in a rebellious, sarcastic voice about how he's planning to do just fine without them all, thank you very much.

Three songs in, Mickey feels confident enough to switch style to ballad and swap guitar for piano. *Lorraine Pt* 1 is in 6/8; driven by a vamped keyboard, decorated with delicate guitar figures from Mo, held together by John's strong bass.

Mickey's singing is plaintive and, if you close your eyes and ignore his cover image, (there is actually one on the inside spread of this album, if not the front), he sounds every bit as black as white.

In comparison, *Nothing Wrong With You* is almost rockabilly. Fundamentally it's a standard twelve bar, but one that's lifted by being sung almost completely in harmony, a la Everlies, pushed along by infectious handclaps.

Somebody In Love is the full Fats. Mickey's piano playing and vocal mannerisms unashamedly mimic Mr. Domino - something too ambitious for all but the best to pull off. Needless to say, he does, assisted by some literal, rather than merely figurative, doo-wop backing vocals.

Goin' To borrows from another slice of rock history: the Hollywood Argylles' *Alley Oop*. This song develops considerably more, though, through some cool chord changes that Mickey cranks out one to the bar. As before, the glue that holds it all together is John's walking bass, overlaid with tasty licks from Mo.

Mickey's vocal is exceptional, while his lyrics slyly subvert their initial meaning: at the start she is the one who is "*goin' to*" love him. By the end he is the one who is "*goin' to....*" well, I think the listener can work out what exactly he has in mind.

Next up is *Anything You Do*, a proper firecracker of a number with Mo and Mickey's guitar phrases intertwined throughout. Bill Fyfield's drums, always solid, now swing, too, and are featured higher than usual in the mix. Mickey's voice cracks and croaks without ever missing a note, while the splendid long fade rings to another impressive guitar line from Mo.

My Typewriter comes straight out of left field. Opening in deep reverb, (he must have tolerated it only as a sound effect necessary to this horror film pastiche), Mickey talks his way through the intro, Boris Karloff/Crypt Kickers-style.

"In the studio I just started singing it like that – it wasn't planned," he remembers. Having decided to keep it in, Hammer Horror-type sound effects were added, groaning and cackling around the vocal. The band recall creating some of these from scratch, using umbrellas and coats to simulate flapping bats' wings. Suddenly the track clicks into sharp, dry harmony-vocal focus. Now it's got a high-speed rockabilly feel with tinkly piano chattering away under Mickey's amused and amusing vocal. The subject matter is an early example of the Jupp surreal tendency with words: this one explaining how his typewriter is more confident about life than he is.

Five Years couldn't be more different. It's an achingly pretty lament for the end of a relationship once meant to culminate in marriage – a similar theme to both the *Lorraine* songs on the album. The gentle acoustic guitar is punched up in places by an electric one, while Bill switches from a cross-snare click in the verses to a chunkier beat in the choruses. From half way through, the famous synth arrives, the one Mickey reluctantly played after Mo suckered him into it. It works well but the figure would have been even better had it been played by a real orchestra, (producer Visconti was after all an ace string arranger). The whole piece is beautifully sung, drawing upon an almost tenor style in the verses yet at full cry in the choruses. As heartfelt as the song seems, it and the playing of it are charmingly polite, perfectly conjuring up the tightly repressed anguish of an Englishman in emotional pain.

Hole In My Pocket sees us slap back in US territory. A boogie-woogie sort of piano and stubbed guitar chords underpin Mickey's lament to his perennial bad luck. The drums swing and the lyrics amuse – it could almost be the Coasters in places, especially with the semi-spoken vocal lines that pepper the verses.

This was one Mickey *was* prepared to perform live from time to time and it's easy to see why. It has single A-side written all over it, unless you worked for Vertigo, of course.

(In fairness to the label, Mickey was always against releasing album tracks as singles. He believed – as did the Beatles – that singles should not be confused with albums as they serve different purposes. In any case, he felt it wasn't fair to make record buyers purchase an album that contained tracks they might already have bought on singles. He has stuck to this principle throughout his career, wherever he had sufficient influence).

In *Lorraine Pt2* Mickey returns to the story he began earlier in Part One - in a different tune - only now things seem to be getting worse. To emphasise this, the pretty piano part running through the piece is deliberately brutalized by fat drums hammering along next to a breathtakingly grungy guitar sound from Mo, later to turn into his trademark guitar howls.

Mickey wails, the vocal seemingly torn from his heart as much as his throat, in front of an almost full choir of harmony backing vocals. It's very powerful stuff.

The album closes with the mighty *I Feel Like Sleeping*, an indolent bruiser of a track whose epic sounds take it to the edge of yet-to-be-invented metal.

The vocals, swathed in a scuzzy reverb as thick as smog, sit well back in the mix, having the effect of making the drier backing vocals more prominent.

Dark, malevolent guitars broodily chug in low register, like a trio of Duane Eddy's after a very bad day at the office. Further up the scale other sounds twang and swirl like angry wasps. The track is altogether too pissed off to accommodate anything as melodic as a solo. The song makes it more than clear that Mickey is far from happy. Best get out of here.

Red Boot has a very clear signature written all over it.
While there are different styles on display within it, it's apparent that everything here is the work of the same collective. Even at the extremes, songs like *My Typewriter* and *Five Years* still sit within the album's overall character.

This is what a good producer can do. This is also what a good band can do.

Legend were a very good band and thus were capable of stamping on the album far more musical identity that any solo artist playing with session men could hope to achieve. This band isn't seeking a refreshingly different ambience for the next track, and the one after that; they want to utilise their trademark sound for the next track, and the one after that.

Strong bands also have the collective clout to tell the singer, songwriter or producer that they aren't going to be playing that sub-standard song or dodgy arrangement, thank you very much. Good bands keep albums honest.

Everything came together on the *Red Boot* album. It was the band's first studio outing, which is always exciting. It was out of time but in a positive, radical way: it could have converted listeners to its style because it contained all the essential ingredients that made rock and roll work in the first place.

Record industry stalwart Roger Dopson's response is typical of many of Mickey's fans, although he admits to buying it purely on a whim:

"The first of Mickey's records I bought was the *Red Boot* album, which I regarded as an antidote to everything that was wrong with rock music at the time of its release."

Wilko Johnson agrees:

"*Red Boot* is one of the great albums. Of all time. Stop. I mean, time passes, then you put it on again and you think, bloody hell, weren't they good. That album is one of the reasons I didn't write songs for years. I'd listen to it and think, I can't do that. When Feelgood got well known I was no longer ashamed to look Mickey Jupp in the eye, but I always remembered he's the boss. I never forgot he always stood in another league from me".

Part of *Red Boot's* power is down to Mickey having built up a stack of those great songs Wilko refers to, brilliant and diverse compositions that made the hairs on the back of one's neck stand up.

Here, after all the traumas of the past few years, was the album the Orioles had been destined to make. What surely no band could have been destined for was that cover – a red winkle picker boot on fire. Once again, dumb art direction had triumphed.

"God knows what the photographer was about, he couldn't even get the boots the right way round," fumes Mickey on the subject.

So the band dreamt up a cover story, (no pun intended), about how this image symbolized the way they were turning their backs on rock and roll, which they duly fed to the media. It might have been an OK idea had it been true, but in fact while the album featured nothing but Jupp originals, anybody turning up at a Legend show was going to experience a great deal of classic rock and roll.

Mind you, not everyone was put off by the sleeve. It was the reason Roger Dopson had bought the LP "on a whim" and he wasn't the alone - as European fan Alexis Reisenhofer recalls:

"I first noticed Mickey in 1970 - I didn't know it was him, though. My local record shop had an LP with a red boot on the cover. The cover looked fascinating but I couldn't afford to buy it, I didn't know anything about the music either. A couple of months later when I had some money the LP had disappeared and I never saw it again. Much later, after buying Mickey's Stiff compilation, I managed to get the other Legend LP's – except for the *Red Boot* album, which I hunted in vain. Finally, after a couple more years, I spotted it in an auction and bid the highest amount I ever spent on an LP. I was lucky to win the auction but was never sent the LP - very disappointing. Got it a year or so later – made it in the end!"

That's the sort of dedication Mickey's work brings out in his fans. But as yet there weren't enough of them.

Whether one can blame the sleeve or the paucity of advertising, (Vertigo did stretch to making *Red Boot* the lead title in a composite Melody Maker ad on Jan 30th 1971), very few record buyers bought the album at the time it came out. Instead it was soon languishing in the discount bins of record shops.

Puzzled fan Will Birch recalls seeing it stickered at 50p in dump bins all over the place, as did I. It was worth more like 50 quid in my book.

As with all Legend or Jupp albums, I bought up any remaindered copies I come across on principle - there was always a new convert-in-waiting to whom a spare copy could be given.

I should have hung on to them. A mint vinyl original would cost you a lot more than 50p on eBay these days. The current Record Collector valuation for *Red Boot* is £300 and the follow-up, *Moonshine*, still more at £350. So why is the even rarer *Legend* Bell album worth a "mere" £175?

That's partly because Vertigo, the label for whom Legend recorded *Red Boot* and *Moonshine*, is one of the most prized labels amongst record collectors. And that, in turn, is because so many Vertigo releases sold very few copies - making used copies hard to find and so inflating their value to a completist. Quantitative proof, were it needed, that Vertigo were blessed with unusually ropey A&R wisdom and promotional skills. (Interestingly, one of the rarest Vertigo albums, by Bill Fay, was produced by Southend-based Jupp fan Peter Eden, and goes for over £1000).

Anyway, Legend were never really up Vertigo's street, something even the music press had picked up on – here is *Music Now* on the subject at the time:

"Legend are a very competent rock'n'roll based group who for some strange reason turn up on the trendy, swinging ultra-progressive Vertigo label. They are quite good – not spectacular but nice, stoned rock music that's performed well. Probably a good live band, too."

So *Red Boot's* low sales were exacerbated because while fans of Vertigo-style music were unlikely to appreciate Legend, fans of Legend-like music were unlikely to expect to find it on a label like Vertigo. But subsequently, as we have seen, views of the albums changed. Some time later *Zig Zag* magazine noted:

"Recently this DJ called Charlie Gillet has been playing some of Jupp's stuff on his radio show and suddenly they're collector's items."

Mickey ruefully reflected on this recently:

"That's the odd thing – when they were out, they hardly sold, now everybody wants them. I'm keeping a few copies of anything else I do in case that does the same!"

Legend had enjoyed critical success with *Red Boot*, but it was only the boot on the cover that had caught fire, not the sales returns. Never mind, they had a two-album deal, so there was still time for them to break through – providing they kept their heads down, kept gigging and the record company stayed committed. Easy-peasy, then.

7 Close But No Cigar

In which Mickey gets the chance to make a record his way, but is anybody listening?

Legend Mk3   **courtesy John Bobin**

It's been said, I'm off my head
To hear me talkin' I'm a fool
But there's a line we've all signed
You think it's you who makes the rules but I've been through another school

Mother and Child by Mickey Jupp, Moonshine

The contract that manager David Knights had arranged with Vertigo called for two Legend albums. Second albums are always tricky: the business is littered with stinkers, even from those who eventually turned out to be successful artists, (the platinum selling Dire Straits being a perfect example of this syndrome: their second effort, *Communiqué*, is a recognised dud).

As ever, though, Mickey had a bucket brimming with songs to take into the studio. However, as is usually the way with second albums, some were newly minted compositions, in a less complete state than was the case at the outset of *Red Boot*.

Perhaps unsurprisingly, Tony Visconti had politely declined the opportunity to produce this one. When Mo explored the possibility with him in a telephone call, spurred on by manager David Knights - a man well-known for his sense of humour, it should be noted - the by now stellar producer professed that he'd prefer not to work with Mickey again "as long as there is breath in my body."

While this refusal no doubt had much to do with the torrid time he had 'enjoyed' while producing *Red Boot*, it should also be borne in mind that he was still producing T Rex, now Britain's biggest band, in addition to being about to start work on David Bowie's breakthrough album *The Man Who Sold The World*.

This time it seemed that he wasn't up to slotting the band into his busy production schedule. In any case, Mickey was determined that this was the band's opportunity to do it themselves, putting an end to all the disagreements about reverb, synths or song selection. He was growing more ambitious for his songs, too: for the first time had visions of string arrangements on some. In part this was down to his having written some particularly powerful ballads on, of all things, a baby grand piano.

It was the property of one of his bosses at the music shop he worked in from time to time: the Southend institution that was the Chris Steven's Music Centre.

Co-owner Roger Stanley needed a temporary home for his baby grand while he moved house. Mickey volunteered to look after it and as a result experienced a new stimulus to his writing, a burst of activity he fondly looks back on:

"At that piano, in my flat at 7 Avenue Road in Southend, I wrote both *Lorraine Part One* and *Part Two*, *At the Shop*, *Another Guy*, *Writer of Songs*, *Mother & Child*. Did I write *Life* then? Not sure. The baby grand was different to anything else, like the Rhodes or Wurlitzer pianos you found in studios or played on stage.

Each of those had different but great sounds. I used to have two Wurlitzers, in fact – one for home, one for stage, because they were a bit fragile – plus a selection of the reeds, because they often got metal fatigue and snapped off. Just before they did that, they started to go out of tune, so you could put a drop of solder on to fix it for a while. In the end you had to replace them. They weren't that robust but a lot easier to cart around than an upright piano, let alone a baby grand!"

Later in life Mickey was to describe a great ambition of his as being "to buy a grand piano and build a house around it," but sad to say he never did.

Looking back on some local media comment at the time, it becomes clear that the band and its management saw the next album as their chance to escape what they were beginning to consider their "rock'n'roll shackles", (somewhat ironic given that rock'n'roll would continue to form the core of Mickey's live act until the year dot). The *Southend Evening Echo's* John Howard was fed input along these lines for an article he wrote at the time:

"First reports are that the album will be a complete departure for the group – there is not a rock and roll track on the LP and many of the cuts feature a full orchestra."

The paper showed a degree of naivety, or conspiracy, by more than once claiming that the provisional name for the album was to be "*Live at the Watford Gap*" – clearly a band joke. According to Howard, he had earlier asked Mickey what he wanted the title of his next album to be, only to be told, "*Led Zeppelin Four*." Well, the sales would have been boosted. Manager Knights linked the change in the band's style in part to the change of drummers, saying:

"This is really great for everybody. Bill is happy and so is Legend. They are getting ready to cut a new album, completely different from the first one, and they feel Bobby will fit in completely."

Many years later, in a radio interview with Stuart Colman, Mickey explained the thinking behind the transition:

"When we started out we were doing all r&b and rock'n'roll standards. By 1970 we were starting to do more of my material." When Colman points out that Jupp had always retained an anchor point of rock and roll, Mickey replies, "Yes, but I wouldn't try to do it for a living! I've got *Short Fat Fannie* by Larry Williams so I don't need anybody else's version of it – and I think most other people who are really into rock and roll think the same."

Exceptional as some of the new material, and fresh line-up, might have been, manager David Knights remained concerned about the new album being self-produced. Elizabethan reel-to-reel demos apart, Mickey had never produced anything before. Eventually, David decided he would have to be there in person to oversee things himself, a caveat with which the band agreed.

Under such circumstances, it might have been a good idea to select a studio where a particularly enlightened and experienced engineer could be found: the sort of proto-producer who was springing up everywhere at that time. Instead Phonogram's own Philips Studios near Marble Arch got the job, maybe for budgetary reasons. Whatever the motive, the studios came complete with technical rather than musical engineering capabilities, to Mo Witham recalls:

"Unfortunately some of the sounds on the Moonshine album aren't very good and it's not a great mix, either. Philips wasn't a great studio and the engineer, Chris Harding, was a nice enough bloke but not brilliant. In some ways Mickey didn't have as much to do with the production as we'd expected. I did a lot of the overdubs on a Saturday morning when he wasn't even there. Me and Johnny Bobin went up and did them, me on my Grimshaw Les Paul copy - it was a piece of junk really, you could bend the neck all over the place, but it sounded great."

Naturally Mickey doesn't remember it the way Mo does: he thought Chris Harding did a great job. When told this, Mo laughed and explained:

"Mickey is contrary about everything. If you're eating lunch and say 'This is a good pie,' he'll respond 'No, it isn't'; if you look at the window and remark that the weather looks grim, he'll tell you it's just fine."

What's perhaps most interesting is the fact that, when it came down to it, Mickey didn't really want to produce the new album. What he most wanted was for *nobody else* to produce it. He simply did not want any control taken away from him, despite his basic inability, or disinterest in doing the job properly himself - something he more or less confessed in an interview with Dutch magazine *De Telegraaf* in 1990:

"If a musician doesn't know which sound fits to my music I can't explain it to him. I snap at so much foolishness. Very unreasonable but still... Besides, I don't know anything about the technical side of the recording process. So I can't explain what I mean. All those buttons and switches and wires for me don't have to do anything with music."

Bob Clouter, by that time firmly ensconced on the Legend drum stool, feels that the album lacked the discipline an objective producer could have brought:

"When you think about it, that's why *Moonshine* wasn't as good as it might have been. Mickey wouldn't have a producer; he insisted we were going to produce it, even though David Knights tried to talk him out of it. And because he wrote most of it on this baby grand in his flat, we were never really able to rehearse it that much before we recorded it. Most of the songs weren't properly finished when we went into the studio."

As the reader might by now have guessed, the other band members' guarded opinions of the album are no guide to Mickey's own. While they harbor doubts, he holds it to be one of his all-time favourites – and judged purely on the quality of the best of the songs on *Moonshine*, it's easy to make that case. At the core of the album are the trio of his songs most usually admired by critics - a suite of beautiful ballads that were given the full treatment, strings and all: *Another Guy, Writer of Song*s and *Mother & Child*. Beyond these three extraordinarily emotional pieces, deeper than anything he had composed before, Mickey had developed a more humorous and observational style of writing for other tracks. The band played these in a less rock and roll style than on *Red Boot* - in some places straight rock, in other places even country-rock. This was necessary to complement Mickey's newer, wittier lyrics.

At The Shop, for example, came out of Mickey's experiences in the gardening department of Keddies department store in Southend:

"I spotted Peter, who used to work with me in the back room at Keddies, walking past my flat one day and out came the line '*Peter used to carry sacks filled with rubbish to the back*'. That expanded into the song *At the Shop* pretty quickly."

Captain Cool, on the other hand, is a backhanded compliment to new Legend/old Orioles drummer Bob Clouter, whom Mickey maintains was laid back about everything in life, "even his drumming - he always hangs back just behind the beat – well, more than just behind sometimes!" (Mickey on the other hand wasn't at all tardy - he wrote this song in the studio on the night the band recorded it).

Will Birch later commented to Mickey that some of the tracks on *Moonshine* were not unlike the sort of thing Free were very successfully doing at the time. Mickey sort of agreed but not completely:

"*Shine on my Shoes* was the closest I got to writing a Free-type song, but we weren't that sort of group. Please don't stick labels on it, Will. I didn't fit in anywhere. I don't want to be stereotyped or pigeonholed. I was like someone going down a supermarket aisle picking up a bit of this, a bit of that. I had no direction." (In actual fact, *Shine on my Shoes* is not a pure Jupp composition; it's one of a couple of rare Legend group compositions as is *Captain Cool* and the instrumental duo on *Moonshine*).

Personally, I see *Moonshine* as only being 50% a Legend album. To me, the stronger 50% of it is effectively the first Mickey Jupp solo record, the band fulfilling the role of support musicians rather than equally contributing band members. This is no reflection upon them: their talents had not diminished; Mickey's had simply grown exponentially.

Mickey doesn't see it that way. What he particularly liked about *Moonshine,* of course, were the drier sounds on it, especially the vocals:

"We used Philips' own studios and produced it ourselves. We kept it pretty dry, no reverb. There are some good songs in there. Del Newman, known for his work with Elton John amongst others, did the strings for us. I did want them on the slow songs, so I got Matthew Fisher from Procol Harum to arrange them for me."

John Bobin recalls that the string players were, in fact, twelve members of the London Symphony Orchestra. After they had played a beautiful first take, the engineer asked that they do it once more – not because there was anything wrong with the performance but in case the band wanted to double the part at the mix stage, to get a fuller sound. The sessioneers looked a bit bemused but did as they were told. By his own admission, Mickey became unusually emotional at this point in the recording:

"I remember the session where Del Newman conducted Matthew Fisher's arrangement for *Another Guy* - top musicians putting the strings on. I was nearly in tears. At the end Del came over and said, 'Nice song, man'. That meant a lot to me because he knew what he was talking about."

There are indeed some nice songs on *Moonshine* - much better than nice, in fact – and there needed to be. The band members were being paid £10 a week by manager David Knights who - subsidising their losses for the time being through his income from other ventures, like his agency work at Shady Promotions - was totting up their meagre income on the other side of the ledger. It didn't balance, nothing like.

The accounts didn't make pleasant reading - the band was fast sinking into debt.

Never mind, the album was finished and the songs were fine. Paul Shuttleworth, an excellent graphic designer - later to be singer in the Kursaal Flyers - was working on the sleeve. Who knew what its release might bring?

All that remained was to go and crack Italy.

The gig was booked; they'd had a hit single: what could possibly go wrong?

The *Moonshine* Album

If *Red Boot* was a firm handshake and a strong voice declaring, 'Hello, we are a rock and roll band', its follow up seems rather more softly spoken - considerably more evanescent than effervescent.

Moonshine is a more subdued album than *Red Boot*, and a less consistent one, too.

It feels unsteady on its feet in places, slightly tentative: perhaps reflecting the less optimistic time the band was going through when they recorded it along with the lack of an experienced production hand on the tiller, to guide and edit .

It's less flashy in production, and so less immediately engaging as a result.

On the other hand, it feels more authentically live, less confected than *Red Boot* - the sounds of the instruments more closely matching the way they would sound on stage. Bob Clouter's drums in particular are less damped than was the recording fashion of the time - mostly to good effect - but his playing style is more intricate and florid than Bill's had been, removing some of the cast iron certainty that underpinned *Red Boot*.

These performance changes might not have been the sole issue at play. Phonogram/Vertigo, doubting whether Legend were creating the sort of material the record buying public really wanted, (as if they knew) demonstrated a marked disinterest in doing much with it.

From their point of view, compared to *Red Boot* no track jumped out as a red-hot single. So the label cunningly chose not to issue one at all – clear evidence of their early capitulation. Yet some of the material was stronger than anything we'd heard from Mickey before. The songs were less in your face, more in your ear – and the very best of them were to live on in the listener's heart.

On *Red Boot* the two parts of *Lorraine* were the spine-tinglers. On *Moonshine* you get three such masterpieces, the baby grand trio: *Another Guy, The Writer of Songs* and *Mother & Child*. That baby grand seemed to have re-set Mickey's musical clock, upping his melodic ambition and the scale of the songs he created. Mo Witham recalls being astonished when Mickey took him through some of these songs for the first time:

"Mickey writes great songs, though often with just a handful of chords in them. This lot was quite the opposite. I remember thinking, 'Bloody hell, where did this all come from?' It was genius stuff, of course."

The *Moonshine* album kicks off with the title track - a great croaky vocal performance from Mickey over quite a funky little riff-based backing. The guitars duel like on *Red Boot* but don't sound quite so syncopated; in stereo they are curiously panned a long way left and right. John Bobin's bass, such a key binding agent on the last album, is lower in the mix this time and the song's ending feels a bit of an afterthought. Overall, a promising start, though.

Another Guy begins with piano and a tender guitar figures which blossoms into great lead lines from Mo, sitting over a running bass and rumbling drums featuring almost random cross stick accents from Bob, to vary the feel.

As Mickey sings his heart out, an acoustic guitar drives the pace forward, aided by Mo's signature electric guitar squeals, pushing the whole thing into the arms of wonderful soaring strings. Bob's drums are in heavier mode by now, pulsing through the long, climactic fade.

Interestingly, when invited on a radio show to choose a single Legend track to be played - long after Legend had ceased to exist - this is the song Mickey went for.

More delicate still is the introduction to *Mother & Child*: a tiny keyboard pattern reminiscent of a child's piano exercise. Clipped hi-hat, almost sounding like recording overspill, leads the song into a lovely, clicky, melodic bass line.

Mo's guitar - aggressively doubled - growls away beneath a fluid string section playing in almost Chinese quartertones. The entire arrangement rises inexorably; in places we hear it echo Mickey's beautiful dry and torn vocal.

As the song turns the corner into the chorus, the piano moves to chords, eventually closing with a lovely suspended feel.

In direct contrast, *Captain Cool* is, (to me) an almost Free-like rock riffer: all guitars and Coasters-style vocal, half sung/half spoken by Mickey in full sarcastic mode:

"He'll never say thank you but he'll say that's nice, In any given minute he won't breathe more than twice, When he talks he talks as though he's running out of fuel, But harken to the words of Captain Cool." Drummer Clouter, the subject of the song, gives a suitably laid back reading, unembarrassed by Mo's girly, breathy line *"Oh, Robert you're really cool"*. It's a clever contrast to Mickey's earlier angst fest, eventually twisting into the Wurlitzer and guitar-led instrumental *Ausfahrt* that leads out Side One.

Eingang rather pointlessly opens Side Two, being the same piece as on the end of Side One and itself fading out rather than symmetrically taking us into a new track. One wonders if some sort of padding might be going on here. If so, it could only be related to lack of recording time; surely Mickey would have had far more songs in reserve than to have run out of options, he always did. (The names of these paired tracks were inspired by the endless autobahn signage the band had absorbed while driving through Germany. Initially they had thought *Ausfahrt* a very large town!)

All is forgiven with the first track proper on Side Two.

Shine On My Shoes is a great rocker: much closer in spirit and soul to the *Red Boot* set. Two guitars working in counterpoint really get going above thumping bass and drums. Still not quite as solid as the Visconti-produced work, it feels like it needed routining for longer on stage to fully bed in – a supposition perhaps supported by the rather ragged ending. You get two guitar solos for your money, though: one straight, one steel. And yes, Will Birch is right: it *is* rather like Free.

Mickey's reflective mood returns with one of his finest ever compositions, *The Writer of Songs*. Beginning with a lovely repeated run down, the piano is joined by soft acoustic guitar and a pretty bass part, beautifully suspended in places. Strings amble in and then kick on, pointing up the dramatic verse which Mickey's supple voice swoops up to. Dark guitar figures echo the melody up to the bridge, where Mo's strings squeal and whine, a wrenched-out sound as edgy as fighting cats, while Mickey reaches the crucial question, *"what comes after once upon a time?"* Bob's drums flop, Ringo-like, until they switch to the main beat as Mo's guitar leads us into a piano bridge to the next song. Unless there is a hidden conceptual reason for this link, it's a slightly bizarre turn for such a gorgeous song to take. The composition surely needs the grounding a proper ending would achieve - something you can't help feeling a third party producer would more than likely have insisted upon.

The song it links to is *Local Folk'ol*, a shimmery, swampy semi-country bopper in which piano and guitar play tag. An amusing tale of town folk and country folk, it comes across a little frothy: the soft drum sound and low bass mix lending it a top heavy feel, something that handclaps and non-Mickey backing vocals only exacerbate. It's catchy enough, though.

At the Shop opens, as did *My Typewriter,* its 'novelty' counterpart on *Red Boot*, with sound effects: this time of a busy shop, its cash till merrily ringing up sales. These atmospherics lead into a medium paced 2/4 number with jaunty 'megaphone equalized' backing vocals. Complete with kazoo solo, it ever so slightly reminds one of the Bonzo Dog Band, (their leader, Viv Stanshall, being another Southend boy).

The album closes - slightly too soon as it's a bit under length - with the head-on *Just Because*: an echo of *Red Boot* and a pre-echo of Dave Edmunds all rolled into one. Nine-tenths a great track, it features an unexpectedly treated lead vocal from Mickey, (how did that happen with him at the desk?), and some great guitar work, but it hasn't been mixed for optimum punch or presence. The drums would benefit from a fatter sound; the whole track remains a bit too fiddly; it maybe goes on a tad too long. And surely the end should fade out, rather than fall to pieces as it does? Sorry: nit-picking. That apart, here's clear evidence that everything is still fine in the rock and roll department. But not everyone was convinced at the time.

Even *Southend Evening Echo* faithful John Howard, normally a stoic supporter of all things Jupp, had a wobble. In an album review entitled 'New Legend seem eager to please', he claimed of Mickey's songs:

"His imagery is as sharp as ever, although often enough the tunes act simply as a vehicle for inventive lyrics." Perhaps more puzzlingly he adds, "Neither this nor the first Vertigo album produced by Tony Visconti match the production of the first Bell recording", a view he may be unique in the world in holding.

Today he still rates the Legend albums in that order but has an interesting view on Mr Jupp's subsequent output, telling me:

"Since then he's put out so much good stuff, yet today I prefer the *Favourites* series to everything else: wonderful tracks like *Seeing Simone*, that sort of thing."

The passage of time has been kinder to *Moonshine* than one might have anticipated, as this extract from a review on the website *Allsounds* indicates:

"The sound is fairly raw throughout, with the kind of loose, relaxed musicianship that comes from pro cats getting down and having fun. Whether they're stripped-down and rockin' or dramatic and string-filled there's an element of toughness that keeps the band from ever sounding stuffy, and it's that same bar-room machismo that makes this record stand out as a near-classic example of down-home, '70s British rock done correctly - with fun and chutzpah in equal amounts."

We shall never know how this album might have turned out if, say, Tony Visconti had produced it. Mickey would maintain less well, the rest of Legend might claim better. What *Moonshine* did do was prove that Legend was more than a one-trick pony, and that Mickey's songwriting strengths were way above most of his contemporaries. Astonishingly, his voice was getting even better.

But was anyone listening?

8 Life

In which Mickey discovers that it's all going wrong – déjà vu once more

Enjoying Italy   courtesy John Bobin

Friends often ask me, Mickey J
What you gonna do in ten years, say?
When you're just an old has been
'Cos you can't last forever on the rock and roll scene

Politics **by Mickey Jupp, Long Distance Romancer**

Having spoken to all four band-members about what happened in Italy, I am forced to conclude that we will never know for sure what actually occurred. Not because of anyone's reticence to tell the truth, rather through genuine differences in opinion as to what the facts really were. This is not unusual when several people attempt to dredge up the same memories from almost fifty years back. On the other hand, such brain fade may be considered a little surprising given the dramatic nature of the episode they are recalling.

What is not in doubt in anyone's account is that the whole affair was a disaster; one so horrible that it brought a fine band to a premature end.

To start with, Mickey nearly missed the whole trip, having decided to leave his employment at Chris Stevens Music Centre the day before the planned departure for Italy and vanish off to Bath. The band managed to retrieve him just in time. As Mo puts it, "He didn't want to go but we had to, so he had to". One of the reasons for Mickey's disinterest in making the trip may have been the fact that at the scheduled time of leaving none of the promised up-front expenses payments had made it to the UK. As John Bobin says, "This should have sounded warning bells, but being young, naïve and dead keen to go to Italy, off we went."

All agree it was a bugger of a journey that nobody much fancied. They drove all the way there with their gear, taking the ferry out of Britain to start what proved to be a long and traumatic journey. The van could only make it over the more severe Alpine passes if the air filter was removed to permit every single molecule of oxygen to make it into the straining engine; at borders the guards made them take everything out of the van so they could search for hidden drugs; on one occasion they even had to play a couple of songs at a customs post just to prove they really were a band.

Their new roadie, Stuart Brooks, (later to become bass player in the Pretty Things), drove until he could drive no more, finally chucking the band out of the van while he had a much needed kip. Mo Witham remembers shivering on the steps of Milan Railway Station at seven in the morning, waiting for Stuart to get his head sufficiently back into shape to complete the journey. They then drove the last leg of their epic trip to Chervia - an Italian resort mostly frequented by Italians. Here Legend had been booked to play at a newly built club/restaurant near the beach, owned by some, shall we say, colourful individuals. This is the point at which accounts of the experience diverge.

Mickey maintains that, due to the building of the venue running behind schedule, they had to hang around for a week without performing at all, got bored with the whole thing, gave up and left.

Mo believes that they were contracted for a month, played for a couple of weeks and then fell out with the management over a request that the band transfer to a club in Rimini to play there for a weekend.

John Bobin has yet another version:

"We did a couple of gigs in a club called the Pathagiro. Then we played an awful club in Rimini called the Ya Ya. The bass player in the other band on the bill was wearing rubber gloves because the earthing was so bad that he kept getting shocks. So in the end we reluctantly did a moonlight flit."

Given the greater degree of detail in his version one is tempted to give John's account the highest marks.

Anyway, what is not in doubt is:

1 The club owners were a particular kind of gentlemen, who wore dark glasses inside buildings and thick overcoats outside them, even in thirty-degree heat.

2 When a disagreement over money did occur, said Italian management produced a gun as the key component in their argument for not providing the band with any cash until their engagement was complete.

3 The band cleared off unannounced and unpaid.

Except that they couldn't quite just clear off. Not out of Italy.

While they had their return ferry tickets to the UK, they lacked funds for the fuel the van needed to reach it. Scared that a call to the British Consulate might require them to sell their gear in order to raise petrol money, the band called their manager, who in turn suggested they get themselves to the offices of Phonogram's masters, Philips, in Milan. Their record label would surely be keen to help these recent hit makers.

This they duly did, as John Bobin relates:

"Philips in Milan said 'How nice of you to drop in, what can we do for you?' At first they seemed to think it was a social call we were paying them. We said we were skint and needed to get work to raise some money to get home. They said that that should be easy to organize but it would take a few weeks to sort out. We explained that unfortunately we didn't have the time. So they advanced us some money against our royalties, about seventy quid I think, in order to get us home. We made it back OK, but by then we were all pretty fed up."

The band's staunch ally, the good old *Southend Evening Echo*, tried to put a positive spin on this debacle, maintaining that:

"Legend are back in town, cutting short their Italian tour. The group have to complete tracks for their new album tentatively entitled *Live at Watford Gap*. Legend sold 100,000 copies of their single *Life* in Italy."

Furthermore, the article claimed that no lesser a light than Stones' manager Andrew Loog Oldham was listening to the new album in his role as talent-spotter for the American Tamla Motown label, which was apparently looking for new UK acts to release in the States. (One hesitates to imagine what sparks would have flown had Mickey Jupp and Berry Gordy been put in the same room to talk record production and artist grooming, even if the man had co-written one of Mickey's all-time favourites, *Money*).

While the resulting morass of confusion and malaise wasn't yet to signal the end of Legend, it was pretty damn close.

Back in Southend again, the band continued to play a reasonable number of gigs, but thanks to the fewer number of performable tracks on the new album, and the lack of any single to plug, they only incorporated one song from *Moonshine* into their act - the title track.

The album was finally released, in the by now traditionally shoddy fashion, in January 1972.

If the marketing of the first album was poor, this time round it was positively negligent. Vertigo chose not to use Paul Shuttleworth's specially commissioned photography of woods by night, both relevant to the subject of moonshine and which the band thought looked great, (no doubt Mickey in particular, as, once again, he wasn't on the cover). Instead they sourced a bizarre stock photo, showing a crowd of people walking down a street within which was a half-secreted man in a lion's head. No, no idea.

Will Birch, however, has an interesting theory on how this may have come about:

"Vertigo records had this special designer chap with a fancy name who did their stuff, knocking out lots of concepts for their big-name bands' albums. Back in those days, if they had what they considered a minor band, they might try and use up an idea rejected earlier by a bigger band. I believe that's what happened with the *Moonshine* cover; I know that the same thing happened to Brinsley Schwartz."

The designer chappie cum photographer in question was one Marcus Keef. It is not known for sure whether he was responsible for the *Moonshine* monstrosity but it is known that he was behind the equally derided flaming boot on the cover of the first Legend Vertigo album. It's art, luv.

Mickey explains away Vertigo's cavalier attitude very simply:

"When we were making the second Vertigo album, having signed for two, they simply didn't know what to do with us. They had bands like Uriah Heap they were far more interested in."

But in fairness, the band had rather changed direction on the label, dropping their rock'n'roll positioning in favour of a less focused one, which can't have helped. Either way, Vertigo's miniscule PR machine blustered away to no avail, whistling in the dark that *Moonshine* was "selling well: there was demand built up by the first one and this is selling better." Really?

One thing Mickey was absolutely right about was the fact that the marketing budget had now dropped from not very much for *Red Boot* to nothing at all for *Moonshine*. In the end, the only advertising that accompanied the album launch was a few small-space press ads, which were paid for by the band itself.

Bob Clouter explains something else he thought was beginning to sour things:

"By then we were getting too old-fashioned. We were playing big venues - university balls, that sort of thing - where they'd had Led Zeppelin the week before playing stuff that was heavier or pompier. This was the stuff that pub rock was eventually a reaction against, but that was after we'd split, more around the Feelgoods time."

Dr Feelgood themselves frequently cited Mickey as one of their musical heroes and have an reciprocal role to play in Mickey's story a little later on. At this early stage in their career it was Mickey's music that helped give them the drive to succeed, particularly the song *Cheque Book*, as Henry Scott-Irvine related in an article about the Feelgoods for *Record Collector* magazine:

"It was a song we used to cover regularly," said Dr Feelgood manager Chris Fenwick. "Mickey was an artist we looked up to. With our first album's advance we bought a 40-seater coach. United Artistes' cheque literally paid for that. There was a loophole in the law back then. If it wasn't a 'Public Service Vehicle', and you taxed it privately, then you could drive a coach with a private license, which is what we did! We put bunks in the bus and extended the boot so we could take a PA around with us. We had a cassette player with Mickey Jupp's *Cheque Book* playing as we drove around Europe for the next three years. So that song really takes me back. When we first drove in and out of Amsterdam it brings back a vision: a joint in my mouth, a can of Heineken in my hand, and *Cheque Book* playing in the background. Now *that* was living rock 'n' roll!"

While it's true that Legend inspired part of the ethos of Dr Feelgood – a right-on, no-nonsense devotion to great rock and blues numbers – there were, as Legend bassist John Bobin points out, crucial differences between the two bands:

"You've got to bear in mind that while there were similarities in music and straight ahead attitude to playing, Feelgood were great showmen. Lee on stage looked so vicious, even though we all knew what a lovely bloke he was in real life. Then there was Wilko as the Mad Axeman, wild staring eyes, playing guitar as if on roller skates. Not the sort of thing Legend would ever have got up to.

Mind you, when Feelgood first got together, I understand Wilko used to say at rehearsals 'It's no good, it's got to be more like the Orioles'!"

Wilko himself is the first to agree that Feelgood's theatricals had a significant effect on their subsequent success, as he told me:

"Neither the Orioles or Legend moved around much or made a show like we did in Feelgood later on, but bands didn't do athletic stuff back then, they just played. It's not easy to develop an image for a band. I might look super-confident when I'm performing but it's not so. I used to get terrible nerves in the early days so we began putting on a front – in my case one of extreme ferocity! Actually Lee was the one who started all the menacing stuff on stage, which I then went along with. It conquered the nerves pretty quickly when you realise you'd intimidated half the audience by machine-gunning them to death!"

But right now it was still pre-the Feelgoods era. It was just too early for Pub Rock. And it was becoming too late for Legend.

The momentum had simply gone out of the band. Bassist John Bobin quit first. He explains what happened in his book:

"I was really down after the failure of our Italian gig and worried about the debt we were building up. I believe now that we should have just had a break and started again after a brief rejuvenation period, but my head was not straight at the time. I remember bursting into tears at a rehearsal, to the surprise of the other guys, and feeling that everyone hated me. So I decided to leave and Bob soon followed suit."

John's replacement was Phil Mitchell, another musician who worked at the Chris Stevens Music Centre in Southend and who is today a long-serving member of the latest incarnation of Dr Feelgood. (Mickey always liked the way Phil played bass and so the two went on to work together in future ventures as well).

Bob Clouter was then replaced on drums by Barney James - formerly of local band Forum, where he had played with Chris East, (Mickey's old school pal, some time songwriting collaborator, and past member of the Bell Records-era original Legend: still more of those Southend rock family tree connections).

Barney went on to play with the band Warhorse and for Rick Wakeman on several of his top selling albums – a CV that tells you straight away his style of playing was probably not going to be up Mickey's street. And it most definitely was not. When he later joined Warhorse, Barney replaced drummer Mac Poole, who himself was later to tour with Mickey. Mac's drumming did not meet Mickey's exacting standards either – it must have been the prog influence.

In Barney's case, bored with the persistent shuffle beat of much of Legend's material, he had attempted to impose a funkier drum feel to the songs, prompting Mickey to yell at Mo one night, "I don't know what Barney's playing, but it ain't rock and roll."

On his website, Barney James refers to Mickey as "the one true curmudgeon of rock", adding, "right from the go I don't think Mickey was enamoured with me or my playing. I did however hit it off with guitarist Mo Witham, so I got the gig."

Mo is of the view that Barney's playing was "a bit too advanced for Mickey."

Barney suggests it was a rather more divisive experience than that, claiming that "Mo Witham and the bass player loved it, Mickey hated it."

Barney points out in his defence that he'd never played in a covers band before and so didn't understand the cardinal rule that when you play a Chuck Berry song it needs to sound a lot like the way Chuck Berry originally played it!

Mickey and Mo were still there from the original Legend line-up, of course, but the band was limping by now, its heart no longer in it.

Moonshine had been launched to almost total silence and the Vertigo deal was dead in the water. Legend were back playing the same old places once more but this time minus the hope and purpose that had been there first time round. (According to Barney James, this final Legend line-up played once more at the famous Marquee Club, further cementing their name in a long list of greats who regularly graced the Wardour Street venue, although the club's website has no record of this last appearance, which would have been their third).

During the few months they lasted, the final Legend line-up's regular support band at gigs was the fledgling Dr Feelgood. One night, during the changeover of gear between Feelgood and Legend, the band spotted an unusual, bedraggled figure in the audience, complete with dirty raincoat, cloth cap and a battered suitcase, occasionally laughing hysterically. Ian Dury, future label mate of Mickey, had either of them but known it, was in the house.

Mickey later saw Dury play with his band, Kilburn & the High Roads, an experience he found both exhilarating and sobering:

"I was blown away when I saw the Kilburns in 1975. They were the best live band I'd ever seen and I thought, 'If that's the opposition, I quit'."

Foolishly, he saw them a second time. They were even better. Mickey should perhaps have had more faith in his own talent, but when did he ever?

For example, in 1975, when Mott the Hoople hired a new lead vocalist named Nigel Benjamin, he was asked about his musical influences:

"Mickey Jupp, John Lennon, Peter Green, Zappa, MC5, Blue Cheer. Lennon and Jupp were the main reasons I joined the business. I roadied for Mickey's band Legend when I was a kid. Now THAT was a band!"

There were further signs that Legend was a band reaching the end of the road - on one sorry occasion, quite literally. Travelling to a gig, they crashed their van head-on, an event fortunately survived by all. When they finally made it to the club in which they were due to perform that night, there was not a single person in the audience.

Bigger gigs might be getting harder to find but they could still pack them in at The Esplanade, a Southend seafront pub where promotions were put on by Will Birch and Paul Shuttleworth, two soon-to-be Kursaal Flyers, under the moniker The Grand Canyon Club. Will remembers how those Esplanade bookings came about:

"We originally did those nights to help promote our then band, Cow Pie. The two main lead acts we put on around us were Dr Feelgood and Legend - the final heavier version with Barney James on drums and Phil Mitchell on bass, along with Mo and Mickey. Every three or four weeks one of them would have played the Esplanade. We only used to get fifty to a hundred in…fifty if it was just us playing!"

On Sunday 16th April 1972, for example, you could have seen Legend there for just 10p on the door – including entry to a 'Free LP Raffle'. But by now it was very near the end for the band. Ironically, the blow fell at the London venue the band had played most; where they had appeared more than a dozen times since first being mistakenly billed as 'Legand'.

"The last gig turned out to be back at the Pheasantry, opposite the Chelsea Potter in the Kings Road, one night in April '72," remembers Mickey. "I loved playing that place, we had some great gigs, but that night we were terrible. Barney wasn't really into that kind of music anyway. Mo and I just looked at each other and we knew that was it."

As Barney's blog records, "I've never been in a band that actually broke up on stage, but that night we did."

Recalling it in 1979, Mickey broadened the blame from Barney to *all* the drummers the band had been through:

"We only split up because we had a succession of drummers that came and went. On about the fifth one, me and Mo just gave up – we couldn't be bothered to rehearse with yet another drummer. It was getting too much like hard work so we lost interest."

However, a trawl of the good old *Southend Evening Echo* suggests whatever the precise reason, the break-up wasn't quite as clean an affair as the participants' memories suggest. The paper reported that the finale was in fact at a local gig, and in any case that the door was left slightly ajar:

"Legend had such a good time with their farewell performance at the Esplanade the other week that Mick Jupp said he 'may do it again if anyone asks us. We weren't expecting anything from it…but on the strength of this our publicity material is going out again inking in £120 for a night, so we could play again'."

Ex-Kilroy pianist John Denton recalls there were so many Legend farewell gigs it became something of a local joke when another inevitably popped up. But he also recalls that they were great fun, being looser and less pressured - to such an extent that other musicians would join the band on stage for a few numbers: sometimes John himself on keyboards, (freeing up Mickey to add another guitar to the sound) other times noted local jazz trumpeter Digby Fairweather.

Whatever the exact moment the deed was done, it was unfortunate timing for Legend to split, as Mickey now recognizes:

"People have said since, 'if only you'd given it six more months.' Eggs Over Easy and others were beginning to kick in; the pub rock scene was arriving. People actually say that us being around helped to inspire that movement a bit – I suppose it's nice to get a mention. In fact, I even get a mention in Paul Weller's autobiography. But we missed the boat. I was always out of step. That's the story of my life, you see - the Jupp timing mechanism kicked in".

Pub rock could have been the chink of light the band needed to keep going:

"I thought the pub rock thing was interesting. The live gig scene had all but disappeared; the only venues you could play were big places like colleges, universities, the Rainbow. All of a sudden the music was back on the streets again, like it was when the beat boom started in '62,'63. There were gigs everywhere, places for musicians to grow up. So while the whole pub rock thing wasn't hugely successful for many of those actual bands, it was good for emerging musicians who were able to continue playing long enough to go on to bigger things."

In an article in *NME* in October 1978, Max Bell, reviewing one of Mickey's subsequent solo albums, summed up the business of his mistiming very neatly:

"Mickey Jupp has always been nearly famous. A native of Southend, Jupp is something of a local folk hero, leastways with them ol' Kursaal Flyers and Dr Feelgood. Legend was Jupp's turn of the '70s vehicle on which he, and many admirers, hoped he'd hitch a ride to the big lights. With one bona fide English rock goodie ticked off, Jupp paved the way for a second generation of aspirant pub rockers. History took its inevitable course and it seemed like everyone had a slice of the action except Mickey."

Some years later the trade magazine *Hot Press* would note that, "Mickey appears genuinely detached from his previous lack of success; there's no obvious grudge burning in his breast. He is aware that Legend's failure was as much the result of his own shunning of opportunity as a lack of record company support – of which there was none."

Will Birch, who *did* taste commercial success with the Kursaal Flyers, (a band who recorded *Cross Country* and at one point planned to record an unreleased Jupp composition, *Daisy Mayes*), believes Legend would have missed the boat, even had they still been around:

"Legend could've been much bigger but they had an appalling image and little idea about the rock scene."

Will is the first to admit that his own career was built the other way round, "I was never much good as a drummer but I knew how to keep my ear to the ground and connect with people," he modestly admitted.

Wilko Johnson was equally astonished that Legend had come and gone, leaving barely a ripple:

"When I went to off university instead of joining Mick and Rob in the Jam, Procol's *Whiter Shade of Pale* became huge hit. I'm boasting to all my new mates that I know this lot, but there's another band from Southend who are going to make it big, too - just you wait and see. I felt Legend *had* to be huge because wherever you looked you could not find anybody else playing like they did. But it was not to be. That's the way this business is, there's no way of knowing how or why it didn't happen, but it didn't. Over and over again with Mick it just wouldn't work out."

Some might blame Mickey's inflexibility for this constant string of failure, yet ironically, after all those years of him refusing to adhere to musical fashion, in 1973 musical fashion was about to arrive at exactly the spot where Legend had been marking time all along. The very place they had so recently and reluctantly vacated.

But it was still 1972 and Mickey had folded his hand.

Now back working in the music shop, he was history.

Or so it seemed.

The Black Art Of Making A Record

Mickey in the only studio he's even semi-comfortable with
Courtesy of Mark Williams

If you are aged under fifty (and if you are, well done for showing such an interest in old stuff like this), you may find it hard to appreciate how very difficult, nay impossible, it was back in the sixties for a British act to make a record, or even a half-way decent tape recording of any sort, unless there was a large record company behind them. All the recording studios of any merit were located in London - pretty well all of them owned by the two big record labels. If you wanted to make a record you had to get signed to EMI or Decca, which between them accounted for 80% of all record sales, roughly half each. If the two smaller players, Philips and Pye, fancied the cut of your jib, you might get a crack at fame with them, often using their in-house studios, but your chances of success were considerably lower.

If those four didn't think you had what it took - hard cheese.

There were few smaller labels back then; nor had independent production taken off. There weren't even local recording studios for hire at affordable rates, where you might self-fund a recording – these were still some years away.

Home recording wasn't much of an option, either. A few middle class families might have owned one of those new-fangled, usually-tangled, reel-to-reel tape recorders but even those expensive, bulky and fragile machines lacked any sort of overdubbing facility, so your only option would have been to record everything, vocals included, in one go, on one microphone. And in this era of hits that dripped with reverb, there would have been no post-recording effects to make the sound more palatable.

So, generally speaking, bands lacked the facilities to send record companies quality audition tapes of their music. Instead they had to wait to be 'talent spotted', either by a label or by a manager with sufficient influence to get them onto a label. Needless to say, such events were a bit random, as the Orioles had already discovered.

It's the reason why there are so few recordings from the early days of many great bands of the sixties. There are no home demos of the Stones and precious few of the Beatles.

In desperation, bands sometimes crammed into audio booths originally intended for the recording of spoken birthday messages to your mum or sweetheart, or spent an hour or two with a local middle-aged boffin in order to capture something of their performance, however rough and ready. The world's most valuable record was made this way.

That'll be the Day by the Quarrymen was just such a one-off. The single copy made of this Buddy Holly song, quickly knocked out by the band that was to become the Beatles, is estimated to be worth a cool £100,000. This is nonsense: the only copy in the world is owned by Paul McCartney, who is no doubt sentimentally attached to it and clearly not short of funds, so I doubt you'd get it off him for a million.

Interestingly, the Beatles themselves got signed to EMI through an early demo tape - yet that tape was, in fact, one that had been made at an earlier failed audition for the other major label, Decca - an event manager Brian Epstein had been able to engineer from his power base as manager of NEMS, one of northern England's most influential record shops.

Once the Beatles had kindly ushered in the beat boom, making a record became more of a statistical possibility. Record companies had overnight become rabid to sign as many cash-generating bands as possible, especially as just about every one of them, including EMI the first time round, had passed on the golden goose that was the Beatles. They didn't want that to happen again.

Not really understanding wheat from chaff, most of the ageing A&R men - who had been suddenly uprooted from their cosy world of sourcing songs from one set of mates in the publishing world and pairing them up with artists signed to another set of mates at the record labels - indiscriminately snapped up good and bad alike. As long as they were purveyors of this new-fangled beat group music – all long hair, jungle drums and incomprehensible lyrics – they might make money. All of a sudden, from not being able to get signed unless you sang songs your Mum and Dad quite liked, you could now only get signed if you played music they loathed.

The resulting explosion of signed acts, and the bloated release schedules this led to, were too much for the few record company-owned studios to cope with. What's more, many of those old recording facilities were physically massive, having been originally designed for full-scale symphony orchestras. This excessive size made them expensive to run and unpleasantly impersonal to record in. And so independent studios began to emerge, often smaller and more comfortably equipped - ideal for bands and cheaper to hire, too. Soon, some even had bars, pool tables and rest rooms - all the better to create great music in.

Studio personnel were changing, too.

When the Beatles started working at Abbey Road, an EMI-owned facility that recorded widely varied material from operas to comedy to jazz, the studio engineers wore lab coats. As you might imagine from their job title, they were members of staff who engineered, modified and repaired the studio equipment: all the recording kit at Abbey Road had been designed, sometimes fabricated, always extensively tested by those forbiddingly technical engineers.

The actual recording process was not their concern - that was the work of mere balance engineers and even more lowly tape operators, under the supervision of the producer, who was often also the A&R man or even - in the case of George Martin - the label boss. And woe betides any tape op that permitted his VU meter needles to stray into the red, signifying the recording of dreaded distortion. Distortion was not yet ear candy, the sonic badge of the respectable rock musician. For now it remained unacceptable and unprofessional: the enemy of high fidelity, the scourge of the audio perfectionist.

Inevitably, alongside these new studios emerged a breed of young, creative, sonically rebellious producers and engineers who didn't obey the old rules. They were soon on the way up, dragging behind them a ragbag of new indie labels, which now had a chance to compete.

But in some cases these were not as independent as they first appeared to be.

Several were, in truth, only faux-indie labels. For once the big record companies got wise to what was happening, they employed cooler, younger managers to front up what appeared to be smart new labels with greater musical credibility but were in fact merely thinly disguised subsidiaries of the flaccid giants.

The big old record companies christened these newly spawned labels 'underground'', giving them groovy names and contemporary logos. Decca had Deram, RCA had Neon, Pye had Dawn, and EMI had Harvest, while Phonogram launched Vertigo, later to be home of two Legend albums and, as we have seen, considerable marketing incompetence.

Here is a quote from past label boss Olav Wyper from the sleeve notes for *Still Dizzy After All These Years,* a CD compilation celebrating the successes of Vertigo (with no mention of Legend, of course):

"Although we set about restructuring the company (Philips), signing new bands and reworking existing artists and records with some success, we lacked the sort of dramatic impact that we needed. At the end of each day we would all gather in my office, have a glass or two of wine and discuss our progress. It was at one such informal discussion that the contemporary rock label concept of 'Vertigo' was born and just three months later we launched the label."

Typically they queered their indie pitch by putting 'A Philips Recording Product' on early Vertigo releases, before realising that was a bit of a giveaway.

Doh.

These fundamental changes in the structure of the record business were down to earlier pioneers, like fifties engineer turned sixties producer Joe Meek: a man who may have been drawn to male performers for the wrong reasons but who exhibited startling originality when it came to production and recording techniques. Joe had set up as a bone fide sound engineer/producer at Lansdowne, following a spell at IBC, a big, traditional studio where he had acquired a reputation for unorthodox recording techniques, (just listen to the presence on Humphrey Lyttleton's *Bad Penny Blues* for an example of how well these could work).

Squeezed out by the establishment for his radical ways, Joe used royalties from a Tommy Steele B-side he had written – which Les Paul subsequently had an unlikely US Top 20 hit with – to build a makeshift studio in his rented Holloway Road flat, designing and fettling reverb, compression and limiting tools in order to realise the unheard-of sounds that constantly played in his head. Joe couldn't master an instrument or sing in tune, but when it came to getting atmosphere down on tape, he was uniquely gifted. He found bands to record, writers to write and then did everything wrong to get the right sound: massive distortion, packing cases or stamping on the stairs for drums, vocals in the loo, tinkering with tape speeds, drenching arrangements in his own unique, hand-made effects.

Johnny Remember Me by John Leyton has it all. It's moody, magnificent and streets ahead of anything any other producer had either the imagination or technical ability to create at the time. (Mind you, it is also a good song, something that can't be said for all of Joe's efforts, especially when he himself was the songwriter).

Early on, when he couldn't get his start-up label, Triumph, and its puny distribution set-up to work, he hit upon the revolutionary idea of "tape leasing".

This was a new concept in which he funded the recording himself (which in his case often cost virtually nothing, apart from his time) and then licensed the finished master to a major label, which would then press and distribute the records for a commission on sales. After a few false starts it worked, and for once the rest really was history.

Tape lease became a major mechanism driving the dynamic growth of the record industry, permitting a following pack of indie producers and their acts to flourish. By the seventies and the arrival of punk, bands were doing even more for themselves, selling easily reproduced cassettes of their cheaply recorded songs direct to record shops, even straight to fans. Radical retailers such as Rough Trade helped bands execute this model, providing the gateway for, amongst others, Scritti Politti and The Smiths. Later, this indie spirit in turn inspired Tony Wilson to set up Factory Records and Alan McGee to form Creation Records, and so we got Joy Division and Oasis. And so on.

But, back in the domestic household of the sixties, recording technology was progressing only at a snail's pace. Reel-to-reel machines were initially the only dish on the menu, but brought with them the frustrations inherent in using clumsy rolls of magnetic tape that twisted, tore, stuck and disintegrated at will. Mag tape technologies had first been developed in Germany during the war, around the time Mickey Jupp was also first developing. Initially these were not to record music but for military surveillance purposes. After the war ended, the Germans' pioneering work came to the attention of occupying American forces, one of whom saw wider applications in peacetime.

Following a demonstration of the capabilities of magnetic tape by an ex-US forces audio specialist in 1947, Bing Crosby invested heavily in the new concept, enabling Ampex, a small electronics company, to develop a prototype model of the commercial tape recorder. As a result, Crosby became the first American performer to regularly pre-record his radio shows. This was allegedly his sole motivation for becoming involved in the project in the first place: Bing preferred to be on the golf course or relaxing at home rather than slavishly tied to the studio when his shows were due to be broadcast. By happy co-incidence his lazy decision to invest was later to make this millionaire into a multi-millionaire.

Ampex went on from these mono machines to develop the first multi-track recorder, Les Paul being given one of the prototypes. He used it to build up multiple performances of himself on guitar, often with his wife Mary Ford on vocals, to great commercial success. The eponymous electric guitar he designed with which to achieve this, arguably the world's first proper electric guitar, went on to do rather well, too. And so another multi-millionaire was born.

By 1963 some domestic reel-to-reel tape machines were emerging with a magical, if crude, "sound-on-sound" capability. By bypassing the erase head, musicians could now overdub recordings of themselves, albeit only by layering up mono recordings, rather than through true multi-tracking. There were serious downsides to this process: in the form of tape hiss that grew exponentially with each generation of added sound, plus an inability to re-mix beyond the balance levels originally recorded, but it was a great boon all the same.

If you had a ton of money you could buy a Revox G36 – a precision machine from Switzerland that was built like a tank. (These machines were so admired that many years later Dr Feelgood were to specify, as a rider to their United Artists recording contract, that each band member had to be provided with a Revox for home use – Wilko's still sits in his living room, propping up his gold discs). But if you were just a budding but impoverished British musician you yearned instead for an Elizabethan.

Unlike the Swiss-built Revox, a sister marque of the unimpeachable Studer range of professional studio recording machines, the Elizabethan was more an example of precision engineering from Romford. It was clunky to use and had wow and flutter figures that would make a sound engineer shudder, but it worked, and until the arrival in the early seventies of Japan's all-conquering Akai 4000D, became the darling of the pop musician, songwriters in particular.

Mickey had inherited an Elizabethan with which, as we have seen, he laid down the initial demos for his Bell debut album.

As we've also seen, it was the instrument through which engineer Eddie Offord got to greet the dawn, linking up the veteran recorder (the Elizabethan, not Mickey) to a far more sophisticated studio desk to run off rough mixes of *Red Boot* tracks for our hero to study.

The arrival of affordable recording kit had another powerful effect - it permitted the creation of a new kind of recording facility, one that hadn't really existed before: the cheap and cheerful local studio. Here was a place where some technical wiz could profitably put his obsessive knowledge of electronics to work, in the hope that by so doing, he – it was never a she – might, as well as making a modest living, add a little previously lacking glamour to his personal image. Back then, semi-pro sound engineers were the nerd equivalent of today's computer machine code writers and hackers, but without the same possibility of life-changing fame and fortune.

Their studios often employed two tape machines, one "bouncing" signals to the other in order to build up overdubs. As the recorders were typically of better quality, often Revox manufactured, and were running at higher speeds than a domestic machine, quality was sufficient to offer a markedly superior end result. With a little egg-box soundproofing the drummer could play with sticks rather than brushes, and with some good reverb effects on tap these small establishments were able to offer local bands a respectable sounding end product at an affordable cost. In the Southend area, perhaps the best of these was a studio in Westcliff called Spectrum Sound, run by Warwick Kemp, which Mickey occasionally used to record his own material.

Back in the commercial world, if the engineer had come on a long way in a decade, the producer's role had developed even faster.

Record companies liked producers. Producers knew how to get the right sound for the market, get the best performance from the 'talent', (sometimes referred to more disparagingly by record labels as "the turns", Will Birch wryly informed me), control their egotistical urges, select and sharpen up songs, optimise arrangements and hopefully bring the project in on-time and on-budget.

This rarely all happened, of course, but it's nice to have objectives. However, even assuming the studio is right, the engineer is right, the producer is right, the musicians are right and the songs are right, there is still plenty of room for things to go wrong.

While some musicians love the recording process, many do not – especially if they see its proper purpose as being to capture live performance, rather than enable pure studio creation. In the early days, the Beatles were essentially a live band who made recordings of the same songs they played on stage. That's how they could make their first album in a single day. Yet by the time they were recording *Sgt. Pepper* they had given up playing live altogether, seeing the studio as the perfect environment in which their music could be created from scratch, as well as recorded. And thanks to the great leaps in technology that had occurred in just five or six years, they could embellish this work in ways they could never have hoped to reproduce on stage, had they still been playing gigs.

If you adore the recording process and have plenty of time and money to spare, it's possible to relax into the whole thing. Pink Floyd, for example, loved it so much that they voluntarily dropped their royalty rate with EMI from 8% to 5% in return for unlimited time at Abbey Road. And this was before they had even finished recording their first album!

For many artists, though - tight on time and money, fearful of exposing their musical weaknesses or under-delivering on performance – it can be as hard to relax into as when the dentist tells you to. For - just as in the dentist's chair - there is nowhere to hide in the studio. Even if the performance is being recorded semi-live, with the full band playing together at the same time, it only takes one prod of a button by the engineer to isolate a single track during playback, for all to scrutinise – unerringly the one on which your hi-hat beat falters, or your bass note bums out. The slightest variation in a vocalist's pitch or a guitarist's tuning will be exposed: there, in the control room, at high volume, in front of the culprit's peers - with costs mounting and time running out. Not fun.

Vocals are usually the worst experience as they are almost always added at the end of the session, often with the rest of the band up in the control room listening hard to the vocalist's performance while time and money run out.

Mickey has less to worry about than most in this respect, having a naturally true voice that is close to pitch perfect. He is also capable of delivering repeated, identical phrasing - vital to the effective multi-tracking of backing vocals.

But the intensity of even his performances will still differ, depending on his mood, maybe the direction given by the producer, even the time of day.

(Mickey prefers to sing lead vocals straight after breakfast, while there is a little sleep and croak still left in his voice. Not many studios operate such hours, though he can record his demos whenever he likes, of course).

If, like Mickey, you are a songwriter as well as a performer, along comes an additional stress, this time about your material. You have ambitions for it, plans for how it is going to grow up. But the producer may have other views. And the session musicians may not grasp the all-important feel that you believe is fundamental - they may have other ways of hearing it, or not be quite the right sort of players, or be a bit hung over, or worse.

Down the years and through the albums he's made, Mickey hasn't always been able to keep consistency in those who played with him. Mo Witham, Bob Clouter, Tex Comer and Frank Mead pop up several times, but mostly Mickey's supporting cast has changed from record to record. Perhaps more disturbingly, on every single occasion Mickey has gone into the studio to make an album, the producer has changed, for nobody ever seemed to want a second bite; no musical relationship ever got built.

No wonder Mickey has always been happier with the total control he can exercise in his home demos. He doesn't much enjoy the process of recording those either, but at least he can *be* every part of the process – writer, arranger, engineer, producer, player of all instruments, singer of all vocals, master of the mix. To do this he has, over the years, made several upgrades in the home studio department, going from that faithful Elizabethan to four and eight track Fostex reel-to-reel machines to a multitrack digital Portastudio. Note that while he may now use a computer to duplicate his privately released CDs, he doesn't use one to record. Mickey is firmly an analogue man wherever he can be.

When it came to making proper, commercial records, though, the studio was often Mickey's biggest obstacle. While he sometimes had a say in who produced him, that producer would usually choose the studio, often the engineer, even which musicians to use. It's interesting to see those choices laid out, examining the effect the process had on the musical outcome over Mickey's career.

Mickey's earliest recordings (the Bell releases) were recorded at Central Sound, a small studio in Denmark Street in London – a short street popularly known as Tin Pan Alley - originally the home street of all the music-publishing companies.

It was a poky place, perched over the 'La Gioconda' café, which soon became a hangout for session musicians touting for work, and the place the Small Faces met up and formed into a band. Not surprisingly, given its location, this studio was created principally for the production of those demos and cheap master recordings that the nearby publishers needed to ply their trade of song plugging, although David Bowie did make some of his earliest recordings there.

Legend Mk 2 and Tony Visconti used the very different, extremely voguish, Advision studio for the *Red Boot* album. This was a place Visconti seemed to have virtually lived in at the time, using it to record T. Rex simultaneously with that Legend LP. As the name suggests, Advision started out as a studio for making advertising jingles but quickly grew, having been the first studio in London to install an 8-track machine, then the first with a 16-track and finally the first to offer 32-track.

While at various points in his career, tight budgets have dictated the use of smaller studios (for example, for *Oxford* and *As The Yeahs Go By*), there have been several occasions when larger labels with larger budgets have permitted Mickey the use of first division studios.

The A&M album *Some People Can't Dance* was recorded at the top residential 24-track facility, Chipping Norton Studios, built and owned by that album's producer, Mike Vernon. During its lifetime, major artists as diverse as Jeff Beck, Duran Duran, Robbie Williams and Radiohead have used Chipping Norton, while big hits like Gerry Rafferty's *Baker Street* and Fairground Attraction's *Perfect* were recorded there.

Basing Street Studios, a former church situated in Notting Hill was chosen by Godley and Creme for Mickey's Chrysalis album, *Long Distance Romancer* and the Gary Brooker-produced half of *Juppanese*. This state-of-the-art facility had previously been Island Studios, playing an important part in the recording careers of countless major acts from Roxy Music, Bob Marley and Led Zeppelin to the Eagles, Dire Straits and Genesis.

But wherever he made his records, Mickey never enjoyed the process. "Something happens to me when the red light goes on," he confesses, "I freeze. I start making mistakes I never made before. I just hate it, wherever I am recording – even at home."

In fact, Mickey hated it so much that around this time in his career he seemed to have set his mind on finally retiring from the business.

But would the business let him go?

9 Not Wanted Anymore

In which Mickey takes a well-earned break from the music business, sort of

At the Shop

Nothing happened today.
Life just went on.
Nothing went right.
Nothing went wrong.
The sun didn't shine.
Neither did it rain.
And they say tomorrow will be 'bout the same

***Nothing Happened Today* by Mickey Jupp, As The Yeah's Go By**

After Legend split it looked as if the record business and Mickey might be due for a parting of the ways. But elsewhere in the industry Mickey's special talents had not gone unnoticed, resulting in a truly momentous event.

If indeed it actually occurred.

Mickey says it didn't; Mo Witham says that he was there and it did. David Knights, Mickey's manager at the time and the third witness to the event, does not give interviews these days. The fourth attendee, Maurice Oberstein, died in 2001, meaning I couldn't quiz him about it.

If it happened, here's what happened.

Maurice Oberstein was without doubt one of the most influential men in the music business at that time. He was Chairman of CBS Records, about to become the boss of industry body the BPI and was respected and feared by all who came into contact with him, from A&R head honchos to his hordes of scuttling record pluggers. One day, Mr. Oberstein is apparently in a meeting room with Mickey - now out of contract to Phonogram - Mickey's long-term musical sidekick Mo Witham and manager David Knights. Maurice tells Mickey that CBS have been watching his career with interest for some time now; that they have him down as a great prospect who writes terrific songs; that they have been really keen to sign him to CBS for a while; that this is the moment. As a tangible indication of their commitment to such an arrangement they propose a five-year deal – with one album and two singles per year. As a further sign of their goodwill, they would be happy to pay an advance of £100,000, (that's around a million pounds in today's money), to get Mickey's signature on the contract.

There is a silence. Mo crosses his fingers beneath the table.

He knows that 99% of musicians offered such a deal would jump at it. He also knows that Mickey is not 99% of musicians. Mickey's talent lies in being amongst the remaining 1%, who do not do the obvious thing.

David Knights must be dreaming of payback for all the time and money he has invested in Mickey over the last few years. Mickey finally speaks:

"To be honest, I'd rather play rock and roll in Southend and go down the pub for a game of darts."

There is another silence, some embarrassed mumblings from a shocked David Knights and the meeting ends. This had been the big one: one with America on the agenda as well as Europe, for that was the CBS game plan.

"I thought 'Thanks, mate', as I watched my career go straight out of the window," remembers Mo Witham. Apart from his personal disappointment, Mo was also puzzled over Mickey's response from his songwriting perspective:

"I don't know how else he thought he was going to get all those songs of his recorded and out there."

And what about the money he was turning down?

"I don't think money ever occurred to him – I still don't think it does."

How could this happen? Surely this offer was an upside without a downside?

At the very least it would have been the perfect conduit for sixty or more fresh Jupp compositions to reach the ears of the public; at best it might have generated enough income to allow Mickey to comfortably go on making music for life.

Mo thinks it was just too much pressure for Mickey to handle, which sort of makes sense when you think about it, at least in a lop-sided sort of way.

With Bell it was all going to happen and yet didn't, but at least it was a simple process, Mickey having already written the songs. One day in a studio, one gig, nothing more. OK, it came to naught in sales terms but Mickey hadn't given up much of his life to do it. And yet through this minimal effort he'd successfully liberated a bunch of his songs - songs that now existed in the vinyl on his shelf and out in the world at large. An honourable and worthwhile failure, then.

But with the Vertigo Legend experience it had been different. There had been promotion to undertake; touring to be tolerated; producers to cross swords with - a punishing schedule with little to show at the end but remaindered records, dashed hopes and debt. Mickey just wasn't that keen on the core drag of promotion: interviews and performing live, night after night, to a set formula.

It isn't that Mickey doesn't like performing: he does. But he likes to play what he likes, when he likes, where he likes - although he recognizes there are sound commercial reasons to play gigs, too:

"Management companies want you to make records. But I want to go out touring, 'cos I make money touring. I don't get paid for making records - the session guys do, the producer might, but not me. I get royalties - in theory. I'm not sure I've ever made money as a recording artist. Yes as a writer, yes as a performer, but as a recording artist? I don't think so, beyond the odd miniscule advance."

While the Vertigo deal meant that there were now more of his precious songs out there, Mickey wasn't very fond of the first of those two records, and the second one - the one he had a freer hand in making - had fallen short. On top of that, the recording process had proved more frustration than fun for him.   Where was the benefit into doing it all over again? The costs of touring, plus the deductions from royalties that record companies make to cover recording and marketing overheads, meant that his bank account was currently far from bulging.

He was actually living the same, largely hand-to-mouth existence that he had for the whole of his life. Did he want another five years of that?

He wasn't that interested in money in any case. And he certainly wasn't interested in fame. He'd never wanted to be a front man – trying to avoid it in every way possible since copping out of that first Orioles gig and ducking the Decca solo session he'd been offered on a plate.

He'd refused to dress for the part of bandleader, or get his hair cut properly; he wouldn't develop any endearing stage patter, nor did he welcome his mug shot on album sleeves.

Most extraordinarily, on stage with his band, he didn't much want to play his own beloved songs. He regarded them as being his personal, almost private, property.

It all felt too invasive. If he signed up with this major label and let them make a massive investment in him, he'd never get out of this vicious circle: he'd be writing material to order, endlessly gigging to build a reputation, undergoing weeks of recording each year, undertaking awful promotional activities to support each release: always on the road or, worse still, in the air, or perhaps worst of all, on camera.

For a man who liked order and a quiet life, the prospect was ghastly. Mickey had ended up making music for a living but couldn't tolerate a lot of what that entailed. It simply wasn't worth the candle - he'd had enough.

How much easier it would be to slip back to the environment he knew – Southend, the old pubs, the games of darts, a straightforward job in retail, maybe some low-key musical involvement. He could still write his songs...

And so, instead of changing up a gear - signing to CBS and setting his sights on UK success, then making it big worldwide - Mickey changed down a gear: spending the next two years working behind the counter at Chris Stevens Music Centre, from time to time sporting a natty bow tie.

He looked like Mr. Retail, but it didn't fool Wilko Johnson who reflected on it in an interview with Will Birch in 2016:

"I always felt that the world ought to know about Jupp. It seemed a shame that he was a local obscurity. I thought it was necessary that he got to the kind of audience he deserved. You'd see him working in the music shop and he's just a geezer...but when he picked up a guitar it was spine tingling. He's not a sparkling wit, but he is the man who wrote 'My Typewriter'! When I saw him working in the music shop it used to amaze me how mundane he seemed, with all the usual shopkeeper's stock jokes, like, 'What can I do you for?' Then you hear some of his brilliant lyrics..."

One last thing; this kind of behaviour is by no means unknown in the business. Here is Humble Pie drummer talking about his band's leader, the legendary singer and guitarist, Steve Marriott:

"Every time success started to come at him he would do everything he could to mess it up. I think his attitude was, 'I'd better mess this up before it messes me up'. I saw him blow a million dollar record deal intentionally because he knew if he didn't they would end up screwing him". I rest my case.

Although Mickey claims no recollection of this alleged CBS episode, it certainly exists in the minds of a number of other Jupp watchers, and is very clear to Mo Witham. If it was all a dream, it sounds a pretty well defined nightmare.

Nor is it the only evidence around that time of Mickey deliberately spurning the clammy advances of the music business, as John Howard recollects with some frustration:

"In 1973 I was doing freelance for BBC Radio London, where Charlie Gillet had a famous show on which he had played *My Typewriter*. Mick was out of contract at the time so I said to him in the pub one night, 'I've done enough for you for nothing down the years – if you like I can make some introductions for you, in return for a small percentage of any deal that transpires.' Mickey said fine, so I took him to Charlie Gillet's house in Clapham for a meeting, an event that was interrupted by Ian Dury – then of Kilburn and the High Roads – trying to blag some petrol money off Charlie, who at the time managed him! It was arranged that Mickey – who was working as a duo with Frank Mead at the time – would go into Essex Studios in London to record new material. On the designated day I get a call from Charlie saying, 'we're all here ready to go, where's Mickey?' At the time Juppy was living in Retreat Road, Westcliff and had no phone, so I went round there to see him. I said, 'Mickey, what's going on, they're waiting for you'. He looked at me and replied, 'Oh, I didn't feel like it'. So that was the end of that; he just hadn't bothered to take his chance. There was no further financial relationship between us after that, although I still love everything he does."

Déjà vu, all over again. But while you may be able to take Mickey Jupp out of the music business, you can't altogether take the music business out of Mickey Jupp, as he himself soon discovered:

"In 1974 and 1975 I ran the Piggies Club upstairs at the Blue Boar pub in Prittlewell. I didn't make any money out of it - it was just something to do. A guy called Max Flitton had been running it but he decided to pack it in so I said I'd have a go. We had some good acts on: Jo Ann Kelly, Duffy Power – what a great but wasted voice: you name it, he was doing it - even Alexis Korner, what a gentleman, and Dr Feelgood, of course."

More surprisingly, on April 10th 1974, Legend themselves re-formed for a gig at Piggies, with Mo, John and Bobby re-joining Mickey, although he made it clear to the local paper that there would be no repeat:

"This is just a one-off appearance – we have already been offered other dates but don't feel we want to get back to that."

The article goes on to say that Mickey now preferred to work as a duo with a harp player, a pairing who would be playing the 100 Club the next week and then recording the following day.

Somewhere around this time, perhaps that very week, Mickey and harp player Frank Mead went into Spectrum Studios, Westcliff to record some tracks. Spectrum was a well-known local studio where Southend musicians could make decent quality demos, even the odd self–released master, that didn't cost the earth. Under the watchful eye of owner/engineer Warwick Kemp, Mickey recorded his compositions *Pilot* and *Wrong Food* for the first time. He also recorded two other new songs which have never been heard of since: *I'm a Car* and *Pocket Calculator*, (although Wilko Johnson is known to have had a go at the latter) along with interesting takes on his own *Hole In My Pocket* and *Guitar Pickin' Slim,* plus the old Elvis standard *Mystery Train*. On a number of these tracks Mickey sings in a style more like a black fifties bluesman than at any other time, before or since. The tape sounds amazing.

While Frank Mead can remember the sessions, (not least because the studio chased him over the non-payment of the bill, which was nothing to do with him) he cannot recollect the exact purpose of the recording. He does, however, recall playing slide guitar on some tracks alongside his more usual harmonica. He also remembers he and Mickey having photos taken in Leigh around that time, the pair of them toting guns – so perhaps there was an intention to use the shots to promote *Guitar Pickin' Slim!*

(Some years later the master tape of these recordings was acquired by this author: through the simple mechanism of settling the outstanding bill for the studio time, which Mickey had typically neglected to pay! It's contents have never seen the light of day but it is hoped that Mickey will agree to at least a selection of tracks being released at some point in the future).

That apart, Mickey wasn't playing much, apart from some outings in a cabaret band to help pay the rent, more of which shortly. But he was not forgotten out in the big, wide world, as he ruefully recalls:

"While I'm working there, musically doing sod all, the bloody *NME* come down; Max Bell turns up to do a double page spread. Where's the justice? It's like having a prial of threes and nobody plays."

That article, published in an October 1975 edition of *NME*, would indeed have been great promotion for Mickey, if he'd had anything to promote at the time. Instead it rather succinctly referenced his dilemma.

"Turn left out of the station and you'll be in the High Street, can't miss it really. The Music Centre is in Queens Road. Mickey Jupp lives in Southend and it's his lunch hour. A more honest, unassuming down-to-earth character you couldn't hope to meet but Jupp also happens to be Local R&B Hero Number One. The Feelgoods and the Kursaal Flyers may have already made it but they'd be the first to admit that Mickey is more than a major influence. With Legend he made three albums not obtainable for love or money. He wrote a whole catalogue of ace songs, played a mean guitar and proved that white bands could not only write original classics, they could play them properly too."

Towards the end of the article, Bell raises the crucial question of whether Mickey will ever shake off his preference for the simpler charms of life behind a counter:

"As time went on and possible success seemed to slip further away Jupp became more stoical, resigned to his situation. He hasn't been short of offers since Legend's demise so why doesn't he go back on the road? 'No, that's just it. Mick Green rang up the other day with a band. All I want to do is play once a week, on this pub scene - I fancy that. I jammed with The Feelgoods once at The Nelson, Holloway Road – smashing, thoroughly enjoyed it. But I suppose you never know. The Kursaal Flyers began for a laugh down The Blue Boar and just took off, on the strength of Feelgood mind, but there you go. Just local lads.'"

Talking to one of those Kursaal Flyers, Will Birch, Wilko Johnson felt that while Mickey may have enjoyed his taste of resurgence, he still wasn't comfortable with throwing himself back into the fray:

200

"I was trying to get Juppy and Mo Witham back together…but there was this powerful reluctance to do it at all - he was disillusioned by then. After Legend didn't happen, I think he lost heart."

I asked Wilko to expand on this tantalising snippet:

"Feelgood had started to go down well in London – in fact we were knocking people out there – and I couldn't help thinking, 'what if Legend got back together and played here right now?' I really wanted to see them do it. At the time, Juppy was working at Chris Steven's music shop, at one end of Queen's Road, and Mo was working at Mighty Music down the other end. I'd go in and see Juppy and tell him he had to do it but he'd say Mo didn't want to do it, so I'd run down the road to try to persuade Mo! I couldn't get either of them to agree, so in a final attempt we took Juppy with us to London for one of our regular gigs at the Lord Nelson, just so he could see what we meant. We did normally did two sets but for the second one that night Lee stepped aside from vocals to play harmonica. Mickey took over singing, while Feelgood became his backing band. It went down a storm, of course – everybody was thinking what's this, who's this? I can remember driving home and saying to Mick, do you see what I mean now? Did he do anything about it afterwards? No he did not. So we were forced to admit defeat."

Confirmation, then, from Mickey's own lips and those of others around him that he felt it a less dangerous option to keep his head down and paddle about on the edges of the business. There were always going to be some mates around who, knowing how good he was, would want to play alongside him, giving him a chance to have a bit of a blow and make some beer money. How hard could it be: all his old cronies were still playing locally. Ex-Orioles and Legend drummer Bob Clouter had continued gigging with ex-Orioles and Legend guitarist Mo Witham, for example. The two of them had joined Chris East from the Bell-era Legend line-up, and local keyboard stalwart Tony Boynes, to play a financially rewarding if undemanding residency at local supper club the Wardroom.

Mickey - now living with his mum in Avenue Road – eventually slotted back into making music within an even more surprising and low-key outfit. The Alan Keys Four (aka the Sid Griffiths Group, Roger Stanley Four or, occasionally, El Sid!), was a decidedly supper-club outfit led by Sid Griffiths, a crooner of the easy listening persuasion who loved the standards. The combo mostly played Golf Club dances, Working Men's evenings and the like. Mickey recalls his involvement with surprising fondness:

"The Alan Keys Four happened in a little gap when I was out of rock and roll. Legend had finished and I was working at Chris Stevens Music Centre with Chris East. I put in a few hours like a guest manager there, and it went on for over two years. Chris' partner in the business, Roger Stanley, had a little dance band. He played organ in it really well, even using the bass pedals and he knew a lot of stuff – dance band music, proper music. The singer was an old feller called Sid, and there was a great jazz drummer called Geoff Larner. Roger was going to move to the Isle of Wight so I got roped in on guitar, to help fill the gap, because in those days I was not a bad guitar player. On bass we got Barry Scanling, who'd been in the Orioles for a little while. It was great and I learned loads from playing functions. Because they knew I could sing a bit they asked me to do some stuff, and so I did half a dozen numbers, all sung gently because it wasn't a loud band and you could actually hear what you were doing! I did my best ever version of Matchbox because the drummer was trying to keep it straight but couldn't help swinging. I found myself enjoying playing things like *The Lady Is A Tramp* - got to learn a lot of different chords. I had a great time. I wasn't the star of the show and I loved it. It was brilliant. If only I could have spent the last fifty years just being the piano player..."

John Bobin got involved in the band at some point, too, and recalls Mickey strapping a bass cabinet to the roof of his old Triumph Herald and driving off to gigs. This meant the Alan Keys Four now regularly had five members, none of whom was named Alan Keys: a fine example of the strength of branding. The name was, in fact, Mickey's elaborate pun on the workman's toolkit standby, allen keys.

But much as Mickey seemed to enjoy this lower-level musical life, he also knew it wasn't the real thing, as he told Max Bell at the time:

"The little band I'm in at the moment, we do rock'n'roll at the end. It's never rehearsed. The drummer's thirty eight, he's always been used to playing a certain way: tss .. ts .. tss.. tsssh and the bass going boom, boom, boom. It swings like fuck. Tremendous, 'cos it's simple. I look forward to my turn and I only really miss singing the blues; stuff like Elmore James' *Coming Home To Dust My Broom At The Crossroads.*"

A *Melody Maker* piece around this time contained the rather forlorn observation: "Shop manager, 30 year old Mick Jupp, plays guitar and piano in a local dance band and was associated with a group called Legend who recorded three albums before they broke up." That sounds uncomfortably like an epitaph.

By night Mickey played for working men; by day he was one himself, happily back in the calm and orderly world of retail. He was still writing songs but when it came to performing them it seemed the fire had gone out. Or had it?

Before too long Mickey had let himself be talked into a workout for an abortive new band, an outfit he christened Kilroy. They rehearsed for a couple of months but nothing much came of it. Fellow band-member Will Birch explains a bit more about the how and why of Kilroy getting together:

"Legend had died a couple of years before pub rock's day, in mid-'73, but Mick's music was made for that circuit. He belonged there but he'd missed the boat. Now he was working in the Music Centre and I was saying to him all the time, as were the Feelgoods, you've got to get up to London, to that scene. The venues and audiences are there and the record companies are signing. So in the summer of '73 we formed a band specifically for that purpose, called Kilroy. I was the drummer. I'd be the first to admit I'm a pretty useless drummer compared to those Mick had been used to, but what I lack in swing I make up for in enthusiasm and keeping my ear to the ground!

Frank Mead was involved, along with the late John Batty on guitar, John Denton on piano and bass guitarist, Ian Slater – it was a six piece. We rehearsed in the garage opposite Chris Stevens Music Centre in Queens Road for six or eight weeks. Mickey sang a mixture of rock standards and some of his own songs. We eventually got a fifty-minute set together, the right sort of length for those types of gigs, but nothing came of it. That was the moment: the moment that the Feelgoods hit London. Three months later me and some mates formed the Kursaal Flyers and suddenly we were off."

Kilroy had looked potentially viable, but it was stillborn. The *Southend Evening Echo* had published a small piece claiming that Kilroy promised to be "one of the best new bands for ages in South-East Essex", labeling the musicians, rather amusingly "veterans in their upper twenties". Mickey spoke of the band having "developed from a few jam sessions" and stated that, "our music is similar to the stuff I was doing with Legend – early country rock and roll," adding, "we'll be doing a lot of our own stuff plus things like early Elvis numbers."

Interestingly Kilroy would have been the only band Mickey ever played in whose piano player wasn't called Jupp - here he was strictly guitar and vocals.

John Denton maintains that they barely played any Jupp compositions, sticking instead to trusted standbys like *Summertime Blues* and *You Talk Too Much*, (surprise, surprise). Also, according to John Denton, the notorious French Henry actually contrived to record the band in that tiny room, though no trace of that tape can be found. Kilroy even played one gig – a private party in a marquee in a field in Hanningfield – the location at which Mickey would later open a demo studio with the owners of the land, his friends the Cooks.

But it was not to be. Mickey simply knocked it on the head. As he put it:

"I never knew where that band was going, it was just a stupid need to return to playing or something. I should have just stayed put and had a normal life - I'm not really bothered whether I play in a group or not."

As if to put a full stop on the whole affair, not long afterwards the out-building in which they and others - including Gil Lavis in his pre-Squeeze and Jools Holland days - had rehearsed, burnt down. The only photo known to exist of Mickey's career at Chris Stevens Music Centre is a slightly out-of-focus shot of him in his quasi-management role, helping the fire brigade sort out the post-blaze mess...

Time passes; more guitar strings and drumsticks get sold; Mickey meets and marries his second wife.

Musically, he may not have been doing much but in the outside world his reputation was still working surprisingly hard for him. Like it or not he was always going to be legendary to those who had seen him play, many of whom continued to bump into him in the shop. The Chris Stevens Music Centre had always been much more than just a music shop. It was a café, rehearsal room, social club and employment exchange for Southend's many talented musicians. There were other music shops in the area - including Tim Gentle Music, where behind the counter at that time you would have found Dave Bronze, future Jupp collaborator and eventual bass player for Procol Harum, Tom Jones and Eric Clapton - but Chris Stevens and his partner Roger Stanley owned the premier establishment. They had bought Wade's, (no relation), an old-style music shop, and turned it into a very progressive enterprise, which quickly grew. Chris Stevens recalls how Mickey came to work there:

"Chris East was the first to get involved assisting in the shop; I can't recall the connection but he was probably in a band with my business partner Roger. He became a full-time employee round about 1971. Through him I would have employed Mick. There wasn't any formal interview or anything – he would have just filled in a few times when were short-handed and it grew from there. He was full time for a while."

Mickey turned out to be the perfect employee for Chris' music store:

"I employed him because as well as a musician he was a retailer, his experience at the builders merchants, St Ann's, and other places was useful – although I'm not sure he really liked the public that much. He's not really a people person, is he? He might get on with the odd individual but en masse - not really, but he was very respected. A lot of people were aware of his musical presence in Southend, so he was a sort of attraction, I suppose."

Long-term fan and Southend bluesman Russ Cottee, (a man whose admiration for Mickey even stretched to giving him a Gibson guitar for his seventieth birthday), remembers that time nostalgically:

"I'd frequently see Mickey playing an acoustic guitar in Chris Stevens Music Centre where he allegedly 'worked'. Work appeared to consist of playing guitar and being a somewhat intimidating figure!"

Steve Hooker, another Southend musician of slightly younger vintage, later to become a close associate of Mickey's, often visited the music shop to try and learn from the master:

"I used to like to go into Chris Stevens because sometimes he would pick a guitar up and play some little thing and you might learn how he played it. He is a great guitarist, as well as a great piano player and singer – I'd put his voice up there alongside the great Delta blues singers and Otis Redding."

Chris Stevens noticed other aspects of Mickey's personality manifesting themselves at this time, like his short fuse:

"I can distinctly remember Mick swearing at a guitar on one occasion because it wouldn't fit into a box - an 'I've told you before' sort of thing, quite Basil Fawlty."

Chris also spotted and admired Mickey's keenness on orderliness:

"He liked to keep things neat – we had a display of guitar strings and I can remember he was always tidying that up and making sure it was fully stocked." In Chris' opinion Mickey was "a total dichotomy", mundanely working in a shop on the one hand and yet on the other, "going to prison for not paying alimony - which is such a rock and roll thing to do".

While Mickey was working there it became a home from home for ex and future members of his bands. He was already working alongside Chris East, twelve-string guitarist in the first version of Legend. Phil Mitchell, ex the final Legend line up and soon to be in another of Mickey's bands before settling as Dr Feelgood bassist, also worked there.

The various musicians employed in the shop played together so often in downtime that they occasionally went public with their efforts. On one occasion Mickey, Chris East, Andy Wade and some others played an acoustic set at The Esplanade. On another there was an attempt to put together a band, tentatively named Beaver.

Through the shop Mickey kept bumping into old mates from the Feelgoods and various other new kids on the Southend block. Many of these visitors were fans, people who knew how good the Orioles and Legend had been and shared in the general air of bemusement at Mickey's failure to make it big.

Touring with their bands, these supporters met other musicians whom they found shared that view. Most importantly of all, they played some of Mickey's songs, even recorded a few, and were thus able to bring Mickey's talents to a new and wider audience.

The Kursaal Flyers, for example, featured long-term Orioles/Legend fan Will Birch on drums, and on vocals, Paul Shuttleworth, (the man originally tasked with designing the cover for Legend's *Moonshine* album). The Kursaals had formed when half a dozen musicians who'd been knocking around the Southend music scene for some time in various permutations got together. Named after Southend's famous but recently closed down seafront amusement palace, The Kursaal, they made their performing debut at The Blue Boar pub in Victoria Avenue, Southend in February 1974, right in the middle of Mickey's fallow period, following the Kilroy episode.

Dr Feelgood, now headliners in their own right, offered the Kursaals some support slots, which got them in front of both fans and record company executives. They duly signed to Jonathan King's UK Records, (previously home to 10cc, one of the few modern bands Mickey ever had any time for, who have their place later in this story.) The Kursaals' debut album, *Chocs Away*, was released in 1975. It contained their cover version of Mickey's song *Cross Country,* from the Legend *Red Boot* album.

In 1974, as the Kursaals were developing, Dr Feelgood recorded their debut album, *Down by the Jetty*. It included a cover version of *Cheque Book*, another of Mickey's more celebrated songs from *Red Boot*. Its inclusion wasn't just down to the quality of the song. It was also intended to be another nudge in the ribs to Mickey's dwindling career, given that earlier direct action hadn't paid off. Wilko explains it thus:

"After we failed to get him to reform Legend, I thought sod it, at least we can put *Cheque Book* on our first album. That way, if it does well people will get to hear one of his songs – plus it could eventually lead to a few bob for Juppy himself. Whenever I do a cover version on an album I think about that: do I like whoever wrote it, as they'll be getting something out of it!"

Released in 1975, the Feelgoods' album *was* a notable success, being cited as an important influence by artists from a wide spectrum that included Blondie, the Ramones, Bob Geldof and, it turns out, Legend fan Paul Weller. (In 1976, before they got their own record deal, Paul Weller's band, another bunch of musicians calling themselves The Jam, went so far as to record their reading of Mickey's *Cheque Book* as part of their audition tape).

It was the Feelgoods in particular who were going to get Mickey back on the scene. As we shall see, that band's leader, Wilko Johnson, had vowed that they would manage to achieve this, one way or another. And he was still trying hard.

What's Goin' On: The Sound of the "Essex Delta"

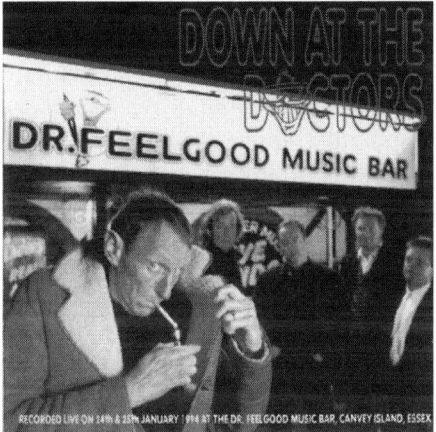

Dr Feelgood's last album with Lee Brilleaux was named after Mickey's song

Southend's musical reputation was now in the hands of Dr Feelgood. The Feelgoods' sound was raw and stripped back, feral and fast. It was a new, higher energy take on the Paramounts and Legend - one better suited to those proto-punk days. I tried to capture their essence in this piece; adapted from one I wrote a couple of years ago for a blog:

Four pasty, sun-starved Essex faces peering out of the mid-seventies gloom heralded the arrival of Dr Feelgood and the birth of music from what they liked to call the Essex Delta. Better known to the rest of us as Canvey Island.

Down By The Jetty was a back-to-basics wake up call to a music business grown fat on the excesses of pomp rock. Unlike the faux egalitarianism of the punk movement that followed, and which they helped inspire, Feelgood were excellent musicians – honed to a cutting edge by constant gigging in nearby Southend (musical home to maestros Mickey Jupp and Gary Brooker) and the low life pubs of east London.

Their devoted adherence to a less-is-more philosophy led to their debut album being recorded overdub-free, live in the studio, by an engineer instead of a producer, effectively in mono. It went down a storm, leading to the release of an equally brilliant, brooding second single: *Back In The Night*.

As *Oil City Confidential*, the recent, glorious Julian Temple documentary about the band illustrates, their music was fundamentally an expression of their attitude – and their attitude was fundamentally an expression of the environment in which they had grown up. An odd, wonky place occupied by outsiders and drifters, sneered at even by the working class citizens of the rest of this frayed cuff of Essex coast.

Essex Delta? Oil City? Full of square pegs in worn, round holes? Canvey had to be worth a look.

So one brooding autumn day I set out for this blurry bit of the Thames Estuary, sullenly reclining between claggy Southend and hazy Kent: home to big mud, oil refineries, rusty tankers and tough, rocking, bluesy music.

Canvey has a sort of seafront, battered and shuttered in the main; yet thanks to the giant sea wall, erected to protect the place from the floods that have regularly decimated it down the years, the sea front has no actual sea view. When you climb up the embankment to reach the sea view, you realise not seeing it may be something of a blessing.

To the east lie the gaunt flaming towers of oil and gas refineries. Straight ahead, a flat plain of camouflage-coloured mud stretches what seems half way to Kent. To the left, where the estuary opens to the sea, giant, shabby cargo ships, bloated with crude oil or fresh Mazda cars, wallow in line, awaiting the appropriate tide.

Everywhere you turn, fat steel pipes rise out of the ground, breaching the sea defences before scurrying back below the mud and out to sea.

Even Canvey's proud boast of housing a Site of Special Scientific Interest turns out to be bizarre, the site being located not upon some vast plain of beautiful wetland but rather on the abandoned foundations of yet another oil refinery, one never built because planning permission was eventually withheld – perhaps a small gesture of mercy towards the island's embattled inhabitants.

And embattled they are.

The pretty coloured legends on the road signs are not there, as they might be in Brighton or Bridlington, to mark out scenic routes for the visitor. They designate the rapid emergency routes off the island locals must take in the event of their imminent immolation.

Away from the front, most of the shops are one-offs, the sort these days that you rarely see in any numbers anywhere else. Gardens are blighted by the permafrost that creeps out from the underground LPG storage tanks. The flat, reclaimed lands behind the sea wall are littered with scuzzy residential caravans. Stray attempts have been made to insert small pockets of executive residences but these prove unconvincing – what executive would choose Canvey in the first place?

More exciting, yet more disturbing are the shacks: home-made by outsiders in an era before planning or building regulation. Small, personal marks on a vast, muddy canvass.

Back on the front, there are sticks of rock and bowls of shellfish and racks of Kiss Me Quick hats , all crammed into tiny wooden stalls dotted along the sea wall. A few indolent jet skis loll in the shallows, awaiting the arrival of tattooed owners in dog-eared BMWs. A couple of tough kids splash in the pools left behind by the outgoing tide, sharing their fun with paddling pensioners, mangy dogs and their excrement, (the dogs' rather than the pensioners', one hopes).

It sounds thoroughly ghastly. But in a peculiar way, it's a little bit brilliant.

It is real and honest and throwback and doing its best.

It is an illiterate child, tongue out, trying hard to read. It is a woman of a certain age doing what she can with what she has left. It is a man sporting a comb over, bravely pretending nobody has noticed.

But it sure ain't the place I would have wanted to grow up.

The sense of failure would be impossible not to ingest. The island would force you to grow a carapace of rebellion, swagger and fuck-you.

It would make you want to make music like Dr Feelgood did: noisy, angry, pumping. Almost industrially mechanical, yet full of feral cunning and intelligent wordplay and spittle.

'Then they will take notice of me, then they won't be able to look down on me', you'd think to yourself. And boy, how right you would turn out to be: Feelgood achieved simultaneous number ones in the UK and USA with their live album, *Stupidity*. They are seen as the fathers of punk. In a form, they still live on, playing today in Mk 4 or 5 or 6 guise.

Nor were they actually as nasty a piece of work as their on-stage demeanour suggested. I met lead singer Lee Brilleaux once, briefly, not long before his tragically early death from cancer, and found him to be a quiet, generous and amiable fellow.

With quite a bit of steel, mind you, courtesy of Canvey.

Sure it's full of dog shit but there's very little bullshit.

10 Doo Wop Shang-a-Lang Shimmy Shimmy

In which Mickey, tempted back into the world of music, goes a bit over the top

Making it big   courtesy of Russ Cottee

Some roads are rocky
Some roads can be long
Count yourself lucky if your road rolls on

Some Roads by **Mickey Jupp, demo**

Observers of Mickey's career sometimes note how he never really sought success for himself; never engineered his own openings; never fully controlled his own destiny. Robin Trower had put him up for the Orioles gig that started it all.

Dave Watson negotiated the Bell deal that first made Mickey's mark as a songwriter. David Knights got him to put Legend together to fulfill the Vertigo contract he'd obtained on Mickey's behalf, which really got him some attention.

And now the Feelgoods, the Kursaals and others were opening new doors for him, through which a fresh audience could hear his songs.

Yet this is not atypical: very few artists develop in any other way.

For many years the great Beatles drifted through managers and gigs, sometimes acting difficult out of sheer boredom, sometimes not even turning up for gigs. Their motto at that time was "something will turn up". In the end something did, something rather big. And because their talent was so evident from early on, they constantly attracted mentors and helpers almost as easily as they did fans, culminating in Brian Epstein, the man who finally cajoled them into success.

Although not producing the same universally successful results, Mickey's exceptional talent ensured that he, too, was often championed by those around him. To play piano and guitar like Mickey does would be enough for most musicians. To sing like that, even half that well, would make any musician exceptionally happy. Mo Witham, a brilliant guitarist so dedicated to his instrument that he gets withdrawal symptoms if he goes a day without playing it, said this about Mickey's vocal prowess:

"I'd swap my guitar playing for his voice in a second, if I could. He makes the hairs stand up on the back of my neck when he's in the mood. He's the best male vocalist I've ever worked with and I've worked with a few good ones. Even Chris Farlowe, who I played with and produced, doesn't get anywhere near him."

And as we know, there are still more strings to Mickey's bow. To be able to write songs of the calibre that he does is a whole other skill layered on top. Finding all these talents together in one person is exceptionally rare.

So who are we to complain that he didn't do things the way we would have done them? We can't do the things he can do, so we should maybe expect him to behave a little differently from we mere mortals. Remarkably, there is evidence that Mickey Jupp's infamously "difficult" side is not born out of the sort of arrogance one might expect from one so talented. Mo, who has played with him longest – still does, to this day - sees the prickliness occurring for quite the opposite reason:

"He's got no confidence – he's the most unconfident person you could meet. Get to know him really well and he'll tell you: he don't like his voice, he don't like his guitar playing, he don't like his piano playing. After all these years I sometimes still have to give him the chat before we go on: 'Come on mate, you'll be fine, like you always are; you could sing the birds out of the trees.' Just to get his confidence up."

(It may seem strange to us that Mickey could hate a voice as good as his, but according to George Martin, John Lennon felt the same, recalling that "John *hated* his voice…he was always asking me to distort and disguise it…I *loved* his voice").

Mo's point about confidence is interesting in deeper ways.

For decades Mickey has been operating in the guise of a solo artist but you will rarely see him play truly solo. There was really only one period when he frequently did, as fan and blues guitarist Russ Cottee recalls:

"I saw him upstairs at The Railway Hotel pub in Southend: on Sunday evenings it hosted a music club called 'Odyssey', or maybe it was 'Expression'. Around 1976 myself and a friend were his support act. Before he went on we were talking to him and asked whether he'd play *Cheque Book*? He replied along the lines of 'No, I've left all that old stuff behind'. That night he did play a blinding version of *Pilot*, though, (it was of course unreleased back then), which stayed in my head for years until it surfaced on *Juppanese*."

Apart from this handful of folk club gigs, when he was trying out songs and short of musical associates, live performances without a full band have always been Mickey plus one, most usually Mo or Frank Mead, as he acknowledges:

"Oh God, I couldn't play solo. Maybe if I was more adept at the guitar I might.

I'm willing to admit that maybe once upon a time I wasn't a bad guitarist but now apart from a couple of good riffs I'm just a good rhythm guitarist. I was never one thing nor the other, what with the piano and singing, plus writing."

It's easy to see that at this particular low point in his career, Mickey's confidence can hardly have been more rock bottom. He appeared to have opted out.

Yet his music was getting more attention now than it ever had when he was thrashing around the country actively trying to cultivate a following. Back in 1973, right after the Feelgoods had made their debut BBC session for Bob Harris, and perhaps sensing their own imminent fame, Wilko Johnson had pledged to "grab Mickey Jupp by the scruff of his neck and deliver him into the spotlight". This generous sentiment is evidence of Feelgood's deep admiration for Mickey, something Wilko was always happy to proselytize about, saying at the time:

"Mickey Jupp made a couple of albums but they didn't really go far. He is one of the greatest singers you'll ever hear, and a great songwriter - a bluesman really, he can sing like Elmore James!"

What broke the dam was the Feelgoods coming good on that promise.

They made him a failsafe offer: if Mickey would get back on the road, he could be their support – a touching role reversal, they having supported Legend earlier in their career. This was Mickey's chance to reach out to an audience bigger than ever before. He would be able to do it amongst friends and without the stress of being top of the bill. The great songs were still flowing out of him after three years working in the music shop, the voice as good as ever, so why not?

But how best to go about it, now it was 1975?

He could have gone out on his own – an intimate singer-songwriter session with Mickey playing his wonderful music at the piano. But that would have been a bit scary.

He could have easily found any number of volunteers to join him in another duo.

He could have recruited another tight band called Legend. But he'd been there, done that. Twice.

Instead he did the least predictable thing imaginable: he formed a big band.

This first ever Mickey Jupp Band - known as the Mickey Jupp Big Band - sometimes went out under the billing Der Grosse Mickey Jupp Band. Mickey explains why:

"My parents met because of the war, so I suppose I've got Adolf Hitler to thank for my existence. Mum was working on secret radar stuff at Tangmere and Dad was in the Navy. They met up at some social do and got together. As a result, I've developed a strange fascination for the story of the rise of the Nazis. I hasten to add I have no right-wing leanings - other than disagreeing in principle with unions, which I think sap the power of the individual. Unfortunately, in the end I was forced against my will to join one before the BBC would let me work for them. Anyway, at the time I put the big band together I was 31, the same age Hitler was when his rise started, so I thought that reference would be amusing. I don't think any of the band objected, except perhaps Joy Sarney."

Keeping track of the opinions of the band wouldn't have been easy, had Mickey even bothered, given that there were ten of them: Mickey on piano and lead vocals plus Frank Mead (harp/sax), John Pugh (sax), Joy Sarney (vocals), Colin Maxwell (vocals), Bob Fish (vocals), Pete 'The Hat' Bloor (vocals), Bob Clouter (drums), Pete Zear (guitar) and Phil Mitchell (bass).

Mickey had pinched the backing singers wholesale after having seen them play in a pub as the Rock and Roll Cadets, a sub-branding they maintained in his band.

This coup was clearly already being plotted when Max Bell interviewed Mickey on the subject of the Southend music scene a few months earlier:

"There's nowhere to play here any more, the place is dead as a doornail. It's all discos now. The group boom happened because of the clubs - that was the original pub scene. There is one band though, all locals, called The Rock and Roll Cadets. They are great. I'm gonna get them when I play."

And so he did. The Rock and Roll Cadets had begun life playing at Piggies as half a dozen acapella singers - including Ian Slater from Mickey's short lived Kilroy and backed by pianist John Denton, also from Kilroy - having initially been billed as the Bob Fish Rock and Roll Choir.

This unit's somewhat shambolic stage delivery paralleled a remarkably eclectic repertoire that included material as diverse as *At the Hop, Three Bells* and *Leader of the Pack*.

Mickey loved to get up and jam with them, both on guitar and vocals, and would frequently announce them by telling the audience, "They think they're crap but I think they're wonderful!"

Looking back, Mickey cites the Big Band as one of his best musical experiences: "None of us were great players, except for Frank Mead who most definitely was: he'd added sax to his harmonica playing and later went on to tour with Paul McCartney. All the same it was one of the bands I most enjoyed playing in, at least for a while, until the egos kicked in."

Frank Mead regularly crops up in Mickey's story. He'd started playing the harmonica as a ten year-old and by sixteen was in his first blues group. He met his "Southend r&b hero" Mickey Jupp and began playing local clubs with him as a harmonica player. Frank's first recording session had been in 1969 with Southend band Wolfe, for whom he played harmonica on *Dead From The Head Down*, a track from their US-only Motown album, *Wolfe*. (We didn't know his full name so on the sleeve he is credited as Frank G Harp!)

That session certainly had an effect on Frank, as he told me:

"After the Wolfe session in that great studio, IBC, I went back to my day job and told my mates that this was what I was going to do with my life. I was 100% converted; it was a revelation - a life changer for me. I was driven to be a musician - I got the shout, and I've managed to avoid working for forty years since!"

Frank first met Mickey just after the Wolfe session, when he was introduced to him at Top Alex. Then, at a party at Max Flitton's house in Argylle Road at which Mickey was singing and playing guitar, he added some harp and found himself being asked if he would like do more duo work.

Frank went on to record with Mickey on a number of occasions, as well as with Gary Moore, Mick Jagger, Squeeze, Beverly Craven and Go West. In 2003 he released his own album, *Shout It Out*. Today he plays with Bill Wyman, amongst others, in his Rhythm Kings.

What's astonishing, though, is that at the time Frank was recruited to Mickey's Big Band he had only been playing sax for a matter of months. He told Will Birch how much Mickey's faith in his potential had meant:

"It was ridiculous…I was so crap! But Mickey gave me the opportunity and I owe him. He was instrumental in setting me on the path to becoming a professional player and I've got a lot to thank him for."

He expanded that memory for this book:

"I only started playing sax four months before Juppy invited me to join the Big Band – so I actually learned to play on the road, with Juppy, in the pubs and clubs. I remember we did an early gig at the old Nashville Rooms – at that time I didn't even know what a key was. I had just learned a few fingering patterns and knew nothing about reeds or any of that stuff. That night it was coming out all wrong, I just couldn't get it to sound right. In the break I slung my alto down in disgust, and a tangerine I'd put in its case as a snack for later rolled out of the horn! Problem solved!"

Frank had an additional reason to imagine he might not be the world's greatest, though, as drummer Mick Brownlee explains:

"Mickey was always pulling Frank's leg. Frank would come off stage after a gig and ask how Mickey thought it had gone. He always replied, 'You were crap, Frank', which Frank always seemed to believe at first, sending him into a panic: 'I wasn't, was I?' he'd ask, and all that. Truth is, Frank is a great player, although I know he played too much for some people's liking - Eric Clapton thought he came forward a bit too often, for example."

However, Frank's gratitude has not blinded him to the deep complexities in Mickey's character, or the issues they can throw up for his collaborators:

"I think he's a man who is riddled by demons. Everybody knows about him. He can be angry, difficult and hard to be with sometimes. But people like him are the ones who come up with the goods, because they are coming from this place of deep hurt. Something happened to him in his past that really fucked him up. It's strange, it's as if his talent is almost like an illness…"

That's quite a thought. A guy singing the blues not because he likes the way it sounds, which is how most white singers approach it, rather because he actually *has* the blues.

A guy writing about the pain in his world; who doesn't have much material wealth; who's always getting in trouble with "the man", not to mention the women; most of all, someone whose angst is created in part by the very pressures of having to write about it for a living!

Blues songs are interesting because they can sometimes be seen as a codified, more acceptable cloaking of what might otherwise be considered the artist's maudlin self-pity.

"Woke up this morning, and I found my baby gone", (parodied by Mickey in *Standing at the Crossroads Again* as "*Woke up this morning, as I usually do*"), typifies the genre. Such a form of words is more acceptable than a blunter version, one that might be closer to the real truth. It might run more along the lines of: "Woke up this morning and the woman I've been mean to for ages, and occasionally unfaithful to, has finally, justifiably, cleared off."

Mickey's most emotional songs – the ones many of his listeners feel might expose the most of his opaque soul – are often, in that sense, self-pitying blues songs:

"How do you say goodbye to five long years of your life"

"The ring on your finger, smiled and laughed out at me and I knew I'd lost again"

"You shot me down, all you said was 'See you around'"

So was the Big Band an attempt to fend off the embarrassment that might result from showcasing songs that exhibited such personal rawness?

(Mickey had, after all, just written *Pilot*, containing devastating lines like the final of the three listed above and another, *"I'm a summer, ruined by rain"*).

Did Mickey feel that more band members equalled less focus on the man with the microphone?

Or was it, as Frank Mead feels, actually a positive step in the man's pursuit of musical authenticity: an important if unfashionable musical crusade upon which to embark?

"Mick was at odds with just about everyone in a musical sense – we were the only band around doing sax-based rythmn and blues and he liked that. For all the showmanship of the Big Band, Mick was serious about his mission and devoted to playing proper stuff."

Whatever his motive, the outfit was certainly a sight to see, as well as great to hear. In 1975 the *NME* ran a series of articles on the highly active pub rock scene, in which Geoff Hill wrote the following:

"Mickey Jupp, with his whole band, is just beginning to let his hair down after some years off the road. With his own vocal performance developing fast and his reputed vast wealth of original material – and if his beautiful *I'm a Pilot* is anything to go by it's wealth indeed – he could be set for the sort of success of, say, a Frankie Miller."

In a second piece, published a few weeks later, Hill went on to write:

"I have actually been moved by this band recently, as well as induced to twitch, hunker and slop beer down my trouser leg. And nobody, but NOBODY, dances at the Nashville as a rule."

As well as the Nashville, the band was becoming a favourite at other cool London pub venues like the Hope & Anchor and Dingwalls in Camden. John Denton remembers seeing the Big Band play Dingwalls one night with them all wearing cardboard masks of Mickey's face. This decidedly un-Jupplike stunt that may have been as big a surprise to him as the audience, for the band were always larking about, sometimes at the guv'nor's expense. For example, the band's set frequently kicked off with Ray Charles' *You Be My Baby*, the first notes of which Mickey sang unaccompanied, using a faint chord from the band to give him the right key. The temptation to give him the wrong chord and leave him stranded in the wrong register sometimes proved irresistible.

The Big Band performed in Southend at numerous venues including Piggies, the club at the Blue Boar pub that Mickey was involved in running, the Queen's Hotel and Southend College. In November 1975, Mickey spoke to Chas de Whalley of the *NME* about his hopes for this exciting new unit:

"Why am I playing the pubs circuit at the moment? Look, I was in Legend three years ago, and we even had a couple of albums put out on Vertigo, but we got screwed by the business every way we turned. So I gave it all up. I went to work in a music shop in Southend until Lee Brilleaux (of Dr Feelgood) and a couple of guys in the Kursaals persuaded me to play again. Of course I'm after the money, I want to be successful, but this time round I'm going to do it my way."

Despite those high hopes, the band's life was regrettably short and unfulfilled, paradoxically because in the end Mickey didn't do it *enough* of his way.

He has always regretted the band's early demise and feels some, but not all, of the responsibility for it:

"Looking back, I could have handled it better. One of the guys was Army and didn't like the stage antics of the Rock & Roll Cadets backing singers, who'd act out mock fights while he was doing a groovy sax solo, but the audience loved it. I felt I was losing control but didn't want any confrontation, so I didn't put my foot down and it all got out of hand."

Southend musician Steve Hooker noticed something else:

"In the Big Band, Mick always gave Frank Mead the solos – even though John Pugh was the more experienced player." Well, John Pugh was bound to be the more experienced player: he was the serving Royal Artillery bandsman Mickey referred to, a chap who had to be collected for gigs from the gates of the barracks and wear a wig on stage to hide his military short back and sides.

Such a long-running spat between guys who shared a mic wouldn't have made life all that harmonious.

Back in 1978, Mickey mentioned other reasons for the band's early demise, joking that by the end he felt so squeezed out he couldn't even get a turn at driving the van. In every sense, some of the cast members seemed to be in too much of a hurry for their guv'nor::

"It was great but some of the band wanted everything at once, they wanted to be big before their time and I wasn't ready for that. I felt that it wasn't my band any more: it was becoming the Bobby Clouter Big Band, so I told them if you're that good, *you* get on with it and I left."

(It's worth noting that any tension between long-term band mates Mickey and Bob wasn't irreparable, as they've played together many times since the Big Band era).

Reflecting on the debacle three years later, Mickey told *Sounds* journalist Dave Brown a similar story, so it seems consistent:

"That band was bloody great but it had too many petty egos to support, too many little pop stars. Some of the band wanted the vocalists out but I thought that was the difference of the band so I quit. They carried on for about three months."

Blimey, I wonder who attempted to stand in for Mickey on vocals. That would have been something of a hospital pass.

Whatever the precise ins and outs of who was to blame for what, these frictions could not have been more disastrous for Mickey: the Big Band offering him musical opportunities that simply weren't there before, however difficult it might have been to keep a balance. On the upside, Mickey had acquired a real show band: one that people could enjoy watching as well as listening to, without him having to be centre-stage at all times. On the downside, such a large unit made it harder for Mickey to exert his will, to get exactly what he wanted. It was always going to be a ticking time bomb.

Handling that many team members would never have been easy, even if they had all got along swimmingly, or if Mickey had shown any sort of diplomatic skill. A band that size had enough scale for factions to emerge, infighting to occur, wounds to fester. Matters like who got the best microphones quickly became the basis for silly squabbles: Mickey claiming that the sax players nicked the best ones when he, as lead vocalist, should have had the pick of them.

There were other pressures, too: economic ones. A ten-piece band couldn't easily fit into some venues. Where they could, they probably wouldn't command a significantly bigger fee than a four or five piece band would have earned, so each band member was going to take home less. That share would be further diminished by the fact that the overheads of running a big band are inevitably higher: there's more equipment, transport and accommodation to pay for.

The Mickey Jupp Big Band's only hope for survival was rapid success. At a critical level this soon came: even Joe Strummer declared his admiration when his pre-punk band the 101ers supported the Big Band at a December 1975 gig at The School of Oriental & African Studies.

But success didn't come commercially because they never got what they needed: strong management and a recording contract. In fact, far from securing a label deal, for years there were only rumours that the unit had ever recorded at all.

"The big band recorded for the BBC, I think – Bob Fish was there. We also did some bits at De Lane Lea", Mickey vaguely recalled some time later, although Frank Mead memory favours Pye Studios, or perhaps, Decca as the venue!

Wherever, there would have been plenty of varied material to record, as Mickey points out:

"We played some of my songs, and re-arranged standards like *Little Bitty Tear* and *Sea of Heartbreak,* the odd Chuck Berry, a version of *Bye Bye Love* that turned reggae half way through…"

Until recently, only a handful of diehards who owned an obscure vinyl album called *Southend Rock,* released by the small Sonet label, knew differently. This LP was a charity compilation issued in support of the Billericay Hospital Burns Unit, an endeavour curated by none other than Southend producer, now record shop owner, Peter Eden – the very man who had encouraged Mickey to write songs in the first place. With the eventual release in October 2014 of *Kiss Me Quick, Squeeze Me Slow*, Repertoire Records' box set of Mickey's collected works, one of only two known recordings of the Mickey Jupp Big Band finally made it onto the CD format and into the wider world. The song selected is a tremendously punchy, rolling version of Mickey's best-known song, *Down At The Doctors*. In fact on the original Sonet album the song was credited as *Down To The Doctors*. Mickey is ambivalent about what the real title is, telling me, "At. To. I sing it both ways so it could be either!" On the original vinyl LP, this ebullient performance was paired with a second Big Band number, a visceral rendition of *The Ballad of Guitar Pickin' Slim*. They just go to show what might have been.

When I asked Mickey why no more recordings were made of such a good band - one surely purpose-built for a live album - I got a surprising reply:

"More than likely, if I'd known a performance was being recorded live for something like that, I would have frozen. I'm not very good when the little red light comes on. I get nervous and start to get things wrong. Performing is not easy for me. Whatever it might look like, it's hard work."

According to the recollections of their drummer Bob Clouter, one of the Jupp originals that the Big Band played on several occasions was, perhaps surprisingly, *Pilot*. This song, which appeared on Mickey's later solo album *Juppanese* and was then covered by Gary Brooker on an album of his, is felt by many fans to be one of Mickey's finest. Obviously very personal, he's habitually uncomfortable playing it live despite endless requests to do so, other than at those intimate guitar-only performances he gave when trying it out at the Railway Folk Club in Shoeburyness. (In down times during the seventies Mickey played such venues for fun and to make a few bob – on one occasion he even played a solo set at the opening of an American Diner in Leigh-on-Sea!).

The Mickey Jupp Big Band did indeed play *Pilot*, and more of Mickey's songs, as the man himself recollected when talking to Mike Davies in 1978:

"We were shit hot. The band did several of my songs, like *S.P.Y., Cheque Book, Guitar Pickin' Slim* and *Pilot* – that's the song everybody raves over, but I've had to do it so many times I'm sick of it".

He elaborated on this point for Dutch magazine *De Telegraaf* a few years later:

"*Pilot* was my favourite song. Once when I was totally fed up again with this business I didn't play anywhere but in a small club in the town where I'm from, Southend. Every night I had to sing *Pilot* four or five times. Once it was recorded I couldn't listen to it any more. I hated *Pilot*. When Gary put it on his first solo album he asked me to do the backing vocals. I almost threw him out - the fate of all my benefactors!"

Vocalist Bob Fish, who shortly after his stint in the Big Band went on to enjoy chart success as a founder member of Darts, recalls that the Jupp compositions played in the Big Band also included *Cross Country*, all the way from *Red Boot*. Bob shed further light on why the break up occurred. In a feature about Darts, (a nine piece - it must be catching), he explained that he himself left the Big Band after a row with several other members, a falling-out he recalls was over the serious underfinancing of the band, who were unable even to afford adequate stage monitors. This meant that Bob and the other vocalists often found themselves singing in a key some distance from that which the instrumental members of the band had chosen!

Bob, who had been one of those originally pestering Mickey to get back on the road, remembers the Big Band experience positively overall. In their short life they played lots of college gigs, as had Legend before them. At one of these Bob remembered a "strange bunch of urchins" turning up and asking if they could be the support band. It was the Sex Pistols.

Frank Mead places the gig at Bedford College, London in Regent's Park. "Mick told them that they would have to ask the social sec, who let them play. This was pre-Sid Viscious and we were shocked by the temerity of them: I noticed how Johnny Rotten was apeing Lee Brilleaux, hand in pocket, etc, but nothing like as good."

John Denton agrees that the Mickey Jupp Big Band was a quality act, singling out singer Joy Sarney for particular praise. Despite being known, if at all, for the novelty hit *Naughty, Naughty, Naughty,* (written and produced by Southend boy and ex-Wolfe member Nick Ryan, with writing assistance from Robin Slater, also of Wolfe and brother of Kilroy's Ian Slater!) Joy had a great voice – one strong enough to hold its own in a call and response duet with Mickey when the band played *Bring It On Home*.

Interviewed in 1980 by Dutch magazine *Muziek Express*, Mickey provided another way in which one might interpret the mysterious episode of the Grosse Mickey Jupp Band: "In '75 we did a small reunion, extended to a ten man band. I never had the intention to carry on with those ten people. How can you ever keep ten people together?"

Good question. But was it always intended to be temporary, a 'reunion'? That feels a bit like a cover story. Whatever the truth, the times were, in any case, changing fast.

"Pub rock was great until punk came in and destroyed it all," Mickey sadly remembers.

Buried deep in a bravely frank 1980 interview by Jip Golsteijn for magazine *De Telegraaf*, translated from Dutch by Jupp fan Ron Bijnen, lies one more possible clue to the reasons for Big Band's disintegration:

"'Is it true, I want to know, 'that Jupp can hardly cooperate with other musicians because it's impossible for him to pay them compliments?' The singer looks at me in bewilderment. 'Who says that?' He lights a cigarette laboriously and gives me a desperate look. 'What a question!' He drains his beer can and stares for a couple of minutes out of the window of the office that the record company people have vacated for us. 'I treat people like I want to be treated myself' he says finally. 'For me a pat on the shoulder is enough but most musicians seem to want more'. And after another long silence: 'It's true I can't give them that much more'."

Whatever the reasons - because they felt unloved or because they became mischievously rebellious - band members began to drift away. After not much more than a year the band had ceased to exist. Almost. On 31st May 1976, the Big Band reformed to play one final gig at an open-air festival. This charity event, called 'Southend Sounds', was held at Southend United's football stadium, Roots Hall. Alvin Lee, Fairport Convention and Budgie shared the bill with Mickey's band. On the advertisements for the event the Mickey Jupp Band's name was sadly underprinted with the words "Say farewell".

The incomparably cool John Peel, a supporter of Legend back in the Vertigo days, compered the event. After Mickey's band's performance was over he announced to the audience of several thousand:

"This rock and roll business is great, isn't it? There's terrific bands like this who have to split because they can't afford to stay together, while there are crap bands going to America to avoid their taxes." Right on, John.

At the point the band broke up Mickey's personal life was not in a great state either, he having just split up with his second wife, Val. Bob Clouter explains what happened next:

"At the close of the Big Band he ended up lodging with me at my place on Canvey Island; a temporary thing while he got himself sorted out. It dragged on a bit, which didn't go down too well with my wife. He had his own room and turned it into a sort of Jupp 'nest ' - all very organized with stuff neatly in cupboards and laid out carefully, almost obsessively." (Mickey was by now an experienced, almost serial lodger, at one point having even spent a while hanging out at Feelgood frontman Lee Brilleaux's pad – also on Canvey. According to Zoe Howe's fine book *Lee Brilleaux: Rock'n'roll Gentleman,* Juppy drove the singer nuts with his constant cooking of fry-ups, although Mickey and Lee's wife Shirley don't share that memory).

Another band was gone and Mickey was once again looking to piece his career back together; carve out some sort of a future. But could he really be arsed?

After all the grief he had just been through it's not surprising that his next plan was notably less ambitious.

By the summer of 1976 Mickey and Frank Mead were going out as a far more manageable and profitable duo, a configuration that also made more space in which to showcase Mr. Jupp's various talents.

"My Brown and Terry McGhee period!" as Mickey fondly remembers it. Frank remembers that period fondly, too, although he never had the nerve to consider it a genuine double act:

"It wasn't a duo, it was Mickey Jupp with me as a bolt-on. I never considered myself to be part of a duo with him. It was just me playing along with Mickey Jupp - that was good enough for me."

It was in this guise that Mickey came across Kilburn and the High Roads for the second, and most demoralizing, time:

"They were playing the 100 Club in 1976, when me and Frank were doing our duo. We did a bluesy first set and then they come on – there was no answer to that. I liked the rhythm, the control of the unit as a whole - every cog knew what it was doing. Dury couldn't sing to save his life but so what? They had a tiny bass player, a drummer in calipers: it shouldn't have worked but it was magnificent."

Most weeks Mickey would journey to the King's Arms in Chelmsford to play rock and roll with a bunch of older musicians – some of whom were the veteran Rockerfellas, once again. Mickey was in his element, as this contemporary quote illustrates:

"We play all the music I love and play it well. You get five quid and all the beer you can drink – lovely. I could do that 'till I'm seventy," How very prescient of him…

In fact it was around this time that Mickey began thinking about his long-term future more seriously. A lot of conflicting emotions needed clarifying and prioritizing. He finally reached the conclusion that it was time to move on - in a profound sense:

"By now I'm thirty-two and thinking about moving up to the Lake District. My brother David was already up there and I knew he could put me up for a while."

The lure of the Lakes, the deep love that Mickey had nurtured since childhood and celebrated in many songs, was calling ever more strongly. What's more, his old sparring partner Chris East had moved up that way and bought a place in Millom, partly on publishing royalties from *My Kinda Life,* a song of his with which Cliff Richard had scored a top twenty hit.

That song had first surfaced on *Hotel in the Country*, an album Chris and the ubiquitous Mo Witham had originally recorded as a duo at John Kongos' studio with producer Ray Cameron. (Ray was Kenny Everett's TV producer, and, it so happens, Michael Macintyre's dad). When the LP finally emerged on GTO Records in 1978 it was credited just to Chris East, as a solo artist. Despite making no headway in the charts a single from the album - *Where do I go now?* - enjoyed a lot of airplay. Eventually the Bay City Rollers took their version of it to the top of the charts in Japan…

The song *My Kinda Life,* off the same album, had somehow come to the attention of Cliff's producer, Bruce Welch – one of those very Shadows Mickey had so notably failed to be wowed by at the Southend Odeon – who played the track to Cliff. Not only did Cliff like the song enough to want to record it, he particularly liked the guitar playing on Chris' original.

And so it was that Mo Witham, one time Oriole and Legend member, found himself back in the studio with his Dobro, playing on Cliff's version, watched not just by producer Welch but by global guitar god Hank Marvin, too.

Apparently Hank asked Mo for a few playing tips – that's how good Mr. Witham is. Later he was retained by Cliff to perform it on Top of the Pops, so he maybe got his own back a little for being left off the original album's headline billing.

Meanwhile, back in Jupp world, Mickey and Frank Mead were still out and about, playing more intimate gigs than Mickey had been used to of late. But on the upside it was an undemanding and unambitious way of making music and a little money.

Nothing much was coming of it, other than a strengthening of Mickey's growing fixation with getting out of Southend for good, getting out of gigs for good, getting out for more long walks in the Cumbrian mountains.

It looked more likely than ever that Mickey Jupp's topsy-turvy musical career would be drawing to a close.

By now, you will have gathered what that means...

Song Writing

Italian sheet music for Mickey's song *Life*
Courtesy of Lasse Kärrbäck

Put "writing songs" into Google and you will get 360,000,000 entries in 0.2 seconds. It seems that a lot of people spend a lot of time writing about writing songs. There's no point going over old ground here, so let's start with a quick précis of those 360,000,000 pieces, (I have to confess I haven't scoured them all but this is the gist):

>There are many ways to do it (melody first, words first, chords first, title first, nicking somebody else's song and changing it a bit, etc.)
>Keep it simple
>Starting is the hardest part
>Write lots and don't obsess
>Get feedback early; make sure to listen to it
>Find new ways to say 'I love you' or 'You don't love me'

This list is directed at the would-be songwriter who is aiming for commercial success. If, like Mickey, that is not your goal and you happen to be highly experienced, it is OK to omit all those rules.

Should any reader need more guidance, go look – and have your credit card handy, for there are lots of "courses" you may want to sign up for.

Here's one thing most of them don't tell you:

>You are probably going to need to be unhappy to write really strong material - for when it comes to impassioned musical inspiration, pain is good, contentment is not.

Here is Mickey talking to a Dutch newspaper about this very issue in 1982:

"About five months ago I got married again. Actually that's the devil for your work because I am in a continuous state of satisfaction, no traumas. You'll understand that this doesn't produce many songs. Normally you have to feel a little sad or angry to be able to write. I don't feel like that now. Not that I worry about it. It will return. The situation which enables you to write best, I mean".

Band colleagues John Bobin and Bob Clouter agree:

John: "He's got an army of people who wish him well"

Bob: "Yet I don't think he's ever been really happy with who he is"

John: "True. Mind you, he writes great songs when he's unhappy"

Mickey's own advice is to keep the tune straight and the words clever:

"I take a lot of trouble over lyrics; I like to keep tunes really simple. I mean, anybody could have written *Cheque Book*: it's just an engaging set of words and a little guitar riff. It's only got to have a little lift or something different - it doesn't have to be ever so different. I have the advantage of not being a very good guitar player or a very good keyboard player, so it naturally suits me to keep it simple. Sometimes I scrap a song because I find it's involving too many chords!"

Easier said than done for we mere mortals.

Here's another tip: try not to get old.

James Taylor – who's written a few belters in his time – recently commented, "it used to be that these songs got squeezed out of every pore, you just couldn't stop 'em – now you have to pull them out with a winch".

It seems a songwriter's success rate falls away dramatically as their age increases, no matter who they are or how good they once were. Yes it's true that Dylan, McCartney, Paul Simon, Jagger & Richards still write some good stuff, occasionally very good stuff, but their song writing salad days - when their output was prolific and consistently great - are gone for good.

That's partly because when maturity arrives, nothing feels as new and fresh and exciting as it once did, and partly because material wealth makes it harder to be unhappy, (I didn't say impossible). Martin Mull, a clever satirical songwriter, once wrote a middle class blues to illustrate this very point. It included a lyric that I fondly misremember as:

"Woke up this morning and I found my baby gone. Woke up this morning and I found my baby gone. Got so angry, I threw the Porsche keys 'cross the lawn".

There may be other factors at play here, too.

A disproportionate percentage of successful songwriters have been male. Their testosterone levels alter as they grow older, as can be seen from their hairlines and resulting fascination with hats. This usually diminishes the blind obsession with sex and the female form that accompanies red-blooded males 24/7 through their adolescence, (there are exceptions to this diminution, mostly past members of The Faces, it seems). Hit songs about women's smart brains rather than their tight sweaters are limited, pop music history suggests.

In his earlier days Mickey was especially fond of a nice double entendre or ten – if in doubt, check out *Switchboard Susan*, (not hard to do, there are no less than ten versions of it on iTunes at the time of writing) or *Do You Know What I Mean*, (controversy rages over whether or not Ricky Nelson would have understood exactly what naughtiness he was singing about, Mickey thinks he would have).

Today Mickey is embarrassed by some of the suggestive songs he wrote in his youth - one of the reasons he isn't keen for his long lost composition, *I'm a Car*, to be heard. It may also account for why the infamous, but excellent, *Dirty the Sheets* demo has never seen the light of day on a commercial recording.

In a past Stiff press release Mickey and his hormones once described what he looked for in his ideal woman as, "long legs that go all the way up to her tits" - suggesting Susan George as a potential candidate for his attentions.

He still has an eye for the ladies, but the mad obsession with all things lustful has mellowed, a right and proper softening 'as the years go by'.

The truly driven songwriter keeps on generating new material, irrespective of commercial outcome or past embarrassments. This may be a form of therapy: many of the songs that get written later on in life are autobiographical, or at least based around real life events: a useful way of handling emotions or settling scores. Max Bell commented on his perception of Mickey's use of such techniques in a 1975 article for *NME*:

"Anyone who gets hold of the Legend albums will notice a marked autobiographical element with a certain depression creeping in at the sides.

'Yeah, *Lorraine* was for my brother's brother-in-law, who fancied a girl with that name, who he saw in a pub 'just sitting there holding a glass'. I wrote it the way I thought he'd feel. *Cross Country* was about being in Bath and coming back to London, *Five Years* a relationship finishing… Most of my good songs were written when I was down, I think most people's are. A lot of it was reminiscing. The best songs I've written were written with me in mind. I've still got an old manuscript of first lines and titles that I'd like to work on, some of them are sad. I suppose they're all mediocre really..." Mickey grins wryly, no trace of self-pity."

These days, perhaps because he has less angst to mine, Mickey tells me his writing is less reliant on real events or tangible grief:

"Not all my songs are about me or what happens to me. Take 1990, for example. I wasn't married but my family, including my daughter Amy, who I still dote on, cleared off to Whitby. My dad died. My cat got cancer. I wrote some great songs that year, nothing in them about any of it.

I'm as likely to put my view of someone else's feelings in a song as it being about mine – I'm often just acting, telling fibs for a living. They're only songs you know!"

Point taken. Well that's what I thought at first, anyway. Until Jupp associates Mick Brownlee and John Howard told me a rather different story about the inspiration for *Lorraine*, one closer to home than a relative's chagrin:

"Lorraine was a real person in Mickey's life. In fact, she was another of original Orioles' bass player Ada Baggerly's girlfriends who Mickey fell in love with – just as he also did with two others, Red and Val."

Whatever the truth about the genesis of that particular song, it's certainly true that not all of a songwriter's songs are autobiographical, as Eric Clapton, a man who has had no shortage of upheavals in his life, spelt out:

"I've always put songwriting down in the past to emotional turmoil. But that's more like a trigger; it sets off something that is actually dormant. It can be something that is set off by an outside stimulus like joy. A lot of people think it has to come from something particularly nasty or a problem of some kind but it isn't necessary."

Clapton's songwriting history illustrates this nicely, given he wrote *Layla* about the pain of not having Patti Boyd in his life, then later wrote *Wonderful Tonight* about the joy of having her with him. (Considering that George Harrison had earlier written *Something* for Patti, she must hold the world record as classic rock muse).

Tracey Thorn, songwriter and singer from Everything But The Girl, suggests another motivation for song writing. Her theory offers a reason why for some writers, creating songs is not as consistent as one might imagine with wanting to share them with the world:

"I'm terrified of everything so I write songs to make sense of it. And then I have to cope with the terror of performing them." Now that is a Catch 22.

Writing is also important as a step up from being merely a musician who plays renditions of other people's songs. It's the next stage on in creativity, taking the individual's status from technical musician to original thinker and author, as Wilko Johnson points out:

"Once we started getting a bit more serious I wanted to write. When we were a local band we were really just together through our enthusiasm for music. I was intimidated by what Mickey Jupp was writing and wished I could write like that."

So how does Mickey actually write his songs? Well, his method isn't peculiar to him but it is slightly unusual and worth examining.

Lennon and McCartney mostly wrote separately and then came together to audition bits of their songs for one another, modifying and merging elements to make whole compositions.

Keith Richards usually first works up a riff that he and Mick Jagger can hang a tune from, Mick then writing the lyrics.

Elton John, who only writes the music, would be sent a complete set of lyrics by his collaborator, initially Bernie Taupin, and then found melodies to fit, rather as Keith Reid and Gary Brooker originally did.

Strangely, this last method is closest to Mickey's style, even though he writes both words and music. Mickey seems to have reached a point where he often compartmentalises the process for himself. Mo Witham has seen him at work this way many times:

"In a funny way he's almost not musical – I sometimes think he should have been just a poet. Nowadays, when he works on a song, the tune's got nothing to do with it at the start. You go round his place - you'll see bits of paper in various places, on the walls, lying around. He'll walk past one, stop, say 'No' and cross something out. He might not replace it with anything, just cross it out. An hour later he'll say 'Oh', go back to it and put something in. The lyrics come first then the song is built around the rhythm of the lyrics."

This is perhaps the reason why Mickey Jupp can be said to be as good a writer of popular songs as anybody, and I mean *anybody*. He can write a melody as beautiful as the best: just check out *Writer of Songs* or *Pilot* for objective proof. He can write a "classic" rock piece of the highest order: take *Taxi Driver* or *Hole in My Pocket*. But most extraordinary of all are those lyrics: peppered with pithy phrases like "*I picked you up, now I'm putting you down*", or "*I guess I'm not the man she was looking for, I'm just the man she found*".

For me the perfect example of Mickey's rare way with words is how he sees right past the obvious phrase in order to find, even invent, a better one. In cover versions of Mickey's *Don't Talk To Me*, such as Dave Edmunds' version, you will hear the following great lyric, which scans with weapons-grade precision:

> *"I've been up all week*
> *I've been burning the candle*
> *At both ends, so to speak*
> *I'm hard to handle*
> *Don't talk to me"*

Pretty damn good, but what Mickey actually wrote is cleverer still. He did not write, *"I'm hard to handle"*, he wrote, *"I'm off my handle"*. This is a new way of expressing the fact that someone has 'flown off the handle', and as such makes a new phrase, the sort of thing Shakespeare used to do when he invented the like of 'Dead as a doornail', 'In my mind's eye', 'Play fast and loose' or 'Break the ice', (no, I'm not going so far as to make a direct comparison). Such ability comes from the same facility within Mickey's brain that does the Guardian cryptic crossword every day. The beautiful symmetry of words coming together, syllables matched, rhythms aligned, give him great pleasure.

To Mickey, such precision matters:

"I believe in doing things the right way – like being on time – and I expect others to be the same. I don't do the approximate – I'm always looking for something perfect whatever I'm doing, from songwriting to crosswords."

This process can take up a lot of time, with the half songs Mo had mentioned earlier all over the place awaiting an important phrase or syllable, as Mickey explained to me:

"You write a framework and leave gaps to fill in. Sometimes it comes pretty quickly, other times you can be weeks waiting for a line or a word and then suddenly, bingo, it turns up."

One good example from the past was *Switchboard Susan*:

237

"Hilary was my girlfriend at the time, the one I should have married. She actually appears on one recording, having been in the studio for the session for *Rooms in my Roof*, on which she sang the one-word girl responses. Well, she was also the one who came up with the word '*invention*' to go in *Switchboard Susan*, to rhyme with "*extension*". All I had to do was drop in '*Alexander Graham Bell*'!"

Another, more recent, classic instance was the third verse of *You Wear My Ring*,

"I'd got the song written except for one bit. I knew what I wanted to say but nothing materialized. It took six weeks but when it arrived it was complete: all there, it slotted in the gap perfectly and the song was finished."

This process is easy to describe, but that doesn't make it easy to do:

"I live on my own and so I'm entitled to walk around the house singing whatever I like – sometimes I dream up some of the most obscene lyrics you could imagine. On occasion the syncopation of that works out, so then I have to find some clean lyrics to fill in the gaps!"

And what about inspiration? Mickey explained a bit about that to DJ Stuart Colman in a BBC Radio London *Echoes* episode dedicated to his work:

"Inspiration is really about whether I'm in a receptive frame of mind to appreciate there is a bit of inspiration floating around. I have to be in some sort of a creative mood. I compose in my head - I don't usually write lyrics down unless there's lots of it. It comes from anywhere. I might go home today and write a song about a dodgy radio station" (at this point there is an embarrassed pause in the show!)

But it's often more about perspiration than inspiration:

"I have to force myself to sit at the piano or pick up a guitar. Tape recorder on, sweat. That's the thing: you can't go on sheer inspiration, though sometimes I write a song within five minutes. *Pilot* was a five-minute song. I just went up to the room I did my writing in and out it came – tune, words, the lot, all in one go."

Many artists feel that the best songs are the ones that arrive very fast – after all Paul McCartney wrote *Yesterday* in a matter of moments. David Crosby of The Byrds and CSN&Y has experienced it, too:

"Many of my best songs come out all in one blurt and at those times I have the distinct feeling that this level of me is just a vehicle for another level of me that has been sitting there cooking this thing up. It often happens between waking and sleeping... this stuff will start to come and I'll turn on the light quickly and write, write, write."

Keith Richards also admits to literally "dreaming up" many of his songs and riffs, saying, "I wake up in the middle of the night and I've dreamt half of it", the riff to *Satisfaction* being a case in point.

This is a situation Mickey has experienced for himself: "When I was touring with Elvis Costello I didn't much like it. My management said that they'd got me on this tour and I'd said 'Do I have to?' So I was irritated and couldn't sleep. I finally fell asleep in the middle of the night but then woke up just minutes later. I was semi-unconscious so I wrote the words that came to me on a notepad to remember them. Next day I found the words of *Old Rock 'n' Roller* on the pad. They didn't need much adjustment, they were more or less fine as they were."

Because these days his routine is clearer and his time his to command, Mickey's daily writing ritual has been more regular and easier to stick to, compared to the past. Back in 1982 he talked of a different process to Dutch paper *Utrechts Nieuwsblad*:

"I'm not productive at all. For instance I write five songs in a month and then nothing in half a year. Actually writing songs is a hobby. If I ran out of work tomorrow because nobody wanted to work with me, then I'd write songs anyway, like someone else makes model planes. Once I panicked. Keith Reid and Gary Brooker had established their publishing company and I was the first songwriter with a permanent appointment - instead of the usual compliments I got money now. For doing something I'd do anyhow! The responsibility was pressing on me. Suddenly I started to believe that I wasn't in one of my occasional dry periods but that the well had gone dry for good. Thank goodness the panic lasted only three days. Then I got back to work as usual."

Yet working every day, as he now does, can take the edge off the appetite for writing, as Mickey confesses:

"I do envy some of these guys the enthusiasm they have still got for making music – I don't have the enthusiasm I once had. I walk around the house sometimes trying to find something to do other than sit down at the piano.

About twenty years ago I first got the glimmer but I'd still spend several hours a day at it. I sort of used to just do it because, well, I had to. Now I'm a bit more thinking 'will people like it?' Once upon a time I only asked myself if I liked it. If I did, that was it. But having your emotions heightened by your surroundings helps with writing, there's inspiration in that. Mostly, though, I just think up a phrase or concept that seems like a nice idea. A good case in point is one of my more recent songs, *Trying To Unlike You*. It was nothing to do with Facebook "unliking", by the way, which I knew nothing about at the time. It just sounded like an interesting way of putting things. Sometimes I wonder if my lyrics are too clever for my own good. It's great playing with words but it can get a bit too much. Once upon a time you couldn't hold a conversation with me because I was so busy listening to what other people were saying - to use in my songs."

These days Mickey's inspiration is as likely to come from conservation as much as conversation:

"I get lots of lyric ideas out walking on my daily hike – it's not why I do it but it's a good side effect. The other benefit is that my walk cheers me up, pretty much regardless of whatever has been getting me down."

It's just as well that Mickey can extract song ideas from such activities, because he certainly can't get any help from listening to the music of others – the man never does and never did. Back in Stiff days he made it very clear:

"I *never* play records at home unless I've got a few people round. I *never* listen to the radio. It's not something I deliberately avoid, it's just something that never occurs to me to do, listen to music. If I want to listen to music I'll take my guitar down and write a song. It seems the only reason I'm in the business right now – because I have the ability to write the odd ditty now and then."

Mickey particularly likes the fact that songs have a theoretically infinite life. While his greatest focus is on writing new ones, he is unashamed of going back into the archive to re-live earlier 'unsuccessful' ones: songs he sees as still seeking the freedom that being released into the public domain would bring:

"Songs last forever. I'm happy to go back. I only say goodbye to a song when it's finally released on a record. It's out there then and it will do what it will. But until then, they're mine. I metaphorically hang them on the wall, but I still go back and listen to them."

It's ironic that this man, a songwriter who professes not to like recording, relies on that very process to "set his songs free". In fact, he justifies recording as the only way this end result can realistically be achieved, as he told *Muziek Express* in 1980:

"I see it this way: because it's impossible to be everywhere at the same time actually playing my songs, the public might like to fill that gap by playing a record of my songs."

The song is always king for Mickey.

And he was about to get his best ever chance to unleash some more great ones on an unsuspecting public.

11 I Should Be Lovin' This

In which Mickey's talent once more shines brightly

Stiff press advertisement

Here I am, on the road again,
Playing rock and roll to young women and men,
I should be loving this, I should be loving this
But all I wanna do is turn round and come home to you

I Should Be Loving This **by Mickey Jupp, demo**

"One day Frank and me are playing a gig at St Martins-in-the-Field in London, when who sticks his head round the corner but Keith Reid, member of Procol Harum. He says, 'we'd like to sign you up for our little publishing company, Bluebeard - we'll lay some money on you'. So they paid me 30 quid a week, which was pretty good in 1976, and that was my re-connection with Gary Brooker and the Procol Harum team – Gary and Keith took on my publishing and Keith and Nick Blackburn at Strongman became my management."

Nick Blackburn was an accountant who had first cut his showbiz teeth at Chrysalis, then in management with the (in)famous Miles Copeland, before branching out on his own, as he explained to me:

"In 1975, when the Sutherland Brothers asked me to manage them, I got five grand backing from Nick Mason of Pink Floyd, who I knew, to start up. Then I took on Procol Harum who I knew from Chrysalis days. Keith Reid wanted to do more than just write lyrics for Procol Harum so we formed Strongman Management together. Then Chris Wright rang me up and said did I want to manage Frankie Miller? I wasn't sure because of his reputation in the business – he was difficult and had certain addictions - but Keith loved his talent so took responsibility for it and we went ahead. Then we decided that Strongman Management should have a go with Mickey. Keith was the driving force behind taking on Mickey but I also thought he was very talented."

Keith remembers the episode very well:

"It started with me hearing his demos, which I thought were great, and suggesting to Gary that we signed him up to Bluebeard, which was the publishing company that Gary and I had originally formed for our own songs. As always Mickey never had any money so I said we would put him on a wage and take it from there. That was when I really got to hear his songs and realised that he was a terrific songwriter: great melodies, his lyrics were really excellent - the whole thing. I was just knocked out at how good he was. We signed him up and I remember playing his songs to all sorts of people, trying to get them interested in recording them. I got fairly close with Art Garfunkel on Mickey's great song, *Pilot* – that would have been brilliant but it didn't quite happen in the end. The posh demo we made for *Pilot* was done at CBS studios, with Mickey singing and Procol Harum playing the backing track! I must have a copy of it somewhere, but who knows where?"

Back in business again, Mickey put together a band at around this time comprising Dave Barnes on guitar, ex-Paramount Mick Brownlee on drums and old faithful John Bobin on bass.

Little is known about what this incarnation of the band got up to, but Lars Karrback's excellent web site, *mickeyjupp.se,* notes that they certainly played at the Kings Arms in Chelmsford on 21st September 1976.

John Denton has a note of Mickey, him and Graeme Douglas (at the point of switching from the Kursaals to Eddie & the Hot Rods) playing at Shrimpers (the club at Southend United's Roots Hall ground) on 18th Feb 1977. That November a reformed Legend played there! There were jams at the Zero Six and – most mysteriously - an evening in March 1978 when Shrimpers saw a performance by Mickey Jupp's Mice: a combo so secret that only Lee Brillaux's involvement can be recalled today.

All the time his 'proper' stage career had been on hold, Mickey had never stopped playing these sorts of gigs. But mostly he had been writing – producing plenty of new material to demo, often at Gary Brooker's home studio. Now he was on a wage, things were looking up again:

"That was the first time I'd ever had a regular deal in this business," he remembers, "it was like the cavalry coming to your rescue when you're surrounded by Indians."

The first thing the cavalry had to do was find a public outlet for Mickey's music, as Nick Blackburn recalls:

"We thought we'd better start by getting him a record deal because he was out of contract and wasn't doing very much. Mickey had recorded some demos - I think Bluebeard may have paid for them, can't recall. I knew Charles Levison, who had taken over as MD at Arista, and he agreed to release *Nature's Radio* as a single in October 1977." Ironically Arista was the label that had grown out of Bell Records, whose inception Mickey's first recordings had marked…another loop in this tale that so often chases its tail.

Nature's Radio was a catchy, poppy little song, which Mickey wrote after overhearing someone using the phrase, or something that sounded like it, during a conversation between two fellow urinal users in the gents of a Cricklewood pub. Proof of his insistence that eavesdropping pays the songwriter. Another Strongman artist, Procol Harum veteran keyboard player and would-be producer Pete Solley, was recruited to oversee the single, although according to Mickey just getting to this stage was a bit of a trial:

"Arista heard a rough demo of *Nature's Radio* and they wanted some band they'd signed up to do it, but when they heard a demo I'd done, with Procol Harum backing me, they asked me to do it. We tried it with Chris Thomas who supposedly produced the Sex Pistols. Useless: all he did was sit and read his newspaper. Eventually Pete Solley did it with us."

(Chris Thomas would have been known to Mickey's management through his production work with Frankie Miller and Procol Harum. Presumably, suitably chastened by his experience with Mr. Jupp, he pulled his socks up and put away his newspaper for he went on to produce Wings, The Pretenders, Elton John, Pulp and U2).

The eventual Pete Solley recording session was packed with top players: Tim Renwick on guitar, (one of three guitarists on the record if you include Mickey himself), who was yet another Strongman client through his role in the band Quiver who had backed the Sutherland Brothers, Henry Spinetti on drums, Jimmy Jewell on sax, Glen Le Fleur on percussion and Pete Solley himself on keyboards. But the end product sounds suspiciously as if the backing track has been slowed down before the vocals were added - giving the whole number a strange air of ponderous ennui. Methinks the tempo itself isn't entirely rock steady in places either.

Nevertheless, the record became something of a turntable hit thanks to copious radio plays. Even Tony Blackburn took to spinning it, proving its pop chart potential, although on more than one occasion he referred to the artist as "Mickey Jump". Now there's a rock'n'roll name. (Way better than Mickey Jubb, which once appeared on posters for a gig) The record could easily have been a proper chart hit, but didn't quite make it. Mickey believes he knows why:

"*Nature's Radio* was never produced the way I wanted – I didn't want drums on it, just percussion. I heard a Phil Spector wall of sound, or a dirtier production, but it didn't come out like that. I don't really care for it, but I wasn't in a position to argue."

On the other hand, in another interview Mickey had a different beef with the final record:

"*Nature's Radio* only took five minutes to write but I loved my demo version of it which was heavy with deep, weird sounds on it: fat overloaded guitar, a big drum sound, me banging pipes! Whereas the record is nice and polite - it has no power at all."

For a little while though, there was hope, as co-manager Keith Reid recalls, "*Nature's Radio* got some good airplay, particularly on Capital Radio but it didn't pan out".

However, nestling away almost unnoticed on the B-side was a simple acoustic recording of a little song called *Down At The Doctor's*, a composition that in the long term was to prove of far greater significance.

"The B-side, *Down At The Doctors*, I wrote in about five minutes," Mickey laughs, and the track didn't taken him much longer to recor, either. Top session drummer Clem Cattini had originally been lined up to play on the track but Mickey decided he wanted less, not more. So Clem was sent home and instead Mickey indicated the beat by tapping an upturned snare drum with a rolled up newspaper! Mickey may have knocked this one out pretty quickly but its eventual effect on his career was to be long lasting, once in the hands of Dr Feelgood – something Keith Reid was determined would happen:

"I will claim credit for that! I took a demo copy of *Down At the Doctor's* along to the Feelgoods' studio because it seemed so right, especially given the name."

Arista records, who were only committed to one single release, agreed to keep the faith and see how things developed, going so far as to part-fund some live gigs for Mickey's new band. Mickey was reported at the time to have lined up *Switchboard Susan* as a follow-up single, should the opportunity for one arise.

In fact, *Switchboard Susan* was not to be the follow-up single because there was never a second Arista release. However, Mickey's version of that song of his did come out on seven-inch vinyl in the end - albeit a whopping five singles and two record labels later, and then only as a B-side.

As always with Mickey's story, it's complicated…

Still, he was now back on the road and, if you believe what he told Dave Brown at the time, enjoying it:

"It's great. I've never done so many gigs so close together before. We've been going down a storm, even in places like Glasgow where we're an unknown quantity."

Furthermore, while *Nature's Radio* hadn't grabbed the attention of many record buyers, it had reached the ever-open ears of Arista's music business competitors, and one man in particular – a man who Keith Reid, touring with Procol Harum, was about to bump into:

"It started when we, Procol, were playing a festival in France that the Feelgoods were also on, (*probably the Orange Festival held in France where both bands played on Saturday 16th September 1975*). Jake Riviera, who was involved with the Feelgoods, came up to me in the hotel after the gig and, knowing I was involved with Mickey, said he had this label, Stiff, and what was I doing with Mickey? This led to us going to see Jake, Dave Robinson and Paul Conroy at Stiff's offices. They were wanting to make a record with Mickey, but I was a bit sceptical about it, not least because I had a good relationship with Chrysalis Records who really liked the Mickey demos I'd played to owners Terry Ellis and Chris Wright, who now also wanted to sign him. At the end of the day I went with Stiff, which really fucked off Chrysalis – though to their credit they forgave us and gave us another shot, signing him later after it hadn't worked out at Stiff."

Jake Riviera and Dave Robinson were joint owners of Stiff Records, set up with a £400 loan from Feelgood's Lee Brilleaux and already the most independent of independent labels. Stiff had been enjoying considerable success with Elvis Costello, Nick Lowe and that weird bloke in the raincoat from the final Legend gigs, Ian Dury. Noticing how many of their acts and mates kept referring to a certain seminal figure from Southend, Stiff decided to put a toe in the water with Mickey, although they were not exactly cut from the same cloth.

Early on in the relationship, Dave Robinson was driving Mickey back to Stiff's offices at his normal high speed, causing Mickey – who doesn't like to rush about even when he ought - to ask him why he didn't stick to the speed limit. 'I'm not interested in anybody who wants to go anywhere at thirty miles per hour' Dave replied, pointedly. Not a good omen.

Alan Cowderoy, possibly the only person at Phonogram who had taken a shine to Legend way back when, had long wanted to produce a Jupp compilation – and now he, too, had signed up to Stiff. Between them they opted to do just this: re-release a selection of previously issued but overlooked Jupp gems on a retrospective album. It was to be called, with startling unoriginality, *Mickey Jupp's Legend*. The album itself, though, was startlingly original, containing fifteen of Mickey's greatest pieces of work, one after a glorious other. This recognition of the man's importance by the coolest label in the country made his fans very happy. Mickey was pleased, too:

"It was nice to see someone was taking an interest. Also, I thought 'there'll be a couple of bob in this'. I can be a bit of a Chuck Berry when it comes to that!"

1500 copies of the vinyl LP were manufactured, each individually, if randomly, numbered. (The numbers go right up to 40,000, presumably to mask the relatively small actual pressing run, making it look like a bigger seller than it really was - a typical Stiff stunt). They even advertised it in the music press with the slogan "Jupp, Jupp and away". The run out grooves of the first side have matrix marks reading "yesterday's sound today", while the second side proclaims "a legend in his own pub" – both accurate summations of the man.

The tracks formed a great sampler of Mickey's career up to that point. Included were songs from the Bell *Legend* album and both Vertigo Legend albums plus singles *Georgia George, Don't You Never* and *Nature's Radio*.

Rumour has it that the Bell tracks were speeded up on the instructions of label boss Robinson, in order to give them a bit more 'oomph'. If so, this proved to be another omen; a warning of interference ahead...

For now though, everything looked hunky dory. In a glowing five star review, *Sounds* magazine commented:

"This is undoubtedly the most played album in my collection this year...to say Jupp was merely ahead of his time doesn't do enough justice to a writer who captures all that's right about rock and roll in short blasts. If a new band emerged with material as good as this they could do no wrong - there's not one dodgy track on the whole album. Jupp is the missing link in the British rock tradition."

Another review in June 1979 put it equally strongly:

"Mickey Jupp is a legend. Now in his thirties, he's had several shots at the big time...this could be his last chance. This isn't a case of the critics making a fuss because he's a seminal figure or a handy name to drop. This is simply about the best album I've heard this year. R&B, rock and straight commercial pop – Jupp can write it all and sing it in a clear, ringing voce."

To capitalize on the album's warm reception, Stiff released a single, sort of.

The A-side was *My Typewriter,* that endearing oddity from Legend's *Red Boot* album. It had been written with long-term friend and collaborator Chris East, but his name had somehow fallen off the credits from the day it was recorded.

(In a subsequent press interview with Mike Davies, Mickey confessed to "diddling Chris out of a few royalties" over this episode but felt his mate would be OK on the strength of other royalties he was getting from Cliff's bigger hit!).

Despite Mickey hating its arrangement and production, the B-side of this single was the dreaded *Nature's Radio.* Clearly Stiff were calling the shots this time: they would release what they wanted, thank you very much Mr. Jupp.

This whole enterprise was another Stiff con, for only 500 copies of the *My Typewriter* single were pressed, (catalogue number UPP 1). *Record Collector* – an authority on such matters - was not taken in by Stiff's tricks, firmly adjudicating every copy of this single to be a promo copy, even if not marked as such.

The sham single's release had a noble purpose: it was aimed at getting those DJs who had ignored the album to listen to a couple of Mickey's numbers and maybe garner some extra radio play. This was the sort of thing Stiff were famous for: marketing stunts that the bigger boys at the major labels thought beneath them or simply couldn't be bothered to mount - the type of 'sharp practice' for which the label was celebrated. But it wasn't Mickey's way of doing things, as Will Birch pointed out to me:

"Mick and Stiff were a real mismatch. Dave Robinson, Jake Riviera, Nick Lowe and all those people were huge fans of Mick, but he lacked the required arrogance for their way of doing things. He's shy and uncomfortable about it, but that isn't a reason to rubbish him. I always say that Mick seemed to have ticked X for no publicity. He was his own worst enemy for promotional purposes. So when he got together with Stiff, who were a hip yet cleverly gimmick-heavy label - which is how they launched Elvis Costello, Ian Dury, the Damned, etc, people prepared to go along with their process – it was never going to work."

Mind you, Mickey wasn't above pulling a few stunts of his own - to achieve the opposite effect. Against his better judgment, he agreed to have new publicity photographs taken to promote the Stiff compilation. At the time he was a man with a 'tache. As soon as the pictures were taken and one shot selected for circulation amongst the music press, he shaved the moustache off, causing some journalistic confusion and no doubt ensuring that Stiff stopped issuing the images.

All this massaging of the media, either way round, took place while Mickey's latest band was getting assembled. With a lot of touring planned, auditions were being rapidly held, but it wasn't looking good:

"We tried a number of people. Paul Riley, Tim Roper from Ducks DeLuxe on drums for a while. Eventually we got Mick Grabham in on guitar – he was ex-Procol (*surprise, surprise*). Because we were running out of time to get on the road we got in Ron Telemacque on drums and John Gordon on bass - they were already an established rhythm section."

They were no slouches. Ron had seen action with the Equals and John had been on bass for The Pirates, as well as playing on some of Roger Waters' first solo outings. Grabham, above all, was a real coup. He explained at the time how he and Mickey got together:

"I wasn't enjoying Procol Harum any more so I left. Then I became frustrated in my intentions to form a band, so I went to the States, before doing sessions in France. I had a call asking if I'd be interested in working with Mickey - I'd heard of him through Procol, of course. So we did a Hope & Anchor session. The gigs are going great, getting better all the time. Not bad for one week's rehearsals, eh?"

Mickey agrees that the musicians came together well – although he has since described Grabham as "a technically very good guitarist but someone who musically didn't know his place". Mickey was far from happy at a deeper level, too, maintaining, "I was a complete social and musical outcast in that band" - something some observers of those performances claim was evident on-stage.

Yet despite having told journalists that this time he was "going to stick with it", cracks were already appearing in his resolve. "It was a good band," Mickey adds tellingly, "but I was already starting to feel a bit old for all this."

This would prove something of a problem as there were big commitments coming up, including a stint supporting Elvis Costello on an extensive UK tour - twenty seven shows in all - culminating at London's Roundhouse. At the time, Mickey's only comment about the star attraction of this tour, Mr. Costello, was discrete - just "he's not my cup of tea".

Recently, he explained more of this to me:

"We started the Elvis Costello tour in this run-down cinema in Dublin, called La Scala. I didn't mind that tour because it was him they'd come to see, not me, so there was no pressure. I called him Albert when talking about him - I never called him any name to his face – because for me there is only one Elvis, and it isn't him! His music wasn't bad though. *Watching the Detectives* was pretty good and I really loved *I Don't Want to go to Chelsea*. I thought that was terrific. His band, the Attractions were alright, too, as players – but they all had a bit of an attitude..." (If you're interested in knowing more about that attitude, there's a whole book about it: *The Big Wheel* by Bruce Thomas, bass player in the Attractions. It's a book sufficiently incendiary for lawyers to have become involved at one point. In it we learn that Mr. Costello's bass player also refuses to call his boss Elvis, referring to him throughout as "the singer").

By all accounts of the tour, Mickey's band was cracking, too. Dave Brown, reviewing the 11th April Penzance gig for *Sounds* magazine, gushed:

"If he's been practicing for the past decade or so, then the wait was certainly worthwhile. If the line-up looks workmanlike on paper then the live reality is a certified stunner. Hard and tight, with an emphasis on rhythm, Jupp's lyrics offer pure honest and simple stuff. Jupp has never achieved more than cult fame and admits to 34, but generates enough sweat through his outfit to send Grabham's strings out of tune. It's never too late to rock and roll and Jupp and band have hit a winning streak at last."

In addition to tightening his performance skills, the experience of the tour was helpful in getting songs together for what was to be a new album - again for Stiff but this time featuring Mickey's first newly recorded material for six long years. While he didn't in the end enjoy the gigging - "I didn't want to do the tour any more; I felt too old and way out of touch" - he had no need to worry about his ability to write, sing or play, as the resultant album proved. It was to be called *Juppanese* and it turned out to be a great record. Most pundits would say it is one of Mickey's best, if not the very best although unsurprisingly the man himself doesn't agree.

So let's look for an objective judge, someone with the ears and experience to really know. Muff Winwood, himself an ex-rocker from Spencer Davis Group days and by this time head of A&R at Legend's old label, Vertigo, thought a lot of it. As producer of 1978's top selling album, *Dire Straits,* also on Vertigo, he was asked by trade magazine *Music Week* which other album he most wished he had produced that year: he chose *Juppanese*. So it's officially good, OK Mickey?

Mind you, Muff might have thought twice about getting involved had he been there for the actual recording. It was not a fun time, by any account.

Splitting the production duties between Gary Brooker and Nick Lowe - one side each - might appear to the outsider a clever plan to showcase Mickey's two modes of outright rocker and sensitive ballad writer, but it wasn't that simple.

In fact it wasn't even intentional.

In truth it was a cock-up, the end product of a nasty bout of high tension and acrimonious falling out, as Mickey sadly explains:

"I had all the songs ready - too many in fact - so I whittled them down with the band – Chris Spedding on guitar, Bruce Lynch on bass, Dave Mattacks on drums – and Gary Brooker, who was producing. Half way through the recording process Dave Robinson, the label owner, has a listen to what we've done and says he isn't happy; says it 'isn't cooking'. I was called up to Stiff in the middle of the sessions and Dave dropped this bombshell: 'I want to you start again, this time with Rockpile'. Now I was an old friend of Gary's and I was happy with what we we'd done up to that point, so I though 'Holy Shit'. I had to tell Gary, who was a naturally a bit unhappy".

Well, someone had to tell Gary. Keith Reid remembers this onerous task falling to him:

"*Juppanese* was kind of a bad situation from my point of view because I'd asked Gary to produce the album with a hell of a good band. We were in Basing Street Studios and it was going very well, we were very happy with what we were doing, and then Dave Robinson came down for a listen and pronounced it 'fucking rubbish". He just wanted Mickey for the in your face rock stuff; that was what he liked. Chris Spedding was so angry about that. He loved tracks like *Brother, Doctor, Sister, Nurse* so much, I think he would have joined the band even though he was a top session guitarist. So I had to fire Gary, which wasn't great for our relationship, and then clear off to Worthing to work with Rockpile, which was gonna be great – but it wasn't. Some of it worked but lots of stuff didn't, because Rockpile are very good at doing just the one thing, while Mickey's stuff had a lot more subtlety in it; it wasn't just rock 'n' roll. Plus Nick Lowe was producing, whereas it would have been much better if Dave Edmunds, also in Rockpile, had been producing. So we got done what we could get done – we didn't run out of time or money, we just ran out of material that worked. But there wasn't enough, so then I had to ring Gary and ask him to finish up the stuff he'd started - most embarrassing. We went back to trying to make the sort of album we'd set out to make in the first place."

So how come Mickey - well known for digging his heels in when he felt like it - agreed to go along with his record label's change of plan? He owns up:

"I could have said 'No' to Dave Robinson but, to be honest, the thought of playing with Dave Edmunds and the guys from Rockpile, with Nick Lowe behind the mixing desk with his vodka and orange in hand - it seemed thrilling, and so it was easier to just go along with it...."

There was another reason, too: Mickey's inherent distaste for confrontation, something he admits to when he says:

"I never had enough strength in me. I could get as far as saying 'this is how I'd like it' but there are times I wish I'd had the strength to say 'if you don't like it, bad luck - I'll work with someone else'. I just don't do confrontation – it stays with me for days. I should have said to Dave Robinson 'I'm happy with the way it is' and waited to see what happened. I shouldn't have acquiesced."

Will Birch, a man close both to Nick Lowe (whose biography he is currently writing) and Dave Edmunds (with whom he has co-written songs like *A1 on the Juke Box*), noted that the feeling of excitement to be working together was mutual, at least at first:

"Nick and Dave were as keen to work with Mick as he was in reverse. But when he goes in with Rockpile he's got seven days to do the job, because time is money. After about four days Mick felt it was getting a bit thin and decided he wanted to go home. Apparently, Mick was a pain in the arse all week, although he'd wanted to be there...."

Mickey picks up the story again:

"Rockpile were very enthusiastic so it all started off really well. A few days later we're running out of time and money on this new stuff, so we have to stop."

Nick Lowe well remembers those turbulent times, as he told Will Birch:

"We were all staying in his hotel by Worthing station. I nearly had to throw myself across the tracks to prevent Rockpile from leaving town, they were so unhappy. Mickey and I had a chat over a few drinks and he told me he wished he had a normal job and would have preferred to be a plumber than be burdened by this creative thing. He was tormented by it."

Falling out apart, there was no doubt that Rockpile were a band who could rock - after all Mickey had nearly joined them at their inception - but perhaps they didn't roll quite well enough for Mickey. (If so, they were in good company, for this was a criticism he also leveled at Dr Feelgood from time to time).

Journalist Harry Doherty shared these doubts, writing of *Juppanese,* "Rockpile, my favourite band in their own field, haven't managed to give Jupp's material the kick it needs", and "the second side, produced by Gary Brooker, is far superior."

With hindsight, Mickey, too, feels that the Rockpile experiment didn't work:

"I preferred Gary's side in the end. We got Chris Spedding in and he did a great job on *Brother, Sister, Doctor, Nurse.* Just after it came out I heard some people talking in a lift I was in, raving about that track!"

Remarkably, the song in question was recorded in a single, six minute long take:

"We daren't do it again! We just sat there listening to it back going 'Wow'. On the album it's been edited and cleaned and polished so all the nice rough edges have come off, like it's just come back from the laundry. I only play my cassette of the original, dirty rough mix – I never listen to the finished album. Chris Spedding was right up my alley, he plays guitar just how I wish I could."

While that track may have given Mickey a buzz, overall he felt pretty bad about what he termed "the whole Gary thing". In an interview with Dutch magazine *Muziek Express* in 1980 he elaborated:

"Looking back, what I did was terrible. I thought it was the chance of a lifetime and didn't think of Gary. I let myself be dragged in by the status of Lowe and company. Musically, the co-operation didn't hit it off. It became a schizophrenic entity."

Was Dave Robinson right to get involved and demand a change of direction? Well, he certainly had a reputation for being hands on: for example, he rejected the original tape of Madness' hit *Baggy Trousers,* insisting they wrote a better chorus, which then had to be cunningly spliced into the already completed recording, making a massive hit of the song.

On the other hand, all he heard of the Brooker sessions were backing tracks without vocals or overdubs. "Dave was still trying to get me do what I have been doing long ago, back in the days of *Cheque Book*. They wanted to push me to be ten years younger," Mickey grimaces.

What the label boss' intervention in *Juppanese* did achieve, albeit accidentally, was to give the album's production two interestingly contrasting points of view. It's also an album of two halves in terms of musicianship, both good but very different. While Rockpile speak for themselves, Gary's side features some great players, highly experienced in session work, all playing at their very best for Mickey.

Drummer Dave Mattacks, (inherently musical having trained as a piano tuner and a dab hand at bass and keyboards as well as the drums), is a Southend boy who'd made good as a member of Fairport Convention. His session CV includes stints with Elton John, George Harrison, Paul McCartney, Brian Eno and Jimmy Page. These days he lives in the States where he teaches at the prestigious Berklee College of Music.

Chris Spedding was also a session veteran having played for Jack Bruce, John Cale, Elton John, Mike Batt and Paul McCartney, even The Bay City Rollers. He was particularly incensed that the Brooker sessions were cut short and took the trouble to pay Dave Robinson of Stiff a personal visit to forcefully explain that what had been recorded was well worth keeping. Keith Reid recalled Spedding had described *Brother, Doctor, Sister, Nurse* as "some serious shit".

Bruce Lynch was a wonderfully interpretive bass player who had worked with Gary Brooker on his records as well as the likes of Leo Sayer and Richard Thompson, plus having been a veteran of six albums with Cat Stevens. He went on to produce music and write film scores. Bruce's blog references Mickey and the *Juppanese* sessions:

"I have played on many songs by original artists and then found myself playing another version by a well known one. *Pilot* was written by Mickey Jupp - a great songwriter who deserved better recognition. Jupp was an English musician and songwriter mainly associated with the Southend music scene. *Pilot* was apparently written in 10 minutes after the break-up of an affair."

In 2010 he posted the following on Facebook:

"Just listening to my UK copy of Juppanese (blue vinyl) for the first time in 30 years. It still sounds good after all these years. Great songwriter; would love to know where he is and what he is doing." (Just buy the book, Bruce).

As he notes, after *Juppanese*, Bruce went on to play on the Gary Brooker version of *Pilot*, produced by George Martin, no less, for the album *No More Fear of Flying*. When I asked him how he felt about the Beatles guru producing and arranging strings for one of his songs, Mickey ruefully remarked, "I have been one degree of separation from fame many times."

Another near-miss in the story of his life.

But the *Juppanese* episode was a souring experience that went a lot deeper, and was a lot more debilitating, than Mickey's earlier "errors of judgment". So much so it persuaded him to open up way more than usual in an interview he gave to Dutch magazine *De Telegraaf* a couple of years after, in 1980:

"I had put myself in a traumatic situation. Gary is my best friend, and also my publisher. My manager Keith Reid and he wrote all the legendary material for Procol Harum. Keith did also agree with Robinson's demands, but I got the task of explaining to Gary why he was dumped. To make everything even more tragic, things didn't work out between Rockpile and me. They were sick and tired of me. I had no other option than asking Gary to finish the album. At first he didn't want to, he was hurt. But eventually he agreed, out of friendship for me. The first day of the renewed cooperation in the studio I was very nervous. I'd planned a sort of festive reunion and rehearsed a 'mea culpa', but when Gary walked into the studio I just said 'Hi Gary, how's things?' And he just said, 'How are you?' The following days we pretended nothing had happened, which made the atmosphere even more tense. In the end I told him that it was all my fault - I should have told Robinson to fuck off. "

In a radio interview a year earlier, the painful experience was even fresher, as was Mickey's memory of the whole drama's effect on recording with Rockpile:

"This was Gary's first production, and he and Keith and me were like a tight family, so it was a political situation. Keith had to come down on my side of the argument, as he was my manager, even though he'd been Gary's musical partner for years. There was quite a lot of nasty, edgy feeling; every one was upset with everyone else. Gary's wife in particular was hurt, as she was very loyal to Gary: she just cut me dead at the time, but I'm glad to say it's OK now. All that business was in the back of my mind when I was making the Rockpile side – I couldn't relax or concentrate on the record as much as I should have done."

The discomfort hung over Mickey's attempts to complete the album like a curse:

"During the final stages, Gary and I were almost at each other's throats about *Partir c'est mourir un peu*. That song is about a French girl I once knew. I loved her but I was not the only one. She went back to France, I wrote five songs inspired by her. In the studio I sang the wonderful *Partir*. I was touched, I was sitting there with tearful eyes, being very happily unhappy, when Gary said 'Can't you put a bit more feeling into it?' I almost killed him."

The French girl in question was Marie Elizabeth, better known as Babs. She was the muse for four released songs of Mickey's: *Partir, Barbara, In Her Chair* and *Make It Fly*. Mickey recalled that when she headed back to France in her 2CV (what else should a pretty young French girl drive?), "I went back to my flat and cried my heart out". But the experience wasn't entirely negative, he recalled:

"It was great in a strange way. In the summer of '76 she came and she went, and I was destitute, forlorn: but something good came of it, as I wrote half a dozen songs about her. That put the lid on it."

For now, though, he was facing a different sort of grief. This was clearly a period of friction between two old mates, as Procol Harum biographer Henry Scott-Irvine sensed:

"If you get on the wrong side of Gary it can be difficult and although Gary was diplomatic and denied it, I'm pretty sure that they fell out over *Juppanese*."

All the same, the material on *Juppanese* was so strong that covers seemed inevitable. Roger Chapman, for example, has released several versions of the track *Short List*, even naming his new band Short List after it, while Gary Brooker himself covered *Pilot* on his next album. But the most obscure cover was a version of a track that didn't actually make it to the album's final cut - for there was at least one track missing from *Juppanese's* intended running order.

As we have seen, Mickey had written *Switchboard Susan* some time before, and the Searchers had already recorded it for their 'comeback' album on Sire. (Apparently they had started out trying to do it in their own trademark jangly style but eventually gave up and settled for a pretty faithful copy of Mickey's demo – very wise, most people do). When laying down his tracks with Rockpile, Mickey had agreed to try a rockier version of the song than the one he had originally demoed. After the backing track was complete he had serious second thoughts, never getting around to putting a vocal on it. So, despite the paucity of material that had been recorded – *Juppanese* could not be called a long album – *Switchboard Susan* never made it onto the final record. Nick Lowe himself explains why:

"When we cut *Switchboard Susan*, we all thought it was great and we were jumping up and down. The next morning we went to the studio and Mickey pronounced it shit from top to bottom. I waited until he calmed down a bit and told him if he didn't want it I would buy the tape and put it out myself. He said 'All right, all right. I never want to hear it again, it's rubbish.' But he was wrong about that one. It's cracking."

So Nick Lowe bought it from Mickey - a figure of £150 has been mentioned - added his own vocal, put it on his next album and released it as a single. It promptly became a hit in the USA, something Mickey had never managed. Oh dear. Oh very dear.

Mickey had to wait a long time for another opportunity to release his own version of the song, and worse still admits that by the time he finally did, he felt obliged to arrange it in a totally different style to avoid appearing to have copied Nick Lowe - on the version originally recorded for Mickey!

Ironically, the version he always plays on stage is the Rockpile/Nick Lowe one, not the Searchers-like demo version he began with, nor the slower, slinkier arrangement that emerged when he eventually recorded it for a later album of his, *Long Distance Romancer*, more of which later.

Despite all the toing and froing, *Juppanese* was released in October 1978 to a chorus of critical approval. The album contained songs inspired by The Man From Uncle (*S.P.Y.*), Mickey's dread of flying (*You'll Never Get Me Up in One of Those*) and Wild West hero Billy the Kid (*The Ballad of Billy Bonney*).

On a more romantic note it also included *Partir C'est Mourir Un Peu*, the number about the French girl Mickey fell madly in love with but went back to France. And then there was *Pilot:* that beautiful song Mickey had written in minutes at the end of a failed love affair, when the object of his affections had dismissively cut him off by saying, as she does in the song, "*See you around*".

Sounds magazine gave *Juppanese* five stars in a paean of praise titled "Love and the poetry of monosodium glutamate" (the MSG reference relates to the lyrics of *School,* which the review stated were "worthy of Ray Davies at his peak"). The review closes by confidently stating, "Mickey Jupp is one of the finest songwriters to come out of the UK", bracketing his talents with those of JJ Cale and Allan Toussaint.

Top critic David Hepworth considered it "a fitting exhibition of the songwriting and vocal skills which had graced all manner of failed projects for too many obscure years".

In the *NME*, Max Bell wrote highly of it, too, commenting, "As with all Jupp's best stuff, the songs are whimsical, witty, sad, blunt, dependable - like an English Sunday afternoon", although he broke ranks with just about everybody else by describing *Pilot* as "coming over like outtakes from an Elton John/Paul McCartney bash – a rather feeble, impersonal slice of schmaltz".

Mickey himself didn't even bother to listen to his new work – the first time he actually heard it was when a selected track was blasted out of Murray's record emporium in Grafton Street as he happened to be walking past - while there on a tour to promote it! He already knew it wasn't what he wanted it to be, as he told *Hot Press* at the time:

"I would like to make a real pearler of an album. There was a time when I thought this one might be it, then there was all the upheaval half way through and that blew it for me – all I wanted to do was get it finished."

Stiff Records, to their credit, gave *Juppanese* the works, with releases in the UK, Germany, France, Spain, Holland, Portugal, Belgium, Japan, Australia and New Zealand. There were versions on black, blue, yellow and white vinyl, plus a limited edition picture disc – meaning that Mickey didn't simply appear on the cover, for once, he also appeared on the actual disc as well. Unheard of.

There were even ads in the music press – not only in the UK but also, notably, in Japan, where a magazine ad features Mickey pulling the same, these days rather politically incorrect, "slitty eyes" pose seen on the album's cover. The sleeve is a particular mess as the images, in an attempted pun on the title, *Juppanese*, show Mickey having just finished eating his, er, Chinese, meal. Chinese, Japanese – well they all have strange eyes, so what's the difference? Presumably this was another example of Stiff's famously "edgy" marketing, something Mickey went to some lengths to distance himself from almost as soon as the album was released, in an interview for German rock magazine *Sounds*:

"It was typical of Stiff, the cover: again I had no say whatever in what was going on. I didn't like the idea of pulling these faces in a Chinese restaurant, that's not nice. We took a whole pile of photographs in three different places. I just happened to drop into Stiff's offices two days later and they said 'this is the cover' – no options, that was it. They were always coming up with ideas I didn't like, or they didn't want to do what I suggested. We just seemed to be arguing all the time."

Stiff also broke Mickey's tradition of not plucking singles off albums pairing *Old Rock and Roller* with *S.P.Y.* to be released as a single at the same time as the album came out. At around this point, Stiff's pluggers had managed to get Mickey a valuable radio interview - those who recall the event believe it was on Radio One - in order to promote the single.

This was a big deal and wouldn't have been easy for them to pull off given Mickey's low national profile at the time.

It could have been just the thing to break Mickey to a wider, younger audience – something the label knew it needed to do if he was to make it as big as the other stars in the Stiff stable.

Live on air Mickey is asked by his interviewer, "so what do you think about your new single?"

He replies, "I don't like it much. Robbo wanted it out as a single, so I had to go along with him. I don't think it's that good".

One can barely imagine the reaction of the interviewer, let alone how that went down back at Stiff. But maybe Mickey had a sort of point, for a highly commercial track had been recorded around the same time as *Juppanese*, apparently as part of the Gary Brooker Basing Street sessions for that album, yet was mysteriously omitted from the album.

You Made a Fool Out of Me was not released as a track on *Juppanese*, nor as the single it so deserved to be, appearing only as a one of two songs Mickey contributed to a dodgy compilation LP called *Can't Start Dancing* - a budget release solely distributed via the UK music paper, *Sounds*.

One can't help wondering whether it might have originally been held back from the album because Mickey was expecting it to be the first single – it would surely have made a stronger contender. All these years later he can't remember, but if that was the plan he eventually got his way.

You Made a Fool Out of Me was indeed Mickey's next single release.

But in the convoluted way of this story it was a totally different version, with different producers and musicians, released on an entirely different label.

You really do have to pay attention to this stuff, don't you?

The *Juppanese* Album

Given how much grief went into its making, *Juppanese* turned out superbly.

It's probably the strongest, that's to say most commercial, collection of Mickey's songs ever put on a single original album, (ie not a 'best of', of which there have been several.)

His management liked it a lot and were confident it would do well, feeling their investment in Mickey was about to come good.

Even the two sides/two producers aspect of the record, which may in real life have been an unfortunate accident, works well: the fact that each side has its own 'feel' only adding to the variety of listening experience without over-fragmenting it. If you like, there's a rockier side and a gentler side, although there are exceptions even to that rule.

It isn't perfect, of course. It would clearly have been stronger still with the never completed Jupp/Rockpile version of *Switchboard Susan* in the track listing.

Not to mention had it included the brilliant yet inexplicably cold-shouldered *You Made a Fool Out of Me*, (see later for my full rant) and some other rumoured missing tracks.

All in all, though, there can't be many artists around at the time who wouldn't have been mighty proud of it, had it been their work.

Makin' Friends opens the album, Mickey in rollicking Fats Domino mode, both in piano and vocal terms. Behind him is a backing that might be described as relentless, with bass and bass drum filling every space they can. Apart from the opening and closing sections there is no guitar part and the piano solo is rather clumsily upped in the mix to compensate. Light and shade are nowhere to be found, resulting in an album-opener that is powerful, but perhaps a little too powerful. Could this be the "too much rock but not enough roll" fall-out in action?

This might be a good place to explore just what this criticism of Mickey's is all about.

Put simply, the fact is that if everyone hits their mark together, with enough power, a band can "rock" - in the sort of way, say, Kiss does. But to get someone's foot tapping and bum wiggling requires rather more than that. A great band also "roll" – they stay in time overall but each instrumentalist strays a little from the absolute perfect beat, advancing or retarding some notes slightly; using accents that don't fall exactly on the tempo. This syncopation creates a seductive, constantly moving aural experience that draws the listener into the music and so creates an interaction between sender and receiver.

As a band gets to play together more, they instinctively learn how this interplay between one another works. The right musicians melding in this way gives performances a magic that can tower over the technical proficiency of the players. The Rolling Stones are probably the best-known proponents of this style, drummer Charlie Watts playing on or sometimes even fractionally ahead of the beat, while Keith Richards always lays back from it.

Ringo, in that other band, tended to play a whisker *behind* the beat, while still keeping great time. (And despite John Lennon's famous jibe, Ringo in his heyday was one of the very best).

At the opposite end of the engagement scale lays the dreaded drum machine. Even if it has the best sounds around - and Mickey's never did have - its metronomic perfection means it can't help but sound inhuman and unengaging. In fact, the best drum machines have patches that deliberately re-introduce some human-style imperfections into this relentless accuracy. I know I'm a fully paid-up member of the drummer's union but it's not just we drummers who maintain this to be true. Singer, musician and non-drummer David Byrne of Talking Heads insists, "The emotional centre is not the technical centre...funky grooves are not square". Musician and neuroscientist Daniel Levitin devised an experiment to prove this theory. He got a classical pianist to play Chopin into a recording computer with a program that permitted the timing of individual notes – but not the pitch - to be adjusted later. As the computer played back the performance with increasing degrees of correction, becoming more and more 'in time', the emotion in the piece disappeared. At the level of perfect accuracy it was dull to listeners. But turning the dial too far the other way, losing too much discipline, created musical chaos.... so it's a fine line. The right amount of slipping and sliding around the core beat, by vocalists every bit as much as by players, is what our brain interprets as feeling. But the bad news is that if you haven't got it, it's hard to learn – it is essentially innate. Mickey has always had loads of it, of course.

Lecture over, back to the album.

Short List is pretty head-on, too, but that's fine because it suits the song. Storming doubled guitars flank piano, bass and drums while Mickey tells the "story of his life" in one of his cleverest lyrics, complete with a nod to the Coasters in the form of the spoken line, "*someone gonna let you know*".

Things click up another notch with *Old Rock'n'Roller*, in which irony and Jerry Lee Lewis, not normally comfortable bedfellows, are conjoined. Double-tracked drums, full doo-wop backing vocals, chugging guitars and a hard working bass line set the scene for Mickey's inspired piano and vocal. After name checking both Chuck Berry and Bo Diddley, Mickey throws a flaming Lee Lewis piano performance over the final chorus. Phew! (Those really old rock and rollers, the Swinging Blue Jeans, were so impressed they recorded a version of it themselves – perhaps they remembered Mickey from the Orioles at the Cricketers).

School cools things down nicely. This is one of those contradictory songs Mickey writes so well: a delicate ballad describing a heavy issue. In this case it's all about how society's overzealousness is destroying personal freedoms. Billy Bremner, who as part of Rockpile played on the track, is on record as saying that Mickey didn't rate the song at all and had to be talked into recording it for the album! Serene acoustic guitars interweave above delicate bass figures. The drums turn up suitably late to give the ending more punch. Mickey amusingly acts out his vocal in places, as if he's presenting '*Jackanory*'. All very smart stuff; including the aforementioned lyrical reference to monosodium glutamate.

If Only Mother is a song of thinly veiled sarcasm, reflecting Mickey's mock delight at the importance of his continuing musical career, typified by the lyric, "*I'm only in it for the money, I'm only in it for the bread*". The Duane Eddy-like twangy solo feels a bit uncommitted, indeed the whole thing - a medium paced rocker - feels a bit subdued. Had the musicians fallen out by the time they got to this point?

266

Down in New Orleans starts off with some terrific double guitar picking (as suits the lyric "*I'm a guitar picker and my name is Slim*"), soon joined by shuffling snare/bass drum and bass. Yet despite an interesting switch of rhythm half way through the number, there isn't that much life in it. Mickey's vocal is tentative and it cries out for a bit of piano to lift it later on. Anyone who has heard Mickey do this live will know how much better it could have been. It is interesting that this song, which Mickey had been performing for some time as *The Ballad of* G*uitar Pickin' Slim*, got re-titled for this album, against his wishes: further evidence of the extent to which artistic control had been wrested from him by this point in his career. He ensured that later recordings he made of this song reverted to his original naming.

The Rockpile side ends on a real high with a track that shows no interest whatsoever in taking prisoners. *You'll Never Get Me Up in One of Those* has a great lyric, explaining Mickey's reticence over flying, that's breathtakingly witty throughout, even managing to rhyme "*Foreign Legion*" with "*Southern Regi*on". Instrumentally, it opens with fabulous groaning, discordant Edmunds guitar figures over a belter of a track, the drums sounding as if Terry Williams is playing them with tree branches, and the bass aping the menace of Peter Gunn. While the track slightly loses impetus in places, Mickey's vocal does not. His spirits are so high that he even feels it OK to nick a little Jerome Kern melody going into the fade, twisting Oscar Hammerstein II and Otto Harbach's famous lyric into "*I won't fly, don't ask me*". Summing it up so far, Mickey put it simply, "It was great to play with Rockpile but their side is a bit too simple and hasty – 'let's record it and fiddle about with it later' – not enough technique, too rough and ready."

Side Two, the Gary Brooker produced set, begins with quite a challenge: *Pilot*.

This song, much loved by his fans, had been part of Mickey's canon for a while, having been played solo, in a small group arrangement and later by the Big Band and as a duo with Frank Mead. So what to do with it in the studio?

The best answer was probably keep it simple, perhaps even simpler than this, but the *Juppanese* version makes a pretty good fist of it. Delicate piano, fine acoustic guitar and a tasteful bass part create a feel that's almost minuet-like in its halting charm. Dave Mattacks keeps the drums clean and sparing. Accents are provided by organ and what sounds like a fretless or double bass. Mickey's vocal could maybe be drier and a little further forward in the mix but no matter, it is lovely.

S.P.Y rather scotches Stiff boss Dave Robinson's criticism that the Brooker-produced stuff "wasn't cooking". Gargantuan wailing guitars that you'd think were Dave Edmunds if it wasn't on the wrong album side, (in fact it's Mickey himself on lead guitar, "I'm the only person who can play it, people say how do you do that but it's actually easy – you push the strings before you play them") usher in a rocking track with stomping bass and fat cowbell supplementing driving drums. Mickey roars through the lead vocal - he'd been singing this one for years, too – while his backing vocals swish around in juicy reverb. B-side material? I don't think so, but Stiff did.

The Ballad of Billy Bonney is Mickey's touching tale of Billy the Kid, sensitively handled by the band. Halved drums and a clever bass line sit alongside something sounding wonderfully like a distant freight train. Every here and there a bit of Hammond pops up and, less expectedly, a touch of synth drum (!)
Mickey sings in a suitably outlaw voice.

Partir C'est Mourir Un Peu is another slow piano vamp of a number but without any attempt at black vocal phrasing. A very personal song, Mickey is almost too controlled singing it. There's a tremolo guitar and a tremolo organ, a gentle drum pattern and a nice bass part that might have worked better fretless or on a double bass, as on *Pilot*. What it cries out for is a Muscle Shoals-style brass section, pushing the vocal to tip over into Otis-like cracked despair. But that's probably just me wanting too much: it's pretty damn fine as it is.

The album closes on an outstanding note. *Brother, Doctor, Sister, Nurse* is a bubbling gumbo of a track: bass popping around in a jus of dirty, simmering guitars, garnished with thick drums and sharp organ licks. Mickey sings it at about eight tenths (maybe the ten tenths at which he does it live would have been better) but it could hardly be improved.... other than if we'd had the original long take and rougher mix, or perhaps a discrete splattering of piano over the final choruses. Anyway it's a right old corker to end with – one that Lulu, of all people recorded, having been blown away by the demo, although it never seems to have got a release.

Yet something was missing from the *Juppanese* album, over and above the obvious lack of *Switchboard Susan*. There was another number that seems to have been recorded at the same sessions. Nobody including Mickey can recall the details how it was actually recorded, although production credits go to Gary Brooker and other evidence corroborates this. All Mickey can say about it is that he "doesn't rate the song much"! I am referring to his utterly awesome original reading of *You Made a Fool Out of Me*.

This brilliant song, brilliantly arranged and brilliantly played is, not surprisingly, a completely brilliant track. Mickey wails a lead vocal in front of his own choir of banshee backing voices, while drums thunder, phased guitars menace and the glorious bass fretlessly swoops. It's got the presence of a Phil Spector production and the power of a force ten gale. Surely it was held back to be a single; surely it had the best chance of any song on the album to make it big? Wouldn't that be the only way any sane A&R man could justify leaving it off the album?

Well, it was left off the album, all right, but not to be a single. It was never released at all, except on that cheapo compilation LP from *Sounds* magazine. It finally resurfaced on a re-mastered CD of *Juppanese*, allowing Mickey's fans to weep copiously at the sheer idiocy of leaving it on the shelf all those years.

Although Mickey himself isn't a great fan of the song, he nevertheless re-recorded it later for his Chrysalis-released album *Long Distance Romancer*. That version is good but in relative terms rather too cool and self-knowing. It gets nowhere near this epic, raw Stiff version. To check it wasn't just me who feels this, I sent a copy of it to Keith Reid to get his opinion. He agreed.

There might be even worse news, though. According to Henry Scott-Irvine's excellent book on Procol Harum, *Ghosts of a Whiter Shade of Pale*, another track that Brooker produced for the *Juppanese* sessions was *Down At The Doctor's*.

A fully realised studio version by Mickey has never been heard. If recorded – Mickey cannot recall - it failed to make the final cut, too. And although he has forgotten the detail today, in an unbroadcasted interview, recorded just after *Juppanese* was released, Mickey spoke of other lost treasures:

"There were four or five tracks we recorded with Gary that never made it to the album. One of them was *Switchboard Susan*, which Gary has now put on his own solo album. Also *You Made a Fool Out of Me* and *You Could Have Been an Army*."

So a third version of *Switchboard Susan* now surfaces: recorded before both the Rockpile failed attempt and the eventually released Godley & Crème-produced version. And nobody has ever heard Mickey sing *Army*, (except perhaps Elkie Brooks and Derek Green, who might well have been listening to this unreleased master, rather than a demo, in a few months from this point – don't worry, all will become clear.)

The disappearance of these tracks was depressing for Mickey at the time and a major disappointment to his fans today. Album sales were what disappointed Stiff. According to Mickey's memory, a few months after it came out, "*Juppanese* sales amounted to about £25000 worth, but that's about what it cost to make and promote, so I've never seen any money from its record sales."

There were downsides ahead on the live performance front, too – but in that instance Mickey himself was the culprit, as we are about to discover.

12 You'll Never Get Me Up In One Of Those

In which a tour, and a career, hit the buffers and fail to take off, to mix one's metaphors

Mickey and Hilary on tour   courtesy Adrian Boot

I've been up all week
I've been burning the candle at both ends, so to speak
I'm off my handle
Don't talk to me

***Don't Talk To Me* by Mickey Jupp, Oxford**

It's 1978 and out in what he has always considered the real world - that's to say playing gigs rather than suffering the rarefied experience of recording - Mickey was a busy bunny. After just a week's rehearsal, on 16th and 17th March, the Jupp/Grabham/Gordon/Telemacque incarnation of the Mickey Jupp Band played a couple of warm-up gigs over in Ireland: Dublin first, then Belfast.

The next day they were in Cardiff supporting Elvis Costello on tour. They continued to open for him all over the country, right through March and April.

Their set list kicked off with a couple of old Legend warhorses, after which, under strict instruction from Stiff, the rest of the show was dominated by tracks that would shortly make up the *Juppanese* album. Typically the show would feature *Cheque Book, Shine On my Shoes, S.P.Y., Chevrolet, Anything You Do, Daisy Mayes, Further On Up The Road, The Ballad Of Guitar Pickin' Slim, Switchboard Susan, Down At The Doctor's* and *Old Rock 'n' Roller*.

Mickey and Stiff were evidently taking the new album very seriously. Any exceptions to the rules were for good reason: *Daisy Mayes* was a song Mickey had high hopes for but eventually never recorded, except at one live BBC session, while the inclusion of that knock-off Arista B-side, *Down at the Doctor's,* would have been explained by the recent activities of old mates Dr Feelgood. They had recorded their own version of *Down at the Doctor's* that year, for the album *Private Practice*. In September the track was released as a single, whereupon it made it into the UK top 50, managing to linger five weeks in its lower reaches. This first version of this song by Dr Feelgood - and there are many - is notable for the accidental omission of a harmonica solo. At one point singer Lee Brilleaux calls "eight bars of piano" to remind the band to leave space for it, which they do, but for some reason the solo was never added. The following year the band re-recorded the song live, as the B-side to their single, *As Long as the Price is Right*; some say following their discovery that Mickey didn't particularly rate their first version, ("they're lovely lads but I didn't like it at all" was his verdict.)

In total Dr Feelgood recorded the song on no less than eight (!) separate occasions, including live albums, meaning that *Down at the Doctor's* eventually appeared on more than a dozen Feelgood albums or compilations. This list includes their UK and US number one live album, *Stupidity*. To many fans, *Down at the Doctor's* became the bands 'signature' tune. To Mickey it became a nice little income generator. But it nearly didn't.

The word is that Lee Brilleaux had been aware of the song for quite some time, no doubt since the release of Mickey's Arista single of which it formed the B-side, but didn't much rate it or fancy covering it.

Apparently he had to be persuaded by the rest of the band, and no doubt Keith Reid, to record it in the first place. (Eventually, perhaps bravely relishing the gallows irony of it all, Brilleaux chose *Down at the Doctor's* as the title of the last LP he was able to record with the band before advancing cancer tragically claimed his life in 1994).

Mickey is typically matter-of-fact about the song:

"That's been a good little earner, that one. Thirty-five years later I still get a few hundred quid per PRS statement from Feelgood's recordings of it. I never wrote it for them or about them, it's nothing to do with the doctor in the name, Dr Feelgood. In fact as a band, I never really cared for them that much: a bit too frantic for my taste".

Even though *Juppanese* had to an extent been toured in advance - through Mickey's support spot for Elvis Costello - it was now time to support it properly post-release, when people could actually shell out good money to buy it. Ideally, Mickey and his band should have played some prominent headline sets to do this. That might have been what Mickey had in mind when he told journalist Mike Davies, who interviewed him during the Costello tour, "If I'm going to keep gigging, in future I'm going to do it my way."

Unfortunately, like so much that Stiff Records did, odd and offbeat ideas were preferred to traditional music industry practices. Sometimes this paid off, putting them ahead of the game; other times it backfired leading, some would claim, to the label's eventual collapse. In particular, Stiff's management had a penchant for elaborate tours featuring a broad selection of their acts in a sort of variety show format, reminiscent of the sixties multi-band tours. It had worked previously so another such extravaganza was now planned. As well as sharing this joint bill, it was decided that to help promote the tour each artist concerned would contribute to a collective EP a recording of his or her own cover version of the Devo song, and early Stiff single, *Be Stiff*. This was to be made available only to concert goers who sent ticket stubs and £1.15 to Stiff's press department. Mickey did not relish recording it:

"I said I don't want to do it – it's a bloody stupid idea. Their only stipulation was you had to use the title so I wrote some rather pornographic lyrics around that. It was a pretty lewd tale about erections but I was buggered if I was going to do it their way."

He was equally derisory about other Stiff attempts at marketing him:

"On the tour they tried to get me to dress up in this and that – certain types of awful 'New Wave' clothes. Kosmo Vinyl, their PR man, is a great lad: loads of mouth and the sharpest brain I've ever come across. But he was telling me, 'we're gonna get you dolled up in these shoes and stuff'. I just turned round to him and told him he'd never ever get me to wear anything I didn't feel comfortable in. He shut up after that and we got on fine." (Er, not sure Kosmo agreed about the getting on fine, as we shall see shortly…)

What Mickey may have agreed to bear were a few judicious red highlights in the old barnet. Certainly John Denton, who took time off from a Wilko Johnson's Solid Senders sound check in Birmingham so that he and Wilko could drop into the Be Stiff dressing room prior to the Aston gig, believes that the Jupp locks were looking surprisingly lustrous.

The Be Stiff tour was a juggernaut, running across October and November 1978, featuring five acts: Wreckless Eric, Lene Lovich, Jona Lewie, Rachel Sweet (backed by The Records, featuring Jupp fan Will Birch on drums; ironic given The Records were actually signed to rival label Virgin) and Mickey. Each night the running order was rotated, to give each artist a fair crack of the whip – one night the opener, another night top of the bill.

For this tour Mickey had assembled yet another group of backing musicians, this time converting an existing band – the Oval Exiles – into what they, at least, referred to as Mickey Jupp and the Treatment. The line-up was Pete Gosling (guitar), Vic Young (bass), Mac Poole (drums) and from time to time Geraint Watkins (keyboards), who, as Mickey puts it "could also sing a bit".

The whole tour was a costly undertaking – some say that Stiff more or less bet the farm on it, committing £40,000 up front and expecting a final bill of around £100,000.

They were gambling it would do as well for them as the previous year's "Bunch of Stiffs" tour, which had helped kick-start the careers of Nick Lowe, Elvis Costello and Ian Dury, (all of whom had left Stiff in the interim; perhaps evidence that the label was already not a happy ship).

In the end it didn't work. Of the assembled cast only Lene Lovich went on experience significant record sales - but nobody could blame lack of effort for the failure of the others. The five week schedule was daunting, taking in Bristol, Liverpool, Birmingham, Burnley, Middlesbrough, Manchester, Lancaster, Carlisle, Glasgow, Dingwall, Wick, Aberdeen, Dundee, Edinburgh, Stirling, Belfast, Dublin, Aston, Hemel Hempstead, Hull, Huddersfield, Leeds, Sheffield, Salford, Warwick, Loughborough, Nottingham, Blackburn, Guildford, Oxford, Plymouth, and ending at the Lyceum in London. Manager Nick Blackburn attended several of the shows and particularly remembers the Hemel Hempstead gig, one of those where Mickey topped the bill. "We had trouble with a guy who jumped up on the stage and wanted to join in with Mickey on the encores. He was well out of it so the crew were trying to get him off, but it proved tricky – they had to be careful as it was Elton John."

Many of these gigs were in big venues – places too big for Mickey's liking – he believes that rock and roll is a form of blues, an intimate form of music:

"I don't mean that only thirty people can listen to it at the same time, but as it originated in America this music had its natural environment in clubs. Nowadays there are plenty of artists who think that you can bring rock 'n' roll into sports halls or stadiums. I suppose that you can perform a show there, but you fool yourself if you think that the music you bring is still real rock and roll."

Much more to Mickey's liking - delight even – was the fact that the physical touring was to be undertaken entirely by train, with only the Irish leg being conducted by coach, for what any self-respecting rail company would term 'operational reasons': no tracks. As we know, the train was Mickey's life-long favourite mode of transport. Believe it or not, at the time a particularly avid trainspotter noted down technical details in a blog unearthed by my extensive, sometimes rather sad, researches:

"On 17th November 1978 the Stiff Records Exhibition Train arrived at Margate from Oxford. This train was hauled by 47070(CF) to Kensington and by 33059(HG) from there. The train was stabled overnight at Ramsgate and departed there at 12.36 the following day for Guildford via Canterbury West, Ashford, Orpington, Brixton, Clapham Junction (W) and East Putney, hauled by 33056(HG). The train was formed of an unidentified Motorail flat, S38744, S38745, E321E, E13306, E14050, ADM44404."

So now you know.

Not only would Mickey be close to his beloved railway, he was also going to be close to another beloved. He was getting to be paired up on tour with his girlfriend from Southend, Hilary Bevan-Jones. Now a top film producer who regularly works with the likes of Richard Curtis, (and a recent chairwoman of BAFTA), she got the gig because she was at the time a teacher at Southend's Alleyn Court private school and so able to act as official tutor to another tour act - fifteen-year-old Rachel Sweet - whose continued education was a condition of her participation. It's likely that one of the ways Mickey got through the long weeks of touring was by having his girlfriend with him, at least for part of the time. And she was quite a girlfriend in Keith Reid's estimation: "Hilary was a very nice woman who put up with an endless amount of shit from Juppy. She was terrific and he was a complete pain to her." This may explain why she did not respond to requests for an interview for this book...

Inevitably, despite Hilary's presence, it was not all plain sailing. Will Birch, fellow musician on the tour, explained the point at which it went wrong, big time:

"Half way through the tour we all get sent home to get our passports, because it's suddenly announced we're going to the States to close the tour. I'd never been – most of us on the tour had never been: we were all so excited. Mickey hadn't been either but he simply says, 'I'm not going'. Mick announced this when we were playing Oxford. Some of us were in the bar at the Churchill Hotel that night having a few scotches - last knockings - and Stiff boss Dave Robinson said to us all, 'I'll have him, I'll get him to go'. He tried everything to counter Mickey's objections: we'll get you a passport, your girlfriend can go with you, you can go by boat if you won't fly, etc.

But when Mickey finally said 'If I go by boat I won't be home in time for Christmas', that was it. Dave said afterwards, 'I'm dropping Mickey Jupp...from a great height'; and that's exactly what he proceeded to do.

First off, as if to rub Mickey's nose in it, Stiff paid for Mickey's band to go over to New York and play a little set of their own, without him!"

Did Mickey refuse to go because of his famous fear of flying? Or was he scared of setting out his stall in America – the very continent whose music had always been his greatest inspiration? Or was he just being bolshie Juppy again – happier down the pub playing darts?

Earlier in the year he'd told Dave Brown, "I don't want to see the world particularly. I quite like England. I'm not that bothered, you know. I am enjoying getting up and playing and shouting my head off, though!"

Will Birch adds a further perspective: it wasn't about not wanting to go it was about wanting to do it his way; to go only when he was ready:

"When I quizzed Mick about why he wouldn't go, he said, 'When I do go to America, I want to make sure I'm ready: that I've got the right material, the right album out and the right band behind me. I don't feel that now – and I only want to go on my terms'. I thought to myself, well you'll never go, then. He sort of did later, in a song writing capacity, but never as an artist."

Mickey elaborated on this theme in an interview taped just after the tour ended: "I don't want to play for just 25 minutes. I don't want to play in the same club for four nights as they did in New York. I don't want to play with that band: I wanted to change the drummer. My plan would have been to go to the States for at least a month, spread myself about a bit, give it a good whirl; do it properly. Then come back and say we succeeded or we failed. I told my band, 'if you are my band, don't go to America; stay here with me and we will get things sorted, do it properly. But it was America and so they wanted to go, even though I didn't! I know its one of the reasons Stiff dropped me but I still think it was the right thing to do."

Worse still, because the band went without him, Mickey missed out on something he really *did* want to do:

"Ian Dury – who by now was bigger than Stiff - did a little tour of London venues that Christmas and he wanted me to support him. But I couldn't because my band had gone to America, just because they wanted to visit. That would have been a much better, more professional thing to do. It was very frustrating."

In Mickey's defence, given that the very album he was on tour to plug contained *You'll Never Get Me Up in One of Those*, a song written expressly about his disinclination to board aircraft, it doesn't sound as if Stiff had thought things through very thoroughly. As he was fond of saying, and singing, "*If the good Lord had meant us to fly, he'd have given us tickets as well as wings.*"

Will Birch glumly concluded, "Jupp had walked away again." On the other hand *New York Rock* wrote that perhaps Jupp was wise to keep his powder dry for a later solo assault on the US. Except that it never came.

Right or wrong, the label continued to get its own back. For example, on the poster for the US leg of the tour, designed by Stiff's guru art director, Chris Moreton, instead of simply leaving Mickey's name off the whole thing, they kept it on the bill but with a thick line through it, effectively branding Mickey a deserter. All these years later Keith Reid still rues the debacle:

"At the end of the tour he famously refused to go to New York - we tried everything but we couldn't persuade him to go. In any case, the label had had enough of him by then. So we had to go cap in hand back to Chrysalis…"

Mickey has another perspective, which he aired at the time: the old chestnut relating to the material he was required to play in his act:

"I don't particularly like doing my own numbers. I'd rather do rock and roll, but you can't make a living out of that."

Typically, Mickey used the experience musically. Although it has never been heard, lurking in his archive Mickey has a song, or at least a set of lyrics, entitled *I Said No to New York*.

But Mickey's problems with the Be Stiff tour were more fundamental than this single disagreement. The truth is he wasn't enjoying being on tour at all, long before the US episode.

He was travelling in the company of far younger musicians who played a very different sort of music to him and were at a different point in their careers. They were less experienced, more impressionable and infinitely more optimistic, revelling in the same big venues that lacked the intimacy and audience contact Mickey sought. Plus he hated the pretence involved in dealing with the media in the way Stiff wanted him to:

"I had to do an interview on the tour with BBC local radio - some chap who looked like a schoolteacher – and he asked me 'Well Mickey, what's it like being part of the New Wave?' because that's what Stiff had fed him. I said, 'you what? I'm a 34 year old rock'n'roller!' Another song off the album should maybe have pre-warned Stiff about that, too…

Regardless of such promotional squabbles, Mickey's performances on the tour were often too good for his fellow artists to stand up alongside. According to an October 1978 *NME* article by Max Bell, who was given access to gigs and some of the train travel, the only act whose performance got close to Mickey's was Will Birch's band The Records who, having tagged along to back Rachel Sweet, were given a slot of their own. Bell's piece recognises Mickey's superior musicianship but also points out his inherent weakness on this kind of tour:

"Mickey Jupp, age after beauty, is last on tonight. He's looking as miserable as ever, the sort of guy who is happiest when he's got something to moan about.

Kitted out in a pair of tartan baggies that are louder than Eric's whole set, white jacket and titfer, old Juppy provides a sterling example of his Southend craft.

One of the South East's most respected, premier rockers, his music, whether with the late Legend or here with the Treatment (formerly The Exiles), exemplifies a cosy understanding of roots, light and shade. His songs mean something; they are intelligible and wry. His pianist, Geraint Watkins, a squat Celt who has done service with Carl Perkins and won the undying admiration of Dave Edmunds for that kudos, turns out to be the best musician on the bill.

There's no false front to Jupp either, take it or leave it. Jupp is stubborn. He won't compromise his principles.

He won't join the Musicians' Union or fly in a plane to a gig (Bowie got plenty of mileage out of that one). This means he can't appear on *Top Of The Pops*; no great loss but business is business. If he had a chart hit? 'I still wouldn't go on. I'd want to but I won't join.' Juppy picks up steam as he progresses through *Old New Orleans, S.P.Y., Short List* and *Sweet Little Rock'n'Roller*. By rights he ought to be in Nashville or Baton Rouge on the Billy Swan, Delbert McLinton trip with an ace band and an audience who gets off on R&R country bop. The Bristolians applaud politely but don't understand where Jupp's coming from at all. He won't force the pace or jump up and down, he sings about being an old rock and roller. People start drifting off, bludgeoned by the nonstop fun.

Jupp's game is too tame. He gets an encore, but it's one of those 'Well we've paid two quid and he is the last act on the bill' type encores." (In a *ZigZag* article published around the same time, called 'Stiff on the Tracks', John Tobler agrees that the Mickey Jupp band were the best thing on the bill.)

Is Bell's article damning with faint praise or wryly observing the impossibility of Mickey's position?

It seems to be the latter; and as for the audience's apparent lack of enthusiasm at Mickey's encore, this is perhaps hardly surprising given that the whole show ran for as long as three and a half hours some nights! As Mickey recalls with a shake of his head, "we were all supposed to do 25 minutes each but some acts just don't know when to get off". As if to prove that point, at The Stardust, Dublin - which the tour had reached by October 30th - the promoter voiced his displeasure at the show's overrunning by pulling the plug on Mickey - top of the bill that night - after just four numbers. Mr. Jupp made no complaint; he could get off stage and into the bar quicker that way.

On 19th November 1978, the influential national broadsheet *The Observer* published a photo-article about the tour, devoting the front cover of their colour supplement to a shot of the Stiff 'stars'. Mickey's facial expression in this shot clearly conveys his disinterest in being there.

What's more, accidentally or deliberately, either way tellingly, the photographer has got him, and him alone, slightly out of focus...

In the article within, the Observer neatly put its finger on Mickey's dilemma:

280

"This year the five featured artists, who each have their own backing bands – take half hour sets apiece and swap roles as headliners – are bewilderingly diverse specimens. Of them, Mickey Jupp registers in the theoretically most deserving but least likely to succeed department, holding down the hard and heavy r&b end of things. It's a style that befits one who is something of a legendary figure among the booze blues musicians from Southend".

As a result of Mickey's mental distance from the proceedings, his physical attendance, even at the UK gigs, was not exactly 100% either: acquiring him the nickname 'No Show Jupp' to some. Writer and broadcaster, Henry Scott-Irvine recalls an occasion when Mickey famously never made it to the stage. It was the Edinburgh leg:

"I was only about eighteen at the time. I knew Bert Muirhead, a dour Scot who later wrote the Stiff books. We went to Bennets Bar, a lovely old bar in Edinburgh round the corner from Clouds disco, where the Be Stiff tour was playing and which we were going on to see afterwards. I noticed that Keith Reid had turned up in the bar because I'd already interviewed him for my Procol Harum fanzine, *Shine On*. He said to me, 'Hello, oh by the way this is Mickey' and I realised it was Mickey Jupp standing next to him. I said something about looking forward to seeing him on stage later and he replied, 'I don't think you will, actually, because I won't be playing'. Keith was frantically waving both arms behind Mickey, as if to signal to me, 'drop it!' So I went to the gig and left him in the bar with his management, thinking he was joking and would go on. But he didn't. He didn't like the tour - not sure he much liked the band they'd picked for him, either. Instead Mickey's band came on and did some kind of a set, they were on second from top of the bill that night – I think Wreckless Eric did a couple of songs with them, maybe even a Jupp song. Anyway, when Bert later did his book on Stiff, he played a trick on me and wrote 'Henry missed the show (which I didn't) and prevented Mickey Jupp from turning up because he got him drunk in Bennets Bar' (which I didn't). I'm not sure that it wasn't Bert himself who stayed in the bar with Mickey all night, actually!"

Mickey's own explanation adds another dimension to the story, without denying the core issue of missing the show:

"Ah, Edinburgh. Rumour says I was talking to Henry Scott-Irvine all night. Actually there was a girl involved - I got chatting with her and ended up staying in the bar all evening." Girlfriend Hazel, who didn't attend all the gigs, would not have been pleased.

Overall, Mickey recalls his experience of the whole tour with a shudder:

"I didn't enjoy it at all. I was feeling old already. I was thirty-four – the oldest bloke on the train apart from the train driver himself! As a result I didn't mix with the others much. Six weeks on the road was too long for me. The best bit was going up to Wick; it was lovely up there. I found the further South we got, the worse the audiences were: the pits was Guildford, where there was a mass spit at Lene Lovich. The poor girl just stopped her act. Later on, after we'd all gone, the dressing rooms got trashed. Lovely."

He summed up his attitude to touring at his age in an article published in *Hot Press* – a record business mag – while still on the road, or rather, on the rail:

"It's not like I'm an 18 or 20 year old going through it for the first time. I'm 34 and like I said to Annie Nightingale, I've got a pipe'n'slippers mentality now. Sometimes I'm a bit annoyed that I'm being dragged from relative obscurity on to this train to go round and play to people I don't really want to."

Despite his overall distaste for what he saw as a pointless charade, Mickey seems to have cultivated a protective, almost father-daughter relationship with teenage label-mate Rachel Sweet, one that doesn't quite fit the curmudgeonly tag he is so often given. He even went so far as to pen an unrecorded song - *Rachel, Rachel* - in her honour. On the other hand, his views of the remaining characters he was spending all that time with were less charitable. In a blog about Mickey, Ron Bijnen captured Jupp's view that "Jona Lewie is weird, Wreckless Eric was constantly drunk and Lene Lovich talks too much". He then added a particularly intriguing comment, which might seem surprising coming from the lips of such a fine musician:

"Look, I can't talk about music: I like a song or I don't and that's it. But them, phew, they talk for hours and hours about it. I'm quite prepared to go and find a compartment of my own and just look out the window at the scenery going by. I don't want to talk about music."

One suspects that this is the point at which instinctive musicians like Mickey, and manufactured musicians like most of the rest of us, including most if not all of those on the Stiff tour, part company. We talk about it for hours; he just does it.

But the differences between the various members of the travelling cast went deeper than mere social friction. There was a difference in ambition, too, as Mickey explained to me:

"I wasn't into this business about strutting my stuff on a big stage. I'd rather play a smoky little club, packed to the rafters with two hundred people in it - like Quasimodo's in Berlin - what a great place that is to play. I hate the lights in your face; I want to see what the audience is doing. One night I found myself up on stage in Newcastle, just going through the motions once again, thinking 'what the fucking hell am I doing here?' I just wanted to go home."

As he'd made clear at the time, "I'm not bothered. I write songs as a hobby, like some people make model aeroplanes. I'm not really that into music, I'd rather talk about football. I've always felt like this, trying not to get too fed up with it and then leaving..."

Kosmo Vinyl, MC on the tour, was another Stiff stalwart aware of Mickey's powerful reputation yet who found the experience of being around him a bit deflating, whatever Mr. Jupp may have thought:

"Mickey's name was often mentioned at Stiff in rather hallowed tones, by those who went back far enough: to the Brinsley's, Chilli Willi's or now The Feelgoods. He had a lot of fans amongst those people. I had never heard of him before I worked at Stiff, but he was considered a major talent that hadn't happened. If I had to pick a word to describe Mickey in person, or on the tour, I would say "grumpy". I have no memory of him ever being happy or pleased, so I tended to gave him a wide berth."

In his book *Be Stiff*, Richard Balls reflects that the Stiff management had a similar view, recognising Mickey's "reputation for being recalcitrant" and dryly noting that he turned out to be "a reluctant passenger" on the tour. In fact, pretty much the only person Mickey got along with on the tour was Lene Lovich's drummer, Bobby Irwin:

"We got on very well, seemed to hit it off - we didn't have to look for an opening to say something, or have an awkward conversation."

Was Mickey simply bored and feeling old, or was there more to it than that? Dutch magazine *De Telegraaf* unpicked something else in an interview at the time; something that would have been considered extraordinary by his fellow musicians on the tour:

"I used to be self-confident that I was a good singer. Still I'm not too bad but lately I'm thinking too much on stage. For example in the middle of a song I think: what if I were there in the crowd, would I still like it? And then I break it off in utter panic. Once I was sure there were only two singers better than me: Paul McCartney and Paul Rodgers of Free. But they've slumped down, too.

McCartney could sing anything. Anything! From *I'm Down* to *Michelle*. Nowadays you can't bear to hear him. Frankie Miller was also good, but not any more. He's drowned his talent."

Frankie Miller's fall from grace, which eventually led to a massive stroke, often features in Mickey's conversation, arising again in interviews for this book:

"What a twerp, what an absolute twerp Frankie was. A voice like that but he just burnt himself out stupidly; treble cognacs all the time. Too many people get like 'Hey, I'm in the music business' and then start behaving like idiots."

Certainly, Tex Comer, bass player for both Frankie and Mickey, noticed the difference between working with the two of them, observing:

"I'd always been in bands that drank, took drugs and partied all night. Then all of a sudden I'm playing with this guy who had two pints and a cheese sandwich, and that was it!"

(Ed Deane noticed the same difference, when he joined Mickey's band later on:

"Mickey wasn't into late night drinking and would mostly go back to the hotel after the gig. It was usually Tex and I who would prowl around whatever city it was after a gig, looking for all-night bars. Sometimes we'd be joined by Big Figure, or Henri Grecourt - who was our soundman and drove the van.

We all got along well and I don't remember any kind of friction. The band's behaviour on the road was kind of jokingly anti-rock'n'roll cliché.

We had all been around for a while and had witnessed a fair amount of stupid behaviour. Nobody saw any reason why we should leave our hotel rooms or dressing rooms in a mess for some other poor soul to clean up after us. The main thing was the music, and if we played a great gig, everybody was happy, including Mickey.")

Despite being more sober than the average rock musician, it sounded like Mickey's insecurities had finally come to a head on this long and gruelling tour, leading to his confidence finally blowing. In his heart he felt - in his head he was sure - that like Vertigo with Legend before, Stiff simply didn't know what to do with him. They had their one way of working and were unprepared to be flexible about how to apply it to Mickey's talents. Rarely having spoken to Wreckless Eric on tour, he would have been unaware that Eric felt exactly the same way about their mutual label. In his memoir, *A Dysfunctional Success*, Eric complains:

"Stiff Records just didn't know what to do with me. Success, in their terms, was hit singles. I didn't have any hit singles; therefore I was a failure. I was an embarrassment to them. Dave Robinson boasted that he could sell anything to the public, even a recording of total silence entitled: *The Wit and Wisdom of Ronald Reagan*. But he couldn't sell me. He once told me I was his Achilles Heel."

It appears that Dave had two Achilles Heels – the other one being Mickey Jupp.

Mickey felt Stiff traded in too many trendy marketing gimmicks, trying to invent eccentric images for artists like Lene Lovich, while Mickey felt he *was* the real deal: a genuine outsider, a proper musical lone wolf. He didn't need embellishment because he already had the important stuff – talent and attitude:

"I was already eccentric so I didn't have to dress up like Wreckless Eric or Lene Lovich. I never had to try and be different, I already was."

Yet instead of accepting him as a true one-off and presenting him that way, Stiff perceived Mickey's disenchantment as further evidence that he was simply an awkward bugger. He was, of course, and admits this – "I never really get on with anybody!" he grins - but great talents frequently are, and truly pioneering, entrepreneurial management and record labels recognize this, even seek it out.

Alan McGee, the enfant terrible at the helm of Creation Records, famously never signed an act that wasn't stubborn and principled; he couldn't see what more you could ask for in an artist. And after nearly being bankrupted by difficult acts like Primal Scream and My Bloody Valentine, he ended up a millionaire, thanks to those difficult sods, Oasis.

But Mickey's brand of obstreperousness did not inspire respect, only aggravation; despite his attempts to better understand it:

"Nick Lowe, Jake Riviera and me once had about a two hour friendly discussion on why I'm difficult to get on with. You see, I often keep quiet because I'm not very good at saying I don't like something. When I do like something I don't go around shouting 'it's great!' - I'm not usually outgoing, I don't enthuse about music - so people only notice the negatives. It's a vicious circle. Because I have this reputation, I try to be more easy-going, so I go along with things until it all builds up, then it gets explosive in the end."

It was clear to all that Mickey and Stiff were never going to see eye to eye, as Mickey and his management had finally been forced to conclude:

"We had been toying with the idea of having to buy ourselves out of the Stiff contract, but at the eleventh hour they got their first; they said they were going to let me go. We heaved a big sigh of relief but because we knew it wasn't ever going to work. They aren't really pushing their artists; they're pushing Stiff – keeping up the image of their label. Every artist they want to be malleable, to mould how they wish. I was way too straight for them."

So the two split up, rather acrimoniously.

It was hard to see how the two parties could ever co-operate again. Not to work together. Even talk to one another.

They did, of course. Nothing in the story of Mickey's life is that straightforward.

But this chapter was certainly over for now.

How The Music Scene Changed

Mickey comes off the rails   Courtesy Adrian Boot

Mickey's first recordings came out in 1969. The big single hits that year were from the Beatles (*Get Back*), the Stones (*Honky Tonk Woman*), Marvin Gaye (*I Heard it Through the Grapevine*), Creedence Clearwater Revival (*Bad Moon Rising*) and the original, bluesy Fleetwood Mac (*Albatross* and *Oh Well*). A catholic portfolio of quality music, typifying the tastes of a sixties audience educated to appreciate a variety of styles. This eclectic mix of great music is even more evident amongst the top albums that year:

1	The Beatles	*Abbey Road*
2	Led Zeppelin	*Led Zeppelin 2*
3	The Rolling Stones	*Let it Bleed*
4	Original Cast	*Hair*
5	Led Zeppelin	*Led Zeppelin*
6	Blood, Sweat & Tears	*Blood, Sweat & Tears*
7	The Who	*Tommy*
8	Johnny Cash	*At San Quentin*
9	The Beatles	*Yellow Submarine*
10	Blind Faith	*Blind Faith*

Right behind them in the album sales charts were The Band, Bob Dylan, Cream, Chicago and Crosby, Stills & Nash.

The sixties might have been drawing to a close but in even its final year the decade was mining a rich vein of quality pop, rock and blues music - a great deal of it home grown.

Now let's move ten years on: it's 1979 and a decidedly odd decade of popular music is thankfully drawing to a close. Reading about it in the cold light of day one realises that to love such an era one clearly had to be there. And be the right age: which was about 16, as it always is with pop music. Just look at the ten top selling singles of that whole intervening decade (warning: you may want to do this through half-closed fingers):

1	Wings	*Mull Of Kintyre*
2	Boney M	*Rivers Of Babylon*
3	Travolta & Newton John	*You're The One That I Want*
4	Boney M	*Mary's Boy Child*
5	Travolta & Newton John	*Summer Nights*
6	Village People	*Y.M.C.A*
7	Queen	*Bohemian Rhapsody*
8	Blondie	*Heart Of Glass*
9	David Soul	*Don't Give Up On Us, Baby*
10	Slade	*Merry Xmas Everybody*

There are only two songs on this list don't make one ill just to think about. (OK, three if you give Noddy Holder the benefit of the doubt – it is, after all, the best Christmas single of all time, although there isn't much competition on that front).

Too many of these records are what might be termed "manufactured pop": indicators of how business forces (for this read corporate greed and accountants) had wrested control away from artists, in particular artist/writers – previously the arbiters of musical creativity and song selection.

It's not just this seventies' overall toppest of the poppest that causes one to squirm. Crap was rife. Other 'acts' enjoying Number One singles during that decade included Lee Marvin, the England World Cup Squad, Lieutenant Pigeon, the Royal Scots Dragoon Guards, Peters & Lee, Paper Lace, Carl Douglas, Windsor Davies & Don Estelle, Roger Whittaker, Brotherhood of Man, Brian & Michael, Lena Martell and Father Abraham & the Smurfs.

Our musical world had once again degenerated into a jamboree bag of sweet, pappy pop, with singles being bought largely by teenyboppers or their mums in roughly equal proportions. Producers and A&R men were now kings, albeit without clothes, because they had fathomed the secret of how to fob off audiences with just about anything. Their acts were often just that: actors, mere vessels for the sounds the labels wished to market. Many didn't actually play on the records they purportedly made, sometimes even the lead singers didn't sing on them – yes, we mean you, Milli Vanilli.

Mickey clearly wasn't going to make it in amongst that lot.

What had gone wrong? And how did it go wrong so fast?

After the music industry's panic and confusion at the sudden rise of teen record buying in the late fifties and the sham-pop of the very early sixties, things had become easier for record company executives to comprehend. The beat boom lasted long enough for them to get comfortable with the concept of what the market was now looking for: guitar groups, ideally from Liverpool, who wrote their own material and dressed in an interesting fashion. Towards the beginning of the '70s came Glam Rock. At first the business found this even easier to grasp: it was the guitar-band beat boom all over again, but this time with familiar showbiz traditions like fancy dress and eye-liner thrown in for good measure.

But in the middle of all this pantomime came punk: a couple of years that recalibrated the musical aspirations of many an angsty teenager, while confusing just about everybody else.

The purpose of punk was to have no purpose; the rulebook contained no rules other than when in doubt piss on the chips. Punk's misbehavior grabbed the imagination of the kids, in exactly the same way the Rolling Stones had fifteen years earlier by urinating up a wall.

Unsurprisingly, Mickey was not a fan of punk; though that was less to do with the music than the behaviour that surrounded it, as he commented upon at the time:

"Violence seems to be an integral part of today's music, which I don't like. Back in the sixties it was a sort of fringe benefit! Now it's what this new wave stuff is all about - some of these groups almost inviting a punch-up. These days they have to have bouncers down the Nashville, unheard of in my heyday. I really don't like it; just like my Dad didn't like Elvis Presley!"

Punk didn't just create a new sort of music; it created a new attitude towards music and towards the business of music. This ultimately led to a new kind of record industry, at long last. For punk's DIY philosophy encouraged the rise of the indie labels, run by people with a very different set of values from Corporate Biz, Inc. So while punk didn't deliver enormous record sales, importantly it tore up the old rulebook. The new wave of acts and actions at its core also permitted other - technically non-punk - acts to hang onto on its coat tails and sneak into the party. They called themselves, with startling originality, New Wave.

The best of these artists soon achieved significant chart success, once they had demonstrated a similar swaggering image, yet also established the fact that they possessed levels of musical talent their punk brethren mostly did not. Acts like Elvis Costello, Joe Jackson, The Police and Squeeze all emerged from punk's shadows, while visually punk-ish pop bands like Blondie, Tubeway Army and the Boomtown Rats each scored Number One singles in 1978/1979.

The singles charts had always been volatile, though - whereas album charts had historically been a different matter. This was where the bulk of Britain's more mature youth was now spending its cash. Surely this was where Mickey could expect to meet an appreciative audience?

In the early part of the seventies the old guard had still ruled the album charts, just like they had in the sixties: the Beatles and the Stones, Simon & Garfunkel, Led Zeppelin, Rod Stewart, Pink Floyd. New big-selling artists of musical stature then emerged - the likes of David Bowie, Elton John and Abba.

But so did new and gimmicky marketing methods, such as K-Tel's TV advertised hits compilations and the first of the true boy bands: the talent-free zone that was the Bay City Rollers. A plague of Greatest Hits albums clogged the charts as the industry - eagerly, profitably, foolishly - ate yesterday's lunch all over again; thus avoiding the troubling issue of which fresh talent to put its money on for the future. As the decade drew to a close there were some signs of new shoots emerging, although the acts themselves - ELO, The Police, Supertramp or Leo Sayer, for example - were not exactly in the first flush of youth. But still their contemporary efforts remained stubbornly intertwined with retro No 1 albums from Buddy Holly, The Shadows, Barbra Streisand, Nat King Cole and Don Williams.

However, while the fat cats at the big labels, (A&Arse men, the punks called them), wallowed around in well-paid, well-dressed confusion, newer, savvier forces were emerging.

The record store Virgin had turned into an influential label with its very first release in 1973. Mike Oldfield's *Tubular Bells* was exactly the sort of record with which no major label would sully their bargepole: two dense sides of multi-layered instrumental music from an introverted nerd who wouldn't play live or promote his record. Yet with some airplay help from that old radical and sometime Jupp supporter, John Peel, it went to number one and stayed in the charts for several years (yes, years). It began to look like there was a niche for new labels with a fearless attitude and good ears, and Virgin were not the only ones.

Chrysalis Records began in a tiny flat in West London in 1967, when former university social secretaries, Chris Wright and Terry Ellis, merged their flair for managing and booking bands to form the Ellis Wright Agency. After a couple of nasty experiences trying to get their bands' records released via major labels - notably Jethro Tull on MGM, a label so uninterested in the band that they accidentally released its first single under the misprinted name of Jethro Toe - Wright and Ellis decided to go it alone.

At the end of the sixties they signed a licensing deal with Island Records containing the proviso that once Wright and Ellis' acts had scored a pre-agreed number of hits the pair would be awarded a label in their own right.

The required tally was reached within just one year and so Chrysalis - an amalgam of Wright's first name and Ellis' last - was born. Not long after that point Mickey's soon-to-be manager Nick Blackburn joined them, firstly on the booking agency side and then in the record company itself.

By 1979 - the time Mickey was to work with them - Chrysalis had already turned into a broadly based (for this read increasingly unfocused) label, having lost Procol Harum in 1977. By Mickey's era they were releasing a successful but fragmented grab-bag of material from artists like Ian Hunter, Leo Sayer, Pat Benatar and UFO, while concentrating their main efforts single mindedly on, er, two objectives: on the one hand developing the juggernaut that Blondie had become, and on the other launching the influential multi-racial 2-tone label. All this while they also tried to keep their flagging New Romantic catalogue alive. Not much time to pay attention to an old rock and roller from Southend, however much they liked what he did.

Stiff Records, Mickey's recording home in 1978, had appeared from nowhere a couple of years earlier through hits from punks the Damned, and New Wave non-punks Elvis Costello and Ian Dury. By the time Mickey's *Juppanese* album was released, Stiff had already started to fade. Founders Dave Robinson and Jake Riviera were always a fiery combination and after a series of disagreements Riviera left Stiff in early 1978 to form the short-lived Radar Records, taking Elvis Costello and Nick Lowe with him as his settlement package. Stiff's energies were thereafter directed mostly at breaking the band Madness, the success of whom kept the imprint afloat for a few more years, before it finally sank in a sea of debt.

Mickey's 1982 guvnors, A&M, had enjoyed perhaps the strangest journey of all. The world's biggest independent label had well and truly put its foot in it on 10th March 1977 by signing the Sex Pistols after that band had already been signed and promptly dropped by EMI, due to objections from its senior management.

Within a week A&M, too, had bowed to pressure: in their case from other artists on their roster and the management's own second thoughts after the Pistols' entourage physically attacked 'old fart' DJ Bob Harris, (the label boss in question, MD Derek Green, would make a better decision in a few years when he signed Mickey).

So the label dropped the band. In so doing they missed out on decent sales plus the massive PR the Sex Pistols then clocked up for Virgin; a label that, thanks to the buccaneering spirit of Richard Branson at the helm, didn't give a fig about pressure from anyone. (It's a shame Mickey himself never signed to Virgin, which was famous for persevering with its artists; even difficult ones like XTC, who also refused to tour, although that relationship finally ended in tears, once Branson's reign at the helm was over and the label had been sold to granny EMI).

By Mickey's period of tenure at A&M, that label too was facing several ways at once. In the same year as his first album for them, A&M launched output by pop diva Janet Jackson, prog-rockers Supertramp, post-punks Joe Jackson and Squeeze, power pop band Split Enz and country rockers the Ozark Mountain Daredevils, while also re-issuing jazzer Quincy Jones, old rockers Humble Pie and the cheesy Carpenters. No sign of a direction there, then.

Back in the sixties, when John Schroeder had produced Southend group Sounds Around's debut single *What Does She Do?* for Pye Piccadilly, he told the young band members that trying to get a pop hit was like "throwing shit against a wall to find out which bits stick". Mickey had the misfortune to time his solo career in a period where the business, having lost judgment and confidence, seemed to have returned to those random principles. But he had no control over that; you have to make the best of a bad job if you play music for a living. It is easy for those of us who aren't professional musicians to imagine the lives of those who actually are as being a sort of musical version of our own: a regular, sometimes better-paid job making music, rather than whatever it is we do - teaching, digging roads, writing adverts. In fact, this is almost never true.

Only the highest-selling artists can afford a life made up purely of writing and playing music, (or swanning about on a yacht/down the golf course/in a heroin den in the me-time between albums and gigs). Most professional musicians have to also have other jobs, just to make ends meet. If they are lucky, they get to work in a music shop or a recording studio to supplement their income. If not, they must do whatever they can – from working in a builders merchants to being a delivery driver for a hymn book publisher, (Mickey and Mo respectively), dipping in and out of playing and recording as the opportunity arises.

If a label subsequently drops them, or their band breaks up, they must start to climb the greasy pole again. Each time they do so, it gets harder: for while the artist may have gained more experience, he or she is also getting older and - worse still - has a growing track record of failure with which to frighten callow record company executives. Record company A & R men do not like failure, fearing it might rub off on them. Instead, they look for the sharpest, freshest newest thing they can lay hands on.

Probably the best way of understanding all this is to read John Niven's brilliant book, *Kill Your Friends*. He calls it a novel, but he used to be an A & R man himself and has assured me that most of it, (just short of actually killing his friends), is based entirely on real events....

13 Cheque Book

In which Mickey gets another bite of the cherry, but it tastes a bit weird

Chrysalis press advertisement

> *Out of the woods*
> *Into the trees*
> *Trouble to trouble, with the greatest of ease*
> *I wouldn't wish anybody times like these*

***Times Like These* by Mickey Jupp, demo**

Post-Stiff, Mickey was back in a familiar place. No record company, insufficient income from songwriting, not many gigs – and several years older than the last time he was in exactly the same place. But now someone had gone and moved the goalposts: punk was everywhere, while established artists were being ejected from the balloon by a panicky record industry that had really lost the plot this time.

Yet Mickey wasn't ready to fold; nor was Strongman, his management company, in the persons of Keith Reid and Nick Blackburn. They had good connections with Chrysalis, the record label for whom Nick had worked and to whom both Keith's band Procol Harum and Gary Brooker, Mickey's publisher, had been signed. Chrysalis had already expressed interest in Mickey's songs a couple of years earlier, when Stiff nabbed him. These connections led to another Jupp album deal being reached. It was just for one album, but there was talk of big names and big budgets - so there were great expectations.

By 1979, Mickey had put together yet another iteration of the Mickey Jupp Band. Local bass player, Dave Bronze, last heard of in this story working at Tim Gentle Music, took on bass playing duties, while that man Bob Clouter turned up for the umpteenth time to play drums. They were joined on guitar by Ian 'Chuck' Duck, a former member of Elton John's early associates, Hookfoot, and allegedly the man behind the harmonica part on one-off hit *Groovin' with Mr. Bloe*, (though quite how he was originally located is a bit of a mystery, not least since he hailed from Southampton rather than Southend). This band, however, was not destined to feature on the forthcoming album.

Chrysalis and Mickey's managers had asked him whom he might like to produce his next record, which gave Mickey something of a problem, what with him being such a devoted stranger to contemporary music and the producers of the day. So his short list was by now precisely that: short. Mickey would have liked it to be even shorter:

"I should have produced my own studio albums but my management company always wanted to get a big name involved, as much as anything for publicity. Dave Edmunds was always on my short lists, but I would have preferred to do it myself, or at least not to have anyone else do it, except perhaps a good engineer.

On the other hand I find recording studios a bit uninteresting anyway. I've got a very short attention span – after a bit of knob twiddling I'd want to pack it in and go down the pub."

At the top of Mickey's very short list was the name of just about the only band he had actually taken a shine to in the previous quarter of a century: 10cc. In fact in a Stiff publicity hand-out that is clearly mostly fictional, (Mickey claimed his middle name was Aaron, no doubt another subtle dig at Elvis Costello), he had named 10cc's *Original Soundtrack* album as a personal favourite, alongside Elmore James' *Memorial* - a most unlikely pairing. But this was no publicity stunt:

"The only current band I like is 10cc. I have all their albums; I think they're marvellous. I try to analyse why I like them and I reckon it's because they are always tongue in cheek with witty, punning lyrics, and always well produced – they spend ages on it." (This latter point seems an odd admiration for Mickey to express, given his lifetime of tetchy impatience with elaborate recording techniques or lengthy studio schedules.)

10cc were famously known for being a four-piece band that fundamentally consisted of two duos collaborating with one another, namely Kevin Godley & Lol Creme and Eric Stewart & Graham Gouldman. They wrote great songs, usually in those pairings, often about unusual subjects, featuring witty lyrics: so far, so right up Mickey's street. However, their recordings were somewhat self-regarding and fiddly; scratchy of sound, complex of arrangement, heavy of audio effects compared to what Mickey always looked for. They had spent more time recording the single track *I'm Not in Love* than Mickey had ever spent making an entire album. What's more, the pair that had agreed to produce the album was Godley and Creme, who, as Mickey was about to find out, were the more experimental wing of 10cc, the ones whose excesses were only just kept under control by the band's more sensible other half. Given that Mickey had elsewhere cited Stewart & Gouldman as one of his favourite writing teams, he seems to have been insufficiently specific in his suggestions for producer candidates, ending up with the less suitable, certainly the less sensitive duo: the pairing who tended to wear their creativity ostentatiously, like a Day-Glo armband.

According to Keith Reid, this was, in a perverse way, what Mickey was after:

"Mickey wanted to make a 10cc record - that's what he really wanted. Godley & Creme's way of working in 10cc was to absolutely never do the obvious thing: 'whatever the song sounds it should be like, do the opposite'. So it was a lot of fun making that record, really enjoyable. Mickey had been respectful of players on the Gary sessions for *Juppanese* but didn't enjoy them much, and he certainly didn't enjoy the Rockpile ones – so in comparison this was fun to do."

The other discovery Mickey was to make, although not until considerably later, was that Godley and Creme were not doing this just for a percentage of sales - what the business calls "points", or even for points and a modest fee. They were on an eye watering production fee, one that would have to come off sales income before Mickey could see any royalties at all. Mickey maintains that the total production costs for the album came to £28,000 - that's around £150,000 in 2015 money. Even had the album sold well, which it didn't, Mickey would have been lucky to see a penny once the record company had recouped such mammoth upfront costs. To Mickey, this dilemma highlighted what is perhaps the biggest conundrum in a musician's career. Every artist needs to make records in order to build a fan base and thus a career, yet most artists never make money out of recording. They can earn cash in hand by performing, or generate a steady income stream from songwriting royalties, but with recording it's a case of shit or bust: you make a fortune or you make nothing. And it generally doesn't much help if the label puts a gigantic promotional budget behind the release, either: the artist will be picking up the tab for that, too.

The record business operates on a simple downside risk model: if an artist fails to generate enough income to cover his costs, the label loses money. A modicum of success should see the upfront costs recouped, after which the label can only win – it's just a question of how much. Given the label chooses both whom to record and its terms of business, a decent record company ought not to go wrong too often.

When the label does drop a clanger it has to swallow the costs, although it is sometimes able to write off certain losses against tax liabilities incurred through its successes.

If, on the other hand, the artist is very successful, the label quickly recovers every drop of its costs, often including big wodges of overhead the artist had erroneously imagined were part of the record company's contribution: like all those long lunches and the wages of their art director, despite him putting a man in a lion's head on the album cover against the artist's wishes. When this ocean of deductibles has finally been drained, royalties begin to accrue to the artist, minus the record company's substantial contractual share. Even then, the amounts that get through to those who made the music won't add up to a lot, unless those sales are really, really big.

Royalty rates have improved since the days of the Beatles, whose penny-per-single deal (half that for foreign sales) meant that a million selling single in the USA would make each of them, as performers, a grand total of £375 less tax (and tax back then was as much as 98%: hence George Harrison's ode to the *Taxman*). But they still aren't overly generous. Big, successful artists now employ accountants with the power of audit to keep the record companies in line, making sure that the creators of the music get their due. Smaller artists can't afford to. (I should know, Motown promised my band, Wolfe, a 'small royalty cheque' in 1972 that has yet to arrive, something which *Record Collector* magazine deems to be 'standard practice' for artists whose sales figures were modest, quoting similar tardiness affecting the Pretty Things, also on the same label as us. Worse, I once toured with a band that had recently experienced number one hits in both the UK and USA, yet were still on £20 a week each until the money men had recovered every imaginable upfront cost. The group actually broke up before they ever saw any major league royalties).

Mickey's view is that the only musicians who make guaranteed money out of recording are the session men, and he's right. In the case of the *Long Distance Romancer* album, the session men selected by the producers were all rather famous: Andy Mackay and Gary Tibbs from Roxy Music plus Godley and Creme themselves. More fees, vicar? Since the record was made, Mickey has been asked several times what these musicians brought to the album, the Roxy Music personnel in particular. His regular deadpan response - "Andy played sax and Gary played bass" - speaks volumes about his view of their contributions. The most I could get out of him on the subject was the word "underwhelmed".

As would befit such a stellar cast (and budget), recording was to take place at the trendy, swanky and rather pricey Basing Street Studios, with pre-rehearsals at Strawberry South in Dorking - a studio in which Godley and Creme's previous outfit, 10cc, had long held an interest.

Manager Keith Reid later explained to Will Birch, "Kevin and Lol were such fun to be in the studio with. They were very creative - in hindsight probably too creative! Mickey really enjoyed it, but I don't think it was what people wanted from him."

Whether he appeared at the time to enjoy it or not, looking back Mickey is not a fan of the finished product, as he made clear to me:

"*Long Distance Romancer* is not my favourite album. I just let Godley & Creme get on with it. I couldn't be bothered to argue. I didn't have the personal clout to say, 'Look, No'. I should have stood my ground and stamped my authority on things, but I didn't. Instead I just thought, here we go again. I felt that proceedings were totally out of my hands. Story of my life."

Interestingly, this was not how he felt just after he had recorded it, at which time he told Southend reporter Mick Walsh, ""It only took about 21 working days to complete and I was really happy with the way things went".

The album title - *Long Distance Romancer* - came from a line in one of its tracks, that old warhorse, *Switchboard Susan*. A Jupp rendition of this song - first destined for *Juppanese* and by now already recorded by several other artists, not least Nick Lowe with his US hit version - had finally broken surface.

The LP was released in October 1979, exactly a year after Stiff had put out *Juppanese*. There was still no picture of Mickey on the sleeve, though he did appear in cartoon form – something he claims was his own idea, in order to wriggle out of any photo session! Keith Reid remembers that cover less than fondly:

"The label seemed to like the album, though the artwork didn't work very well. It was just one of those things. Peter, the art director, was very nice and went on to do very well out of the Mad Max franchise but it didn't turn out that great - Godley & Creme couldn't believe how bad it was."

It was later put to Mickey, by Dutch magazine *Muziek Express*, that *Long Distance Romancer* was a less straightforward album than those he had previously made. After all, it even included him flirting with a genre as unlikely as reggae. He didn't agree, of course:

"That's a bold statement. They're just a number of songs together. There's no question of a concept, they don't even date from one particular period. It's just a bunch of Mickey Jupp's stuff."

Certainly, some of the songs went back a way, as Mickey reflected more recently: "I wrote *Politics* in about 1976. I used to go down to the Odyssey Folk Club: that was my proving ground for any new songs I'd written. I can remember first playing *Pilot* there, just me and my guitar. Well, *Politics* was another one from that era."

This idea of the album being nothing more than a grab bag of songs is worth examining. While nobody would suggest that Mickey should have been aiming for a concept album in the grand sense - such as The Who's *Tommy* or The Moody Blues' *Days of Future Past* - there is a construct that lies somewhere between that level of dogged thematic adherence and a mere random collection of tracks. The Bell *Legend* album was made up of songs recorded in a very similar sound and style – perhaps unsurprising given it was knocked out in a day - but also reflective of a focused writing style and band performance. *Red Boot* had been clearly watermarked, *Moonshine* a little less so; the glue on both being the consistent playing style of Legend. *Juppanese* had two clear moods; true, a consequence of the ham-fisted way in which its production was allowed to run out of control, but quite good for establishing some sort of character per side.

In stark contrast *Long Distance Romancer* feels like a refuge for lost songs; an impression exacerbated by the fact that each track has been deliberately played in a wildly different musical style, so any common ground the material may have once had is lost by the time the session musicians have finished with it. Instead, each song becomes a strident advocate for itself, rather than part of a cohesive album.

As far as production techniques are concerned, the songs are even more willfully differentiated - as if striving constantly to be novel represents some sort of kaleidoscopic vision. In fact, it represents the opposite: a lack of clarity, an absence of a binding vision. Was it thought, as John Schroeder had suggested to Sounds Around all those years before, that such random disparity might increase the chances of something 'sticking'? Instead, it has the opposite effect: confusing the listener and puzzling the critic. It is hardly surprising that, once again, Mickey wasn't very happy with the end product: the production, the sound of the record, even the playing. It lacked guts. It was a terrible waste. The music press did not receive it with open arms. Mickey was no longer a cert for critical acclaim.

Chrysalis, to their credit, attempted to overcome the album's deficiencies through aggressive marketing. They put out a single of You *Made a Fool out of Me*, backed by *Do You Know What I Mean*, this B-side being another of Mickey's occasional nudge-nudge innuendo songs, a la *Switchboard Susan*. This was probably the strongest pairing to put out.

"I can remember there was a Friday night review show on the radio that played *You've Made a Fool Out of Me*," Keith Reid told me. "Dave Edmunds happened to be on the panel and said he thought it was fantastic. We all thought maybe we'll have a hit but it wasn't to be."

Despite its lack of sales success, Ricky Nelson's management contrived to get hold of the song on the B-side and Ricky put a version of *Do You Know What I Mean* on his last ever album, originally released on his own Silver Eagle label but which MCA picked up later. Every other track on this LP had previously been a hit for Ricky (now Rick, to be pedantic) bar the Jupp song - something of which old rock and roller Mickey is rightfully mighty proud:

"When I was a kid, Ricky was like second man down from Elvis - so I've always considered this as a huge feather in my cap. The Jordanaires have sung on a few of my songs, too, which also gives me a sense of pride." (The Jordanaires, Elvis' original backing vocalists, have appeared on several recordings of Mickey's songs by Henning Staerk, a Danish rock musician who's covered the best part of a dozen Jupp compositions down the years - including the rare *Over'n'Out* – a song of unrequited CB love!)

Given the low-key nature of Ricky's release, of which neither Mickey nor his management had initially been aware, publishers Bluebeard Music had to rapidly go chasing after royalties - as their solicitor's letter put it, "to assuage our concerns." This aggressive pursuit didn't appear to put Ricky off Mickey, there being an Austrian bootleg in rock journalist John Howard's possession of Mr. Nelson covering another of Mickey's songs, *So Long* - although this seems never to have been officially released.

But putting out Mickey's version of *Do You Know What I Mean* as a single, albeit on the B-side, didn't do the trick in the UK, so Chrysalis followed up with *True Love,* another track off the album, backed by, er, *Do You Know What I Mean*, once again. Pay attention, Chrysalis. A third single was then concocted. The B-side was good old *Switchboard Susan*, but the A-side was a newly recorded track with which Godley and Creme were thankfully not involved.

Rooms in Your Roof was a rollicking Fats Domino-style track, very smartly produced by proven hit maker Pete Wingfield. Wingfield had started his recording career in a band called Jellybread, whose early output was produced by one Mike Vernon – a fellow who would shortly get his own crack at producing Mickey.

In an odd way, both sides of this single feature Mickey's then girlfriend, Hilary. She'd earlier helped with the lyrics of the B-side, *Switchboard Susan*, while on the A-side she now contributed the female vocal that delivers answering phrases in the verses.

Despite Mickey and Hilary's best efforts this excellent single also failed to get anywhere and so the Chrysalis arrangement timed out - the fourth label to do so thus far. As manager Nick Blackburn pointed out, neither Procol Harum nor Frankie Miller were doing well for the label and so there wasn't much traction to keep Mickey in their good books, other than how many copies he sold.

And he hadn't, leaving Chrysalis with a big, fat loss on the deal. There may also have been the mandatory clashes between label and Mickey behind the scenes; certainly there was a difference in priorities. The label had initially had ambitions to break Mickey in America but he remained uninterested, as he told *Muziek Express*:

"It all leaves me cold. Those Americans don't have any taste. Suppose they like me over there? Then I'll start getting doubts about myself. I don't need it."

Mickey maintains that this was a misquote, saying today:

"America is everything: it's rock'n'roll, Leiber& Stoller, Chuck Berry, Elvis Presley, Ray Charles, the Blues, Hank Williams, Country. America asked me to marry it, but I said No!"

Nevertheless, the underlying logic of the first of these quotes is quintessential Jupp: if people I don't respect start to like me I will lose my self-respect, perhaps even lose my way. I may be tempted into doing things I would not be proud of. Much easier to stick with what I like, even if only a small group of followers agree.

You can call that foolishness, or you can call it true independence. Peter Gabriel, a man known for not hiding his opinions on the inadequacies of the business, put it rather well when speaking of similar traits in the legendary Kate Bush's way of working, saying, "you can be positive and call it courageous or negative and call it bloody-mindedness". I guess the difference in descriptors depends upon whether or not you have already sold a few million records. (Kate could also add to this the fact that *Wuthering Heights*, a recording that she - a teenager with no track record - insisted had to be put out as her debut single against the advice of experienced EMI executives, had gone to number one. There wouldn't have been much arguing after that).

Most artists of value have more or less stayed true to "their way of doing things", even when that principle hurt. But being stroppy doesn't guarantee success. What it is guaranteed to deliver is a lot of conflict, an atmosphere of tension and an environment of pressure.

Some artists who create these conditions revel in it: Van Morrison is a past master, by all accounts. Mickey created a lot of friction, too, but he truly hates it.

Despite his disappointment with the end product, Mickey worked hard to make the best of the *Long Distance Romancer* period, going out on the road as ever. This band was one of his best, featuring Ian Duck on guitar, Frank Mead on sax and harp, Pat Donaldson on bass and Dave Mattacks on drums. Donaldson and Mattacks were both ex-members of Sandy Denny's bands Fairport Convention and Fotheringay. As we know, Dave worked with many artists from Nick Drake to Paul McCartney, while Pat went on to play for the likes of Richard Thompson and Stevie Nicks. And while Ian "Chuck" Duck might not have been the most technically proficient guitarist Mickey had played with, Juppy liked his style, recalling, "Chuck was one of the few lead guitarists who was happy to not get in the way and drop back into rhythm when I was doing something."

Astonishingly, Pat Donaldson later married Kate McGarrigle and in so doing became Rufus Wainright's stepfather!

On December 17th 1979, this line-up performed in WDR Studio A for a German TV show, *Live at Rockpalast*: from which Chrysalis used cuts to promote Mickey across Europe, but to no avail.

Thankfully for his fans, Repertoire Records have finally released this show on DVD/CD – all 66 minutes of it. Frank Mead told me, "I got sent the DVD but I've been too frightened to watch it so far." Don't worry, Frank, it's great.

That a label thought it worthwhile releasing footage of this show nearly twenty-five years later is testament to Mickey's lasting popularity amongst an avid hard core of admirers who buy everything of his they can lay their hands on. But back in the seventies Mickey's records required much bigger sales figures to keep his record labels happy.

And that, once again, hadn't happened.

The *Long Distance Romancer* Album

The much-respected magazine *Record Collector* succinctly put their finger on the problem with *Long Distance Romancer* when they reviewed the re-mastered CD release in their May 2014 issue. "Too clinical for its own good", they said. To which I will add, "Too clever for its own good". Mickey himself said at the time that he didn't have much choice because "10cc were my heroes", later describing it as the album of his that people either liked most or least. (Well, I've spoken to a lot of people in putting this book together and have yet to find a soul who cites it as their favourite while meeting quite a few who have problems with it.)

When it was first released, David Hepworth – top journalist as well as *Whistle Test* and *Live Aid* co-presenter – perceptively noted in a review for *Sounds* that this album was "one of those Jack Nitzsche or bust scenarios". Blaming both Mickey and the producers, he went on to state, "the less comfortable moments occur when the producers' instinctive sarcasm colludes with Jupp's bitterness and inclination towards tiresome innuendo and winds up demonstrating how clever people can be". Hepworth's view is blunt: "he has done, can do and hopefully will do better". Luckily, he was right about that.

Recently, Mick Grabham, one time Procol Harum guitarist and sometime Mickey Jupp collaborator, put it more forcefully than most would dare. He told Michael Heatley, who wrote the sleeve notes for the CD re-issue, "I can't stand it! It screams of trying to find an angle and cash in on who is kind of hot at the time. His own demos were the best it ever sounds."

Dave Edmunds agrees with that sentiment. He confessed to Bernie Keith on BBC Radio that it was always a struggle for him to improve on Mickey's home demos when he came to record masters of those songs for his albums. Yet *Long Distance Romancer* is as far from Mickey's demos as it has ever got, which is why it sounds so odd.

In parts - most parts actually - the album comes across less like a Mickey Jupp album and more like an audition tape for Godley and Creme: a sort of calling card to tout for further production work. The pair insensitively impose a wide variety of unsuitable styles over Mickey's fine songs - although it could be argued that this may not be his best ever collection of compositions. Maybe he'd used up his usual deep well of quality material on *Juppanese*, because as a solo artist this counts as Mickey's "difficult second album", (if one discounts the three Legend band-based efforts and the one compilation that preceded *Juppanese*).

You Made A Fool Out Of Me makes a good start point, however. It opens with a dark and malignant guitar riff, hiding like a shark beneath the fattest, richest backing vocals Jupp ever recorded. Mickey's lead vocal is sinister, brooding, unsettling. The overall effect is spooky, like a handwritten note from a stalker. The saxophone then arrives and commandeers the bridge sections, slipping into interesting discords while the guitars ring on. The track feels stronger than the song in places, though, and Mickey's lead vocal is a tad passenger-like, as if he's clinging on for dear life. While not as visceral as the original Stiff reading, it's clearly the right single to pick and a fine way to kick off the album.

Were it all this good...

Chevrolet is a bubbling Bo Diddley of a number, featuring Messrs. Godley and Creme playing their parts well but all too evidently. Mixing themselves considerably louder and drier than Mickey's vocal, they seem to be vaingloriously promoting their own contributions. Mickey's voice has never before been so drenched in reverb. Slap back and straight echo merge to pin him to the floor of the mix like a wounded moth. Strange Doppler-effect guitars and backing vocals flutter past - interesting but diverting. The guitar solo is on the one hand fairly pointless, yet on the other as show-offy as you're likely to hear.

Mickey only sounds himself for two unsoaked bars at the point of the false ending - which leads into an unnecessarily, almost comic, sequence of key changes, (count them). This simple song has lost its inherent power, drowned out by a flood of reverb and a host of gimmicky overdubs. Repeat after me, "I must remember less is more".

Barbara is far simpler and all the better for it. In his delivery of this lovely yet wittily pragmatic love song, Mickey sounds much more at home, although the bass part is still too fussy and too high in the mix. Bruce Lynch would have had the measure of it. Nice acoustic sounds, though.

Do You Know What I Mean? is sung by Mickey with a big fat wink in his voice. The vocal is pure 1950's slap back. Given the full rockabilly treatment, right down to the cymbal-free drumming, the track really does swing but again the novelty treatment slightly overpowers the song. Mickey is a master of backing vocals, so Godley and Creme's 10cc-style backing contributions aren't needed, thank you. This shouldn't be the sort of pastiche that 10cc records like *Rubber Bullets* or *Donna* were: Mickey is a guy who respects this genre of music – don't make it sound like he's belittling it.

True Love is one of those simple slow rockers that Mickey writes and performs so superbly. He sings it well, but his voice is again heavily treated - this time, I swear, with ADT and a touch of phasing! Plus his backing vocal parts are sopping wet, though pleasantly choir-like. These shortcomings might have been survivable, but the fussy producers couldn't leave it there. Fuzz guitars fiddle, anvil percussion pings, snare drums double flam, male voices growl, and soprano saxes wiz around as the thing grows to Spector-like proportions. All that's missing are the Ronettes and Emerson, Lake and Palmer's giant gong at the end, (and where is the end, by the way? This track is way too long, seriously outstaying its welcome).

Politics is a pithy, witty song; an intimate little number - or at least it would be without the pantomime-style production from which it suffers. Let's do jazz: mmmm, nice. Or not. Noodly guitars and be-bop cymbals; harmonies in 7ths, 9ths and no doubt 13ths; the whole thing delivered the way Spike Jones and his City Slickers would have done it on 78rpm shellac. A waste, a crime: truly god-awful.

Hard Times shapes up as though it's going to restore some sanity. It's a nice song, taken relatively straight. OK, Mickey's backing vocals have become a Welsh male voice choir, (and, then less forgivably, a Welsh female voice choir), but his lead vocal only has a modicum of reverb to battle through. True, the drums are too prominent in pattern and volume, as are the guitars in places, but compared to previous offences this one is minor. Until it all starts to unravel as it runs on: it's too long again and towards the end Mickey's vocal performance loses any pretence at interest, rather mirroring the listener's predicament.

Switchboard Susan is a very different arrangement to the one that nearly made it to *Juppanese* but it really swings along - the lowing Muscle Shoals brass part working a treat. Mickey's voice would have been better with a click or two less reverb on it, and why do we have to listen to more 10cc backing vocals in the choruses when the guvnor is on hand? Worst of all, the guitar solo is eight bars of your life that you'll never get back. By the end, Andy Mackay's sax has uncannily begun to resemble a lost, distressed duck. So it's nearly, but not quite.

I'm in Control is presumably ironic, Mickey never having been less in control in his life. It's the ultimate evidence that Mickey has given up, for it clearly should have been left on the editing room floor. It's played (and more depressingly partly sung) as cod reggae. The guitar part sounds like a first run-through while Mickey sounds as if he is only singing it because someone is holding a pistol to his head. It's probably the worst thing he has ever recorded in his entire career so it's a real pity that it's so bloody long, (again).

Make it Fly opens with such simple dryness that it shocks. You soon have your hands together in prayer that things will stay that way. It's a tremendous song with gripping lyrics and some unexpected melodic twists. Personally, I would have chosen a more standard Hammond organ sound behind the gentle acoustic, rather than the Baptist Chapel one that appears here. That apart, it was nice of the producers not to plaster goo all over at least one of the tracks. That, plus the quality of the song and Mickey's vocal delivery, makes it an all too rare highlight.

Some redemption then; right at the very end.

As a whole, though, nil points. As *Sounds* noted on release: "Even the higher points lack the wit and charm they should have, as if the object of the exercise had been to spotlight Jupp, songwriter. In attempting to effect this, they've removed him from the very element that made him: twelve bar rock and roll".

It's a shame to be so negative but overall this album is a bit of a stinker - despite probably costing as much to make as all Mickey's previous albums put together.

Stronger characters would surely have binned it and gone again, freshly alert to the dangers of using radical experimentalist musicians to produce an album by a man whose songs already speak for themselves. But the money had been spent.

Long Distance Romancer is proof that it isn't always true to say you get what you pay for. If this were a school report, one would be tempted to write at the bottom, in red ink, "Must try less hard".

As if to prove the point, on the 2013 CD re-master there is a bonus track: the Chrysalis single-only release, *Rooms In Your Roof*. It has a rambunctious arrangement, lots of fat sax parts, hefty drumming and a non-Jupp voice (as we now know, girlfriend Hilary). But it's oh, so much better put together; an object lesson in how to introduce additional colour into a Jupp song without crushing it underfoot. If only Pete Wingfield had produced *Long Distance Romancer*.

So why wasn't *Rooms in your Roof* a hit, then? Well, while it's great fun, it had been a while since Fats Domino or the Coasters had sold many records...

It was a fine final effort but it, like Mickey at this point, was out of time: its lack of sales success spelling the end of the Chrysalis experiment.

14 Standing At The Crossroads Again

In which Mickey is forced to tread water for a while, but still manages another fine album

In concert   courtesy Lasse Kärrbäck

I'm standing at the crossroads again
With an empty heart and a dollar ten
Maybe I'll bump into some famous names
Robert Johnson, Elmore James
I'm standing at the crossroads again

Standing At The Crossroads Again by Mickey Jupp, As The Yeahs Go By

The Chrysalis deal was history and the phone wasn't exactly ringing off the hook with enquiries from other major labels. All the same, when an artist possesses real quality there will always be pockets of interest in his work - sometimes from the least expected of places.

312

Over the years, Mickey Jupp's records had been released all over Europe, a few even more widely, in the US and Australia. It is sometimes the case that an artist is better appreciated outside his home country than within. ("Big in Japan" is such a truism that the cliché eventually became adopted as the name of a real band). Overseas success happened to Legend with the *Life* single: the one that made it big in Italy, and for a long time interest in Mickey as a solo artist had been growing in Northern Europe, particularly in Germany. A label in Hamburg called Line Records had shown faith in Mickey's work by releasing some of his earlier UK material. Mickey had often repaid the favour by gigging across Germany in support of those albums.

Keen to keep their artist active and in the frame, Mickey's managers now pulled off an inventive deal. Mickey would sign to make an original recording for Line in the German market, which would also be licensed on to Smash Records in Sweden. It might find an outlet in the UK; it might not. The search for a new UK recording contract would continue regardless. In the meantime the message to Mickey was clear: keep going.

Given the narrow geographical scope of its planned release, resources to make the new album would be restricted. What wouldn't be restricted, as usual, was the supply of songs. Mickey had been as fecund as ever: another tall pile of candidates awaited the selection process. The other key element to be sorted was who would produce this time. There wasn't the budget, nor probably the inclination, for any more star names. In the end the issue proved surprisingly easy to resolve. Strongman Management still represented the Sutherland Brothers who, out of contract with CBS, had broken up their band in 1979 in favour of more production work. They might be a good match for Mickey: not least because they, too, were songwriters at heart.

Gavin and Iain Sutherland had been Scottish folk singers and writers who, after a couple of albums as a duo, had teamed up with a band called Quiver to form the ingeniously named Sutherland Brothers & Quiver.

Together they recorded several albums, spawning a sizeable US success with their debut single, followed by an international hit with *Arms of Mary*. However, more profoundly, back in their earlier days the brothers had been clever enough to write a little tune called *Sailing,* which, once in the hands of Rod Stewart, became their pension. Now the Sutherlands could afford to spend much of their time at Trick Sounds, the home studio they had built in Stoke-on-Trent. Great: the producers could provide a studio, too, and it probably wouldn't cost that much to rent. Their wives, eventually credited on the sleeve for their efforts, would provide the food.

As for a band, Mickey already had one, ready-made. The current Jupp/Clouter/Bronze/Duck variant of the Mickey Jupp Band had been playing together for a while and would do just fine for the sessions. Dave Bronze recalled how he'd first got involved with Mickey's revolving band of sidemen:

"Well, in time honoured style, my day job in a music shop was to help finance my musical career. I actually knew Mickey before, as he also worked in another local music shop. He was a bit of a local hero. One day he came into Tim's shop, where I was working, to buy strings. We were chatting over a coffee when he said he was about to go on tour in Europe and didn't have a bass player, so I volunteered. That was it! When I joined Mickey, I already knew how to rock, but he taught me how to roll. There is a very elusive and beautiful roll in well-played rock'n'roll and R&B that is not always obvious to fledgling players. Mickey has it in aces, and that was the first time I was exposed to it full on. It was a most important period for me. Incidentally, I played with Mickey again on a one off gig in Southend for the first time in over 15 years. The guy was still awesome!"

The album that Dave and the band recorded in a studio in Stoke was, naturally, called *Oxford*. As before, the title was chosen merely because it forms part of the title of one of the songs on the album, *Oxford Dick and the Words*. Right. (Recently, Mickey privately released a CD of his songs called *Cambridge*, simply because this earlier one had been called *Oxford*. Given his way with words it is remarkable that decent album titles so elude him). Bob Clouter remembers recording *Oxford*:

314

"Although *Oxford* says it's produced by Ian and Gavin Sutherland, it was mostly Gavin who did it. Ian had the bigger house up in Stoke on Trent, with a studio built on, but Gavin spent the most time in the control room. I remember Keith Reid lent Mickey a Saab convertible to drive up there because his old Triumph Herald had broken down. Mick isn't the greatest of drivers, so it got quite hairy at times! It was a good atmosphere on that album. In the evenings Gavin used to trot us around all the local hostelries 'cos he liked a pint as much as we did."

Following the recording sessions, the *Oxford* band toured Germany, Holland and Belgium, recording a number of radio shows along the way. Bootleg copies of several of these gigs remain in circulation and illustrate how strong Mickey's live performances were at this time.

The most commercial track on the *Oxford* album was undoubtedly a rumbling half-pop half-blues number titled *Don't Talk To Me*, the strength of which was immediately apparent to Keith Reid, who had no doubts about its potential, "*Don't Talk To Me* came out great – that was a bit of magic."

While the album didn't have any planned UK release, managers Keith Reid and Nick Blackburn thought this song would make a strong single over here and so put it out on Keith's own tiny Good Foot label, with another *Oxford* track, *Junk In My Trunk,* on the flipside. Despite the lack of clout this minnow label and its second-division distributors were in a position to muster, the excellence of the song prevailed and radio DJs began to play it more and more as Keith recalls:

"We had a really good song plugger working for us, so we put out *Don't Talk To Me* as a single on our own little label and got great airplay."

But thanks to puny distribution, record shops quickly ran out of stock, just at the point of take-off; something Nick Blackburn remembers with a wince:

"It got to about number 70 in the charts. We had a Radio One Record of the Week on it from one of their DJs. I remember ringing up the distributors, Pinnacle, and screaming at them because they hadn't got enough records into the shops and people couldn't buy it anywhere."

However, Mickey's previous label but one caught wind of what was going on and offered to re-release *Don't Talk To Me* on their imprint, to give it better distribution and some extra momentum.

And so it came to pass that Mickey Jupp found himself back on Stiff, a label that had previously unceremoniously dumped him. Duly tarted-up with a picture sleeve, (which did feature a photo of Mickey for a change), the record was re-issued, though without any greater chart success, despite continuing airplay. But the song was too good to go away, which is why many major artists including Chris Farlowe, Dave Edmunds and Joe Cocker have covered it. Each regularly played the song in their live acts while Edmunds put it on an album of his. Joe Cocker even sang it with an all star band including Eric Clapton and Ronnie Lane at the Cow Palace in San Francisco in 1983, one of a series of concerts from which an LP was eventually released – but Mickey's song missed the final cut, so no royalties came his way, (although you can find it on YouTube).

Another sad chapter, it seems, in the story of his life.

The *Oxford* album came out as planned in its designated territories. The resourceful German Line label even followed up their release of *Don't Talk To Me* with a 12" maxi-single (the new name at the time for that old favourite, the EP), featuring a proper version of *Switchboard Susan*, ie Mickey's live BBC studio version of the Rockpile, rather than Godley and Creme, arrangement. (It can be found on the recent *Kiss Me Quick, Squeeze Me Slow* retrospective box set).

Yet the *Oxford* album wasn't officially released in the UK until as recently as 2014, when a suitably re-mastered CD finally saw the light of day. As Nick Blackburn says, "It was made quickly and fairly cheaply. It wasn't a very good album, partly because it wasn't a very good studio."

What it did do, though, was act as a placeholder: something to keep Mickey ticking over while better future options were located. During this relatively quiet period Mickey continued to play with a band sporadically and also jammed with various musicians: on a number of occasions Suzi Quatro, for whom Mo Witham now played guitar.

He was to be seen out with brother Dave from time to time. He set up a Friday night card school with friends like John Denton and Colin Crosby. He also briefly took up one of his most unlikely personas: M Jupp, session musician.

In 1981, the Texan, Mac Curtis - a veteran Sun rockabilly star from the fifties, no less - was recording a new album called *Truckabilly*, (no, no idea why). Later re-issued on a privately pressed CD as *Rockin' Around the World*, Mac was backed on the original sessions by a group called the Rhythm Hawks, with one Mickey Jupp manning the steam piano on four songs! Mickey has no recollection of this happening, or how or why it happened. As the CD has proved very hard to track down, being a US private release, nobody else knows what it turned out like either. Along with a tiny dabble in production work for Steve Hooker's band, The Shakers in February 1982, this was long thought to be the extent of Mickey's extra-curricular activities as musician or producer. However, evidence of further endeavours has recently come to light.

It turns out that since the late seventies, Mickey had been making a little extra income by renting out his modest studio facilities to other artists who wanted to make demos or simple albums, the 8-track Tascam machine Mickey owned being good enough to record a basic album on. Even if a pro could have spotted the difference in quality compared to a full scale recording studio, it was good enough to illustrate a song or satisfy the demands of a fan for a cheap recording by their favourite local act. Mickey explained to me how this facility came about in the first place:

"My little studio over in Hanningfield was a converted stables that belonged to some friends of mine, Jill and Martin Cook. We were great mates and they were well into their music, although not my sort of genre, more Pink Floyd. Martin said what about putting a recording studio in that building we don't use any more? So he put some money up and I put some money up and we bought the gear and soundproofed the place as best we could. We had an enormous carpet in there as dampening but it was basically a live room, not too live but live, and great for drums in the alcove.

We had Sure 57s on snare, bass and two overheads, and it sounded great. In fact Mike Vernon liked it so much, he used it to record simple blues albums; he loved the place. It was mainly for my own demos – I wrote *Modern Music* in there, for example, but I did twiddle knobs for one or two other people to earn a few bob. Bands used to rehearse there, too - one was called Holy Joe, I seem to remember. And I used it to rehearse the *Some People Can't Dance* album – in fact, the first time I played with Tex Comer was there. I also recorded local musician Steve Hooker there, and the Bottles. Still got the tapes but they and a load of other things are in this ex-lady's house in Southminster."

One such demo tape remains in the possession of occasional Jupp associate John Denton, member of the stillborn Kilroy and former keyboard player with Wilko Johnson's Solid Senders, who had interviewed Mickey in the mid-eighties for a planned book about the Southend music scene, a project he never completed. At the time of the interview – the transcrips of which have predictably but frustratingly disappeared – Mickey gave Denton some of the demos he was working on. These included *Playing the Machine, In the Country, Dream Song, My Female Friend, Lover By Night, The Usual Crew, Heartbreak Today, Right Now I'm Down, Ohio, Stranded in Manhattan* and *Marnie's Song*. (This last song, named for his long lost daughter, may well have been inspired by him meeting her for the first time, backstage at a Dickens Inn gig in the eighties).

Amazingly, in March 1982 Mickey also produced some early electronica at the studio for City 19, a band he was surprised to find he enjoyed working with, despite the unlikely musical fit.

But it wasn't all sweetness and light in the new studio. Back in 1979, Bobby Harrison, last heard of in this story as drummer of Procol Harum, (who else?), and before that the Rockerfellas, (who else?), joined forces with bass player Walt Monoghan, formerly of Bobby's band, Freedom, plus an ex-Raider from Romford, guitarist Clive Mulcahy, to form a blues band.

After playing a few gigs in parts of Essex as far flung as Brentwood and Southend, (ie not very), it was decided that the time was right to get their music down on tape.

They chose Mickey's place in Chalk Street, Rettendon for the job - by now named Cookhouse Studio after Martin and Gill Cook who owned the premises - with Mickey as engineer-cum-producer. Band guitarist Clive Mulcahy takes up the story:

"Mickey was, I believe, between marriages at the time, lodging with friends on a farm in West Hanningfield. The owners had stables and several outbuildings, one of which had been converted into a rehearsal studio with a control room to enable demo recording - I was told Susie Quatro rehearsed there. Bobby felt it would be good to meet Mickey and take a look at the studio, so after a swift pint we drove over there. Mickey was drinking a cup of coffee, reading the paper at the kitchen table. 'Ah Mickey, I would like you to meet Walt and Clive who are playing on the album' said Bob. 'Ullo' came the gruff reply, barely taking his eyes from the paper. After a difficult silence Bob said, 'Mickey, I thought we could just see the studio while we were here?' 'Well I haven't got all day Bob, I've got a gig tonight'. Driving back, Bobby was quite embarrassed by Mickey's behaviour."

All the same, the sessions did proceed, though the recording didn't go smoothly:

"I wanted to overdub some lead guitar fills and a solo, but before the take Mickey spent considerable time at the desk getting a sound he liked. Eventually he was happy and I said 'That's great Mickey, let's go with that, it sounds just like Clapton's Blackie Strat!' His response? 'Yeah - never liked him.' The irony - that I was actually playing a Les Paul - seemed lost on Mickey! Another song, a Bobby co-write, was *Over the Bridge*, a rock ballad with some interesting chords.

Mickey piped up from the control room that he could possibly add some keyboards and asked what the chords were in a certain section. I believe there was a major seventh, an eleventh and a thirteenth chord and the song modulated between two keys. I went to some lengths to explain this and the voicings I was playing, to which Mickey responded 'That sounds like Musicians Union stuff to me, perhaps I won't bother - (long pause) - 'ere Bob I thought you were doin' a blues album?"

Clive did meet Mickey one last time at a gig/party in another outbuilding on the farm after several acts including Mickey had played a set.

"He was really good," recalls Clive, "and I told him so as we were queuing at the bar afterwards. 'That was really good' I said, 'I enjoyed that'. A flicker of a smile came from Mickey, 'Oh I'm no one special - just play a bit and write a few songs now and again.' he responded. Unfortunately, as a bit of a joke I nodded my head and agreed, 'Oh yes we know that!' His face turned to thunder and he responded 'I don't think eight albums is doing too bad, do you?' and stormed off!"

It's interesting to think for a moment about Mickey's response there. Is it the response of a cocksure, arrogant, self-confident artist who knew he had more than earned the right to respect? Surely one might have expected a man of Mickey's proven talent and broad experience to laugh off Clive's facetious comment. But he didn't, or couldn't. It's this vulnerability, and the prickliness it can accidentally create, that so often brings about a response from Mickey that others can find disappointing or offensive. Indeed, it can sometimes be that the any miscommunication works the other way, as my brother Andy Wade once of Southend band Wolfe and subsequently a pro musician in Las Vegas, and thus no mean guitarist himself - recalls: "I was a big Legend fan so did unofficial roadie work, ferrying Bob & John to gigs mostly, so I didn't really know Mickey that well. Basically, I was in awe of his talent and wasn't sure that I had a right to talk with him. Years later I got the chance to meet him properly but found myself still tongue-tied. I said something dumb I think - I guess I blew it because I had so much respect for him; I was still a bit scared of him."

As a result of these sorts of situations, in which one or both sides are on their guard, there are legion tales of Mickey's grumpiness floating around the business. In fairness, though, you would be hard pushed to hear any one of these negative stories without also hearing the high regard in which the alleged 'victim' holds Mickey's musical talent. As Steve Hooker, who got to know Mickey well down the years, affectionately puts it, "Mickey only really does Jupp", but then adds, "he can be very kind, a good mate, too."

Mickey himself doesn't recall that many of these painful occurrences, but this should not automatically be assumed to be the result of a conveniently selective memory. Mickey considers much of his bluntness to be simply a manifestation of his honesty, and thus more forgivable than deliberate rudeness would be. Of course, the other reason he might not remember many such events is that all this stuff took place a long time ago. Mickey has a pretty good memory for the big issues but there was so much occurring, involving so many people, over such a long period, it's inevitable that some detail gets lost in the mists of time:

"There's a clip of me on YouTube singing *Memphis*, in fact three songs - quite a good little set - with Tex and Chuck, but I don't know who the drummer is! Can't remember at all." (We think it was Lester Gordon, Mickey).

One of the things he does remember from around this time was yet another brush with Rockpile. The first time he had decided not to leave Legend to join them at their formation. The second time he had fallen out with them while recording the *Juppanese* album. Now they were falling out with themselves. Messrs. Lowe and Edmunds were feeling that the fun had gone out of the enterprise and that solo futures might be more rewarding. And so it was that the band was looking for a replacement for one or both of them. Mickey had made it to the short list, in fact to the top of it, as he confirmed in a radio interview a couple of years later:

"My name was put forward more than once, if they were going to keep the band together. But in the end they decided to scrap the whole thing."

The story of his life once again…

The *Oxford* Album

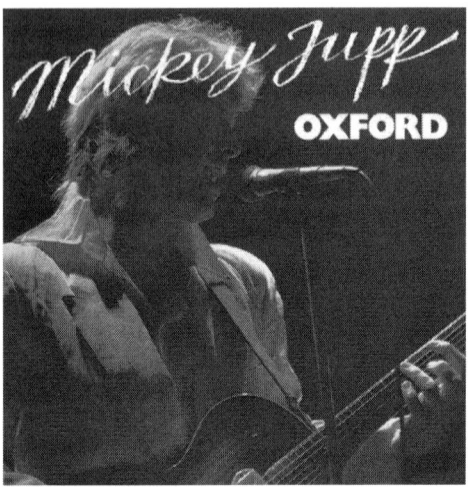

It's a shame that *Oxford* had to wait so long for its UK release as it's a respectable enough piece of work, offering up some good material and a rare chance since Legend days to hear a Jupp stage band at work in the studio. Bob Clouter is back on the drummer's stool in his best form, while Dave Bronze's bass playing is exactly the sort of revelation you might not have expected at the time but would now take for granted, given his subsequent career as Clapton's long-term bass man, Procol Harum alumnus and current member of Tom Jones' backing band.

Certainly these tracks feel relaxed: the product of a group of musicians who knew each other well, recording in the presence of a producer who considered himself there to serve the needs of the music rather than the other way round. And the style is engaging, having even been referred to as "barrelhouse" by one observer. On the other hand, the production can be on the flat side in places: the sound of the instruments uninspiring and varying little from track to track, which eventually grows wearying to the ear. Mickey himself is on the fence about it, commenting, "Mmm, I'm not displeased with it. It was recorded very cheaply…"

However you look at it, it's way better than the box of fireworks/dog's dinner that preceded it.

Oxford opens with the simple but slinky *Blues on Their Own*, neatly described by *Record Collector*, in their May 2014 review of the CD's release, as "chug-a-lug".

Drums, bass and rhythm are flanked by slide and tremolo guitar figures, in turn joined by a warbling organ as the song develops. An neat yet modestly understated bass part slots in beneath Mickey's half sung, half spoken vocal. The song boasts one of Mickey's favourite wordplay games: ending with a line that's slightly different from the one with which he began. Here Mickey ends singing not about how he loves the blues "*on their own*" but how he loves the blues "*on my own*". Keith Reid thought this number had broad appeal, trying hard to get Robin Trower to record a cover of this song, sadly to no avail.

Don't Talk To Me is Mickey at his snarling, sarcastic best, *("I picked you up girl, now I'm putting you down"),* made all the more effective by being overlaid on a backing track of creamy mellifluousness. The glowing Wurlitzer, steroidal drums and athletically pumping bass blend together perfectly in the mix, becoming almost a single instrument, the track progressing as if on rails. Twin guitar riffs and a reedy synth pick out the higher, hypnotic motifs. Great stuff. No wonder Mickey's management put it out as a single; no wonder Stiff picked up an option on it; no wonder it was a turntable hit with radio DJs. The only wonder is why it wasn't a hit? Oh, yes - no distribution. Also, perhaps, the subject matter might be touch too vindictive for Joe Public. However, it remains one of Mickey's finest lyrics – even though those who cover it, missing the extreme poetry of "*I'm off my handle*", tend to sing, "*I'm hard to handle*" instead. Mr. Jupp is smarter than that, boys.

The slightly curious *Soon Enough for Me* pops up next, all vamping piano chords and Leslie-treated guitar. The musical influence of Fats Domino is easier to spot than the purpose of the lyrics, which are often charmingly echoed by a chorus in the Roman sense - ie third party observers drily commentating on the singer's narrative - which in turn is beautifully, sadly sung.

It's tempting to put the next track, *Oxford Dick and the Words* straight in the box marked Novelty Song, but it's too good for that. This tawdry yet true-to-life tale of an egotistical rock band on the road offers an almost Spinal Tap vision of the awfulness of tired musicians trapped with one another in a fading career. It's wrapped in a strange percussive arrangement of drum machine, piano and bass, plus a weird synth sound evidently borrowed from the mighty Stylophone.

Junk in my Trunk gets us back on track with a boogie woogie piano and guitar core, the bass pulsing eight to the bar while the drums play an odd rhythm, just the second beat of the four. It's a simple but effective song of impending desertion, one of Mickey's favoured themes.

Monte Bronte & the Sisters is next up and I must confess it pretty well defies description. The lyrics may be a humorous little knock-off but the track is more Jerry Lee Lewis - rolling double piano part, double shuffle drums and a vocal sung in Mickey's best USofA rock and roller voice.

More than Fair is a sweet little song of devotion, given a highly unusual production. An extremely vintage-era drum machine, (cool or simply outdated? You decide), announces the song, to be quickly if unexpectedly met by a guitar sound one can only really describe as "US soft rock flange", a la *Bette Davis Eyes*.

Paired with a growling bass that cunningly plays only half the time, an unusual feeling of space expands within the track. Over this, Mickey sings the lead vocal in a kind of half patois, backed by thick wedges of harmony. With some power drums thrown in, it could have made it big in the States on AOR FM radio, REO Speedwagon-style!

Homework is a delightfully sleazy twelve bar with Frank Mead's scuzzy harmonica marinated throughout. Mickey sings his Chuck Berry-style set of words in an appropriate Chuck Berry manner, while Coasters clones appear on backing vocals. Yet more proof that musically, if it ain't broke, Mickey has no intention of fixing it.

324

Even For You is a slow piano lament in the Fats style, percolated by a Latin beat and an unexpectedly low harmonica chug, later joined by a thin church organ. Against this, Mickey sings in an unfeasibly high key, proceeding through some interesting chord changes, especially in the bridge. At the end the lyrics once again switch meaning, this time from *"even for you"* to *"get even with you"*.

Technique is Mickey showing off a rare Noel Coward touch. This stagey, jazzy confection is all witty lyrics, brushed drums, high bass lines and brittle vocal, almost as if delivered through a megaphone. I was about to say that it reminds one of the stylistic excursions of 10cc, but perhaps that would be an unfortunate reference, given the mauling Mickey's reputation had just taken at their hands.

The album rounds off with *Poison Girls,* an aptly named gobbet of bile that's almost punk in its gritty anger. A song about very bad girls indeed, it features some beautifully precise dual guitar riffs from Mickey, (not unlike those in the yet-to-be-recorded *Taxi Driver)*, which the band rumble around with economic menace. Towards the end there is a brilliant little Chuck Berry instrumental nod before the song fades away to a terrific bass line.

A neat little album, indeed, but no UK record company wanted it, even after Line in Germany, who had commissioned it, swallowed the production costs. One of the problems with UK take-up may have been the lack of an obvious second single to follow the very obvious first one, *Don't Talk To Me*.

A further factor may simply have been Mickey's growing history of non-achievement. It was beginning to look as if a combination of reducing sales volumes and advancing years were going to deny Mickey any further crack at musical success.

Not true, of course.

15 Never Too Old To Rock

In which Mickey finds a new label and a fresh start

Shorts on stage   courtesy Jo Meijs

Today's tunes are over my head
Let's make a million and get back to bed
All my rock and roll heroes are dead anyway

Modern Music **by Mickey Jupp, Some People Can't Dance**

The A and M initials in A&M Records stand for Herb Alpert (of Tijuana Brass fame) and Jerry Moss (of no fame at all, other than being a top promotions hustler in the record business with great ears). Started in 1962, the same year as Mickey's musical career, A&M had gone on to become the biggest independent record company in the world, thanks to the success of artists like The Carpenters, Supertramp, Peter Frampton and Squeeze.

It turned out that A&M's UK Managing Director, Derek Green, had been keeping an eye on Mickey for a while, not least because of his long term friendship with Mickey's co-manager Nick Blackburn, (for whom he had played as a ringer in the Chrysalis football team, taking the role of striker alongside Mickey Most's brother and ace record plugger, Dave). All the same getting a new deal was nevereasy, as Mickey noted just before he completed his 'escape' from the Stiff contract:

"Last year I did two tours – Elvis Costello and the big Stiff one – and after that I didn't want to go out and play anymore. I want to tour again now, I've got the taste back, but I've got no band or record company at the moment – legally I am still signed to Stiff but once I find another label we will draw up papers, pay them anything we owe them and say bye-bye. It might be Chrysalis next. There was talk of A&M but they've just dropped right out of the picture..."

Nevertheless, in 1981, Strongman managed to re-enthuse A&M, turning that slim prospect into a two-album deal, the start of which Mickey recalls vividly:

"Derek Green was an OK bloke. He took me to lunch in his Roller, I suppose to welcome me to the big time, even though the restaurant we were going to was only just around the corner so we could have easily walked. I remember his motor was always full of family rubbish and stuff, a bit of a tip inside. Apparently, he took Elkie Brooks out in it a while later - she was on A&M, too. He'd been playing himself a cassette of some of my demos, so it came on when they set off, I guess. That's where she first heard the song *She Could Have Been an Army*. Elkie loved the song and right away wanted it on her next album, which was in the planning stages."

Though that wasn't exactly what the song would end up being called, as Mickey points out:

"It was, of course, written as *She Could Have Been an Army*, so it had to be switched to *He Could Have Been an Army*. If it was about anybody, it was about Hilary – she and I were an item from 1977 to 1981. Elkie really did love it, and still does: she plays it on stage to this day, I believe. I'm afraid the demo Elkie would have heard disappeared ages ago, along with loads of others. Left at one of the houses of various ladies I've seen down the years, I guess."

Another part of the plan for Elkie Brooks' next album, eventually to be released as *Live and Learn*, was for it to be produced by music business veterans/writing legends Leiber and Stoller: the very two guys whose writing and production for the Coasters had sparked Mickey's first interest in pop music back in the fifties.

Surely, they would be bound to do his great song justice?

In the event, not only did they make a great job of producing Mickey's composition, they even paid him the extraordinary backhanded compliment of 'improving', or you might say muscling in on, his song. In this quaint showbiz custom a small part of an original song is replaced by an element the interloper has written, in this case part of a single verse. For this 'upgrade' Leiber and Stoller got a split writing credit with Mickey and, more importantly for them, a slug of the writers' royalties. This practice goes on right up to this day, known as "add a word and claim a third" - surely the basis upon which one recent Rita Ora song was credited to no less than *twelve* different writers.

These days, Mickey is fairly philosophical about what happened:

'I still get a kick out of that co-credit. But they didn't have to do what they did – they threw out a perfectly good verse of mine, put one of theirs in and nicked half my money. They're a couple of old-school shysters, I guess."

As it turned out, Mickey's loss wasn't as great as it might have been:

"The album didn't do too well, unfortunately. They even put my song out as a single but that didn't work, either. They thought it was going to be a hit: they'd done the TV session for Top of the Pops, but it never made the top thirty."

Album and single prospects were not helped by the fact that, while recording the album, Elkie had become pregnant - curtailing what promotional work she could undertake to support the record. If this seemed an extreme example of what Mickey often refers to as "the story of my life", there was still worse to follow.

After the failure of *Live and Learn*, and given the fact she was now a new mum needing time off the road, A&M decided to issue a compilation album of Elkie's previous material, spiced up with a few new tracks.

It was to be called *Pearls*.

This was a reference to her big hit, *Pearl's a Singer,* which had been co-written by Leiber and Stoller, yet originally composed, (as well as performed), by Ralph Dino and John Sembello – which sounds like another strange writing arrangement. What's more, the compilation would be TV advertised: a new, risky and very expensive promotional strategy.

"The next album of hers, *Pearls*, sold tons," explains Mickey ruefully. "My track was supposed to be on it but it got left off - no one could say why, not even Derek Green, it just didn't happen. 'We can't tell you why, Mickey' he told me when I asked, because we all knew Elkie loved that song."

Pearls got to number two in the UK, staying in the charts for an extraordinary 79 weeks. At the time it became the biggest ever UK album by a female vocalist, going on to sell 1.2 million copies. Elkie certainly loved Mickey's song enough to put it on later compilations, (there have been thirty in all!), sending a trickle of income towards Jupp, Leiber and Stoller, but it wasn't the torrent that inclusion on *Pearls* would have generated.

"I remember going round to Elkie Brook's place, after she'd recorded *He Could Have Been an Army*, to say hello and sit at the piano and see if anything else might work out, but it didn't. She signed an album for me, though, writing 'Love from Elkie – what a nice chap you are'!"

So not everyone falls out with Mr. Jupp.

Looking back over his entire career, Mickey believes that this cock-up was probably the turning point; the one thing he would most like to change, if he had the chance. The exclusion of *He Could Have Been An Army* from the *Pearls* release meant more than a loss of income.

It marked the point at which Mickey began to truly believe that, whatever he did, he was never going to make it; that the fates were always going to work against him. A bit of hope had slipped away for good: from now on Mickey firmly expected *not* to succeed. This was a critical time for such doubts to begin to enter his mind: he was with A&M to make his own records, not other people's, and needed all the confidence he could muster to get through what, for him, was already going to be a trial.

The above story is, though, version one: Mickey's honestly remembered tale of what occurred, and I'm sticking with it because I love the symmetry of it – which is why I also put it in the prologue. But Keith Reid has an alternate take; one that, given his unusual powers of recall, plus the fact that he was both Mickey's publisher and manager at the time, may be more accurate, if less satisfying:

"At Bluebeard, where we published Mickey's songs, our admin deal was with Rondor Music, who were a pretty good publishing company. They would have been helping us get Mickey's songs out in the world for other people to cover.

Through them we got *She Could Have Been an Army* to Elkie Brooks for inclusion on her next album, which Leiber & Stoller were signed up to produce. After they had recorded the song, A&M found out that Leiber & Stoller wanted a share of Mickey's publishing on it in return for a ludicrously small change they had made to the lyric. So Derek Green rang us up, shamefaced, and said, 'Look, I'm really in trouble: we've made this album, which cost a fortune, and Leiber & Stoller have a clause in their contract that means they can stop me releasing it if they aren't happy. They are insisting on a credit on Mickey's song - you've got to help me out!' When we told Mickey that the producers wanted a shared songwriting credit, he was absolutely delighted to be sharing a song with his idols! So it wasn't a problem. On the back of that agreement we asked Derek if he would make a record with Mickey, and he agreed – which means we actually have Leiber & Stoller to thank for A&M signing him up."

You've paid your money, (unless you nicked or borrowed this book), so you can take your choice.

Either way, the line-up for Mickey's first A&M album seemed to be taking shape rather nicely.

First came the choice of producer: the widely respected Mike Vernon, a man who had worked with countless major acts including John Mayall, Eric Clapton, Fleetwood Mac, Focus and Ten Years After. He loved bluesy music enough to have left his job as a staff producer at Decca in order to form the Blue Horizon label. This was surely the man to finally get Mickey the sound he wanted. Mickey confirmed afterwards he indeed had been:

"*Some People Can't Dance* was with Mike Vernon – a good lad, we're still in touch. We did it at his own studio in Chipping Norton, a really good place."

The heavy lifting - the slog of arrangements and run-throughs - took place closer to home in the slightly less salubrious Cookhouse facility at West Hanningfield:

"It was in my little studio that we'd rehearsed the album. It was the first time I met Tex Comer, the bass player – I remember picking him up at the railway station. We found him as he'd played with Frankie Miller for a while, who had the same management as me."

Tex was quite an industry character, having started out in Warm Dust, before joining Ace in 1972. Ace's big hit *How Long* was not, as might be assumed, about a chap's anxiety over the potential infidelity of his girlfriend, ("*How long has this been going on?*"), but rather Ace writer/singer Paul Carrack's concern over the potential infidelity of his bass player. That bass player was Tex, who had allegedly been planning to join another outfit. (Interestingly, the band he was rumoured to be flirting with was none other than the Sutherland Brothers and Quiver, the leading lights of whom Mickey had just recorded *Oxford* with.)

The rest of the musical crew were equally interesting choices. Especially the always-tough job of drumming for Mickey - but this time Mr. Jupp was happy:

"Steve Holly out of Wings was on drums. He was good and he enjoyed it so much he even played a few live gigs with us when the album came out."

Tex Comer recalls the importance of getting the right drummer for Mickey:

"Steve Holly on drums was fabulous. Mickey had a thing about drummers: he was always very difficult to please. He wanted it really simple – as soon as they started to play fills he'd get agitated! We ended up going through quite a lot of drummers over the years I was with him."

On guitar, it was the return of Mickey's old musical sparring partner, Mo Witham. He was relishing the chance to play with Juppy once again, and was impressed with the quality of the set up at Chipping Norton:

"We had great players in a great studio: a pool room, a Scalectrix room, beer on tap in the kitchen, lovely meals cooked there for you every evening, after which you could go on recording or maybe visit the pub opposite. Dream studio, dream producer in Mike Vernon, what else could you want?"

It should have been a smooth run, but inevitably it wasn't.

Even before recording began, there was trouble brewing, as Bob Clouter - at that time drummer in Mickey's live band - recounts:

"We were aware the album that turned out to be *Some People Can't Dance* was coming up. I already knew Mike Vernon as I'd done some sessions for him before.

The band played Dingwalls in late 1981 and Mike came along to see us. He took Dave Bronze and me to one side after the gig to tell us how much he was looking forward to getting us down to Chipping Norton and working with us on the next record. Then everything went quiet for a bit and one day we heard Mick was indeed in Chipping Norton, but with other musicians."

Bob was taken aback, but given how long he'd worked with Mickey not entirely surprised:

"The next time I saw Mike Vernon, long after the album had been made, he said how shocked he'd been that we'd got dropped on the eve of the album being made. But that's what it's like with Mick. I still like him, though."

Mickey hedged his way around this later, saying in a radio interview, "At the time this album was due to be made I didn't have a band as such on the road - I wanted to play with Mo again if I could." But later in the same interview, he admits that he had "a little band until last summer that Bobby Clouter was in."

When you talk to Mickey's musical friends, this is the sort of story you will hear more than once. They may feel slighted from time to time but they know two things for sure: firstly, the man is musically brilliant, so you take what you can get, and secondly, he doesn't really mean to hurt them - it just happens. So they tend to shrug it off or turn a blind eye. Here's Dennis Masterton, the man whose time with Mickey stretches from recording demos for the first Legend album in the sixties to playing bass on stage with him now, nearly fifty years later:

"Of course he can be difficult, but we all love his music: I've got everything he ever recorded, I think. He doesn't realize that he offends people. It just doesn't occur to him. He's a genius in my eyes, and all geniuses are a bit different, a bit odd I suppose. In fairness, his standards are very high for himself, too. I've heard him say 'I wish I could have played better' after a really good Mickey & Mo gig.

The problem is that when it came to being really successful, he maybe bottled out. So he wasn't the star he could have been – but we all know how extraordinary he is. He's his own worst enemy: a genius - but a flawed genius."

As the writer Eric Sykes memorably noted when commenting on fellow writer and comedian Spike Milligan's brilliance and attendant instability, "Geniuses are multi-faceted. Like diamonds … and hand grenades."

Mickey's short fuse, his apparent rudeness, also comes about because he is one of life's more solipsistic souls: a man who can't help but see everything through the lens of his own priorities. What is important to him is only whatever matters most to the current project. Past friendships or future prospects are irrelevant to achieving this goal. All he does is what he considers right for the job in hand - even if that means scolding musicians whom he generally respects and has played with for decades. He doesn't understand the hurt of others because he remains unaware of what others feel - indeed he wouldn't truly understand their hurt if he did. As Dennis commented, "Even when you're playing in his band, he keeps himself to himself - you don't socialize or talk the music over with him."

Much of this reticence is down to Mickey's self-confessed reluctance to confront sticky issues. For example, in the case of *Some People Can't Dance,* explaining well in advance to his stage band that they were not going to have a role on his next record. But might there be a deeper reason still?

Could Mickey's lack of confidence, combined with his desire to maintain control of pretty much everything, put him under such severe stress that he ends up unconsciously creating the very dramas that plague him at crucial moments?

If it's going to go wrong anyway, why not get one's retaliation in first? That has to be a possibility, when you hear him say things like this:

"I've never liked recording studios - it's like writing a book twice: you've got the song, got the feel for it, lyrics all written, demo made and then you've got to go to the studio and do it all again. It's at best a necessary evil. When you're in a studio with your band and a recording team, you know you're at the office. You can't muck about: you've got to do the best you can. Sure you've got all day and tomorrow, maybe all week, but not forever. I remember recording *Taxi Driver,* which opens with my guitar riff, the one that slides up the frets. As I recall we only played one take. Steve Holly, who played great drums on that album, said at the end, 'Thank God that's done.' I was amazed because I felt sure I was the worried one, the one most likely to muck it up."

With these doubts and fears in the back of his mind, it isn't surprising that, on the first day of recording *Some People Can't Dance,* self-imposed disaster once again seemed to be the order of the day, as Mo Witham recalls with a shudder:

"That very morning, just before the first session for the new album, Mickey had cut his own hair with scissors - so it was all over the place - and decided to give up smoking! Within an hour his Gretsch was flying across the parquet flooring. He'd made it go wrong when it was all set up to be great. He had a bunch of really good musicians ready to go but instead of exciting him it seemed to unnerve him."

There are plenty of artists who tend to do this, almost revelling in their problems: setting things up so they are bound to go wrong; providing themselves in advance with the alibi that they had always said it was never going to work. Yet another chapter in what they might choose to term 'the story of their life'.

While the atmosphere did improve over the next few days of recording, Mo recalls that the traditional 'Mickey versus the producer' flashpoints still occurred:

"He's happy recording his home demos because he does it all himself and so can control every note and every sound. For a long time he's used a particular synth voice that is peculiar and very dated. Years before, Gary Brooker had asked me if I could get hold of that synth and throw it in the sea, so horrified was he by this particular setting that Mickey kept using. Now he tries to sneak this horrible sound on to the new album. Mike Vernon said, 'It's a nice part, Mickey, but look, there's a lovely Hammond over there - try it on that.' Mick says, 'I like it sounding like this.' Mike replies, 'Yes, but most people don't, including me, and I'm the record producer!' So it got left off, thankfully."

There was a synth on the album, though, and a most unusual one, as Mickey explained:

"I took my Wurlitzer to the sessions but never used it. They had a proper Yamaha grand piano and I used that instead. In fact the thing I'm disappointed with throughout the album is the sound of the piano – I'd rather have used a Yamaha electric piano. The organ sound is a Casio M10 synthesizer – it cost £69, is eighteen inches long, has only four pre-set sounds but when you run it through a box of tricks it comes out sounding like a Hammond! They had a real Hammond but it sounded over the top!"

The only "real" synth on the album was one added later by session man Bias Boshell on the track *Modern Music*.

Unsurprisingly, that old chestnut of reverb on vocals came to the fore again, prompting Mike Vernon to gently chide, "Tell you what, you write the songs, Mickey, I'll make the records."

Perhaps that's one reason why the process of mixing the album turned out the strange way it did, as Mickey recollects:

"With Mike Vernon producing, I used to sit in the TV room long after all the musicians had gone, keeping out of the way while he was doing the mix. They'd call me in when they'd done one and I'd make the odd comment and then go back to the TV room. They must have thought it very odd. But it's so boring. I'd want to keep in all the rough edges, like they used to in the old days. I mean they just recorded *All Shook Up* several times and picked the best take, no overdubbing or anything."

Despite the odd flashpoint, Mike Vernon recalled the process of making the album with a degree of pleasure when he talked about it to Will Birch for some later liner notes:

"I liked Mickey actually. It's a team game, making good records. We had a lot of fun rehearsing the material in Essex and we also spent some fun time at a local pub – eating, drinking talking about music and playing darts...mostly darts!"

The quality of the original material was particularly impressive, as the producer recognised:

"I loved *Taxi Driver* – Chuck Berry could not have written it any better. Another song I really loved was *Joggin'* ...but it didn't make any charts. I've always been proud of the album and disappointed that it didn't sell much better than it did. Maybe it was the right record but the wrong time."

At the same time, he recalls the odd tension:

"Mickey was never in a great mood at the best of times...he could be a bit awkward, doubtless as a result of always having been in charge of his own destiny. He probably didn't welcome having someone telling him what to do."

Mickey finds it difficult to talk about that side of his character - the aspect of it that drove him to create a drama at the outset of recording an album of such good songs, with such a good crew. He has been careful to keep such feelings out of most of his past interviews, but in 1990 Dutch magazine *De Telegraaf* found him in a confessional mood:

"At home, with my own equipment, I often get better results than in a completely equipped, super-modern, million-track studio. I've made singles with producers I didn't know and with musicians radiating that they were only hired for the job.

In a situation like that I get full of hatred. Mainly self-hatred. I don't like my own voice. I cannot communicate. I can't explain anything. That's why my musicians become gloomy and sometimes resentful. And on top of it I blame them for the situation. Moreover my sense of humour is rather black. I'm not difficult: I'm peculiar. I know that all too well."

And so did everyone around him. In an article in *Sounds*, David Hepworth remembered Mickey being described to him by a close associate as "undoubtedly the most miserable individual in the entire music business".

Given all the tension and bad temper involved in making it, one might expect Mickey to express a dim view of the album that finally emerged in February 1982.

Wrong: it's one of his favourites. So it should be. It's a cracking album with some great songs, terrific performances (including super sax from Howie Casey on several tracks) and – at last - really good sounds. Still no Mickey Jupp shot on the cover, mind you. Soon after it was finished, Mickey glossed over the pain and tribulation, telling BBC Radio London DJ Stuart Colman:

"Making an album is like a day job. I've found in the past I don't really get on with people in studios. But this time with Mike Vernon producing at his own studio we all had a great time – the band was great, I was particularly superb (laughs), Mike was lovely. I like it – the whole album I play a lot."

Knowing what a gem they had on their hands, A&M swung behind it, issuing a suitably fictionalized Press Release, (claiming that Mike Vernon had been bewitched by *Don't Talk To Me* which brought about the label's signing of Mickey), for the release of the first single. This was a remixed version of *Modern Music,* (an edit that is now finally available in CD form on the *Kiss Me Quick, Squeeze Me Slow* box set), backed by *Taxi Driver*. That didn't click, so in April another slightly beefed up and re-mixed version of an album track - this time *Joggin'* - came out as a single, with *Feel Free* on the flip.

A&M's marketing boffins had also come up with a wizard wheeze to promote this one, managing to get *Joggin'* adopted as the official song of the 1982 London Marathon. This distinction was celebrated with a picture sleeve, (no, of course there wasn't picture of Mickey on it). Mickey remembers the record coming out to a small fanfare:

"Chas & Dave reviewed it in the paper and said 'Mickey Jupp deserves a hit, but this isn't it.' They mentioned *Pilot,* so they obviously knew what I'd been up to, which was nice."

There was some touring to support the album, particularly in Europe, where
Mickey fondly remembers a concert on the Callantsoog beach in Holland, August 3rd 1982, recorded for the radio show *VARA's lijn 3*. (A picture of Mickey at this show – wearing shorts, what informality – graces the opening of this chapter.)

Other concerts took place in France and Germany. In May, Mickey had also recorded a short set for French TV, with an introduction by a very youthful Antoine de Caunes, no less. It would have been great promotion, had the album been released in France...

In the UK there was very little happening, Mickey admitting to only fancying playing pubs like the Golden Lion in Fulham and the Half Moon in Putney, claiming on radio that, "I'm getting a bit fed up with playing bigger venues and chancing my arm."

To everyone's disappointment, despite having made a great album and releasing two catchy singles, Mickey had still not troubled the charts. He wasn't surprised himself, though:

"At that point it was the best record I'd made. Some people had high expectations for it, but to me it was just another album done. Already I had an expectation not to sell records. That's the way it is. I sometimes get a lot of airplay but that doesn't make a hit."

Some People Can't Dance turned out to be the last time Mickey was to play with Mo Witham for almost a decade. Having turned down the chance to replace his disciple, the departing Wilko Johnson, in Dr Feelgood in 1976, ("their touring schedule and lust for life would have killed me"), Mo had accepted a role in Suzi Quatro's hard-working, (but less socially OTT) touring band. Mo became Suzi's lead guitarist and from time to time Mo's wife Kellie joined the line-up as a backing vocalist. The pair made their living together playing music while this new adventure took them around the world for the next nine years.

But even after that, there would still be plenty of time left for Mickey and Mo to make more music together.

In the meantime, Mickey had a second album to make for A&M.

The *Some People Can't Dance* Album

A&M must have been very pleased when they heard the tapes for this one. Great playing and production; Mickey singing well; strong new compositions - even if, to quote the standard industry observation, one "can't quite hear the single." In part this may be because of Mickey's penchant for writing songs about unusual subjects, perhaps still under the influence of Leiber and Stoller. His more oddball lyrical diversions really come to the fore on this outing: we've got the benefits of fitness, the evils of smoking, cartoon heroes with human foibles and inhuman cab drivers without foibles as subject matter for songs.

We've also got a great band.

Alongside Mickey there's Mo, in top form on guitar – so much so that producer Mike Vernon made him his session guitarist of choice for years afterwards. On bass is Tex Comer - previously of Ace, the Sutherland Brothers, the Danny Kirwan Band and the Frankie Miller Band – who never does less than a great job.

Drummer Steve Holley was a sessioneer who had experience with Elton John, Joe Cocker, Kiki Dee and Paul McCartney and had been drummer in Wings for three years. He's on fire, too.

Finally, on sax, Howie Casey, a veteran of the Liverpool beat boom – an actual contemporary of the Beatles from Hamburg days - who also played with McCartney in Wings, (as did long term Jupp associate and Southend saxophonist, Frank Mead). Howie was also a particular favourite of one time Legend producer, by now Bowie producer, Tony Visconti: more wheels within wheels.

Yet while it didn't produce the hit single everyone wanted, the album features an exceptionally high quality collection of tracks, as BBC Radio London DJ Stuart Colman noted in the 11th April 1982 edition of his radio show *Echoes*, a broadcast devoted to interviewing Mickey about his career and the new album. Colman opens the show by saying, "It's very rare that I pick up an album where just about every track is a winner - just one or two times a year – but this is one of them."

Mickey's response to this praise is typically low key. When asked by Coleman, a long-term fan of Legend, "How do you think those old Legend albums of yours stand up these days?" Mickey replies in an offhand way, "I don't know, I don't play them. It's water under the bridge really." The best he can manage is, "I'd like to do some of the songs again, re-record some of them."

Not a particularly positive way to drum up demand for the back catalogue!

(On the other hand, Mickey later spoke of his Legend albums to a local Southend paper in rather different terms, saying "they are long deleted but I'll pay good money if anyone has got them to sell. I wouldn't mind hearing them again.") Luckily, Coleman played much of the new album on his show, hopefully re-enthusing any deflated listeners.

Fittingly, *Superman* is up first. Starting with a flourish that parodies the famous theme of, er, Batman, we get a groove of intertwined guitars from Mo and Mickey over a cool, funky bass and some very classy drumming. This is one of Mickey's sort-of "novelty" songs: in it he taunts Superman for being a fake goody-goody *("you'd give a ton of Kryptonite for just one drag")*. There are two fine Mo solos and a top-drawer sax solo, too - the whole piece driving along very competently and reassuringly beneath Mickey's full-voiced, confident vocal. A stonking start.

Joggin' is also a bit of a novelty, but can be forgiven as it was a very topical subject at the time, jogging and marathons having unexpectedly taken hold of the UK public's consciousness and conscience. The original idea for it came from Keith Reid who had prompted Mickey to write a song about the subject, a suggestion that was initially rejected, "I said I can't really do that sort of thing, but after a couple of days I thought I'd better have a go..." Mickey famously hates the idea of writing songs to order, as he explained to me:

"Bob Fish wanted me to write songs for Darts, Wreckless Eric wanted me to write for him. But it's a completely different ballgame; I'd have to think of them. After five minutes I think, nah: I'll just write my sort of song and if anybody else likes it, that's great." (This was a point of view Mickey would temporarily adjust in the future but at this time he was adamant).

Joggin' gets the full Bo Diddley - the constant tremolo guitar laced with acid-sharp lead figures, bubbling drums and bass, plus a classy touch of organ. There are some lovely and unexpected blues chords in the bridge and some very big harmonies on the chorus. One can see why it would get picked off the album to be a single, and why it would get airplay, being unusual and topical, but one perhaps wouldn't expect tens of thousands of punters to buy a copy, given the cheesy subject matter. Taken a twice the pace it could have been Chas and Dave.

For our third song in a row on an unusual topic, we get the lovely *Virginia Weed*, a song all about Mickey's devotion to, and helplessness in the face of the dreaded nicotine, (oddly, we now know he had given up smoking just before recording it).

Delivered through an aching yet ironic vocal, Mickey sings over a smartly kicked tempo - delivered by drum, bass and guitar figures - that feels very late fifties Americana. A honky-tonk piano arrives in time for the neat solo, before a spoken word bridge, complete with backing vocals in observational third party Roman chorus style once again.

It all ends with a gospel feel and a rasping cough – how else?

DJ Stuart Colman noted the Dixie Chicken feel of the whole thing, to which Mickey replied, "We were doing it straightforward at first. Then I said to Mo, 'let's just try putting the *King Creole* riff across it', and that's how it came out. We didn't set out to sound like Ry Cooder or anything."

Maybe Baby, is not the famed Buddy Holly song but a US-style rocking blues on the traditional subject of boy and girl and love; more specifically in this case the recovery of a boy's love for his girl, (*"maybe, baby, I'm beginning to love you again"*). This is not an outstandingly original song by Mickey's standards but it's an excellent ensemble piece, showing off nimble drumming, some superior Chuck Berry-style guitar from Mo and an extremely complicated triple set of backing vocals, setting up a kind of "round". It must have taken quite some time to achieve, notwithstanding Mickey's exceptional pitching and phrasing abilities.

Feel Free is another love song, although of the opposite emotional persuasion to the last: this one is about fearing the imminent loss of a girl, (*"feel free to feel free"*). It features a highly original chord sequence vamped on piano with a soft organ alongside. A terrific sax part echoes Mickey's sensitive, pain-wracked vocal while Mo contributes a wonderful spacey multi-tracked guitar solo. It's hard to categorise this one, being Fats Domino influenced in places and yet more like an Otis Redding soul ballad in others. Either way, it's excellent.

Title track *Some People Can't Dance* is a pacey rocker with shuffled snare, fast rhythm guitars and urgent sax blasts. There's a groovy walking bass, a scorching Mo solo, a honking sax solo, an organ that sounds like Chris Montez' *Let's Dance,* a closing riff borrowed from *Watch Your Step* and some archetypal fifties doubled-up handclaps. I couldn't quite make out the kitchen sink but I've no doubt there's one in there somewhere. All in the best possible taste, mind you. Mickey relishes his vocal: "*Some people just can't dance, Some people can't rock and roll, These people got no chance, These people ain't got no soul*".

342

He is, of course, half-singing about himself: a man famous for not being prepared to dance, a soul that he confessed had only entered the portals of a dancing emporium once in his life, very briefly. As for "no chance", he most likely refers to the resulting reduced opportunity for getting together with females.

Taxi Driver opens with Mickey and Mo playing infectiously slinky intertwined guitar figures, setting up snapping drums and stubbed bass, to create a rhythmic stew that rolls and simmers on slow boil. Mickey barks out his sarcastic lyric in the first person, as the mouthy cab driver himself, while Mo interjects a fine steel guitar solo. It's the perfect example of rock that rolls. I would have considered it more suitable as a single A-side than the B-side it became - it's certainly a big favourite in Mickey's live act to this day. It's also a lyric dear to Mickey's heart:

"I have experiences of taxi drivers and truck drivers, and I do get uptight. It's an attitude people have towards their fellow man these days – nobody seems to give a damn about anybody else, and taxi drivers are the worst."

Modern Music is the track that first brought Mickey to Ry Cooder's attention, (as we shall see), which is interesting because while the subject matter is quintessential Jupp - the old songs are the good ones - it isn't sung by Mickey in his typical style. Perhaps in deference to the semi-latin arrangement the band opted for, Mickey croons this one, never stretching or cracking his voice along the way. As always on this album, it's beautifully played with an authentic old-style sax solo in the middle. Sublime it may be but the lyric is barbed, as Mickey explained at the time in an interview:

"I got a bit fed up making up excuses for why I didn't like most of the music going around for the past few years. You watch *Whistle Test* hoping there will be something good on - and then think no, maybe it's a generation gap thing - but actually I think a lot of it is simply rubbish. Some of them haven't got a clue, not an ounce of talent", quickly adding, "I'm not bitter, either."

The finished product sounds more benign though and, unusually for Mickey, feels less Coasters and more Drifters to me, though I can't quite put my finger on why - perhaps it's the creamy consistency of the whole thing.

So That's What It Is feels a little lightweight in comparison. The 'M. Jupp gospel choir' hums under a spoken introduction before this piano-led 12 bar shuffles into life. Doo-wops and a fat sax chorus set off Mickey's somewhat reverby voice, (no doubt a matter of some debate at the mix). It ends with a short bass solo!

The album closes, to my ears a little strangely, with *The Gospel Song*.

In theory a big gospel-style number at the end of an album could work well, but this one doesn't quite pull it off. Firstly the tempo seems more country than gospel, as does the bendy, picked lead part. Under this lies a funky drum and bass bed, slightly undermined by a parpy organ synth – an unwelcome whiff of the dreaded Jupp demo sound. Mickey sings passionately enough, but something here doesn't quite feel sincere, coming across more like Elton John in his ersatz *Tumbleweed Connection* phase. Maybe some brass would have helped lift it. Anyway, it ain't bad – it's just got a lot of very good competition to measure up against. For this is a truly fine album, as Mike Vernon himself maintains, and he should know.

In fact, it's hard to see how it could have been much better, other than by the inclusion of an example or two of the sort of song Mickey seemed by now to have stopped writing: the totally tortured ballad that featured so strongly in the Legend Vertigo era. Perhaps he needed to get back to writing on a baby grand?

In fact, his writing was starting to go in the opposite direction.

16 Nashville

In which Mickey makes it to the States, if not in the States

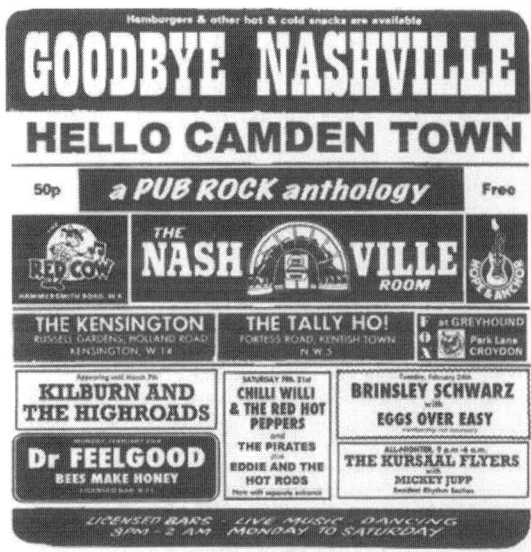

Sanctuary CD Box Set cover

They can keep their money,
I'd rather be nobody,
At least that way I get to be myself

Nashville by **Mickey Jupp & Chris East, X**

The track *Modern Music*, a single from the *Some People Can't Dance* album, turned out to be more than a song. It was to become a calling card.

Although not released in the US, Mickey's label, A&M, was an American organisation and information about artists would have been freely swapped between the UK domestic operation and HQ in the States. Plus Mickey had an active publisher at the time, one looking to encourage covers of his songs, everywhere and anywhere. However it happened, *Modern Music* somehow came to the attention of highly respected US songwriter and performer, Ry Cooder.

Ryland Peter Cooder, three years younger than Mickey, is best known for his seminal slide guitar work and his support for roots music of various types - sparking collaborations with traditional musicians from many countries.

Ry produced the worldwide hit soundtrack album *The Buena Vista Social Club*, for which he was nominated for an Academy Award. He has also written several film soundtracks, such as *Paris, Texas*. He has won Emmys and played on the Rolling Stones' *Let it Bleed* album, falling out with the band over his claim to have originated the riff on *Honky Tonk Woman*. He was ranked eighth on *Rolling Stone* magazine's 2003 list of "The 100 Greatest Guitarists of All Time", his many playing styles having featured in collaborations with some of the world's top musicians, including Eric Clapton, Van Morrison, Neil Young, Randy Newman and The Doobie Brothers.

Now he wanted to collaborate with Mickey Jupp. Not bad.

"Ry Cooder wanted me to write songs with him. He'd heard *Modern Music* and really liked it. So my management people fly me and my wife to Santa Monica, where he lived. We're in this apartment a couple of days when there's a knock on the door and lo and behold it's Ry Cooder. Apparently his record company wanted him to have a proper hit, not another cult success, and thought I might be able to help. At the same time, though, it transpires he's in the process of drying out. So I went round to his place a couple of times to try and write with him, but it just didn't work out. Firstly, there was a kid of his there, who kept being awkward and getting in the way of things. Then Ry wouldn't settle down; he was going for jogs and not concentrating properly on the writing. It just didn't work, perhaps partly because I wasn't used to writing with somebody else. With Chris East, one of us would take a bit away to work on or add a verse or something. Not just sit staring at one another, waiting for an idea to emerge. I can't do it like that."

Within three or four days Mickey felt that he'd had enough of getting nowhere, and quit the process. This might just have been a rash decision, and not only from a songwriting perspective.

Not long afterwards Ry formed Little Village - a sort of supergroup involving, amongst others, Nick Lowe on bass.

Some believe Mickey's visit wasn't just a writing trip but also an audition for that band. Either way, writing or playing with Ry Cooder could have opened up the US to Mickey's talents.

Perhaps the reason why they didn't hit it off was simple. As has been pointed out, Ry Cooder was pretty damn close to being America's own version of Mickey Jupp: a stubborn, independent purist, uninterested in doing anything that looked likely to be an obvious commercial success. Mickey himself hints at this when he says, "we were both loners, really; he's his own man like me, so we cancelled each other out".

Keith Reid spelt it out a little less charitably:

"All I know is Mickey finally met his match: somebody more moody, more cantankerous, more bloody-minded even than him", he observed with a knowing smile. With the benefit of hindsight, this bringing together of two difficult and fiercely independent strangers wasn't ever likely to succeed. They knew little or nothing of one another's music; they were meeting in manufactured circumstances created by business interests they loathed - interests looking for both to be more commercial, against their wills.

"It wasn't working", Mickey recollects, "so they flew me down to Nashville. We stayed in this nice apartment block but the weather had turned, so there weren't that many people around to write with. I met Guy Clark but not much more, so me and the wife switched our tickets and went to Orlando, where she came from, for me to meet the in-laws. Not a great idea, actually."

Despite the trip turning out to have been little more than an impromptu holiday, Mickey and his publishers were keen that he should try again in the USA, especially when, a little while later, one of Mickey's compositions literally turned to gold: the Judds' cover of Mickey's song *Tears For You* ended up selling more than three million copies. We will get to that shortly.

Mickey recalls a number of subsequent writing trips to Nashville, some paid for by him, others by his publisher, all in the hope that Mickey's UK freshness could be combined with the experience of a US country music 'old hand' to create a magical songwriting blend.

A few more million-plus sellers would be a ticket for the gravy train, and with publishers taking 50% of the writing royalties, it was worth them investing in a little seed for their potential golden goose.

"I went to Nashville three or four times in all," Mickey recollects. "'We're going to put you on a silver bird to twang town', they told me - they really did say that. Overall I suppose I quite enjoyed it, although I honestly don't think I learned that much. I co-wrote a song with a bloke called Spady Brannan called *Heartline*. It wasn't bad, actually. Then I worked with another guy called Kent Robbins, who also wrote for the Judds. 'Nice people, great cheeseburgers', is what I'd say about Nashville."

Nothing concrete seemed to come out of these trips. And given that Mickey's main aim in life was to spend his time in the Lake District, and an important secondary objective was to fly as little as possible, these unfruitful forays were distracting, costly and maybe a touch counter-productive, as well:

"Trouble was, every time I got on the plane to come back home I'd think 'What was that all about?' You see their ideas over there and ours over here about country music are very different. I'd got a song called *Seeing Simone* on the way already and was working on it with Kent, so we moved it around a bit, but after I came back I had a listen and then switched it back to my original way. Trouble is, I spent the next ten years or more of my life trying to write country songs. Waste. Of. Time."

Mickey was at least now getting on aircraft, something he had previously, famously, been unprepared to do. It turned out that Mickey's original unwillingness to be airborne was not the result of some ghastly flying episode; the sort of experience that might cause him to vow never to do such a thing again. Rather it came, child-like, from a feeling that he probably wouldn't like it if and when he ever got around to doing it... The flying phobia came to an abrupt end one day, out of the blue - no pun intended – when Mickey was left with no choice but to get himself on board a plane:

"The first time I flew was in Norway – Oslo to Sondheim. I was doing a radio interview out there one day and the DJ asked me where I was playing next. When I told him he seemed a bit surprised and asked me how I felt about having to fly, because he knew I didn't fancy it - yet apparently that was the only way I was going to be able to get there in time. It was news to me but I thought I'd better do it: there wasn't much choice, was there? Three quarters of an hour it took and I was fine. I don't mind flying, actually – it just gets a bit boring on long flights like the US ones."

In one bound, our hero had overcome a problem that it turns out he never actually had. Each time Mickey flew back to the UK from his American jaunts, he kept on gigging, although he was finding the collapse of the local live scene particularly depressing:

"Shrimpers on Sunday nights – at the football ground - is the only place to play in Southend these days, since the discos took over. Most of the bands are very bland these days; God knows where they even find to play to get experience - although I do like Ace Bentley and the Traffic Lights. I get to them support me so I can hear them again!"

In London, things were not so bad. January 1983, for example, found Mickey's band recording a full set live at the Dublin Castle, a couple of tracks from which were released by Ace Records on their *Live in London* LP series. The whole performance exists on a bootleg, if you know who to ask. In May he was playing the Grand in Leigh with Gary Brooker, which led to the idea of a Shades reunion gig, something that duly followed on 20th June - a charity event at the Dickens hustled together by Mick Brownlee, the original Paramounts drummer who had also played with Mickey on occasion. The packed-out show featured the Rockerfellas, the Orioles, the Paramounts and, er, Suzi Quatro.

From Mickey's point of view, live performance was very much the core of what he did. It was the part of the job he liked most, or at least hated least. It was the thing he always got paid for. It was something he could always rustle up a bit more of if in need of a few extra bob. So it's perhaps surprising that there aren't more live recordings of UK gigs in existence.

Thankfully, though, over the years Mickey made a number of radio appearances that were recorded for posterity. Recently, the best of these were polished up and released on CD, much to the delight of Mickey's loyal fans.

The quality of these performances is incontrovertible evidence of just how good he was at his peak – and for just how long that peak lasted.

Mickey Jupp Live At The BBC **Album**

Sorry, but there's no absolutely correct place in the book to locate an appreciation of this album. It was recorded in separate sessions – two in 1978 and one in 1979, around the time of the Stiff episode. Yet it wasn't released until 2004, when Hux Records very kindly unearthed the master tapes from the BBC vaults - something the label specializes in - and gave them a little sonic tweak before releasing them. Some tracks, however, had already been made available on the German Line Records CD release *Oddities*, which came out there in 1987. It had to go somewhere, so I've put it here, OK?

Cheque Book kicks the whole thing off – and what else? This is the first of three tracks from a John Peel session on 29ᵗʰ June 1978, recorded in the brief downtime between the end of the tour supporting Elvis Costello and start of the Be Stiff tour promoting *Juppanese*. The tracks feature John Gordon on bass, Ron Telemacque on drums and Mick Grabham on guitar - the line-up from the Costello tour. Mickey gives a very spirited rendition of this Legend classic, which had become more widely known by then thanks to various cover versions. The sound isn't the very best but the playing is first rate, the whole thing slipping and sliding with a masterful, syncopated precision – no doubt born of recent consistent gigging.

Daisy Mayes is a terrific, gothic beast of a track, boasting a Roger Corman of an arrangement: packed with thunder from the drums and lightning from Grabham's screaming guitar. These heavy, spooky sounds match the sullen menace of both the lyrics and Mickey's sly, knowing vocal delivery. It's heavy, man and would have been perfect for a single. In the end it was never recorded for anything at all, other than this session. Big shame.

Anything You Do also harks back to Legend days, but this slinky performance by the band is subtler than the original version. Another great guitar solo is matched by a terrific, animated vocal from Mickey, who was clearly on particularly good form that day.

Making Friends is the first of five tracks recorded on 21st November 1978 for the Stuart Coleman show, taped just one month after the release of the *Juppanese* album on Stiff. This time the band is the Cable Layers, with whom Mickey collaborated on the Be Stiff tour that had finished (in the UK at least!) just two days earlier, so they should have been pretty well rehearsed. They were Vic Young on bass, Mac Poole on drums, Pete Gosling on guitar and Geraint Watkins on piano. On *Making Friends* the sound is rather muddy and some of the mixing and stereo imaging is frankly a bit odd (for example, the guitar panned hard right), but once again the playing is excellent. Mickey's vocal is perhaps over-reverbed and gets a bit swamped as a result, but as consolation there's a great bar room piano sound when Geraint takes a solo. Does Mickey sound a teeny bit tired from all the touring, or is it one's imagination?

Down at the Doctor's is something of a rarity, for while it's in some ways his best-known song, there aren't too many recordings of Mickey himself singing it. This version starts out acoustically, quite similarly to the original Arista B-side, with Mickey singing conspiratorially. One by one the instruments pick up: piano first, then a strong bass driving to an almost jazz-like guitar solo. Mickey even name-checks Radio One in an amended lyric, and ends with a full blues, "Yeah". It's a great reading of this newly minted classic.

Switchboard Susan finds Mickey's first-rate vocal awash with the hated reverb, although it does suit this number better, contrasting with the venom of the backing. The rhythm track cooks like a cauldron, although the solo is a bit weak. Interestingly, this version is based on the abandoned *Juppanese* arrangement – making its inclusion a bizarre example of Mickey promoting a song he'd recently chosen to leave off the actual album! (A different, apparently studio-based, recording of this arrangement appears on the box set *Kiss Me Quick, Squeeze Me Slow*, the provenance of which is unclear.)

Guitarpicker Slim is a real shock, being taken at a mighty pace and in rockabilly style, rather than the gentler *Juppanese* album version, (where it's called *Down in New Orleans*) or the subsequent, even slower unplugged version found later in this same collection. This rendition has great backing vocals, stonking piano, Latin rhythms and eight to the bar bass at its chugging heart. Top quality stuff.

So Long brings this particular session to an end with a very energetic Rockpile-like arrangement of a song that appears nowhere else in Mickey's canon. Why he dropped this song from his repertoire is unclear, but he didn't waste it entirely as a good chunk of the lyrics (and a riff from the bridge) resurface later in his more successful composition, *Don't Talk To Me,* (while there's a hint of the *Standing at the Crossroads Again* lyric somewhere in there, too). The song was officially published, though; and Dr Feelgood's rather good reading of it can be found on their twelfth album, 1994's *Doctor's Orders*, while Rick(y) Nelson also recorded it although it never got an official release. Mickey's version of this out and out rocker must have been great to see on stage: the perfect closing number, given that title.

You Made a Fool Out of Me ushers in four tracks from a BBC In Concert session, recorded in front of a live studio audience a year later, on 22nd December 1979, just a couple of months after the release of the Chrysalis *Long Distance Romancer* album. It is perhaps typical of Mickey's uncommercial ways, or - more charitably - a lack of rehearsal time, that of the four tracks captured here only one came from his new album: that track being this song, the single. The band featured Dave Mattacks on drums, Pat Donaldson on bass, Ian "Chuck" Duck on guitar and Frank Mead on sax. The sounds are great, with big fat drums leading a rock steady arrangement that relentlessly drills a hole through the listener's head, while Frank Mead's sax perfectly mimics Andy Mackay's on the record. Mickey gives another fine vocal performance, which the audience clearly appreciates.

Short List is a survivor from the previous year's *Juppanese* album. It's a true four-on-the-floor stomper that's sung by Mickey with great projection and Coasters' humour. Here, guitar twins with sax to create a wide sound. Again lots of reverb everywhere, big key change moments (both up and, unusually, down!), evidence of a super tight band. The audience loved it - wish I'd seen that session.

St James' Infirmary is Mickey's tribute to Bobby Bland, in a number he had been playing live for years and still does to this day. Nevertheless, the inclusion of this great blues standard may not have had his record label's fulsome approval, given that a song from the new release could have been plugged instead, but the band makes a good fist of it. Strangely, the fundamental simplicity of the song means it feels slightly underwhelming up alongside Mickey's own compositions, (I know Mickey won't agree and will find this comment embarrassing, but this is my review, not his). Frank Mead's excellent, if slightly strangled sax lifts the drama in places although it, too, now drips with excessive reverb.

354

Bony Maronie/Sweet Little Rock and Roller is a medley of further excerpts from Mickey's stage set. The full barrelhouse onslaught is only disturbed by one small snatch of a bizarre piping organ, a la Del Shannon's *Runaway*, (as this never recurs one is tempted to read it as player error). The whole thing sounds like a brawl in a bar, just like it should. It goes on long enough to warrant a fade ending, unusual in a live concert recording, (or was the guy mastering the CD running out of time?)

Guitarpicker Slim returns to open the final set of six songs: five of which are taken from the April 1978 *In Concert* recording, in which Mo Witham joined Mickey for a two-man acoustic set. This recording went out just before Stiff released the compilation of Mickey's earlier albums, in order to drum up interest in it. In fact this session was recorded in a gap between dates on the Elvis Costello tour, on which Mickey was playing support for the same purpose. It's therefore something of a mystery why Mickey didn't use the band and elements of his set from that tour, preferring instead to rely on his old faithful musical companion, Mo, for an interesting but comparatively low-impact broadcast.

He can't recall why himself, because the touring band, (the same line-up of Gordon/Telemacque/Grabham who played the Peel session a couple of months later), was fully immersed in a bunch of tracks that made it on to the subsequent *Juppanese* album, which would have benefitted from an advance airing.

Anyway, all that aside, this is a very interesting diversion for the Jupp listener: this rare chance to hear some of Mickey's best songs played in an unplugged format is fascinating.

Guitarpicker Slim suits itself well to an acoustic treatment and Mickey has fun wrapping his mouth around the lyrics in a way that would be impossible while fronting a full and noisy band. Mo's guitar work is delicate and intricate, embroidering patterns around Mickey's underlying rhythm, although the balance favours the flourishes rather more than the basic drive, which is a mixing error.

Wrong Food is a real rarity: only one other recording of the song is known to exist and that has never been released. This drowsy blues lament is a little gem, beautifully sung - in places almost acted out - by Mickey. Once more the mix of the second guitar elaboration is slightly overpowering for such a gentle number.

It would have been interesting to hear how it would have sounded in the studio, with a nice classy/lazy arrangement – it surely having been a candidate for the *Juppanese* sessions, where the song would have sat well on the side Gary Brooker produced.

Next up is *Pilot,* sounding as close as it could to how Mickey would have first sung it when trying it out in the folk club. The strength of this performance is its intimacy, although anyone familiar with Mickey's usual sweeping backing harmonies in the chorus will miss them. The two guitars sound much more integrated on this number, working well to weave beautiful patterns together.

Make it Fly is the star of the collection. This simple but beautiful composition is perfectly suited to the acoustic treatment it gets here, standing up brilliantly to the scrutiny such a sparse arrangement places upon it. Mickey's vocal switches from conversational in the verses to angelic in the choruses. It is the best version you will ever hear, Chris Farlowe's excellent cover notwithstanding.

Hole in My Pocket slyly squirms along, worming its way into the listener's brain, despite lacking the thump of the full band version. Mickey's vivid vocal brings each lyrical scenario to life in an almost cinematic way, reminiscent of - yes, you've guessed it - the Coasters at their very best.

The version of *Cheque Book* that closes the selection is a complete mystery.

The CD sleeve-notes claim that this sixth track was recorded at the same Mickey and Mo session as the previous five, but this is clearly nonsense as it features a complete electric band! It's hard to say which line-up incarnation might feature on it, other than to note that it's faster and less nuanced than the track that opens the album, and the playing is not of the highest standard. One small clue is the fact that it contains a sax part, almost definitely played by Frank Mead, but that apart its origins remain shrouded in mystery.

We should be grateful for the existence of this set, the odd misattribution notwithstanding. In part because it is the only way to get an official CD on which Mickey has recorded some rock and roll originals, something he never permitted on his other commercial releases, for a variety of reasons:

"What would be the point of that? I've got too much respect for the originals. And I don't want to be labelled a rock and roll singer – six months and you'd be dead. So I've made myself a promise that the only rock and roll I'm ever going to record is the stuff I write myself."

Live at the BBC also proves beyond doubt that Mickey Jupp is one of those super-rare musicians whose live performances sound as good as - frequently even better than - studio recordings. And by live I mean *properly* live: no auto tune, no overdubbing, no use of backing tapes, no subsequent re-patching of vocal fluffs. Stark, bollock-naked live. There really aren't many around you can say that about.

Sadly, there is nothing more lurking in the vaults, Lasse Kärrbäck and Rupert Williams having thoroughly scoured the files: everything else has been wiped and re-used, in order to save the BBC a few bob on recording tape!

17 Wrong Food

In which Mickey gets to boogie with the big boys but to no avail

Guitar Man   courtesy Lasse Kärrbäck

I'll play you a tune on this here guitar
Tell you 'bout the time I was nearly a star

The Ballad of Guitar Pickin' Slim by **Mickey Jupp, Juppanese**

It's 1983 and Mickey's A&M deal calls for a second album.

Like Tony Visconti before him, Mike Vernon has passed on the chance to make a second album with Mickey. A new visionary is needed at the helm.

Mickey gets out his by now somewhat dog-eared shortlist of candidates, with the 10cc now crossed off the top. He recalls that the few remaining entries included the name, Status Quo. If so, this turned out to be most fortuitous, as Keith Reid explained:

"After the failure of *Some People Can't Dance*, we were back in front of Derek Green who frankly didn't really want to do another record with Mickey. Now Derek Green loved Francis Rossi - not sure why but he did - so Nick and I hatched the idea of getting Rossi to produce Mickey's second A&M album. It was nothing to do with Mickey's choices, as I recall. Derek duly became much keener: 'Well, if you can get Francis Rossi to produce it, I'm definitely with it', he told us."

Francis Rossi was duly approached, sent some demos and, having had a good listen and liking what he heard, agreed to produce Mickey's next A&M LP. The musicians on it were to be, for once, the latest incarnation of the Mickey Jupp Band. Despite being left off the last album, Ian "Chuck" Duck would be on guitar, Tex Comer from *Some People Can't Dance* was back on bass and Paul "The Youth" Atkinson had assumed drumming duties.

With Francis Rossi at the helm you could hear in your mind's ear pretty much how it was likely to turn out: a chugging wall of guitars and tub-thumping drums; the mighty driving engine that would bring new life and punch to a selection of the latest Jupp compositions. It could be tasty and it could be commercial. In fact, it shot off in a rather unexpected direction. For starters, the album was required to be recorded as close as possible to Francis Rossi's home in Purley, which threw up The Factory in Woldingham, virtually next door. It was a small facility owned by producer and string arranger Dave Mackay, a man who had earlier produced Frankie Miller's one real hit, *Darlin'*. Mickey outlines the reason why it had to be round the corner from Rossi's place:

"At the time Rossi was going through a bit of a bad marital patch so we were forced to work near his place and do office hours. As a result I'm stuck miles from home in a little hotel, spending evenings in the pub thinking 'we should be working now'. Instead we were hanging around doing nothing."

There were a couple of other significant drawbacks:

"On the first day, there's one of his mates with him behind the desk: a bloke named Bernie Frost, who we'd never heard of but who just turned up with Francis. And they had this new gizmo, a keyboard thing called an Emulator, which they wanted to put on everything."

Rossi had retained top engineer Barry Hammond from the last album, so there was a degree of sonic continuity with *Some People Can't Dance*, at least in theory.

The whole team was enthusiastic, too, and well in tune with Mickey's songs. Along with his usual stash of fresh material, Mickey had a half-finished song he was still mucking around with - inspired by his new home in beloved Eskdale - called *Catseye Cam*, the name of a nearby Lakeland peak. Rossi liked what he heard, getting Mickey to play it to Tex Comer for a second opinion. In no time they were rehearsing it for inclusion on the album. Two of the other songs selected for inclusion, *Orlando FLA* and *Little Miss America*, were inspired by and dedicated to Mickey's new American wife, Dina.

(After five years with girlfriend Hilary, a period which Mickey - fast approaching forty and already twice a husband - had decided should not end at the altar, a whirlwind romance with Dina, plus a desire to help her overcome visa issues, suddenly resulted in a new Mrs. Jupp. Unfortunately, by the time the album was released Mickey and Dina had already parted.)

In a 2011 interview with Henry Scott-Irvine on *Resonance Radio*, Francis Rossi, like many before him, considered his experience of working with Mickey to have been a mixed blessing:

"Oh, Mickey Jupp. He's a silly arse, 'cos he's good. He's a very hard man to work with but he's extremely talented. He really is excellent. Great songs, great performer, the band all round him love him, want to do well. But he's shot himself in the foot time and time again. He's busy trying to trip you up, or himself, all the time. I'm trying not to knock him because I think he's great and I enjoyed working with him - it's just one of those things. That track *Orlando FLA* – I loved it! *Catseye Cam* was a great track. I really thought he would do well - that with those songs it couldn't fail...."

In fact, Rossi reckoned he'd got what he called a 'free ride' when it came to the production of the record:

"I thought what does he want me for? I can't do it as well as he could do it."

It was great that Rossi - a man with vast experience stretching from early Flower Power hits to opening the proceedings at Band Aid - was a Jupp admirer. But he was nevertheless taken aback by how hard to handle Mickey could be:

360

"I didn't realize the man was difficult - I don't think he sets out in his life to be difficult, he just can be. Some people will try to get their own back on you in this business...it seems a lot of people want to get him back for being difficult and I think that's a bit unfair..."

This ominous suggestion raises the question of whether Mickey was by now running out of road. Had his reputation for proving prickly started to close doors around the music business? It seems unlikely that Mickey was that worried, mind you, having not much relished the recording of the Rossi-produced album, as Keith Reid points out:

"I do remember taking Mickey down to Crawley to meet Francis, who loved the songs - we had a bunch of really good ones. But the recording process was less smooth. It was a little bit like the Rockpile situation, I suppose. Mickey didn't act up that much in the studio but he didn't enjoy the experience very much."

Tex Comer recalls the recording as being worse than just uncomfortable:

"After the fun of making *Some People Can't Dance*, the Francis Rossi one was hard work; we didn't really enjoy that one. There was a lot of stuff going on that Mick didn't like – drugs and stuff were always an issue for him. He just wanted to get on with it, as he does: play it and move on, but Francis was a bit of a stickler and kept wanting us to go back and do things again, try different tempos and all that kind of stuff, which ruffled Mick's feathers. I'm surprised in a way that we actually finished that album; there were times on the way back to the hotel when I was thinking, 'this is going to go pear-shaped and Mick's going to go home'. He was perfectly capable of it. I mean that's what Mick did; if he didn't like it he just went home."

Tex can see why these conflicts blow up so often:

"Producers all want to put their mark on things, whereas we want to do the best job we can of capturing live music. This leads to all sorts of problems. Recording is a slightly alien environment, which it takes a bit of experience to get used to, time to settle into. And then everybody gets fed up with the mixing stages that go on and on and on, while people have different ideas.

I used to let them get on with it and go for a walk but it was Mick's album, meaning he sort of needed to be there so they could drag him in to hear things. But in his mind he's already finished it: played it; sung it; all done."

Mickey himself had pointed out this conundrum very clearly in an interview with *Hot Press* a few years earlier:

"I write a song and after I've written it, the thrill is never...well...I've written it, and that's the big thing. I never experience the same thing with recording...I really don't know what to do with it sometimes. The song is there; I've done it. I've written it; that's enough for me. That's the trouble, I've got no direction in the studio."

Nevertheless, it was clear from what Mickey told a Scandinavian interviewer at the time, that he didn't want anyone else to direct him. When asked the question "Is it true you didn't like Francis Rossi producing it?" Mickey replied, "I didn't like the idea of *anybody* producing it. This is my 9th LP and I haven't really had a chance to do it myself..." That's one confused artist, then.

With or without sufficient direction, in September 1983 the album, *Shampoo, Haircut and Shave*, (named once again after a fragment of a lyric from a track within it) got its release. For once the package came complete with an image of Mickey on the cover, taken by renowned rock photographer Graham Hughes. However, it's rather indistinctly shot - so while Mickey is there, he's barely there. Many years later, Mickey talked about the process of shooting that cover photo in an interview with Roger Dopson for the sleeve note of the CD re-issue. He had found the whole enterprise a bit odd:

"It was daft – like all my other LP sleeves! My abiding memory of the photo shoot – which was done at Heston Services on the M4 on a very hot day – is that when we came to leave, the M4 had been closed because the tarmac was melting!"

The final audio product turned out to be a mixed bag, lacking the production focus and crisp musicianship of *Some People Can't Dance*. As a collection, the songs probably weren't quite as strong, either, and the sound was once again a bone of contention. So it was all a bit of a disappointment, as Mickey sums up:

"I don't like it much. I don't like the sound - it's too thin. At the time of the actual recording it seemed OK but something must have happened in the mix, it's rather tinny. I wanted some of Rossi's energy but it didn't work out like that – the production was never as up front as I wanted."

(It is perhaps significant that this LP was the last of the major label albums to be re-issued on CD. This was because Mickey's usual reissue outlet, the German Repertoire label, decided to pass on releasing it at all. Eventually it came out in 2014, years after the others. Even then, Mickey's dislike of the sound nearly scuppered that. Hux Records, who put it out, had to continually pester him to get him to agree to its release, after he had initially vetoed the idea).

Back in July 1983, as a taster for the LP's original release, two album tracks were issued as a single in a picture sleeve: *Stormy Sunday Lunchtime* backed by *Reading Glasses*. In September, to coincide with the album release, another picture sleeve single came out: *Boxes and Tins* backed by, er, *Reading Glasses* again, (why does this keep happening?) Unfortunately, neither single troubled the charts. Although that isn't to say that Mickey wasn't still making his mark in the business.

But the most significant event in Mickey Jupp's life in 1983 wasn't musical at all.

This was the year he moved up to Cumbria to start living in the Eskdale area - something that had been on the cards since he started dreaming of it, and writing songs about it, nearly twenty years earlier.

His brother David had found some cottages in the tiny village of Boot and had moved there with his family in 1971. Now he had gone abroad to work and needed somebody to keep an eye on the place for him. This was Mickey's chance to get up there for good, and rent-free to boot, (that was an unintended pun, so I've kept it in). He pulled no punches in telling Mick Walsh of the local Southend paper about his desire to re-locate, "I've wanted to get away for a long time. I don't like the state Southend is in. I know where I want to go. I can't wait to leave this place." Nice PR, Mickey.

Despite his new geographic fixation, Mickey was forced almost at once to temporarily abandon his beloved home, so that he and a band could tour hard to support *Shampoo, Haircut and Shave's* release in Europe. They were busiest of all in Germany and Sweden, where his fan base remained strongest. Between the 1st and 12th December alone, Mickey and his band played in Hamburg, Hutzel, Bremerhaven, Bochum, Cologne, Darmstadt, Freiburg - and back to Darmstadt for a second night! Unfortunately, they gave almost no performances in the UK, which can't have helped penetration of the album or the singles from it. Dave Vickers recalls one of the few that they did play:

"I had the privilege of seeing Mickey play live on the 11th August 1983 at the Red Lion in High Street, Brentford. *Shampoo, Haircut and Shave* was about to be released, so many of the night's songs came from that album. One recollection was that his new wife was in the audience - there are a couple of songs on the album inspired by her. I also particularly remember that Mickey kept referring to how young his drummer, Paul Atkinson, was."

In fact, the band line-up around this time variously incorporated no less than three different drummers: Paul Atkinson, Lester Gordon and the redoubtable Bob Clouter, (there is something vaguely Spinal Tap about this).

Whoever was drumming, the band usually played *Orlando FLA*, *Boxes and Tins*, *Don't Go Home*, *Reading Glasses and Little Miss Am*erica from the new album. The *Stormy Sunday Lunchtime* single was rarely played, although there is a clip of it from the German TV-show *Lieder & Leute* on YouTube.

By now Mickey had largely defaulted to his old phobia regarding playing his own songs on stage, something new fan Stuart Hopper fell foul of when he discovered Mickey's past work and went to see him play live:

"The first time I saw Mickey was mid-80's at the Dublin Castle. What I remember of that gig was that he refused to play any of his own songs. He did covers which was great but I'd been looking forward to hearing live versions of some of the songs I'd heard only on record."

Disappointing as that must have been, it no doubt sounded great and Mickey may even have looked fairly happy doing it, but you can't help but wonder what was going through his mind at the time. He'd just recorded another album, an experience he never liked. It hadn't turned out as well as he'd hoped, something he was used to yet always disappointed by. Once again it hadn't sold well. He was miles from his new home which would have upset him – especially as it had become a marital home, new wife Dina having moved up there after their marriage in March 1982, but that hadn't worked either.

Now he'd started missing gigs again, as a good friend who prefers to remain anonymous, recalls:

"There was a Jupp gig at the Dickens in Southend around that time. The thing was sold out, which meant around 200 punters had bought a ticket. My girlfriend and I had a beer at our local pub en route. To our surprise in walked Mickey and Dina. Mick mentioned something about soundcheck problems then joined us for a beer....and another...and....well, they spent the full evening with us, most convivial. Both Mickey and Dina were in good spirits but what about the 200 punters? And his band? I never did find out how the Dickens management were able to explain all that."

With his latest recording contract now out of time, he was having one last throw of the dice at nearly forty years of age, which would have depressed him. Yet this hard work formed a last desperate attempt to bring about something Mickey wasn't in any case all that interested in: achieving fame and fortune.In fact, by moving to Eskdale, Mickey already realised how much he had compromised any musical future, as he later told rock journalist Chris Welch:

"I wanted to get out of touring and be my own boss. I admit moving here was a bad career move. But as I got older and the road got harder I thought it was time to stop. I don't want to do gigs any more. I never was Ethel Merman - desperate to get up on stage and be a star!"

Surely his career was at an end now?

Actually, no, his bestselling song of all time was still ahead of him.

But what was true was that Mickey's major label recording career had finally come to an end. Five big recording companies had given him a good go. The songs he had recorded and the performances he had turned in had always been of a high standard. His producers amounted to an impressive bunch, but they changed too often, discouraged by Mickey's unquenchable talent for souring any artist/producer relationship.

Taken as a whole, Mickey's career had never really followed a clear trajectory. Instead it had meandered unstructured, sometimes seeming laissez-fare, other times almost willfully random. Mickey hinted at one possible explanation for this on the original *Shampoo Haircut and Shave* LP. In its sleeve blurb he thanks Keith Reid and Nick Blackburn 'for making me an overnight success', something he clearly wasn't and, by definition, by now never could be. While the comment was ironic, might it also have been barbed?

Had Mickey taken time to look back over the years and conclude that what seemed best at the time may have been unhelpful in the long run? Mickey's professional handling – management, publishing, production - had so often been about serendipity and working with mates, rather than any career strategy. He remembers times when he and his managers' priorities seemed at odds:

"It's true that a lot of my management, like Keith, were rather playing at it.

I think they only wanted me to make records, really. I was always much more keen on doing gigs and touring, because that's the only place I ever really made any money. I got bugger all profit out of records."

But when it's suggested to him that he might have benefitted from more objective, better-connected, stronger management, Mickey is unsure:

"Strongman and Bluebeard both paid me a retainer. They showed more faith in me than any body else had ever done: I've had lots of promises in the past but they paid me money: I call it folding faith! For these fellahs I tried to keep going, smile at the camera, attempt to be a pop star. But I haven't got endless drive.

So I wasn't sure I wanted a manager with loads of it, going round doing what I didn't want him to do."

Those who actually did manage him endorse that last sentiment, as this comment from Keith Reid, delivered in a carefully considered, evidently painful fashion, makes clear:

"He was very difficult. He didn't like performing his own material. I think he finds it easier to handle people saying 'Mickey's great; it's such a shame it isn't happening', rather than to commit himself to really trying, putting himself out there. At the time you just deal with it on a day-to-day basis and cope with it; the problems only became apparent as we went along. It's only in retrospect that you stand back and see it wasn't ever going to work."

Certainly *Shampoo, Haircut and Shave* was not the album to put thing right. Writing in *Record Collector* magazine in May 2014, Terry Staunton it sums up:

"Though always a witty and insightful writer, and with a strong voice, studio outings have never quite captured the joie de vivre of the man on the stage live."

Spot on, Terry – but it turned out there would still be time to put that right, even if not at the very highest level...

The *Shampoo Haircut And Shave* album

I hadn't much been looking forward to revisiting this album in order to review it for this book. It was probably the vinyl album of Mickey's that I'd played the least, certainly of the major label outings, and I suspected I'd bought the CD re-issue as much out of loyalty and completism as anything else, the *Record Collector* having given it a non-committal review. In fact, it's very existence was only as a result of a twelve-year campaign of attrition mounted by Lasse Kärrbäck to convince Universal, who owned the tapes, to permit its re-release – although even his persistence was insufficient to persuade Mickey to allow bonus tracks to be added to it.

So I was surprised and more than a little pleased to find a lot more to like than I had expected. And despite Mickey's disappointment with Mr. Rossi's input, it's actually a weeny bit Quo-like in places, you know.

Stormy Sunday Lunchtime is a case in point. While it sounds in many ways like a typical Jupp rocking blues, it also enjoys a very Quo locomotion – all heads-down guitar and solid-as-a-rock drums. On the other hand, the sentiment is very non-Quo. Would they have written a song about a chap having sex with his girlfriend's mother because the daughter had gone out unexpectedly? In fact would anyone other than Mickey Jupp? What an imagination he has: assuming it's all made up, of course. And as for the record company - given the subject matter it was hardly likely to attract much airplay when selected as a single, chaps! The heavily treated backing vocals sound like more than just Juppy, too. I can't help wonder, was Mr. Rossi singing along?

Orlando, FLA comes up next. With the dial now set at 100% Quo chug, this twelve bar, (with typical Juppesque inventive chordal departures in places), sits firmly in the boogie groove, tracked guitars mixed over Mickey's tinkling piano. Quite a bit of reverb fills out Mickey's well-handled vocal. Thin sound? Not a bit of it on the CD re-master: if anything this one sounds relatively bottom heavy, led by Tex's highly effective but primitively simple bass part. Even Mickey admitted, "the one that has the best production on it, my favourite sound is *Orlando, FLA* – that worked out reasonably well." The whole shebang ends with a wolf whistle, no doubt an appreciation of the new, American, Mrs. Jupp. Why not a single? Good question.

In Her Chair is pure late 1950s US upbeat love ballad. It's beautifully sung in multi-harmonies by Mickey, almost Jeff Lynn in their intensity, (from me that is a compliment) and tremendously well played by all, especially Paul Atkinson on drums and percussion. There are some nice slidey guitar parts from Ian Duck, but listen carefully and I swear you can just make out a hint of Mr. Jupp's mouldy old synth sound lurking within the darkest recesses. Mickey's long-time friend and musicologist Roger Dopson recalls that Mickey once told him whom this was written about, but he forgot. Mickey confessed to me that it was the French girl again, a woman who was the subject of four or five of his songs, lucky thing – I hope she aware and suitably grateful.

British Rail Blues (All Change) pounds in with typical Mickey intensity, only to be halted by open chords, left hanging. A big guitar figure and some train-sounding keyboards, (that pesky Emulator?) add edge to a song that's an interesting combination of two of Mickey's obsessions: rock songs and railway trains, and not for the first time. Listen harder and you'll wonder to what extent the lyric might also be a metaphor for Mickey's then hectic patchwork of a life: work all over the place for little financial reward might be obliquely expressed as, *"all change, there's no buffet on this train"*.

More Than Fair slows the tempo and transports us across to the pretty melody side of Mr. Jupp's songwriting. It's a little lightweight by his standards, and possesses a rather inappropriate synth solo, mixed too high, but it drives along well, thanks to Paul and Tex's well-drilled engine room performances.

Boxes and Tins is a great semi-Fats slow rocker, once again not without Quo feeling, especially the one chord guitar solo. It's tempting to think that the subject matter of the title might have been inspired by Mickey's recent experience of moving home, but according to Roger Dopson's sleeve notes, this song had been around for quite a while, pre-dating Mickey's big move North.

Don't Go Home slows things down a notch further, living off its synth sound so much that you can almost hear the ghost of Mickey's demo hovering in the background (but thankfully not that *actual* synth sound!). Intertwining keyboards weave around dead-straight drums and bass. As is often the case with Mickey, the song features a delicious and unexpected bridge, which he sings brilliantly the first time round, and over which Ian Duck plays a cool solo second time round. In places it's almost Stax-like in feel, so a sax part would have been nice, (couldn't the Emulator have emulated that?).

Hot Love sees the Bo Diddley beat spring back to life: a halting drum pattern with handclaps setting off a shimmering bank of guitars. There's an amazing half guitar/half harmonica sound from time to time, including the solo, which may be further Emulator evidence, in which case it wasn't all bad. Mickey's immaculate backing vocals reach banshee proportions in places. The track makes a nice sound but doesn't add up to much in the end, (although the end is actually quite musically witty - a deliberately clichéd key change occurring just moments before the song finishes).

Reading Glasses - the song so good it made it onto two singles - gets a real harmonica; uncredited, but presumably played by Ian 'Chuck' Duck, the artist previously known as chart-topping harp player, Mr. Bloe. This 'Dear John' song pleasantly plods along the on beat, Mickey's jangly piano poking through the deep bass and drum bed of the backing track.

Catsteye Cam is delicate and country - that country being the countryside of Cumbria, despite the Americanization of the lyrics in places. (Mickey has always preferred to sing of dollars and dimes than pounds, shillings and pence).
One has to love the folksy harmonica, along with great lines like "*I'm only lonely when there's people around*". The song could have happily stood some strings, had the budget been able to. Thirty year later I'm sure that Mickey would still swear by every word of its sentiment.

Little Miss America, which closes the album, has a Quo opening (with a bit of Abba thrown in!) and a generous dressing of reverb glooped on Mickey's lead vocal, which delivers a Chuck Berry lyric and overall feel. It's an irresistible live song, a great opener or closer. It's also a great album track. But it's probably not something the public in its millions were going to buy as a single.

In fact that's a big part of the problem A&M must have faced over *Shampoo, Haircut and Shave*. Despite Francis Rossi's oft-stated belief that the album was packed with potential singles, it wasn't - at least not for an artist in Mickey's position. It might have been true for an established band like Quo, whose followers were looking for another one, just like the other one, but there isn't much here that could be expected to break a near forty year old with a disinclination to play the showbiz game.

Mickey commented on its shortcomings himself, "Being honest, *More Than Fair* and *Hot Love* I was never overly happy with, while *Catsteye Cam* is one of my worst vocal performances ever - I cringe when I hear it."

(Not everyone agrees. Lynn Wagstaff, a leading light in Mickey's fan group, certainly doesn't. "My favourite song has to be *Catstye Cam*. Beautiful tune. Brilliant lyrics. The first verse alone is worth its weight in gold. Mickey has a knack of describing feelings I have actually had, with that wry humour he does so well. I did climb to the top of Catstye one year, intending to sing the song up there, but having reached the summit I couldn't bear to break the amazing silence... I know Mickey does not like the vocals on *Catstye Cam* - I do wish he'd record a version he *does* like!")

Beyond those specifics the album maybe feels a little aimless. There's not the naïve freshness of the first Bell *Legend* album, nor the inclusion of stunning ballads of the sort that gave *Red Boot* and its Vertigo sister *Moonshine* their special stand-out, and *Juppanese* its gentler side. Nor does it boast topical material like *Joggin'* from *Some People Just Can't Dance*, or that album's confident sense of musical accomplishment.

Those albums seem to represent the times that Mickey's career came closest to breaking through – the way everyone was sure it would, but eventually never did. If those great records couldn't do it, it was hard to see how this one would.

Shampoo, Haircut and Shave is good enough but it's beginning to evidence a narrowing of vision in song selection, or maybe even songwriting. Apart from the almost accidental selection of *Catsteye Cam*, the album pretty much ploughs a lone rocking furrow. Chances are Mickey had songs of a more varied nature in his bag; he always does. But chances also are that he, or perhaps his producers, didn't see the need to make room for them. He hinted at this when talking to a Scandinavian radio interviewer while touring it:

"This last album, well, we didn't have a good time doing it, we were glad when it was finished. I thought songs had gone to waste and the production was nowhere near as good as it could have been".

All the same, many artists would have been proud to have made this album. But Mickey had done better before, making this outing something of a disappointment.

The good news, had he but known it, was that he would go on to better things, although not quite yet.

18 No Place Like Home

In which Mickey bids farewell to the majors and starts doing things his own way

Loving the Lakes   courtesy Chris East

I won't play what I don't want to play
Even for two thousand dollars a day

The Ballad of Guitar Pickin' Slim **by Mickey Jupp, Juppanese**

In 1984, Towerbell Records - an obscure independent label with an eclectic, in fact downright bizarre artist roster featuring Snowy White, Shirley Bassey and Chas & Dave - approached Mickey about releasing *Only For Life,* a song he had recorded in demo form.

The details of how this odd coupling came about are now long forgotten, but in August, *Only For Life* was released in 7" and 12" single forms, the 7" backed by *Animal Crackers* and the 12" backed by *Princess*. Both were in picture sleeves, (no, of course there weren't any pictures of Mickey, but in fairness to him he was by now past his most photogenic years - he claims there never were any, of course).

Like the A-side, both B-sides were also home demos that had gone straight to commercial release, although some web sites erroneously credit the Sutherland Brothers with an involvement in production. *Animal Crackers* is a song of which Mickey is atypically not proud, having gone so far as to sign one fan's copy of it "you fool" – which makes it all the more surprising that it was selected for his career-spanning box set *Kiss Me Quick, Squeeze Me Slow*.

As with so many other of Mickey's recordings, the A-side, (and *Animal Crackers*) was loyally picked up by Line Records in Germany who issued them as a single heralding a forthcoming German-only Jupp compilation album called *Oddities*. This rare collection was to include material selected from Mickey's earlier albums plus a few rare BBC radio recordings, later to resurface as part of *Mickey Jupp at the BBC*, (although with markedly different sound quality). *Only For Life* also got releases in France and South Africa.

Releasing demos as singles on tiny labels wasn't exactly premier league stuff - but Mickey wasn't downhearted. He'd never been overly happy with big budget production in any case, and had long ago grown tired of the grind of touring. He was forty now; a good age to concentrate more on his first love - songwriting - because to Mickey it was always the songs that mattered most:

"Someone recording one of my songs is to me the great thing. Never mind me going out there and rock and rolling. I've always liked it if more people record my songs – it's nice when other people pick up on them."

In fact the following year Mickey managed to visibly square that circle by demonstrating, in a live gig, the act of writing – or at least appearing to. He took part in an unusual German TV documentary called *Rock and Roll Feeling*, during which he and a collection of musicians played a short concert before attempting to collectively write a song, which they called *Wait*.

It has to be said that the whole thing comes across in a rather stilted way, while the song eventually produced is a pretty lame one by Mickey's standards, but it is nevertheless a unique opportunity to see Mickey's writing process sort-of in action: which, inevitably, involves a certain shortness of temper with his collaborators! It's out there on mickeyjupp.co.uk for anyone who wants to see Mickey in rehearsal with a bunch of musicians he doesn't know, looking decidedly uncomfortable. Mickey himself barely recalls the event, other than to say:

"I've never seen me writing this song on German TV. I seem to remember most of the guys were English musicians living in Germany. It was after I moved up North, so it was post '83. I can remember that I had to fly from Manchester and then use several trains in Germany to get to the studio. In Germany you can do that because they all run on time!"

It sounds like a lot of effort for not much return. But these were thin times for income, given that Mickey was now ensconced in the Eskdale village of Boot and doing relatively little local gigging. Sometimes there was an appearance when he was back down South, playing with Mo Witham, at venues like the Dickens Inn in Southend, but not much else.

On one such return to Southend a re-union night was put on, featuring the Paramounts (minus Robin Trower, who was presumably busy elsewhere being the platinum-selling international superstar he had become), the Orioles and - back from prehistoric times - the good old Rockerfellas. Dougie Sheldrake dusted off his Gretsch and stepped back twenty years in time to take part in it, once more joining Mickey in the Orioles. "I loved it", he remembers with affection, "Mickey could be awkward but it's always great to play alongside him."

These infrequent trips back to the old town proved a rare opportunity for Mickey to play the music he loved to play, (ie not his own stuff), make a little money and see his old mates. In December 1985 two charity gigs were set up to help fund the restoration of Southend's Pier Head, which had burned down (again!). The first of these was to take place, understandably, in Southend: that's where the pier was and that's where local musicians biggest following lay. Except that this time it wasn't just to be local heroes on parade:

"The first time there was Gary Brooker on keyboards, Eric Clapton on guitar, Mick Fleetwood on drums - the other time it was Henry Spinetti on drums - Darryl Way on violin – can't remember who was on bass but it was someone famous - and me on guitar. The first song I sang on at the first gig was after Gary had done a couple of openers. I chose *Kansas City:* we all knew it so I said 'Let's do it in E', and off we go. As I started singing I heard Eric behind me exclaim, 'what a voice!'"

Some time earlier Gary Brooker had become a sleeping partner in a pub called The Parrot, situated not far from where he now lived in Dunsfold. So the second show was performed there, this time the participants also including legendary guitarist Alvin Lee, in a glorious evening that went on until 3am thanks to that great British institution, the pub lock-in. But much to Gary's chagrin Mickey decided not to sing on that night, saying his voice felt rough. So Eric didn't get to hear any more of the Jupp pipes.

All the same, Eric was happy, keen even, to do more of the same and not long after these two gigs Mickey bumped into him once more:

"Geoff Keane - the bloke who got up to stand in for me with the Orioles when I got carted off to the nick - had one night been playing at the Dickens Inn in Southend with his band Geoff Keane and the Rockin' Machine. He was a big guy and at some point in the evening didn't feel too well, so he went outside to recover, where he unfortunately died. So they organized a benefit gig for his wife, which Gary and Eric kindly came down for. They were staying at a little hotel on the cliffs at Southend, where I went to meet them. Eric walked over and said, "Hello Mickey, do you remember me, I'm Eric". How great is that: the genuine common man touch. I always thought he should have done *Standing at the Crossroads* – right from the moment I wrote it. That was never going to happen with me, though, that's the rules, isn't it?"

Another example of the story of his life, it seems.

In November 1986 Mickey played at the final night in the history of the Dickens in Southend. Times were changing and the old haunts were going dark.

What's more, his returns to the hurly-burly of rock and roll reminded Mickey of why he so valued his Lakeland solitude, to which he was always careful to return pretty sharpish. Chris East, a friend since school days and member of the original Legend line up from Bell days, had beaten Mickey in moving to Cumbria, relocating to Millom a couple of years earlier.

(Amazingly, not long after, that mainstay of the Vertigo Legend line up, Mo Witham, also upped sticks and moved to Burton-in-Kendal, within a few miles of Mickey and Chris).

Now virtually neighbours - twenty miles apart is very little in Cumbrian terms - Mickey and Chris got stuck into writing together, as they occasionally had before. Both had the time and Mickey, as ever, had a home recording facility, now supplemented by a little studio in Millom in which he and Chris both had an interest. For a couple of years they made an agreement that whatever either of them wrote would be co-credited: what Mickey calls a 'Lennon and McCartney' deal, because that's how the two Beatles operated. Material that pre-dated the agreement remained credited to whichever of them had written it, as did anything written after the arrangement ceased. From this association came dozens of songs, a few of which made it into the recording repertoire of other artists, such as Chris Farlowe's cover of their song *Function to Function* and Dave Edmunds' version of *Stockholm*.

A number of these co-writes were later used by Mickey on subsequent albums, while still more have recently been privately released on CD compilations put together by both Chris and Mickey (detailed later on in this book). But, as mentioned earlier, the big event in Mickey's writing career didn't occur in the UK at all, but far away across the Atlantic.

The Judds were an American mother and daughter country music duo comprising Naomi Judd and her daughter Wynonna. Signed to RCA Records in 1983, the duo released six studio albums between then and 1991, becoming one of the most successful acts in country music history. Among other honours they won five Grammy Awards for Best Country Performance by a Duo or Group. They accounted for twenty-five country music chart hits between 1983 and 2000, fourteen of which went to Number One. Not bad at all.

For their 1985 album, *Rockin' with Rhythm*, they recorded one of Mickey's songs, *Tears For You*. Mickey recalls how this important event came about:

"Bluebeard, my UK publishers, were affiliated with the big Rondor publishing group who got the song to their publishing arm in the US, as part of a cassette of four of my compositions. Dave Conrad, who ran their Nashville branch, rang me and said he loved *Tears For You* and had got it to the Judds. But I didn't know the Judds had actually done it until I was with Dina, my second wife, in Nashville one day when I heard it playing on the radio! They used all of my demo arrangement, even the little guitar lick I put on – I'm rather proud of that. I eventually met the Judds when they were over in London at the Kensington Garden Hotel, long after it had been a hit. Rondor persuaded me to go all the way down there from my home to say hello to them. In fact I only got to meet Wynona and then only for a couple of minutes - Naomi wasn't feeling well so stayed in her room..."

No doubt this wild goose chase reminded Mickey of the extreme shallowness of show business and how much better off he was out of it. However, the Judds' album had sold squillions. Equally importantly, the Judds issued several 'best of' compilations after they called it a day in 1991, and Mickey's song was on all of them. Or was it Mickey's song?

Tears For You was written during that collaborative period with Chris East, when all songs were going to be jointly credited as 'Jupp/East', yet the Judds' album credits the writer just as 'Jupp'. What's more, the original cassette tape of four songs that Mickey's publishers had sent to the USA contained another composition that US publisher Dave Conrad was keen on, as Mickey remembers:

"He also liked *Claggin' On* which was on it. A guy called Michael Johnson did it over there, though he recorded it as *Hangin' On* - apparently the Americans wouldn't have understood what "*claggin' on*" meant." (This seems pedantic, given that most Britons wouldn't understand it, either.) *Claggin' On*, which later features on Mickey's album *X*, is clearly credited there as a joint Jupp/East composition. So were all the tracks on that tape of four songs joint compositions? Certainly at least one early cassette of demos exists in which *Tears For You* is credited to Jupp/East.

Did Chris miss out yet again, as Mickey admitted he had on *My Typewriter,* way back in the Vertigo days? No. Mickey is adamant that the mis-crediting was an accident, later rectified, and that Chris has always received his fair share of royalties from *Tears for You,* despite Mickey's equally strongly held view that it was a song he actually wrote on his own, without help from Chris. As a loyal friend, Chris maintains a diplomatic silence.

However the cash ended up being divided, *Tears For You* was quite a big earner. Naturally Mickey and Chris, separately or collectively, wanted to repeat that success. But despite relentless effort, including several more co-writing trips to Nashville by Mickey, as covered earlier in this book, the magic formula could not be re-created. Or perhaps it was just that those songs of theirs that might have made it never quite reached the right ears. Several of those written in this failed attempt were eventually released privately and sound pretty good, but lightning refused to strike a second time. Although it very nearly did. In 1990, Muscle Shoals veteran Barry Beckett was scouting material for a 'comeback' album by much-admired US singer Delbert McClinton. Mickey took up the story of what happened next in a BBC GLR interview some time later:

"Barry Beckett just happened to be in the office of my publishers in Nashville when my song *I'm With You* arrived there and got played by Dave, who ran the place. Barry wanted it for Delbert's album right from the off – in fact this was a Monday and they'd done the backing track by the Thursday!"

So Curb Records put it on the new album. They then called the whole album *I'm With You.* They then released Mickey's song *I'm With You* as the first single from it. And they made a video for *I'm With You,* which was all over MTV.Despite all this promotion this great track was not the smash everyone expected it to be. That's the problem with the music business: it defies logic, which can drive an artist insane. He or she therefore needs some stability in their lives, to help them withstand these slings and arrows of outrageous fortune. For some that's a false prop such as drink or drugs; for others it's a genuine one, such as partner, close friends or family, even a faithful dog.

To others, it's a wonderful place to call home.

The Lake District – Mickey's spiritual home

Lakeland lads make music   courtesy Mike Wade

To help understand why Mickey loves this place so much, it's best to start with a bit of geography and a bit of geology. The Lake District, also commonly known as The Lakes or Lakeland, is a mountainous region of North West England: a popular holiday destination famous for its lakes, forests and mountains (or *fells* as they are known locally). Historically shared by the counties of Cumberland, Westmorland and Lancashire, the Lake District now falls entirely within the modern county of Cumbria. All the land in England higher than three thousand feet above sea level lies within this National Park, including the mountain, Scafell Pike. The area also contains the deepest and longest lakes in England: respectively Wastwater and Windermere.

400 million years ago the Lake District's mountains looked something like the Himalayas do today. Millions of years of erosion have worn them down to their present size, but the folds and faults that created them can still be seen, while the volcanic, igneous intrusions that cooled and crystallised hundreds of metres below the surface are now exposed around Eskdale, Ennerdale, Shap, Skiddaw and Carrock Fell.

About 350 million years ago most of the land sank beneath a tropical sea. My, how weather patterns have changed in these parts – there's still plenty of water but even Lakeland's most avid fan would refrain from ever calling it tropical. This sea soon teemed with life, its floor becoming covered with a thick layer of sediment that ultimately formed into pale grey carboniferous limestone, in which fossil corals, brachiopods and snails are sometimes found today.

During the latter part of this period this sea eventually silted up with mud and sand, to be colonised by swampy forests whose remains now form coal.

Today there are over eighty bodies of water in the Lake District, although confusingly only one is actually called a Lake. Most are bigger, called meres, or smaller, called tarns. Don't ask; I don't make the rules.

Down the ages the Lake District has been exhaustively mined and farmed, although these days its commercial activities are mostly based around tourism – especially the hikers who throng the place - and groovy galleries flogging local art and other trendy, artisanal items. However, to describe the Lake District as being about mountains, valleys and bodies of water, even about hordes of hikers, is accurate but inadequate. It's like calling a pristine LP copy of the Legend Vertigo *Red Boot* album 145grams of black vinyl. Each is so much more to do with the overall experience conjured up, the way they can make you feel, rather than their mere physical attributes.

This is a place that is powerfully rugged yet endlessly beautiful, which makes it profoundly inspirational. As a result, the Lake District is steeped in artistic associations, being especially strongly linked with early 19th century poetry, in particular the writings of William Wordsworth and those others known as the Lake Poets. More recently the region inspired famed children's author Beatrix Potter, who lived there for almost 40 years.

In the twenty-first century, the Lakes' many appreciative visitors may be of a less exalted artistic cut but they include enough global celebrities to make the area famous worldwide.

Hollywood power couple Angelina Jolie and Brad Pitt, Oscar-winner Charlize Theron, teen queen Kristen Stewart, country crooner Taylor Swift and Baywatch star David Hasselhoff are just some of the stars who crossed the Atlantic to sample the delights of Cumbria in recent years, according to the proud local Tourist Board. They will have enjoyed steam trains, steam ships, wildlife parks, treetop treks, farm parks, Roman forts, fishing trips, heritage museums, climbing centres, off-road driving, aquariums, leisure centres, watersports and no less than ten National Trust sites. Best of all, they should have discovered the space in between all these mass attractions and activities: precipitous passes, empty valleys, proud peaks and those deep, dark, strangely wise stretches of water.

The landscape unfolds on such an epic scale, beneath skies wide and frequently biblical, that the place seems at its most comfortable when darkly brooding. That's when one encounters piercing shafts of sunlight darting between sharp, blustery rain showers. When the heavy clouds part to grudgingly permit the visitor a fleeting glimpse of a glorious rainbow. When it doesn't matter that the wind and rain are blowing in your face: one is so aware of the joy of being alive in such a place that discomfort becomes a trifle.

In fact, in bright sunshine the place can look positively startled: as if surprised by the unexpected warmth it knows better than to expect to last.

Now imagine how much more engaging still these charms must appear through the eyes of a small child, especially one brought up mostly in the flat and densely populated plains of the South, back in a greyer time. Then multiply that by frequency of visits over the best part of a lifetime. Multiply again by the sense of relief each visit would bring, especially later on when the setting came to symbolise blessed relief from a severely pressured musician's life. It would make you want to write songs about it, would it not?

However, it's slightly more complicated.

Within the overall magnificence of The Lake District lie two distinct sub-groups: the beautiful but busy chocolate-box Lakes and the rather more brutal backwoods.

On a good summer's day on the most famous Lakes, sailboats bob around while spectators in hotels, shops and restaurants look on in rapture. Not so in Eskdale, over which the vertiginous Wrynose Pass stands sentinel, challenging any vehicle on its right to enter. There are few caravans or charabancs here, just a squiggly half-road and some precipitous drops. For the wilder part of the weather year, no one gets through that way. Ulpha is another way in – as bleak and windswept a high plain as you will find anywhere in the British Isles. The area's big water feature is the awesome Wastwater. Deepest, steepest, roughest and toughest of them all, it sits brooding in its lair at the heart of the least navigable part of the Lake District - daring visitors to brave its single road and precipitous mountain tracks.

It is here in the rugged, hidden heart of the Lakes that Mickey chose to settle. Here, where only the hardiest of visitors pass muster; where small communities of kindred spirits cling on to nature red in tooth and claw; here where you can easily lose yourself, both metaphorically and literally.

No wonder it appealed to Mickey, a man by now worn down by show business demands and busted half-hopes. And no wonder it inspired him to write so many songs about the area. He's even written songs about the journey he undertook to get there.

By rail, just before arriving in the Lakes proper, the visitor passes through *Foxfield Junction* - subject of the faux-Legend track that appeared many years before on Vertigo's compilation, *Heads Together*. Now Mickey no longer needed to pass through Foxfield Junction. He was a permanent resident of the Lakes, free to wander, to gather inspiration, to write all the songs he wanted. No more locking himself away in a flat in Bath or sitting in a rented room with a borrowed piano. He could walk the fells and dales at will, welcoming the muse wherever and whenever it might visit him. And fit in a bit of painting, too. He was addicted to the place, as he had once told BBC GLR in a radio interview, joking, "I've often said that wild horses and a million dollars wouldn't drag me back down South...well, perhaps a million dollars would."

Now a sudden, temporary move away from the area proved his reliance on the place to him. In the early nineties one of Mickey's local flames, Mitch, decided to move to Whitby, taking with her four and a half year old Amy, the daughter they had together produced:

"The day I put them on the train from here to Yorkshire I went back to my place and cried for hours. I wanted to see at least one of my children grow up – and so I moved away, to a rented cottage in Holmrook, to be able to do that. It was worth it because Amy's a great mate these days and I love her to bits.But I grabbed the chance to get back to Boot at every opportunity. I'd always use any excuse to return - I continued to get my car serviced there even when I was living in Yorkshire, driving all the way back!"

In all, Mickey has had three wives and has four children. He had son Gary, named after Gary Brooker, with his first wife, Pat. This was the child whose maintenance issues ended so disastrously for Mickey, and whom he has not seen since.

With his second wife Valerie, who later married Legend band-mate John Bobin, he had Joanne, with whom he is loosely in touch.

Third wife Dina – real name Dawn – lived up in Boot with Mickey for a while. They had no children, but not long after they parted and Dina had gone back to America, Mickey struck up a relationship with a local girl called Michelle - Mitch for short - with whom he had Amy, now twenty nine and in very close contact.

(Much earlier, another brief liaison, this time with ex-Oriole Ada Baggerly's ex-girlfriend Scarlett, known as Red, had produced Marnie, now in her forties and living in Australia).

Mickey is the first to admit that to this day he continues to fall in love rather easily, a side effect of his susceptibility to all things romantic – whether symbolic Mother Nature or real flesh and blood female.

Returning from his brief sojourn in Holmrook, Mickey was back in Boot and alone again, happy with his little recording studio, in his little dwelling, in his little village, set in the vast and beautiful Cumbrian emptiness he loved.

How he spent his hours and days was entirely up to him. He could see people coming and hide before they arrived, if needs be. He could be as grumpy as he wanted because he no longer needed anybody else.

He could be Cumbria's Greta Garbo.

Which was great for him; but now that he was miles away – out of contact and out of contract - how would the rest of us get to hear the new songs he wrote?

19 Up Snakes, Down Ladders

In which Mickey discovers that smaller recording budgets can end up costing you more

Piano Man   *courtesy Fans of Mickey Jupp*

When the writer of songs is lost for words
And the songs he sings have all been heard before
Does he tear it up and start again
Does he swear not to hold a brush or a pen anymore?

The Writer of Songs by **Mickey Jupp, Legend Moonshine**

It's 1988 and not much is occurring (again).

Mickey is still up in Boot, writing away, but not many acts are buying the new material and he is no longer a recording artist himself.

Yet his reputation continues to hold strong in pockets, not least in Germany where, since getting involved in the funding and release of the *Oxford* album, Line Records have been re-issuing some earlier LPs - for the first time in the new-fangled Compact Disc format.

In 1985 they'd put out *Long Distance Romancer*. In 1987 it was the turn of *Juppanese* and *Some People Can't Dance*. In the same year they compiled *Oddities*, on vinyl and CD, made up of tracks from the three Legend albums, some solo singles and a few rare live BBC recordings.

This programme of releases was a treasure trove for fans across Europe who had not been able to obtain Mickey's music on CD before. Here was the music they loved in clear, crackle-free form, often with bonus cuts of B-sides and other rarities. UK fans were happy to pay a premium to have copies imported, although getting one's hands on them was no easy feat in those pre-Amazon, pre-eBay, pre-PayPal days.

Now Line was to get an album of brand new material to release. Mickey recalls its inception:

"Dave Hatfield was a local guy who ran a record shop in Leigh. I'm playing the Dickens pub in Southend one day and he approaches me, wanting to know if I fancy making a record for his little Waterfront label, which he ran with Steve Hooker. I had bags of material and wasn't doing a lot so I agreed."

John Howard, who apart from being a music journalist and DJ was also managing a local band called the Bottles, adds a bit more detail:

"Dave, as owner of Waterfront Records, had pressed some Bottles records for the band to sell at gigs. He maintained that part of the payment for this was still outstanding, despite me having thought it had all been settled. One night at a Jupp gig at the Dickens, he says to me, 'What about this £300 you still owe me? Tell you what: you're friends with Mickey and I'd love to get him to make a record on my label, if you can persuade him to, I'll forget the debt'. So I walked across to Juppy and said 'Do you want to make an album for Dave?' and he said 'Yeh'. That's how the deal was done."

(Dave Hatfield, a founder member of the Kursaal Flyers was to have multiple musical careers from resident double bassist at the Cambridge Folk Festival to running several record shops - most ended badly – to playing bass for Chris Jagger's band, which has occasionally resulted in him backing brother Mick!)

Mickey had been playing 'down South' on and off for some time now - at The Dickens, the Zero 6 in Southend and occasionally The Greyhound in Fulham - with a band consisting of Ian 'Chuck' Duck on guitar, Dave Bronze on bass and Bobby Clouter on drums – sometimes supported by Steve Hooker's band, the Shakers, another part of the Waterfront scene.

Southend's Waterfront Records (not to be confused with an imprint of the same name in Sydney) began life in the early '80s as a punk label. Amongst other records, it released an album by The Shakers, on which Mickey is credited as co-producer of two tracks: *Nothing but Talk* and *She's Afraid to Come*. Mickey was scheduled to play piano on the latter, but it never quite happened, despite his enjoyment of both the riff and the double entendre! These tracks were recorded in 1982; a year later Wilko Johnson produced four other tracks that ended up on that same LP.

Many of the songs Mickey was referring to when he said he had "bags of material" had come from his years of collaboration with Chris East. This stockpile included *Claggin' On*, the song that had intrigued the Americans a couple of years earlier. Each of their compositions had been turned into a high quality demo, either at Mickey's home or at Chris' and Mickey's AO Studio in Millom, the two musicians playing all the instruments (including the synth with "that" sound) to drum box rhythms.

A selection of songs from this stash was to form the basis of the new album - a record to be made by Mickey, Chris and stalwart Mo Witham, who would both play on it and produce it. Engineer Barry Vernon would take care of bass on some tracks, old confederate Tex Comer on others, while Lee Brilleaux of the Feelgoods would add in some harmonica. Mick Brownlee, ex-of the Paramounts, would handle drums, (preferred over the record company's suggestion of Feelgood's Big Figure because Brownlee was also playing live with Mickey at the time), as he well remembers:

388

"I was working at that time at a local car dealer's. Mickey rang me up and asked if I would play the drums on his new album. I said 'Yeh, but I've got to do it at certain times to fit it round work'. He said that was OK so we met with him in a pub - me, Mo, Tex Comer - to ask him what he was going to record. 'I don't know' he said and chucked five CDs of demos on the table. We had to go through them all and sort out what to record. We did a few and then he went off to Cumbria. It took a long time to do nothing, really."

Mickey recounts in more detail how the album developed, or more accurately, didn't:

"We started recording in a studio in Boreham, near Chelmsford, called Indigo Blue. It was all right but it seemed to be run by kids. We got three tracks done, Lee played harp on one of them. Then, all of a sudden, the studio went bust. Overnight. All we had left to turn to were our original demos. We did some more work on them at Henry's Place – which was a cottage in Great Wakering owned by a colourful local character called French Henry. I think Mike Vernon lent us a tape recorder to help out at some point."

The resulting album, released in March 1988, was called *X*: not to reflect the X-certificate experience of making it but in recognition of the fact that it was - depending how you do the counting - Mickey's tenth LP. Regrettably, it contained only those three proper masters: *Claggin' On, Lover by Night* and *Heartbreak Today*. The rest of the tracks were Mickey's original publisher's demos with some overdubs added, and weren't really up to commercial release standards.

X emerged on Waterfront in the UK as a vinyl LP, from which a single – *Claggin' On* b/w *Driving on Your Lights* – was taken. Line Records took the album for Germany where it came out as a CD. Despite agreeing to put it out, Line complained about the quality of the offering they received, requesting of Mickey that in future they "weren't sent any more of your demos to release."

Perhaps the sole breakthrough that *X* could boast was the fact that in both markets and both formats a clearly legible picture of Mickey had finally made it to the album cover!

The UK release's photo is a poor shot, Mickey not having been informed that a picture was due to be taken that day.

The German CD carries a much better portrait of Mickey and guitar - apparently taken at the same session, so it's a mystery why Waterfront chose the naff one.

Now while this is the commonly heard story of the genesis of the X album, there is another interpretation of events – one that explains rather better the mysterious gap between the recording in 1986 and eventual release in 1988.

Steve Hooker - who by this time had effectively become Mickey's troubleshooter and tour manager – was executive producer on the album for Waterfront. He has a clear recollection of things being rather more complicated than the usual version suggests:

"A whole album was recorded by the band at the sessions. The problem was that Mickey wasn't happy with it when it was finished and didn't want it to come out. Well, he was the artist. We were so pleased to have such a great talent on our label that we considered it his prerogative and agreed at first. The album sat on the shelf for a good year before I felt we had to do something with it, given what had been invested in it and how much we knew people wanted new material from him. So I approached Mickey about releasing an EP of the handful of tracks he was happier with. At that point he kindly offered us a batch of his home recordings to make up the numbers for a full album, so that's what we did. It wasn't what we intended but we were pleased to be able to release it – especially as he hadn't had anything out for quite a while by then."

John Denton, who played keyboards on the initial recordings at Indigo, confirms this version of events:

"We did a bunch of tracks one snowy day but Mick didn't like them. He wasn't even happy when we were recording them, which was a shame for me because that was the only time I got to record with him. I seem to remember Mo thought they were OK, but I felt they were a bit iffy. We had a good time – especially in the pub afterwards - but I wasn't surprised that those tapes never saw the light of day."

Tex Comer's recollections are a little fuzzier but also support the idea of an entire album having been recorded in the first place:

"*X* was a weird one; it just sort of disappeared. We recorded the album but things were falling apart a bit so I just left Mick to do what he wanted to do because it was his project. I didn't particularly like the end product, which seemed a bit amateurish compared with most of the stuff we did together. Mick was always a little bit prone to going too far that way, in my opinion. His demos are good but they are still demos. I think that's part of what let Mick down in the end – he wasn't always wanting to be quite professional enough."

Eventually a little bit of extra work was done on the final running order before Steve Hooker mastered the assembled tapes with engineer Warwick Kemp at Spectrum Studios, Westcliff, on January 21st 1988.

Whichever story is the true one, given the smallness of the label and the relatively makeshift quality of some of the recordings it was little surprise when *X* failed to shift many units. This wasn't for want of trying, certainly as far as gigging was concerned. Steve Hooker and the Waterfront crew kept the pressure on Mickey to play shows in support of the album. At the time he had a great band featuring Mo on guitar, Tex on bass and by now Dr Feelgood's original drummer, Big Figure, on the kit. But the prospect of performing with them was always counter-balanced by the lure of the Lakes, as Steve Hooker, now arranging Mickey's live bookings, recalls:

"They would do half a dozen gigs before Mickey would say he'd had enough and wanted to pack it in."

Mickey mostly played in Southend – particularly at the Grand, the Dickens and the Cricketer's (of course) – or in London. There the most regular venues were the Weavers and the Half Moon in Putney, but there were also key shows at the Borderline and the 100 Club. The 100 Club gigs were promoted by Steve Beggs, who had become a devoted Jupp fan since first booking him into the Dublin Castle years before.

One night at Rochford's Zero Six an especially mouth-watering event occurred: Legend reformed without Legend! Brilliant Southend Hendrix sound-alikes The Hamsters, who have recorded many Jupp compositions, learned a whole bunch of tracks off *Red Boot* and backed Mickey on them in concert. How come nobody recorded that?

There was some overseas outreach, too, both in Holland in August 1989 and even a couple of Paris shows Steve Hooker arranged for September through his connections over there, (Steve himself had earlier been signed to two different French record labels). Steve remembers the Paris gigs particularly vividly:

"The audience loved him. He kicked off with *Schooldays* and you could see them metaphorically turn up their collars and really get into it. I'd managed to get a big article in one of the main newspapers over there as advance publicity and persuaded Mickey to smarten up for the gig and wear a jacket. I recall him saying to me, 'All you're interested in is image'. Not true, of course!"

Sporadic bookings stretched into 1990 - with trips to Brighton, Bristol, Dudley and Farnham, and another foreign jaunt to Belgium thrown in, too - but it was difficult to keep a regular band together when only playing a handful of gigs in the time Mickey was down from Cumbria, as Steve recollects:

"Every now and then one of the band wouldn't be able to make a date, so we'd have to substitute someone. On one occasion Mo was pre-booked with Suzi Quatro, so Mick only went and sacked him! It seemed a bit harsh but it had an unexpected side benefit in the end. The bloke Mickey wanted to get in to replace Mo – Dave Kelly of the Blues Band, who had also played with Tex before – said he couldn't do it but knew a man who could, and that's how Mickey got hold of Ed Deane. Other times Figure couldn't make a few gigs so we got Malcolm Mortimer in on drums – from a white reggae band!"

Ed Deane himself, now living in Ireland, filled me in on a bit more detail about how he got his slot Mickey's band – which turns out to have been a considerably longer process than Steve's story suggests:

"I first came across Mickey Jupp's music through Ron Kavanagh. I had just returned to London after a spell of a few years in Paris playing with an Anglo French band. Ron and his wife were very kindly letting me stay at their place in Islington while I tried to find somewhere to live. We were wading through Ron's huge collection of recorded music, particularly early American R'n'B, Rock'n'roll and Blues. We would also listen to Charlie Gillett and often record his radio shows onto cassette. One of the records we listened to was the *Legend* album by Mickey. It was such a great record and I think we might have included a couple of the songs in our set. One day, Ron told me that Mickey was auditioning for a guitarist so I went along to the rehearsal studio. Paul Riley was trying to put a band together for Mickey and was having a hard time of it. I can't even remember whether we actually played or not but we ended up in the pub across the road.

Mickey seemed kind of despondent and was telling a frustrated but patient Paul Riley that he (Mickey) was 'too old for this lark'. Paul was earnestly trying to convince him otherwise and I said my goodbyes and left them to it. The next time I saw Mickey was when my friend Tex Comer was playing bass with the band. I used to go and see them at the Dublin Castle in Camden Town where I was living at the time. Tex and I had been working together in Frankie Miller's band. Frankie was also a big fan of Mickey's and loved his voice and his songwriting. Mo Witham was playing guitar with Mickey and I loved his playing. It was stripped down, economical and funky. Not a wasted or irrelevant note. Just right for Mickey and just right for his songs. Those gigs were just so great."

But as yet Ed had not joined up. Which was perhaps just as well, given the instability in the band's future, all down to Mickey's continued lack of conviction over his suitability for the role of 'rock star'. A pattern of doubt was emerging, as Steve Hooker noted:

"We would want him to do a gig or two and then after that he'd say he didn't want to do any more but his band members would talk him into doing another six or ten."

But despite the gigging that did occur, X did not prove his salvation: Mickey's attempt at a recording comeback proved to be a career low point.

He finished his relationship with Waterfront and Steve Hooker in 1990, sending Steve a letter announcing that he wanted "to quit live performance for the foreseeable future because my equipment doesn't work and in any case someone up there doesn't want me to be a success."

He ends with this firm instruction:

"To keep my mental health on an even keel, please cancel all my gigs and kindly refrain from accepting any more."

It wasn't the first time he'd wanted that and it was destined not to be the last. As Steve ruefully commented:

"Every time he did that we would wait with bated breath for one of his guitars to appear on the wall at Chris Stevens – it was your one chance to get your hands on an ex-Mickey Jupp guitar, one played by your hero!"

In fact, a little further down the line, Ed Deane's tenure with the band was to end in similar circumstances:

"There was a lull of a couple of months in our gigging schedule as there often was. I think it was May and there were two or three gigs lined up for the following September. Probably the 100 Club in Oxford St, then maybe a gig in Southend and one at the Half Moon in Putney or somewhere like that.

One day in May the phone rang and it was Mickey. He was giving me a few months notice that he didn't want to do those gigs, or any others for that matter, and that he had basically 'had enough'. I was a little taken aback but not really that surprised. The conversation was amicable enough and we bid each other farewell and good luck."

By now, Mickey's long-suffering supporters – let alone fellow musicians - might well have assumed that mementos of Mickey's past were all that there was left to look forward to; that by now his best work was far behind him; that he really had finally turned his back on his musical career.

But they would have been wrong.

In actual fact, Mickey's two personal favourite albums still lay in front of him...

The *X* Album

Oh dear, oh dear, oh dear - what a shame.

There are some good songs here, though few outstanding performances. The overriding problem is that the recording is airless and samey, lacking sufficient conviction or energy to fully engage the listener. Whenever a good number threatens to break out of this malaise, it gets dragged back under by its 'demo' roots, which entangle and protrude from almost every track. If ever there was an example of why demos are demos and masters are masters, this is it. One is forced to the reluctant conclusion that the musicians involved, while attempting to breathe some vitality over the top of the demo tracks, recognized the hopelessness of their task and ended up kind of going through the motions. That said there is some quality material on *X*.

Claggin' On, for example. This is the opening track, and was the single rather optimistically taken from the album. It's properly produced, with real musicians playing real instruments, albeit over the demoish drum box. Mickey sings this charming little country-style number in a relaxed yet positive fashion, backed by his own super-tight harmonies. There are some fine figures from piano and guitar, although the acoustic feel is somewhat compromised by intrusive digital handclaps.

Close to Me is most unusual: a half speed lament sung over a slightly sinister part-oriental/part-Doobie Brothers keyboard riff. Not a guitar in sight, and barely a drum either - handclaps holding the beat for the first half of this unexpectedly fine number. Not Mickey's usual type of song in style or sound, but a very interesting diversion, nonetheless.

Crazy Cowboy Christmas is another, though far less welcome, departure. As corny and ghastly a piece of pointless opportunism as the title suggests, this yodeling oddity would have been better left where it was, scraping the bottom of Mickey's usually impeccable musical barrel, (although I have found one person brave enough to claim he actually likes it – stand up, John Howard). One must assume that this atypical lack of taste came about in the desperate hope of spawning a Christmas hit; commercial imperative eventually won the day and the track was chosen to be included in a Line Records Christmas compilation album! (Bless my soul, a few months after the publication of the first edition of this book, three more Jupp Christmas compositions surfaced - *I Wonder What my Baby's Giving me for Christmas, Christmas Day Dreams* and *The Rhythm of Christmas* – and they aren't that bad, either…)

Next up is *Blues for the Blues*, a very country blues that Mickey delivers in full US country vocal style. It sounds as though it were written to order - as it probably was as part of the catalogue of songs written with US country performers in mind, although the lyrics are very much in line with Mickey's own sentiments. Mickey's vocal performance seems less than enthusiastic, save for the odd flash of passion in the chorus. The oddest thing about this number is that it cries out to be treated as a full-on bluesy blues (or at least a Legend-style rocker), given the interesting subject matter, mourning the dearth of good music on the radio:
"I got the blues for the blues
Nobody plays like they used
The good guys are gone
The new guys are young
Too young, too loud and too loose"

Southend stalwarts, The Hamsters, give it a more muscular treatment on a cover version from their live album, *They Live By Night* - one of around a dozen Jupp compositions they have released down the years.

Lover by Night is a fairly standard Bo Diddley kind of affair, complete with some nice wailing harmonica from Dr Feelgood's Lee Brilleaux. The good news is that it's a proper recording, albeit rather a gutless one. This rebellious song is a thinly veiled threat, yet is played rather precisely and recorded on the weedy side. Bass and bass drum are crisp yet low in the mix, whereas the song surely needs them to be prominent and swampy. Equally, the vocal from Mickey seems uncharacteristically polite.

The Road takes us back to demo land - a shame for such a good song.

The lyric, all about family responsibilities keeping a man from doing what he outta be doing, is appropriately howled by Mickey, adding some drama to an otherwise unengaging synth/drum machine track with some guitar mixed in.

Amusingly, Mickey deliberately muddles his lyrical context, rhyming the US "*dollar bill*" with a decidedly North Country "*over yon hill*".

(This track re-emerged some time later on a Waterfront compilation entitled *The Southend Connection*, the sleeve note of this rare and rather obscure collection noting that Mickey's ambition is "to write the perfect Country Rock song"...)

Big Black Cadillac sums up the *X* album's problem perfectly. It's a pounding rocker in which powerful cars are a metaphor for wild sex, yet this red-blooded message is delivered by what sounds like a lounge band playing in a small restaurant. Its demo origins cannot be concealed, especially the cartoon-like synth sound that actually takes the solo. Mickey must sense the difficulties as he sings the whole thing as a sort of parody. What this track needs is a kick up the arse with a red winkle picker.

(If you want to hear it done properly, look it up on YouTube. No lesser a light than Linda Gail Lewis – that's Jerry Lee's sister– gives it a far heftier reading, complete with Lewis/Jupp-style thumping piano. She has since gone on to record Mickey's song *When Honky Gets Tonky*).

Nashville comes over way better, mostly because it's already a parody - its witty lyric based upon Mickey's entertaining experience of that particular city's music scene. Unfortunately the sourly negative lyric ensures that the song could never be covered by any artist who ever wanted to work there again:
"Dreams are only dreams,
But to me it's always seemed
*At the end of the rainbow it just rai*ns"
Mickey manages to deliver this in part satirical, part wistful fashion. There's some fine guitar picking, a nice rolling banjo from Chris East and a drum box setting that has been moved from "lame" to "lively".

Driving On Your Lights is a terrific song – one of those sad and gentle ballads that really would have made a great track if it could have been produced right. It features an unusual metaphor at its heart, some pleasantly unexpected chord changes and a verse structure reminiscent of Mark Knopfler at his best. But the budget constraints meant its strengths couldn't be fully realized and so, while the synth and drum machine sounds don't damage the feel too much, one longs to hear it with some strings - even brass - over a sensitive rhythm section, to give proper light and shade.

First Things First might be the best pure pop song Mickey has ever written - it has mid-sixties beat group written all over it. Fully realising its potential would have required some electric guitar, of which there is sadly none (although there is some nice acoustic amongst the synth barrage). It features another plaintive lyric about being on the road and missing a partner: *"I leave her when I must, my heart just gathers dust."*

Songwriters Lament is a pretty thin sounding twelve bar demo, outlining Mickey's supposed problems with writer's block, which is a shame because it really needs the full Rockpile treatment to punch home its catchy chorus. As is so often the case with songs Mickey writes from the heart, the personal nature of the lyric renders it virtually uncoverable by other artists. On the plus side, this is proof that while some of Mickey's songs at the time were being cynically churned out, the man still used his writing talent to examine his own emotions every now and then. This track is a favourite of a number of Mickey's fans, including Steve Hooker, the man who had suffered so, throughout the production of *X*.

Heartbroke Today reveals Mickey in lively, slightly Fats, country style. This is one of the tracks that actually got properly recorded, before the money ran out. As a result the sounds are stronger, with drums by Mick Brownlee and reliable Tex Comer on bass, along with some nice Mo Witham guitar flourishes. A mix of synths do their best to stand in for the brass section that would have lifted the whole thing, had funds permitted.

The final track on some pressings is *A Man Always Cries On His Own*, although it's left off others. To an extreme fan of Country and Western, Grand Old Opry style, this might be a truly poignant song. To the rest of us it moves beyond parody and into the OTT world of pastiche. There are fine harmonies and guitar flourishes but there is also a toe-curling Johnny Cash spoken rendition of the title line and some plain dumb words. Here is a sample lyric:
"Babies got mummies and daddies, Doggies can chew on a bone
Woman's got someone to lean on, But a man always cries on his own"
I rest my case.

The trouble with *X* is not what it is but what it isn't; what it might have been.

A few songs probably needed to be substituted, which a strong producer would have done straight away, while a couple of tracks warranted investment in extra session musicians to add strings or brass. But beyond that, a group of very competent players - such as this bunch - could have made much more of it than they were able to, had they been given the chance; in other words, had they had the funding stretched to proper masters.

This hypothesis was to be supported by Mickey's next album, as we shall see.

But for now, the existence of the rather sub-standard *X* can't have much helped the prospect of there ever being *any* further Mickey Jupp records.

20 There's A Thing

In which, against the odds, Mickey returns to sparkling form

Ed Deane, Mickey and Tex Comer on the road

Can't do it, I'm too old, it ain't my gig
The music's too loud and the hall's too big
The sounds I like, well, you wouldn't dig

Old Rock and Roller by Mickey Jupp, Juppanese

Since Will Birch first appeared in the queue for the Orioles outside the Cricketers pub back in the sixties he had been a busy boy.

He'd been drummer in several Southend bands including psyche outfit Surly Bird, Neil Young sound-alikes Glory and country rockers Cow Pie, before founding the Kursaal Flyers.The Kursaals, who had covered Mickey's *Cross Country* early in their recording career, ("It was nice that they did it but I didn't like the way they did it", was the Guvnor's comment), went on to have a hit with *Little Does She Know*, which Will co-wrote.

Following the Kursaals' demise in 1977, he formed The Records who had some success with *Starry Eyes*, which he also co-wrote. The Records were part of the same Be Stiff tour as Mickey in 1977, in which they performed themselves and backed Rachel Sweet. Will's successful writing credits also include *A1 on the Jukebox*, written with and recorded by Dave Edmunds and a number of tracks for Dr Feelgood. Moving into production, he made records with Feelgood as well as Yachts, Any Trouble and Desmond Dekker.

In the 1990's he became a rock writer, producing pieces for music magazines such as *Mojo*, including several about the Southend scene. He also managed to write two books – *No Sleep Till Canvey*, about the pub rock movement, for Virgin Books and a highly regarded biography of *Ian Dury*, published by the prestigious house of Sidgwick & Jackson. No wonder *Record Collector* magazine referred to him as "the Samuel Pepys of the Southend Scene".

Alongside all this, Will somehow found time to form a record label: On The Beach. While the bulk of its catalogue was re-issues of albums by Will's bands the Kursaal Flyers and The Records, it also issued some original material, as Will told me:

"I was working with the Feelgoods, doing some writing and production with them, and I saw how their own label – Grand - worked. So I set up On The Beach. We did a little record with the Hamsters first and then I was wondering, what's next? Mick had started making this new album up in the Lake District and I was up there with the Hamsters in Kendal, so I went to visit him while he was working on it. I thought it would make a great second original album for my label, even though there was unlikely to be any money in it."

What was it that especially inspired Will to consider doing this?

"Two songs in particular made me want to release it – *Standing at the Crossroads Again*, which is just fantastic -Dave Edmunds loves it so much he's put it on two albums - and *Till Honky Gets Tonky Again* - a song Nashville would be proud of."

The genesis of the first of these two songs is particularly fascinating, as Mickey recollected:

"I used to have a little song that me and the guys would run through as a warm up at soundchecks. I had maybe only one verse, but one day Tex says to me, 'What is this song we keep hearing bits of then? It's good, so why don't we do it properly?' I'd started it in 1989, so I finished it up - we played it for the first time at JBs in Dudley, I seem to remember. That was *Standing at the Crossroads Again*. I remember when the key lyric came together – *I guess I'm not the man she was looking for, just the man she found* – I thought, hey, maybe there is a God."

So the album deal was done. Now what to call it? For once it got a great title and a great cover to go with it, as Will remembers:

"Mick had the idea for the album title – *As The Yeahs Go By* - and the 'footwear' album cover, representing the five ages of man in shoe form! I got Pete Knock, a mate of mine, to illustrate it, and he drew the portrait of Mickey on the back. I pressed it up on vinyl, while Line in Germany, who Mickey had done a deal with, did the CD – we swapped copies so I didn't have to manufacture any of those. I was honoured to have the great Mick Jupp on my record label."

In 1992, FOAMCD2 - *As the Yeahs Go By,* by Mickey Jupp - came out.

Mickey was back in business and, it transpired, in very fine form. The album had been recorded up in Millom at AO studios, the one in which Mickey and Chris East had an interest, but this time it was no corner-cutting affair. The band alongside Mickey was one he had been playing with for a year or so, boasting quality all the way.

The Big Figure, one of the original Feelgoods and solid as a rock, was on drums, while Tex Comer remained on bass. Tex is Mickey's all-time favourite bassist.

"He's the best one I ever played with: really good and a lovely fellah. He had a strange way of moving on stage, in a sort of dance, almost but not quite a Shadows step, usually with his eyes shut! He's what I call a deck chair sort of bass player – he'd play a note, then have a sit down, then play another. Perfect."

Tex remembers the album sessions very fondly, as he related to me:

"I remember that one particularly because there was some good stuff on it. In fact, I was playing the CD last night and we're going to put *Not Wanted Anymore* in the set of Blues Patrol, the band I play with these days. We did the tracks for the album in two or three days, something like that, I seem to remember – Mick liked it done like that, none of it dragging on. He never really understood why it should take two weeks to make an album when the songs only took five minutes each to play! When you've been there and done that so many times before, you want to go in, knock it out and finish it. I think we all had a low boredom tolerance."

On lead was the excellent Ed Deane, an Irish guitarist who, like Hendrix before him, played a right-handed guitar left handed, much to the bemusement of every other musician who ever watched him play. He had recently been working with British blues stalwart Dana Gillespie (for whom, coincidentally, Mike Vernon, producer of *Some People Can't Dance*, and Mickey's long term guitarist, Mo Witham, had recently co-written an excellent album track, *Where Blue Begins*).

Both Tex and Mickey have a high opinion of Ed, who played in the live band for some time. Tex recalled, "Ed Deane is a fantastic guitarist, the best bluesy lead player Mick ever had – he wasn't as rock and roll as Mo, but he was like Clapton when he was on form."

Unsurprisingly, given that view of his talents, it was Tex who finally got Ed into the band:

"Tex asked me if I would be interested in doing some gigs with the band. I think the first was at the Pegasus in Stoke Newington. I don't remember any rehearsals except maybe Tex and I running through the songs at Tex's house. I had been given a cassette with the songs Mickey wanted to play. I spent a lot of time listening to it and getting the shape of the songs. I was apprehensive about meeting Mickey again as Tex had mentioned that he could be quite temperamental. I can remember him telling me that Mickey had become so frustrated with a guitar that had tuning problems that he had flung it across the stage mid gig! I also remember thinking that at least the guy was human and alive and not someone who would be content just bluffing along with an out of tune guitar.

When I arrived for soundcheck I set up my amp and we ran through several songs. I loved it. Even the tension in the music was great and gave it a vital edge. Tex was a good mediator because of his laid back, unfussed personality. Big Figure was playing drums and he was both friendly and serious with a very sharp sense of humour. After the soundcheck I sat at the bar with Mickey. He was happy with the way the band was sounding and it kind of broke the ice. I was very aware of not overplaying or playing anything superfluous. Mo Witham was my role model in this respect."

So the band that would record the album was coming together. It needed just one more thing to make it hum: and so the redoubtable Frank Mead - who else - added sax and harmonica in all the right places, although it was a bit of a trial for him:

"I had to get up at 4am and drive up to Cumbria in a noisy 1300 Beetle, wearing earplugs in to attempt to defeat the terrible racket it made. When I finally got there I overdubbed a few tracks – including *Standing At The Crossroads*, which actually has horns on it, though you might not notice because they are buried deep in the final mix. I stayed over at Mickey's place that night for a few beers and then drove all the way back the next day."

Such are the joys of the itinerant session man.

In recording terms, Mo Witham's impeccable guitar playing would not be in evidence on *As the Yeahs Go By*, given he'd been fired from the band by Mickey over his gig clashes with Suzi Quatro. Instead his stabilizing presence would be around in the form of producer, for he was to co-produce the album with Mickey. He remembers getting the invitation:

"Mickey said, I'm making another album - can you come and twiddle the knobs. I said, 'Yeh, for £50 a track.' He said, 'That's a lot of money'. I said, 'Well I've got to sit there and listen to some other guitar player in my place, haven't I?'"

Mo had taught himself to engineer as a result of his frustration over the number of times the sounds he was producing in various studios weren't making it on to tape the way they should. His first steps in this direction came when he and others, including this author, built a 16-track studio in Great Wakering, Essex, back in the late seventies.

Beyond these craft skills, it was particularly useful that Mo knew Mickey well enough to be able to handle the man and his moods. Their long musical history meant Mo was able to point out areas for improvement without generating quite the same amount of friction an outsider would have.

Mickey remembers the genesis of *As the Yeahs Go By* slightly differently, crediting Will Birch with having been the original stimulus for the whole event:

"It was all Will's idea from the outset. He came up to check on progress once or twice but basically we just got on with it. Tex, Ed, Figure and Frank were staying in guesthouses up here so we didn't have long: a week or so on the bits we needed them for. Then lots more time with Mo, doing overdubs and vocals.

We did most of the tracks from scratch. In one or two cases we augmented the basic demo tracks of mine because we couldn't beat the feel of them. *Doo Wop Shang-a-lang Shimmy Shimmy* and *Rock and Roll Peg* were two I think we did that for. We all had a good time and it transmits on the record. It was simply us doing it our way. I knew we had some nice songs on there. Ed's playing was particularly good – to me on that album he sounds like he was half cut and sitting down while playing his parts, although he wasn't! And of course it was our studio, too. I had an interest in it from 1987 to 1990. I sold up my share because my father died in early December 1990 just as we were finishing up the album - I moved away again for a bit to be with my mum, renting a flat near Pickering, where she worked as a nanny."

That would have given Mickey the chance to reflect on the ups and downs of his borderline career, for his Mum was as avid a collector of cuttings and memorabilia as he himself was dismissive of such behaviour. (In her time, girlfriend Hilary had been equally assiduous, keeping a scrapbook of Mickey's exploits – I wonder if she still has it?)

There were other fans emerging, too. Over in Sweden, Jerry Williams began recording several Jupp compositions. John Denton can recall sitting in a car in the Grand car park with Mickey grinning as he listened to these new interpretations for the first time, unaware of the future significance of this moment...

For now the pressure was off: the songs were great and the studio process was simple - perfect for Mickey, as Ed Deane recollected:

"When we recorded *As the Yeahs Go By* in Cumbria, Mickey had already recorded several of the songs using drum machines, playing keyboards and guitar himself. I think the band recorded about six or seven numbers on top. Mo Witham was engineering and we did everything live. There were very few overdubs. I hung on for a day or two to overdub some guitar, particularly on *Not Wanted Anymore*. I remember Mickey really wanting me to just let loose on that song and just wail.

Frank Mead came up later to overdub some sax and harmonica and that was pretty much it: very much a 'no frills' recording and that's the way Mickey wanted it."

Indeed the atmosphere of harmony - the good-time vibe of the recordings - does shine through the tracks of *As The Yeahs Go By*, a fact Mickey attributes in part to that use of original demos as the basis for several numbers. Mickey is not alone in finding that sometimes it's impossible to beat the feel of an early musical sketch. No lesser a proponent of ultra-crisp studio sound than Goldfrapp found it impossible, bigger budget and bigger studio notwithstanding, to match some of the demo material they had assembled for their first album, *Felt Mountain*. As a result, they were obliged to dub some decidedly lo-fi home cassette recordings into what became a much-admired audio masterpiece. Even more notably, megastar Bruce Springsteen abandoned a whole studio version of the album *Nebraska*, releasing his original four-track demos instead.

The Jupp band who had made the record wasted no time in getting on the road to support its release, playing in the UK and touring parts of Europe. Inevitably, Mickey blew hot and cold about this, as Ed Deane recalled:

"I think it's fair to say that he was a reluctant performer in a sense. There was no dressing up to go onstage or anything like that. No real concessions to the visual aspect - just no-nonsense rock and roll. He is primarily a songwriter who takes great pains in shaping his songs. That's his craft. I remember a gig we did that had a dartboard in the outer bar. After our soundcheck, Mickey passed the time by getting involved in a game with some locals. When it came time to go on I was given the job of reminding him that we were on in five minutes. He sort of rolled his eyes in despair, saying something like 'Oh really? Damn! Right in the middle of a game!' I don't remember doing an awful lot of touring with Mick. I don't think he enjoyed touring at all. We would do these short little forays into Europe, playing blues festivals and clubs. We played in Paris, Belgium, Germany, Holland and maybe Norway. On one occasion, after the third of five or six gigs in Germany, Mickey announced that he had had enough and wanted to go home. The last two gigs were the bigger payers and to lose them would have meant coming home with practically no money. I was very pissed off and confronted him, telling him that he couldn't do this to me in the middle of Germany when I had committed to do these gigs with him etc, etc, blah blah blah. He eventually relented and we finished the tour!"

The band's set list for that period reflected songs from right across Mickey's career, plus, of course, a few standards thrown in. On a typical night the running order would be something like this:

Schooldays, Blues For The Blues, Songwriters Lament, Brother Doctor Sister Nurse, Hole In my Pocket, Modern Music, Orlando FLA, Sweet Little Rock 'n' Roller, Till Honkey Gets Tonky Again, Don't Go Home, Big Black Cadillac, Sea Cruise, Taxi Driver, Crossroads, Shine On My Shoes, Memphis Tennessee, Switchboard Susan, Walkin' My Way Back Home, Old Rock 'n' Roller, Bye Bye Johnny.

What a shame nobody taped one of those shows.

But while the band was tight, the gigs to promote the album were not all plain sailing. Henry Scott-Irvine remembers one night in London's Oxford Street that was a bit of a let down:

"The next time I saw Mickey after the no-show on the Be Stiff tour was one night at the 100 Club. Mickey was supporting the *Yeahs* album with the Big Figure on drums, etc. After seven or eight songs he said he had flu and so wasn't going to play any more: it wasn't working and his voice wasn't up to continuing. 'There's not enough people here to make it worthwhile going on', he said, 'that's it.' But there were 150 or so there. He just wasn't happy again."

On the other hand, Mickey psyched himself up sufficiently to appear in the first of two Roger Deakin's TV documentaries in which he features, *Southend Rock*. Shot in April 1992, it featured several tracks from *As The Yeahs Go By*, along with the usual paean of praise from fellow mucicans, critics and narrator Billy Bragg.

Nobody expected Mickey to have hit records any more, but this was a fine album with which to bring any career to a close - for that's what it seemed destined to do. As Will Birch pointed out, it wasn't released to make money; in fact it probably lost money. And great as many of the gigs were – this author saw a couple of outstanding ones - the audiences weren't big enough to boost record sales by much.

But importantly it was proof positive that the quality of Mickey's songwriting was as high as ever.

There was life in the old dog yet.

The *As the Yeahs Go By* Album

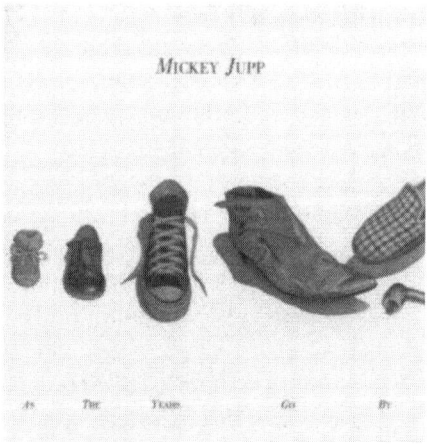

After the false step of *X*, Mickey was right back on form with this one.

For a start there was no pressure: his record company was run by fan and fellow Southender, Will Birch; the co-producer was old friend, Mo Witham; and Mickey had enjoyed a good interlude in which to stockpile some quality material, back writing on his own again after the "Lennon-McCartney" experiment with Chris East. OK, the less sophisticated studio may have slightly compromised the richness of sound compared to what a top London facility could have delivered, but in the end this barely shows, given the quality of songs and performances.

Standing At The Crossroads kick-starts the listener's attention from the off. Funky piano and boogie guitar combine over a super solid yet unpretentious rhythm section performance, (years in Dr Feelgood had taught the Big Figure – then alongside bass partner John Sparkes - that their prime role was to root everything else firmly to the ground).

A very Chuck-y guitar solo punctuates Mickey's splendid delivery of a particularly sardonic lyric, featuring great lines like, *"I woke up this morning like I usually do"* and *"I guess I'm not the man she was looking for, I'm just the man she found"*. The whole thing cooks like crazy. Here's what Dave Edmunds said about the song in the sleeve notes for his album *Again,* which contained his version of it:

"Standing at the Crossroads was written by Mickey Jupp, a talented but massively under-appreciated songwriter. There are several possible reasons for this, one is that his demo recordings capture a feel and performance that are almost impossible to get the better of, but I think he would be happy with my rendition."

No Place Like Home gently feeds off Mr. Diddley's never-ending influence, with some nice subtle drumming (this tempo usually brings out the Animal in drummers, but not here) and bass work, sharply cut by some authentically bluesy guitar licks from the excellent Ed Deane. Held together by Mickey's Hammondy organ, the track is saved from any charge of predictability by an unexpected, suspended, ultra-catchy chorus.

All Sorts To Make a Woman is a bit of a surprise: a soft, lazy, romantic ballad sung over a marshmallow of bass, synths and acoustic guitar, highlighted by darting sax riffs from Frank Mead. While almost a little too sugary in places, (not a criticism one would normally make of Mr. Jupp's work), it has a very pretty melody and an innocent lyric that ought to have rendered it a natural for others to cover – all the way from cabaret crooner to black soul singer: I'm getting Des O'Connor and Wilson Pickett.

Nothing Happened Today opens with Mickey's tongue-in-cheek spoken introduction, a nod to the old Walter Brennan song, *Life Gets Tedious, Don't It?* But it soon morphs into a heads-down rocker of mumbling guitars embroidered with Jerry Lee piano. The arrangement breaks down again before regaining its momentum, driven by some suitably restrained, non-heroic bass and drums.

Not Wanted Any More is a belter, although it's by no means a belter, if you know what I mean. It's actually quite hard to describe. The basic rhythm pattern is made up of an almost imperceptible lightly lilting reggae organ, balanced against a beautiful piece of counterpoint bass. This is suspended in a cloud of superb blues guitar licks, over, of all things, a drum machine. It feels somewhat like a gentle, reflective build on one of Mickey's favourite standards, *St James Infirmary*, beautifully sung, voice cracks and all. There's a bit of the feel of Clapton's *I Shot The Sheriff* in there, too. Look, you need to hear it – it's a brilliant song. In fact, Clapton would probably have sold a million copies of this one had he ever recorded it. (Mickey was pleased to hear how much I appreciate this one as he says it doesn't get much praise – see how he anthropomorphises his songs...)

The Someone Special is one of Mickey's enjoyable, if slightly novelty, country rock songs. It's got a wailing harp, handclaps, a guitar like a freight train and goes at a sprightly lick. Once again, there's a surprising trace of blue beat in the upstroke rhythm.

From a Barstool opens with its catchy chorus, in which Mickey seems to be describing a new evening hobby: drinking to forget. Pushed onward by bubbly walking bass - way up in the mix - and runty sax grunts, the whole thing swings like a good pub band after a few pints, which is surely the point. Mickey sings hopefully of banishing his demons through the liberal application of Cumbrian bitter: *"I'm gonna make that world fold up, and fade away"*.

Old Rock'n'Roller makes a surprise comeback after its original outing on *Juppanese*, only now it's dressed in newer, cooler clothes - opening and ending as a slow, harmonica-led blues. In between, the band attacks the number with a little less rock but a lot more roll than the original Rockpile-backed version, presumably the reason Mickey wanted to re-visit the song for this album. It's a triumph from start to finish - all doo-wop, slapback vocals split by tearaway guitar and piano solos.

There's a Thing is a quality country mid-paced ballad, which Mickey sings over a synth bed reminiscent of a male voice choir, plus vamped piano. This foundation is adorned with some delicious soprano sax, weaving in and out like a wraith. It's simple but lovely – surely ripe for US singers to cover. If only Mickey had written it while he was in his Nashville-connected phase.

The other side of country is evident on *When Honky Gets Tonky Again*, the lyric of which can be interpreted more than one way. It's either presenting the unlikely return of genuine blues music as a metaphor for the duration of the singer's love, or it's a veiled threat that he will remain faithful only as long as his libido permits; it all depends what you think Mickey means by Honky, and what he means about it getting Tonky! Whichever, it's an amusing lyric, its innuendo given a knowing performance by Mickey, right down to the "yea" on the end.

(Linda Gail Lewis recorded a rather heavy-handed version of this one in the US)

In *Rock and Roll Peg* Mickey refers not to a girl named Peggy, rather of his own dilemma having moved way up North. He sings satirically of "getting it together in the country" – that great rock star cliché – while noting that due to the complete lack of musical interest in the place ("*all I ever hear about is sheep and potatoes, these local folk aren't no conversators*"), he's "*gotta get out of here before I get old*". Intricate overdubs are layered above Mickey's original demo, (retained for its unbeatable feel) while some Coaters/Summertime Blues deep voices interject, before Mickey typically revises the song's title in a naughty way. At the start "*I'm a rock and roll peg in a country hole*" refers to him being a fish out of water; by the end it refers to occasional amorous adventures with a country lass, if you get my gist.

Next up is the snappily titled *Doo-Wop, Shang-a–Lang, Shimmy Shimmy*. This smart homage to the music of the fifties chronicles teen love at the prom dance – a subject historically more US than UK, although today's British youth seem to be catching up.

Its twist is that the lyric is written from the point of view of a now long-married man, sifting back through his happy memories to that point. As we now know, it used Mickey's original demo as a bed, the upside of which is that the great, syncopated feel of the original is maintained. On the downside there are flashes of *that* synth sound from time to time. Fittingly, the song finishes with the massed ranks of Mickey Jupp on vocals, a dozen or more of him overlapping in *"Doo-Wops"*, *"Shang-a-Langs"* and *"Shimmy Shimmys"*.

The album ends in a country mood, with *Funny Old World*. Ed's guitar slides, Frank's sax swoops, Figure brushes away, while Mickey croons in his lowest Nashville register. If I'd been sequencing the album I think I would have swapped these last two tracks around, in order to end on a more dynamic note, but I suppose as an overall comment upon Mickey's whole life, *Funny Old World* makes logical sense as the closer of what he probably thought would be his final album.

Mickey, (now sporting a full beard) and the band from the album then went out on the road under the name Mickey Jupp's Cheque Book. They played some substantial venues, like the newly re-opened Town and Country Club, and recorded an excellent live set for BBC GLR but by now there was just too much inertia to be overcome. Had an engaged public been eagerly waiting for this album to come out, it's tempting to think it could have achieved some real commercial success. Had the music business still been paying attention to Mickey, it's hard not to imagine that some of these songs would have been successfully covered. But it was too late for all that by now.

Nevertheless, Mickey had once again proved that he still had it in him.

Mickey's loyal fans bought the record and were delighted to find this out.

But were there enough fans for him to keep going?

It soon transpired that there were, just where one might not have expected....

21 Old Rock And roller

In which, at the age of fifty, Mickey proves that you really are never too old to rock

With the Refreshments   courtesy Lasse Kärrbäck

It's a long lonely ride that I'm takin'
Maybe I'll see you down the line
Baby my heart is breaking
You can have my ticket any time

British Rail Blues (all change) **by Mickey Jupp, Shampoo Haircut and Shave**

It's now 1994. Mickey may be fifty but he isn't over yet.

His consistent touring in Europe plus the release and re-release of most of his past material meant he still had an active European fan base - particularly in Germany, Sweden, Holland, Denmark, Finland and Norway.

These loyal supporters had enjoyed their musical relationship with Mickey over the years and didn't want it to end. Mickey's UK fans may have felt the same but it was Europe that went and did something about it. As had happened so many times before, a third party, rather than the man himself, decided that Mickey's career was unfinished business. This time round it wasn't members of Southend bands Procol Harum, Dr Feelgood or the Kursaal Flyers. It was a chap from Sweden, who worked for Gazell Records.

"I'd been touring over there with a band called the Refreshments, so they knew me a bit," recalls Mickey.

The Refreshments were a very accomplished Swedish band consisting of Joakim Arnell on piano and guitar, Tord Eriksson on guitar, Mats Forsberg on drums and Micke Finell on sax. Mickey had played a number of concerts with them in April 1993 – a tremendous live recording of *Brother Sister Doctor Nurse* by Mickey and the band exists on an obscure CD (and iTunes if you dig a bit).

"Also Jerry Williams – the Swedish Cliff Richard, you might say – had recorded some of my songs and he was connected with Gazell Records." (In fact Jerry is still recording Mickey's compositions, including a rare song called *2 Sunsets and a Dream* on his 2011 album, *Alright*).

"They asked me if I wanted to record an album in Stockholm. I said yes thinking it would be with the Refreshments, a great band including Mats, the best drummer I ever played with. Mick Brownlee is a close second, actually, because he also swings even when he's playing straight."

But playing with the Refreshments was not what Gazell had in mind. They had bigger plans. Executive producer Jerry Williams (not his real name by the way, he is actually Erik Frenstrom) and his two studio producers, Ulf Jansson and Svante Persson, (now those do sound like real names), had a grander vision. They wanted to back Mickey with the musicians they had employed on other big-budget recording sessions. These were classically trained musicians: some played for a major symphony orchestra, others in a five-man brass band. Mickey, on the other hand, was not to play at all; for the first time ever he would purely be the vocalist on an album. There were to be changes, too, in the way the vocals were done, with Jerry Williams singing some backing vocals rather than the pure Mickey plus Mickey harmonies we had heard since the early days.

Mickey's first job was to send over demos of his preferred songs, so the Swedish session crew could prepare backing tracks. Not only would he not be playing on the record, for the first time ever he would have no involvement in it's arrangements or production. On past experience he was surely going to hate it.

But he didn't and he doesn't. The resultant album is one that Mickey likes a lot, although he recognises it's not quite flawless:

"Some of the playing is a bit stilted - they just couldn't let go and loosen up quite the way I'd have liked. It's particularly noticeable to me on *Ring Damn You Ring* and *Part of Your Furniture*. For example, I was mucking around with this thing called *You Wear My Ring* and they liked that a lot, so we decided to record it, but they changed the chords in places and put stuff too high in the mix. Overall it's probably my second favourite album, partly because I think the songs are pretty strong."

Recorded at Atlantic studios in March and April 1994, the album, named *You Say Rock* after a fragment of one of the lyrics it contains, (once again - but this time it's a pretty strong title), was put out later that year on Gazell Records in Sweden and Crisis Records in Holland.

For Mickey it had been an entirely different experience, free of many of the tensions that had made recording previous albums such heavy going:

"On *You Say Rock* I never played a note, I just sang. Even though I had a cold at the time, it was good to be just singing. I recorded the vocals in the middle of a big studio without any sound baffles, really relaxed."

And Mickey was among true admirers, who got the chance to work with a stress-free artist, for once:

"I remember overdubbing some harmonies on *Sonya's Song* and I said at one point that I wanted to improve it, go again. Ulf, the producer, paid me one of the biggest compliments I've ever had, saying 'it's good to work with a singer who knows what he's doing'. They looked after me well there. They assumed that being a Brit I'd want endless cups of tea but the studio didn't have a kettle, so they provided me with a little gas ring and my own saucepan to brew up in!"

While Mickey was generally happy not to be playing on the album there were moments when he itched to get stuck in:

"The only time I felt that I should have been playing was where they were being too precise for rock and roll – which is why, as I said, *Ring Damn You Ring* doesn't quite work. My demo recording of that is the same tempo and key, but it's a completely different ballgame. But the slow songs on that album are just great."

Not playing didn't completely stop Mickey getting involved with the notes that other people were playing, either:

"There were some good musicians there but in *Heave to My Hearties* I did score a point over the bass player. When it goes into the first chorus I wanted the bass to play simple notes along with the other instruments - he said it wouldn't work. But he tried it and he admitted it did, so that's how we recorded it."

Aged fifty, Mickey really was becoming an old rock and roller by now, but despite this he returned to Europe - with the Refreshments in tow - to promote the album in June 1994, paying further return visits in 1995 and 1996. Typically, though, Mickey managed to turn his pleasure in playing with the Refreshments into a small diplomatic incident back in the UK, as Tex Comer recalls:

"We're all mates as well as band mates, playing the odd UK gig still. Then Mick goes over to Sweden to record the vocals for the album and comes back raving about the Swedish backing band out there! Apparently they could do his stuff *properly*, even the backing vocals. I was left thinking, 'Bloody hell, where's me next gig going to come from now?' It was a little bit insensitive, but Mick can be insensitive. When I first started working with him he used to wind me up terribly; we never got to blows but we did have our little clashes now and then. But musically, I just loved what he does. As soon as he sits down to play, I'm a goner. I used to go into a sort of trance. I've always loved playing with him.

So it was one of the things I found a little bit odd about him; that he could be really quite hurtful at times, without even realising he was doing it. He just says what's on his mind, I suppose. You have to get used to it because while he's not the easiest man in the world to work with, deep down he is a lovely fellah."

418

You Say Rock was to be Mickey's last commercially released album of new material, although it didn't need to be. Today, at the age of seventy odd, there are still open offers for him to go back and record another album in Scandinavia, but Mickey isn't having it:

"They want me to do another right now but I haven't got the enthusiasm. They said that if I didn't want the bother of going over to Sweden to record it, I could send them the demos. They'd then record the backing tracks and send them back for me to add vocals here in the UK - but I don't use a computer to record, so that would be difficult. And I know what will happen: next it would be, 'You've got to come over and do touring to support it', and I don't want any of that, not any more. I think I'm entitled to say thanks folks but I've had enough of all that."

Once again, it seems he has no passport, something his current musical collaborator, Mo Witham, finds amusing but frustrating:

"Lars Karbaak said he'd get him a passport to physically go to Sweden. Or I said I could record his vocals over here, overdubbing the Refreshments' backing tracks. But he won't do it. He's sort of had enough. He doesn't listen to music any more; he got rid of his telly - so no American football, he used to love that. He's finally worked out what he wants; got his routine to stick to. And that's that. He doesn't need much money to live off, so he sounds happy enough to me."

The man himself owns up to his reasons:

"As I got, how shall we say, more decrepit, I started to wish any success away. I didn't want to know, really. It would mean hard work, going out doing gigs, travelling – which is why I don't have a passport any more, a good excuse."

The *You Say Rock* album never received a release in the UK, which is a great pity. By this time our domestic record industry seemed to have finally come to the conclusion that Mickey was not going to make it big after all. Or even medium sized. It is to the credit of the rest of Northern Europe that they have continued to stand by him. But even Mickey was unsure about his prospects, selling his *You Say Rock* artist's royalty rights back to the record company for just a couple of thousand pounds:

"I've done it on other albums, too – never got more than about three grand, mind you. But for me it's win-win: at least I get something that way. And I've still got the songwriting if it becomes a hit - which it won't, because they never are!"

Anyway, thanks to Amazon, iTunes and the like, these tracks can be accessed in the UK, while copies of the CD are often on eBay and Amazon.

I don't know Christopher Webb, but I hope he will forgive me for quoting his short Amazon review of *You Say Rock*, posted in August 2013, for it sums things up rather well:

"Highly talented singer songwriter who deserves as much praise as possible. Another great album, one that others could only dream of achieving. You will want all the others after listening to this."

Indeed you will.

However, Mickey was not an entirely forgotten man in the UK, either: praise for, and interest in him was still to be found back in 1994. That year the now late Roger Deakin - well known academic, wildlife lover, (a frequent visitor to the Lakes, where he liked to swim) and writer - went so far as to make a half hour TV documentary for Anglia TV about Mickey and the Southend music scene, called *Long Distance Romancer*. Until recently, bootleg copies - excerpts from which have been floating around the Internet for a while - have been the only means of viewing it. The film was finally released in its entirety as part of the 2014 Repertoire box set, *Kiss Me Quick, Squeeze Me Slow*. In it, Wilko Johnson seizes the chance to praise Mickey some more, saying, "There are so many famous musicians in this country, but they haven't got that thing, and he's got tons of it", while Deakin's voice-over makes the point that "Mickey Jupp is one of those people whose name is always prefixed with 'The Legendary.'"

Well, its certainly been hammered home often enough in band name or album title. Also, it's true.

But whatever interest the TV exposure may have stirred among the UK record buying public was entirely wasted: for there was no new album to buy in Mickey's homeland. Nor would there ever be another.

Except there would be - sort of - as we shall see.

The *You Say Rock* Album

This one is the big surprise, the unexpected gem.

It's Mickey's second favourite album but then he has always had a bit of a down on his earlier work. It's not hard to see why he likes this one, though: the musicians are excellent, the engineering immaculate, the production extremely assured and the songs and their arrangements really strong. And then there is Mickey's singing. With cold or not, I truly reckon this to be the best realized set of vocal performances he has ever recorded – the power and flexibility of his voice in no way diminished by the years, now joined by greater levels of control and interpretative skill.

On the downside, and there isn't much, the entire thing is super controlled - in a sort of squeaky-clean, Abba-like way, which in some places can be a strength but in others a slight hindrance to the feel. Taken as a whole, it's a triumph; absolute proof that Mickey's talent was undimmed as he reached his half-century.

It is also the first time ever that he had recorded an album and not played a thing on it, just sung: a degree of focus that clearly played a part in the high quality of the end product.

You Wear My Ring announces its intentions with a crisp beating opening, unexpectedly punctuated by sliding, sinuous strings. Everything comes together to merge into a great feel, even if the playing is more mechanically spot-on than we are used to on Mickey's records. His singing is rich and animated – well set off by backing vocals which, for once, aren't 100% Mickey. (Don't get me wrong, Mickey's backing vocals are the best around, but the contrast here seems to work for the first time). It's a great start.

Anything You Say is an easy rolling piece, a fragment of whose lyric gives the album its title. Fuzzy bass and glistening guitars hang above hefty drums in the gin-clear mix, embellished with subtle organ touches and first-rate understated drumming. Mickey's voice is in excellent form again.

I Thought I Heard Something opens with Mickey as a deep Elvis, over a faux Dave Edmunds guitar sound. Thereafter, the stepped key changes show off Mickey's still-impressive vocal range, in a fine chorus faintly reminiscent of *Rooms In Your Roof*.

Heave To My Hearties is a lovely ballad with a superb classic fifties rock structure, some unusual chords cleverly dropped in to give it real freshness. The temptation to pastiche the song is resisted, preserving a simple piano and acoustic guitar arrangement, gently assisted by bass and brushed drums - later joined by a lovely delicate string arrangement. Mickey sings it superbly well with no trace of irony, despite the somewhat piratical lyrical influences! I know people (including my wife) who cried when first hearing it.

The Fortunate Few sees us back in dirty blues-with-harmonica territory. The quality of the playing is unquestionable, although it doesn't "roll" quite as much as Mickey would probably have liked, despite some tasty organ playing and fine backing vocals behind his singing.

Modern Music, for reasons not entirely clear, revisits Mickey's original from *Some People Can't Dance*, although this time it's a subtler, almost bossa-nova version. Overall it's simple, immaculate stuff, although rather unexpectedly the arrangement features a spectacularly gymnastic, overly prominent bass line throughout. Mickey sings with terrific animation and skill: a real vocal master class.

Three Little Words is a wonderful musical time warp – a slow, bluesy blend of fretless bass and church organ, blossoming into something much more soulful as the beautifully restrained brass section arrives. This controlled and contained backing track, rippled through with elegant guitar and bass, forms the perfect base from which Mickey can let rip a fine, raw vocal. It really could be Stax.

Ring Damn You, Ring sets off in an entirely different direction - all slapback rock and roll, with a jumping piano line and Scotty Moore guitar licks. The sounds are cleverly authentic of the era: the drums thin and clacky, the guitar stridently toppy, the bass muffled and walking underneath everything else. Mickey sings in his best Elvis/Ricky Nelson manner, his voice suitably treated and bolstered by some vintage-style backing vocals.

Sonia's Song is quite an unusual departure: slightly country-pop and sung in a very straight, sincere manner over an almost easy-listening backing track.

It feels like Mickey means this one – an older man observing an interesting, attractive but ultimately unattainable much younger girl. It's a song that could have been covered a lot – although I'm not sure the narrowness of the title would have helped much in that respect, and these days political correctness might frown on the subject matter.

Part of Your Furniture is probably not amongst Mickey's strongest songs, although I know he likes it enough to have later privately put out his demo version, which he prefers. One can see why he has some reservations about this reading of it: the clean, careful arrangement and playing mean the track struggles to swing in the way the song demands. For the first time the musicians sound like the session men they are: a bit off the pace, but doggedly soldiering on in a professional fashion.

Good Gracious Me – not involving any mock-Indian accents - features nice sturdy brass and jangling piano in an arrangement that pays homage to Jerry Lee Lewis, whose *Great Balls of Fire* chorus it also half-echoes. This perfect live song is draped in rocker echo, driven by insistent bass and drums, interwoven with that splendid brass section. It makes a great, archetypal album-closing number.

And, as it turned out, a career-closing number - certainly as far as third-party record companies were concerned. Mickey's fans will always be sad that he turned down the regular offers he received to repeat this formula and bring new helpings of his outstanding compositions to our record collections. How else were we ever going to hear any more of great new Jupp songs, those precious creatures he was so driven to share with the world?

In time there was going to be a way, but for now the technology, and Mickey's mindset, simply weren't up to it.

424

22 So Long

In which Mickey finally finds a formula for settling down

Mickey's Lake District gallery   courtesy Nessie Haslehurst

> *Well each and every evening, I'm a patron at the same old bar*
> *Sitting on the same old barstool, sipping from the same old jar*
> *Talking to the same old people, about the same old thing*
> *I like my world the way it is*
> *That's why you can't come in*

I Like My Little World by Mickey Jupp, demo

In *I Like My Little World,* a recently written song, Mickey makes his position clear: he wants what he has, and he has what he wants - so kindly leave him alone. In person, he expands his feelings on the matter thus:

"I'll stay at home and mow the grass, somebody else can tread the boards. I just wanted my songs recorded. Basically, I'm quite lazy. Just being a writer would suit me fine. I go for a walk in the morning, write songs in the afternoon and have a couple of pints in the evening, then sometimes a little bit more writing after that".

This might appear a sad and solitary existence to some, but that isn't how Mickey sees it. For him, the solitude is splendid isolation.

Boot, the village he lives in, is a small and remote place where everybody knows everybody else, and everybody else's business. There's a real sense of community, people look out for one another. When Mickey is without a car, (a not unusual situation), another villager lets him borrow his for the odd trip Mickey feels forced to make. There are some incomers, of course. During the day, a gaggle or two of hikers are likely to invade, but most of them will be gone soon enough. It's beautiful round here, yet unlike much of the more accessible, picture-postcard areas of the Lakes, it isn't a tourist trap and so offers Mickey the peace he's always sought. To Mickey's delight, despite the remoteness there's a nearby railway station: 'Dalegarth for Boot' is part of the enthusiast-operated Ravenglass & Eskdale Steam Railway. Its downside is that it bringeth the tourist; its upside is it also taketh them away. For Mickey himself, trips out of Boot are to be resisted as long as possible, other than his regular good long walks – and for regular read daily.

Leaving the village is only ever for unavoidable reasons, such as a round trip to PC World in Workington to get a vital component for his computer, or a gig. Such travel is not welcomed, put off for as long as possible. Even the odd visit to his musical collaborator Mo Witham in Burton-in-Kendal (all of thirty eight miles away) is a bit of a trial, something to be tolerated and minimized. Mo finds this amusing:

"You can't keep him here for long; he has to go back to the valley - it's like a drug. He'll suddenly say, 'I've got to leave now, it's getting dark'. I'll say 'Well you can drive in the dark, or stay over in the spare room if you like', but no, he's got to get back there right away."

Back to his romantic village, waiting for him deep in the romantic Lake District. But as for any other sort of romance, Mickey is these days of a different persuasion:

426

"I don't want any more wives. There is a lady I'm quite close to but she lives a fair way away. There's always a drawback you know - story of my life."

And music?

"I play in a pub now and again with Mo, that's enough for me."

But there was another important element in Mickey's life for quite some time.

In 1998 he opened a gallery in Boot – the Fold End Gallery: a place that was to be the centre of his world for the next fifteen years, except for a brief interlude in 2004 when he "buggered off to Southminster for six months, to be with a particular lady." The Gallery was set up to sell 'arts and crafts and nice things', Mickey's long-term collaborator, Chris East, already operating a similar venture outside Millom, some fifteen miles away. Mickey remembers the moment he took the plunge:

"The opportunity to buy the shop came out of the blue. I was thinking of moving away from rock and roll touring and at that very moment Michael, who owned it, offered me the chance to buy it, his previous sale having fallen through. I said I don't think so but then while I was hoovering a bit later on I thought well, maybe I'll see what he wants for it, because in those days I had a few bob in the bank. I remember thinking if I don't do this I'll be kicking myself for the rest of my life."

At least Mickey by now had some savings. His life had usually been lived hand-to-mouth, not that he seemed to mind too much, according to a comment he made back in 1979:

"I wouldn't know what to do if I made a lot of money, I never have. The other week I got a royalty cheque from PRS for a thousand pounds and that was the most money I've had, ever. It was strange, so I had to go and spend it – all on recording equipment – not clothes or cars; that never occurred to me – and now I'm broke again. I'm quite happy, though. Anyway, not having done well leaves you something to look forward to: the big house and stuff! I've been in the music business for sixteen years now and I have had good times and bad. I look forward to more good and bad times ahead. If we'd made it big early, perhaps I would have been in and out and all over by now."

By now that future had been spent. It seemed a good time for a new beginning.

From the start, one of the key components of Mickey's gallery was his own art. Forty years after leaving Art College he had taken up painting again, producing charmingly simple yet skillful watercolours of the dramatic local landscape, hundreds of which he has sold down the years. So the gallery gave him a small income to supplement his musical one – something that came in handy as the royalties began to dwindle.

The best Mickey could hope for now was the odd advance for re-releases of his old recordings, some modest fees for a few local gigs and perhaps a bigger-earning show once a year back at the Cricketers (now renamed Club Riga) in Southend. Mickey had long ago sold out most of his artist royalties for small lump sums, the cash being urgently needed at that time. Anyway, he never expected to make much as a recording artist, as we have seen.

But playing live was always a different proposition.

In 2000, Mickey played a Christmas gig at Club Riga with a scratch band; one he had first put together when temporarily living down South. By Mickey's account it turned out to be rather more than just a scratch band in performance terms:

"One day in 2000, the band - which was me, John Bobin on bass, Mick Brownlee on drums, Dennis Masterton on guitar - played at a crowded seafront pub in Burnham-on-Crouch, The Anchor I think it was called. That day we were one of the greatest rock and roll bands in the world. Dennis was on fire, the sound was great...but a couple of gigs later it had gone, it just wasn't the same again. You never know how or why that happens."

Dennis, whose last connection with Mickey had been prior to the release of Legend's first Bell album some thirty years earlier, remembers getting back together with him:

"In 2000, long after Mickey moved up to Cumbria, Mick Brownlee, who I had played with before, asked me if I wanted to do some gigs with Mick. He wanted to play a bit locally as he was seeing this woman in Southminster at the time, and was part-living there. We did the Riga, the Grand in Leigh and the Crawdaddy - we knew it was only ever going to be the odd gig over a couple of years."

It might have lasted longer, but as per normal, friction arose, as Dennis hesitantly relayed to me:

"In the end there was a bit of bad feeling between Mickey and Mick Brownlee, who had put in a lot of work getting the gigs together. He'd done the organizing of everything and all the publicity but didn't feel he got proper credit for it.

One time, I remember Mickey saying, 'Publicity? I don't need it, actually'.

So they fell out a bit and I assumed we would never play together again. We did, of course."

No doubt these gigs brought in some much-needed funds, but it is publishing income – his writer's royalties - and PRS payments that have really kept Mickey going down the years.

PRS, the income derived from public airings of various artists' recordings of a writer's songs, can still bring Mickey a few thousand a year, such is the body of work he has built up over time. More than a hundred bands or artists have recorded one or more of his compositions, covering eighty plus different songs in total. So there's a fair chance of some of them getting played, somewhere in the world, every now and then – and every little helps.

Mickey finally closed Fold End Gallery in Autumn 2013 - the strain of hanging around for hours in order to capture decreasing passing trade finally becoming too much for his fragile patience to bear. A man with his love of order expected to have his lunch hour on time, even if there were tourists about to get off the steam train, wanting to look around. Equally he did not like having to stay open longer than the official shop hours, even if he still had a few browsers in the gallery who might buy something. At one stage he reputedly put up a sign saying "Browsers Not Welcome". Such attitudes do not generally sit comfortably within successful retailing practice, so it was perhaps inevitable that the venture would wind down in the end. Mickey sees this as being as much about a change in customer type as his own waning patience:

"The first ten years it was OK. I was painting to satisfy my creative urge – I sold around 500 paintings. Not many people can say that - although I didn't charge much for them. Over the last five years it was nothing but browsers – people with a different attitude: 'We'll just take a look but we won't buy anything'.

That made me want to bang a few heads together so I thought I'd better get out.

Anyway, in the last full year my entire gallery turnover was under £8000, whereas for the first two years it was four or five times that. It didn't work out but I wouldn't say I regret it because it allowed me to stay in the village. And because I live in the downstairs – the gallery was upstairs - and bought the whole thing for cash, I haven't had to pay any rent for the past thirteen years!"

Mickey's long career in retail may have come to a full stop, but his preferred income stream, his music, hadn't quite. In fact, he hoped it might blossom now he could give it more attention, but he was soon reporting problems on Facebook:

"The recording nightmare is with me again. I can (I think) still come up with some good lyrical ideas but I am damned if I can record them. It is getting very worrying and annoying, that something I am expected to do reasonably easily is becoming very difficult. The problem is compounded by the fact that I no longer know what is good, bad or indifferent, musically. My plan - now that I am closing my gallery - was to devote more time and attention to writing songs, but - once again - I find myself wishing that there was something else I could do. Maybe wash pots at the pub!!"

(This thought was to become the inspiration for a future album title).

When he was managing to write them, Mickey's songs were published by Hornall Brothers, a company representing many, shall we say, veteran blue-chip writers, including Mark Knopfler, Joan Armatrading, Leo Sayer, Status Quo and John Fogerty. However, it seems many years since any of Mickey's songs had been placed with any other artists to record, which rather raises the question of what the point was in him writing them:

"Why do I do it? Good question. I've often asked myself that. What's the point?

They go to the publisher but nothing ever happens to them. Anything of mine that ever gets covered is normally from my old stuff. There aren't many old-style pluggers around any more to find new outlets."

Tired of waiting for a chance to set his songs free in the traditional way, Mickey instead turned himself into something of a cottage industry. It was an idea that originally came from his oldest musical friend, Chris East.

Proud of the songs he and Mickey had written together - and his position as the only writer Mickey had ever consistently collaborated with - in 2008 Chris issued a CD of some of the demos he and Mickey had recorded in their jointly owned studio many moons before. The intention was to sell them direct to fans via the web site 'mickeyjupp.com', which Chris registered for this purpose. Mickey did not object when told about the web site plan in advance, but has since maintained that he has no interest in the site, commenting:

"That's nothing to do with me. It is a hobby of Chris East's – I don't even know what's on it."

Unsurprisingly, when invited to participate in the release of vintage material, Mickey decided he wanted nothing to do with that, either - initially doubting sufficient quality could be achieved by simply digitally 'tweaking' old analogue tapes. Not that he was any keener when offered the chance to go into the studio and re-record portions of those songs:

"I don't really want to make another, proper album. I'd rather do what I can at home", was how he summed it up.

As ever, Mickey was interested in the future, not in re-visiting the past. So Chris went ahead on his own, as he was entitled to, the songs and recordings from that period being half his. He maintains that he made a point of giving Mickey his share of any royalties achieved, although this is something Mickey sometimes disputes; these two old friends displaying the same odd flash of discord that Mickey's long-term musical relationships always seem to suffer from.

And so it was that in 2008 *Never Too Old to Rock* was released, known colloquially as the *Red Brogue* album, for the cover was an 'update' of the famous Legend *Red Boot* one.

It's an ambitious re-working of old demos, with past members of Mickey's bands laying down new overdubs on top of the original demo tracks. It is credited to Legend on the cover and Mickey Jupp & Legend on the actual disc, although Mickey himself had nothing to do with it and disowns the CD. Those who are on it - Chris, Mo, John Bobin and Bob Clouter - re-play their way through *Never Too Old to Rock, Good Lookin', You Wear My Ring, Teach You Children, Claggin On', Tears For You, I Need a Woman, Good Enough for You* and *Function to Function*. Mickey's vocals are simply those that remain from the original demos – but these were always going to be fine performances, as we know.

Later Chris released two more CDs of demos, but without any additional overdubs: *Country and Northern* and *Nil Lyricus Shetlandium*. Then came a further "tweaked" collection entitled *David,* which utilised remote sampling of various past Legend alumni - even including former T Rex drummer Bill Fyfield from the original Vertigo Legend line-up - to achieve fuller arrangements and a more muscular sound, (more on these later).

That all the songs were twenty years old didn't matter much - a good song is a good song – but the old technology and old-school sounds from the original demos intrude in places; particularly some outmoded, unrealistic drum machine sounds and dated keyboards.

Mo Witham has always regretted these outdated sounds and would like to help Mickey make his past (and current) demos more contemporary:

"Mickey's publisher isn't pushing them much, but then look at the quality of the demos. No atmosphere, an ancient drum machine or that horrible old snare drum he found in a skip somewhere, the same old manky keyboard. I said to him 'I'll do your backing tracks for you, then you can come over to the studio to put vocals on - I don't want any money for it'. But he gave me a flat No."

Why would he do that, I asked?

"Because Mick hates the business - the way everything works; but the business is the business. It's what you have to do to get on."

Mickey admits as much himself:

"My career was my hobby, acted out bigger. That's why there's never been a game plan or goal – I've just drifted through. I'm kind of reluctant, always have been. These days I don't really even want to get in the car to drive to a gig, especially after all these years of getting in cars and driving somewhere miles away. I'm doing gigs these days 'cos I need the money – times are hard. Truth is I may play rock and roll, but I'm not Rock and Roll. I'm good at doing it, apparently, but I haven't got the other stuff you need to go with it – the attitude, the mental robustness."

There are plenty of other musicians who have drifted through their careers the same way; some washing up on the shore of success while others got becalmed in the doldrums. Because, to a certain type of musician, the music is the point - not the adoration or the business plan. Mickey's dogged adherence to the view that any form of marketing is toxic to his talent means that while he, Chris and Mo are still friends they sometimes fall out. Usually over the difference between what Chris and Mo want for Mickey versus what Mickey wants for himself.

Ron Bijnen found this out when, in an interview with Mickey in 2009, he strayed into the tricky area of those CDs of old demos. Mickey pulled no punches, saying: "Chris East wants to make money. I'm sick of that but they are also his songs so he does as he likes."

Mo Witham is philosophical about that outburst:

"We all know how we feel about each other. It's all been said. I've told Mickey, 'You know Chris is your best friend. You know he's done more for you than any other person on this planet'. Mickey says 'All he does is make money out of me'.

'But he makes money for you, too', I say. But he can be scathing about Chris."

Tellingly, despite all his misgivings, in 2009 Mickey followed Chris' suit and began to issue his own CDs. These are collections of songs that he has written solo and home recorded entirely on his own. They are more simply arranged than some of the earlier Jupp/East demos but due to Mickey's musical abilities often turn out as good or better - thanks to the excellent playing and great feel he generates when left to his own devices.

Drawn from a larger body of work produced over a longer period of time, and with better sounds in some cases, (although the dreaded keyboard sound that Gary Brooker wanted thrown into the sea does surface in places), these CDs are terrific, containing many unreleased gems. Because the recordings are all Mickey, he has had total control over the performances and which songs get released, in what order, and when.

The CDs are sold at gigs and through Facebook (the Fans of Mickey Jupp group has over 600 members), serving two important purposes. Firstly, they generate a little income for Mickey. Secondly, they give life to songs previously unreleased, or as he sees it, songs still trapped in his private domain. It quickly becomes evident when talking to Mickey just how much he cares about his songs, almost as if they were living entities:

"Once they're out in the big wide world, they are on their own", he told me, like a proud parent. As Mo puts it, "then his obligation to the song is done".

This isn't as unusual as we non-composers might think. Top keyboardist and songwriter Greg Phillinganes makes a similar comment about his own songwriting:

"It's from my gut, you can definitely feel it, it's amazing – it's like birthing a child".

And as with children, one loves one's progeny regardless of whether or not the rest of the world feels similarly. The passionate writer wants them to get a crack at a life of their own. For as Pulp's Jarvis Cocker observed, "a song isn't really a song until someone hears it."

As long ago as 1980, Mickey told Dutch magazine *De Telegraaf*, "I make albums that I like myself. If my neighbours like them, I'm satisfied. If the whole street likes them, I'm beaming. But that's about it."

By the noughties, Mickey's "whole street" had become, as well as his loyal gig-goers, his Facebook fan group: people with whom he could never have hoped to directly connect before the days of social media.

It was this web development that enabled him to market his private CDs to a select group of avid fans, who would happily purchase them and properly appreciate them. And thanks to advancing computer technology, he could burn at home the copies he sells, avoiding production costs that would otherwise have eaten into his meagre profits.

Yet while the income is much needed, and Mickey has many more tracks he could yet release, he is rigorous in what he is prepared to put out:

"In the first place, I put them onto CD, off the original tapes just for me - so I could easily locate any composition I wanted to hear again. From those files, the ones I already like most, I've collected what I think to be the best songs and performances."

Typically, Mickey has set the bar for what he will let into the public domain further up than many would – the result of his high standards and low boredom threshold:

"I don't really like recording. It's a bit of a chore and I can make mistakes. When I did the demo of *Trees Died* - a lot of people seem to like that song - I put the tambourine on it too loud in the mix. Did the same bloody thing on *West Coast Mainlining,* a song about the train journey from Euston to Carlisle, with the stations in it in the right order! So neither of them will be coming out on CD - not unless I can find someone with a very clever graphic equalizer to take out just that frequency, and I can't really be bothered."

In general, Mickey reckons his large collection of still-unreleased songs is of good quality:

"I don't write anything ordinary. I'm so critical about my writing that the mere fact that I finish a song means that it's pretty good. Next I want to perform that song perfectly, which is often the main problem in the studio - but what someone else does with it, I don't care. I'm flattered when I'm covered but I can't get myself to have a real interest in someone else's version."

It is interesting that, despite his self-confessed lack of confidence as a performer, Mickey has no such doubts about his songs. "I often think if someone else had written these songs they'd be world wide hits", he told me.

I ask him how it could be that the simple fact of *his* having written them meant they couldn't be successful. He pulls a face and replies, "It's all part of the plan", once again referencing what he sees as the story of his life...

By mid-2014 Mickey had privately released five demo compilation CDs: *Favourites, Favourites Too, Naughty Boy, Cambridge* and *Pot-washing.*

Each contains some great, previously unheard songs that the business had overlooked. The sales of his home made CDs wouldn't mean much to a record company but, with the unit price consisting almost entirely of profit, they provide him with useful income.

And they remind Mickey that he has a lot of fans out there still. But most of all, Mickey is thrilled to release more of his songs into the big, wide world:

"Of all my stuff I still prefer to listen to my demo CDs – all those songs that never got recorded. And I think I'm my own best producer. I reckon my *Favourites* CD series is mostly far better than my studio recorded albums. They're nice and fresh, not overdone, not too much reverb, which I hate: it's false, unnecessary. On my demos there's just a tweak that you'd hardly know was there. A dry vocal hits you right in the face – Otis Redding and Ray Charles didn't need to use much reverb...."

Mickey remains clear that he is better off on his own, as he recently spelt out in some sleeve notes:

"It's been suggested that I should enlist the help of other musicians but, for better or worse, I much prefer to go it alone. That way, if I get bored/peeved/etc, I can just walk away from it without letting anyone down. And, of course, when it all works I can gleefully tell myself 'I did that!'"

Mickey is not alone in holding these opinions. Roger Dopson, a fan who's been close to Mickey for many years, even writing sleeve notes for one CD re-issue, agrees wholeheartedly:

"The quality of the songs, and of Mickey's own singing and playing, on those CDRs of 'demos' that he has been doing for the past five or six years, is nothing short of astonishing. Indeed, some of his strongest-ever material has come out on these low-key, "unofficial releases". And yet no fucker knows about them! It's an absolute tragedy. I think their "demo" status makes these recordings all the more enjoyable. I don't believe Mickey could have greatly improved on any of these performances if he'd gone into a recording studio with a producer, an arranger, and sundry session musicians - they would have all got in the way, and the songs would have been wasted – like on the *Long Distance Romancer* LP."

The quality of Mickey's demos was always high, and this often became a problem, as Keith Reid spelled out:

"It was often frustrating making records with Mickey because his demos were always great – in some ways good enough to release, certainly they would have been if made with today's equipment."

But good as they may be, one day in 2015 Mickey claimed there would be no more CDs in the *Favourites* series.

His strict quality control standards meant the rejection of the rest of his back catalogue, and his current writing output was now too slow to fill up another release, at least in the foreseeable future, he maintained.

(Although, at the time of writing, Roger Dopson and fellow superfan Russ Cottee are trying to persuade Mickey to release another batch of quality tracks that they have identified from his huge back catalogue of unheard demos.)

Meanwhile, out in the big music business world Mickey was still getting releases, albeit of old favourites rather than new work. Over many years German labels Line and Repertoire have released his work, both with Legend and as a solo artist. Re-mastered CD versions with bonus tracks have added to the backlist of available material, taking in B-sides and rare tracks.

In 2004, Hux Records, a UK based label, released *Mickey Jupp Live at the BBC* - a marvellous historic reference, collecting together material broadcast on radio since the beginning of his career. Then in 2012 the same label re-issued *Shampoo, Haircut and Shave*, now on CD for the first time.

Mickey was typically ambiguous about all this:

"When Hux first contacted me about putting the *BBC* one out I said 'No', I didn't like the sound of the cassette they sent. But they kept on at me and in the end I agreed. It was exactly the same story with *Shampoo, Haircut and Shave*.

I guess I was getting a bit fed up with people digging up my old stuff when I had all this new stuff. I suppose it's nice when people are interested in whatever you've done - I just don't like the old sounds we were getting."

2012 also found DJ and former Fall member Marc Riley playing old Mickey BBC Radio I sessions on his new-fangled BBC Radio 6 Music show.

In 2013 we were treated to a re-mastered *Long Distance Romancer* from Repertoire, while *Oxford* - never officially released in the UK – finally made it onto CD here.

On top of that Repertoire issued a CD/DVD set of a German TV performances from 1979 as *Mickey Jupp Live at Rockpalast*.

Most interesting of all is the Mickey Jupp box set, *Kiss Me Quick, Squeeze Me Slow,* finally released on Repertoire in late 2014 - its issue date having been delayed several times over the previous twelve months.

It was well worth the wait, though - *Uncut Magazine* scoring it nine out of ten and *Record Collector* awarding it four stars out of five in their respective reviews, while blogger Stephen Foster commented, "This collection is the dog's undercarriage and will satisfy long-time fans as well as those who may only just be discovering what they've missed down the years."

Lifetime Jupp fan, journalist John Howard, who had reported on Legend's career for local Southend newspapers way back when, reviewed it glowingly for *UK Rock and Roll* magazine, commenting that Mickey "could be heading for the national recognition he has always deserved but never sought."

In the editorial of the same issue, editor Johnny Hop muses, "I've always been surprised that Mickey's songs haven't been plundered by today's rockin' bands."

(In fact, Mickey's recording of *S.P.Y* was included in the original cut of a feature film: Patrick Ryan's *Darkness on the Edge of Town*, although it had to be left out of the final version for copyright and budgetary reasons. Patrick, son of Southend musician Nick Ryan, had learned to love Mickey's music via his father's interest. He and brother Alex - multi-instrumentalist and these days Hozier's musical director - once recorded a barnstorming version of *Cheque Book*, on which they played and sang everything.)

While all this attention is good for Mickey's reputation, re-releases make less of a difference to his bank balance than one might expect, "Mostly with a re-release I get a small advance and then assume I won't see much else after that".

The continued interest would be good for his ego if he cared about such things, but it's notable that when Repertoire sent him four complimentary copies of his box set he passed them all on to other people: one each to long term musical collaborators Mo Witham, Bob Clouter and John Bobin and one to a friend. He is unworried that he has no copy himself.

By contrast, live gigs can provide double income: firstly in the form of his fee on the night, and secondly if it can help sell a few CDs – more recently from the *Favourites* series, or if the gig were recorded to be sold as a CD afterwards.

This process began in 2010 when Chris East's Wild Bird Records issued a CD called *The Mo Witham Band Live at the High Cross Inn*. The singer in the band was one Mickey Jupp – mostly singing rock'n'roll standards, with just two Jupp originals included in the set list. Any reader who might still be harbouring a faint suspicion that Mickey is really a closet egomaniac, merely pretending not to court fame, will be interested in how this strange form of billing came about, as Mo Witham explained to me:

"There's no arrogance with Mick. He's difficult but he's not arrogant. He actually always hated being the front man. That's why we went out as the Mo Witham Band - just for him not to have to be the front man. He didn't want to do it otherwise. 'I don't care about my name in lights', he said."

The following year came *The Mo Witham Band Live at the Riga Music Bar*, a longer set featuring half a dozen of Mickey's original songs out of 21 tracks.

Then there was a small switch in billing, reflecting the time in which Mickey and Mo started performing more as a duo: *Mickey Jupp and Mo Witham Live,* a recording of a gig at Mickey's then favourite local, the Boot Inn.

Late in Mickey's career, Mo was regularly coaxing him out of his shell and back to performance because Mo appreciates what working with Mickey has meant to his own musical life, despite the odd tricky moment:

"I'm just grateful that I met him – because I learned everything there is to learn from him. Let's face it, when you start out with someone who can sing like Mick, everything after doesn't measure up. He cannot sing a bad note – he's incapable of it. He's a complete and utter one off – there is nobody who can do what he does. Mind you, he's the hardest person I've ever had to work with."

And it doesn't seem to get much easier, either:

"I've worked with him for 50 years and I still don't know him. What I have learned is that he's completely unpredictable. There's no pre-agreed set list with him - he plays whatever he fancies doing next. Even then he doesn't tell you what's coming, not even the key. There's no count in; he just starts.

When it's just me and him playing some local pub that's fine, but when you're playing with a band - bass player, drummer, etc - they're all bewildered.

So I have to watch him hit the root note with his little finger and work out which song it might be and what key it might be in. Then I have to shout it to the rest of them! That's why he plays with the same musicians so often – we're sort of used to it..."

Another of Mickey's oldest friends, Chris East, has strong views on Mickey's reluctance to record and play more than he does:

"If you've got talent it ought to be illegal not to show it off for others to enjoy. If he did one gig a week in different local places he could make a lot of people happy and make a better living - but he only wants to work every six or eight weeks. The only way you'll get him to do anything is to put him in a sack and take him there. Finland, Germany, Sweden: he could go once a year, put out an album.

But he's Mickey, isn't he? Whatever you say, he'll say the opposite. He wants to be a free spirit; he doesn't want to get involved in the game. He can still be the same as he's always been: some moments of mellowness now, perhaps, but much the same. Though when he dies people will say, 'what a truly great songwriter'. I'm a great second man – I can maybe make Mickey's stuff a bit better - but I can't come up with the stuff in the first place. Not like he can."

While the Mickey & Mo duo found it handy to play local gigs in Cumbria, that didn't mean Mickey's band-playing days were over. On 16th and 17th March 2012, an astonishing event occurred, something fans thought they would never get to see: Legend reformed to play two gigs together. Mickey was to be joined on stage by Mo Witham, John Bobin and Bob Clouter: the original Legend Vertigo-era Mk 2 line-up.

Even more significantly, the Orioles best line-up was back in Southend at Club Riga, previously the Cricketers Inn: the very place Mickey had first gained his reputation as a crack musician.

Local paper, the *Southend Evening Echo*, made a big splash about the gig, John Howard – who else - quoting John Bobin's excited anticipation:

"It's going to be very good. A bit challenging because Mickey's lived in Cumbria for about thirty years, so I think we can guarantee it will be pretty unrehearsed; we'll have a run through on Friday afternoon then hit the stage running on Friday evening. We've got people from Sweden and Holland, some are staying over and coming to both gigs – they're gluttons for punishment, really."

(Those foreign fans are truly obsessive; one posting on Facebook: "There's no reason to hope that he will play outside England again. In one of the breaks, I got to ask when he would be willing to come to Sweden. Immediately and with emphasis, came the disappointing answer, 'Never! I'm done with that.'

You just have to accept that, and if you want to see Mickey Jupp, you have to go to England. But it's worth it.")

John also commented on the more than usually balanced set list they were planning:

"Mickey's written lots of really good songs over the years and we've persuaded him to do a lot more this time round."

Both nights were packed out as the band played a long two-hour-plus set, mixing standards with more than a dozen Mickey compositions, including *My Typewriter,* which received its first *ever* live outing: slightly rickety but great fun.

Record Collector magazine later referred to the reunion as "a small-scale version of Kate Bush at Hammersmith" - based on audience reaction rather than elaborate stagecraft, one assumes, because, as ever with Mickey, there was precious little of that. The article went on to bemoan the fact that Mickey was "a genuinely overlooked talent" who "remains a mystery to the wide world", referring to *Kiss Me Quick, Squeeze Me Slow* as "a superlative box set".

On the first night, when this author was present to take the photographs used for the album sleeve, the band sounded good despite being short of rehearsal - Mickey, as always, preferring to busk as much of it as possible. Unfortunately the recording gear at the venue was not working properly that Friday.

On Saturday night, Mickey's voice rather gave out – not all that surprising considering the length of the set the previous night plus a touch of unusually vigorous post-gig celebration. While Mickey could have re-recorded the vocals for the ensuing record – Mo suggested he could easily organise this back in Cumbria - he decided not to.

The double CD of the Saturday performance, entitled *A Living Legend* was subsequently released by Chris East via his website. And I was honoured that some of the shots of the band I had taken that night were chosen for the album sleeve.

Since then, Chris has plugged the Legend gap by releasing a further album, referred to earlier, called *David.* Named after a song of that name which it contains – one that many claim Mickey wrote about his brother David, but Mickey vehemently denies - the CD is credited to a band called Virtually Legend.

In truth, this is less a band and more a digital confection, one in which original Mickey and Chris demos have been augmented with live and sampled overdubs by Legend members Mo Witham, John Bobin, Bob Clouter and, more extraordinarily, Bill Fyfield from the Legend *Red Boot* era – despite living in America, from where he seems to have "phoned in" his contribution.

442

David offers up an impressive set of songs, well put together: *Got No God, Tell Me I'm Dreaming, Not Now Baby, Halfway to Heaven* (the slow version), *Big Black Cadillac, Island, The Difference, David* and *Stockholm*, this final song being yet another covered by Dave Edmunds.

With many artists, one would expect private releases of material recorded years before that "never made it" to be less than impressive.

But this material is a million miles from that, and richly deserves a wider hearing...

Mickey 's 'Unreleased' Releases

Some of the 'Favourites' series

While Mickey's professional recording career may be over - his choice, he still has that standing invitation to make another album in Scandinavia - his love for his songs has, as we have seen, led him to release material he considers to be his strongest in a series of privately issued CDs.

Mickey himself has released eight:

Favourites, Favourites Too, Naughty Boy, Cambridge, Pot-Washing, Body-building, Loose Ends and *Grumpy Corner* (copies are available from the man himself via Facebook).

Further songs in demo form have been issued by Chis East, (mostly co-writes between Mickey and Chris), on a number of CDs:

Never Too Old to Rock, Country and Northern (Collector's Edition Volume 1), Nil Lyricus Shetlandium (Collector's Edition Volume 2), David (Copies available at mickey.jupp.com)

As one would expect, the quality of songwriting is very high throughout, especially given that these are anthologies of the writers' very best compositions. The performances and recordings are pretty good, too.

What follows is a personal selection from these sources, a sort of 'Best Of The Best Of The Rest' from this listener's perspective. Everyone will have their own opinion, so I suggest that any interested reader invests in as many of these inexpensive CDs as possible while they are still available. This is particularly pertinent given this sort of view on further production, as stated in Mickey's blog in August 2014:

"Hi all. You've heard this before but you won't be hearing it again I have, for the final time, (last Monday) dismantled and packed away all my recording gear. And I feel gooood!! I daresay I might still write a song or two in the future but I won't be recording them here at home (if I record them at all). It's the recording part of things that I really find difficult. Sometimes I think that I would rather visit the dentist (!) than sit in my corner trying to commit music to 'tape'. This means that there will be no more CDs in the *Favourites* series."

As we shall see, Mickey subsequently changed his mind, and then changed it back again, and then changed it back once more...so you can never be quite sure.

Got No God (Favourites) is probably the most commercial song of Mickey's that no one ever recorded, including himself. (This isn't merely my view, it's Mickey's, too). Written just too late for inclusion on the *You Say Rock* album, it has fabulously wry lyrics, a hooky chorus and a feel that's downright joyful. Beware: once heard it is very hard to get out of your brain. There is a "sexed up" version of it on the Virtually Legend album, *David*. Some listeners prefer this reading – needless to say Mickey isn't one of them.

I Should Be Lovin' This (Favourites) is one of Mickey's most confessional songs; one in which he comes clean about how much he hates the rock and roll life – all of course ironically wrapped up in a rock and roll song: one he frequently plays as part of his rock and roll gigs. But few serious artists other than Mickey would want to go on record singing a song of such non-muso sentiment, which is a shame because it boogies like Chuck Berry at his best.

Written on a plane from Manchester to Stockholm on his way to tour with the Refreshments, the song was inspired by re-meeting a girl after a fourteen-year absence. (Mickey obviously had it bad because he also wrote *Got No God* and *Heave To My Hearties* - on the *You Say Rock* album - about his feelings for her.) The band met him when he landed at Arlanda, drove to Skovde, had a rehearsal, included this song in the set and played it at every gig thereafter. (That show, at a pub called Husaren, was recorded for Swedish radio by Lennart Wrigholm).

Seeing Simone (Favourites) is a sweet ballad that, strangely, gives off echoes of Nina Simone (no relation to the subject of the song), being piano-led before melting into a sweet harmony chorus that sticks in the memory. It was 'sort of' written with a Nashville pro called Kent Robbins, but Mickey re-wrote into this final form having had second thoughts after returning from his writing trip to the States.

The Difference (Favourites) is simply brilliant and out-Chucks Chuck Berry himself for funky swing and witty lyrics. The simple premise of the song is that *"there's a difference between the things we remember and the things we will never forget"*: a thought prompted by something Mickey overheard in a bar, before turning it into a clever and rather moving number.

Function to Function (Favourites) only borrows an intro from Mr. Berry (a very *Memphis, Tennessee* one) before breaking into its own good-time stride, complete with girlie chorus (Mickey and Chris East speeded up, I'll wager). Although the song is written about functions as in gigs, its inspiration was a tape recorder knob labeled 'function'! This didn't put Chris Farlowe off covering it.

Out on the Edge (Favourites) is cosmic jazz-style noodling of a style more closely associated with Mickey's favourites and one-time producers, 10cc. It features a fiendishly clever lyric built around the life of a hydrogen molecule (!), ending with the immortal line *"I look at my clock but it always says sixteen million to nine"*. Mickey says, "I think I'm the only person who likes it". Wrong.

David (Favourites). Mickey claims it's about a girl called Stefanee, (the subject of another of his songs of that name), with whom he was infatuated yet who would only talk about her boyfriend at the time, a chap named David. Just about everyone else who knows him thinks it's really about Mickey's younger brother, David, (who tragically died of leukemia in 2003). Either way it's a great song about being fed up with hearing about nothing but someone else's virtues morning, noon and night. It would have made a terrific single for Mickey, for Dave Edmunds, for Status Quo, for almost anyone.

My One and Only Someone Else's Girl (Favourites Too) would be another single contender, particularly if Mickey could have got Dave Edmunds to produce it. Mickey got close to achieving this goal on a couple of projects but their work diaries never coincided sufficiently for these two mutual admirers (Dave having recorded four of Mickey's songs on his own albums) to have got together. The almost sing-along chorus, vaguely reminiscent of Shirley Ellis' *Clapping Song*, is unusual for a Jupp song, but highly effective.

I like My Little World (Favourite Too) is Mickeys unequivocal kiss-off to the rest of us: his explanation for why he doesn't want to come out and play any more.

It's a sweet shuffle of a song but the lyrics are one long stare straight into any impudent visitor's eye. There's more than a touch of Royston Vasey here.

Some Roads (Favourites Too) features Mickey in the guise of a black vocal harmony group, to great effect. In some ways it sets out his philosophy for coping with the financial consequences of living the way outlined in the previous song: *"As long as I'm losing, I know I'm alive"*. However, it is cleverly celebratory in tone, taken at a fast lick in an upbeat, gospel style. You could almost imagine these sounds floating out of a chapel window somewhere in the Deep South...

I'm Going to End Up in a Home (Favourites Too) is not as bleak as it sounds because the home he is referring to is not actually an old folks home, although in a typical Jupp lyric trick, this doesn't become clear until later in the song. The words and sentiment are reminiscent of vintage Randy Newman, although the vocals are thankfully of a higher Mickey standard (no offence, Randy) – in particular his Deep River Boys backing.

Searching for Andromeda (Naughty Boy) finds Mickey in a reflective mood, star gazing his way through this gentle piano-based philosophical blues.

Somewhere South (Naughty Boy) is a country song of the Jimmy Buffet sort, with a particularly interesting melody. Written in 2011, it surely could have found a taker on the other side of the Atlantic, had it got the right sort of plugging.

Trying to Unlike You (Naughty Boy) has nothing to do with Facebook. In fact it's one of Mickey's reflective semi-ballads, one he likes sufficiently to frequently play on stage these days – a rare compliment to it.

Denial (Naughty Boy) is a simple but fiendishly clever song in which Mickey sings two separate vocal parts: the narrator expresses one view while a Roman-style chorus of backing vocals suggest that he actually means quite the opposite.
Mickey has adopted this very effective technique on a number of songs in the past, but this is the most extreme example.

Song for Holly (Naughty Boy) is Mickey's direct response to a challenge from his local barmaid to write a song about her, leading to quite a heartfelt little ballad. Maybe calling it *A Song For Someone* would have given it more traction for other performers who might want to cover it, but by the time it was written in 2013 Mickey had probably given up any such expectations.

I Beg Your Pardon (Cambridge) is a neat ditty in which Mickey's lyric cleverly showcases both halves of a difficult conversation between two lovers. Must have been a bugger to record, given that on home demos he has to do the backing vocals before the main vocal can be done. You'll understand if you listen to it...

Times Like These (Cambridge) is a sad little story about trying to cope with life's recurring disappointments: "*Out of the woods, into the trees, trouble to trouble with the greatest of ease, I wouldn't wish anybody times like these*". One hopes it's not entirely autobiographical but fears it might be reflective of how he sometimes feels.

Scratch My Vinyl (Cambridge) is an almost skiffly country-folk number with laugh out loud lyrics in which Mickey illustrates the depth of his affection for his beloved by offering to let her "*scratch my vinyl, kick my dog.*"

Alexis Reisenhofer, in proudly posting a photograph of an extensive collection of Jupp vinyl on Facebook, proved the inspiration for this particular song!

I wish (Pot-Washing) is a typically cleverly constructed Jupp lyric, set to a melody line that crosses and teases the basic rhythm. Good to see that he was still writing songs this sharp as recently as 2013.

One More Won't Hurt (Pot-Washing) harks back to 2004, when it was written, and looks back even further in its echoes of Mickey's Legend Vertigo era writing. It's a slow blues that sounds like close relative of *Hole in My Pocket,* complete with classic blues riffs and stabbing piano.

Don't Blame Me (Pot-Washing) is Elvis updated, telling the story of Mickey's bad luck: "*don't blame me when things fall to pieces, just because I'm there when they do*". The great rolling piano and fat vocal chorus have RCA Victor 1959 written all over them.

The Town Had a Night On Me (Pot-Washing) is an anthem to hangovers: short, sharp and hugely catchy. It is yet another contemporary song that could have been a hit in many past eras, and maybe even today if anyone, apart from his fan base, was listening.

Doctored (Loose Ends) is a sort of follow up to *Down at the Doctor's* with a great live feel, some top-notch piano playing and another set of suitably risqué lyrics.

Dirty The Sheets (Loose Ends) is a legendary, head-on propositional song of unabashed directness:
"Come on baby let's dirty the sheets,
Let's do it 'till the floorboards squeak,
I'm a red-blooded boy who's been without it for weeks,
Come on baby let's dirty the sheets."
Naughty but nice, its lascivious stance may embarrass its writer these days, which might explain its exclusion from any of the private releases for so long (and probably also accounts for why it wasn't picked-up on back when it was written!). Its belated appearance is due to the fact that these tracks were picked from a long list prepared by fans Roger Dopson and Russ Cottee, who loyally listened through most of Mickey's archive to pull out what they saw as hidden gems.

Close but No Cigar (Loose Ends) is clearly actually Chuck Berry with a just a bit of Jupp overdubbing! The lyric is brilliant, a witty take on not quite making it to third base.

Monk Moor (Loose Ends) is a great, heartfelt slow ballad, unusually about the resolution to a world of pain. It's a bit *Not Wanted Anymore* in places and a bit *St James Infirmary* in others, but it's a lot more than that. It sounds like a fuller recording than most demos, with some splendid blues guitar (Ed Deane?) smeared across this most bluesy of blues. Fabulous.

I Wish This Car Was a Train (Loose Ends) is a splendid song about a favourite subject, although the demo is a little on the thin side and a tad too fast to settle. Jerry Lee's sister Linda Gail recorded a superb version in 2009 on her album *Lie and Deny*.

450

England From The Air (Loose Ends) is a smart little song, one lyrical element of which later re-surfaced in the song *Short List*. This compact love ballad, fashioned from synth pads and twangy guitars, maybe needed a bit more work but is very fine nonetheless.

If I Could Cry These Tears Again (Country and Northern) is the full Don Gibson with a touch of Everlies thrown in. A terrific, quality country song it seems extraordinary that no one picked up on, with its distinctive chorus of *"Boo Hoo, Boo Hoo"* and handy Chris East harmonica work.

Wallflower (Country and Northern) is a pretty little song with a sad lyric and a great original melody. It's got mega Country hit written all over it but, as Mickey always maintains, we don't write them like they do over there, so perhaps they didn't get it, (or, more likely, I don't).

Halfway to Heaven (Nil Lyricus Shetlandium) is an up-tempo version of a song that I personally prefer in the slower, more reflective alternative version that lies somewhere in the vaults. Either way it's a good song, if a bit bubblegum at this pace!

How about you (Nil Lyricus Shetlandium) may be written by Mickey and Chris but vocally it features Mickey and Michelle Jupp: in that Mickey sings a female part (via a speeded up vocal) as well as his own, presumably in order to market a song directly to the - it has to be said rather small - duet market! Either that or the boys just got bored one day and did it like this for fun. Either way, this is a really strong song – a little slice of pure poppery.

My Turn Now (Nil Lyricus Shetlandium) has to be one of the best songs Mickey and Chris ever wrote. I first heard it many years ago, just the once, yet it struck home sufficiently strongly for me to largely remember it from that single exposure. It's a power ballad with a great chord construction, tune and arrangement – think Bee Gees. And this is a pretty hot demo, too – with strong vocals and a convincing mock string section.

October Mornings ((Nil Lyricus Shetlandium) is a terrific, bucolic song that sets out to celebrate the British weather from the point of view, or perhaps metaphor of, a migrating bird. It's a mix of big twelve-strings and dreamy synths sounding as fulsome as only a master recording can usually manage.

Trees Died (Body -building) is an interesting little number that centres round the fact that precious paper, from precious trees, was wasted in the farewell note our hero was left by his ex-partner. There's a tiny bit of Don Gibson in this one.

You Stupid Moon (Body-building) is a cracker of a rolling lament, complete with amusing lyrics and a touch of *Your Cheating Heart* buried away deep in the verse.

Little Old Me (Body-building) is a gentle, melodic composition; an exploration of Mickey's motivation for writing songs, complete with some cool sounds and rich harmonies.

Friday Night (Grumpy Corner) is a paen of praise to the weekend; one that swings like hell – I would love to hear it as a master recording, but only providing the demo's great feel could be retained – the usual conundrum.

The Last Of Me (Grumpy Corner) is a lovely tune with lyrics that reflects on the fact that most things in life will pass, but "you won't ever see the last of me". Here's hoping.

Now here are a couple of gems that got away: tracks to be sought out on the various bootlegs that sometimes float around:
A Million Stars (unreleased) is a keyboard-led, plaintive love song with an aching bridge and chorus. It would have been great on a film soundtrack.
Close to me (unreleased) is a rather disturbing recording with a spiky, almost oriental arrangement wrapped around a clever lyric that confesses to infidelity while pledging future faithfulness: distinctly oddball but most interesting.
Go have a dig on Facebook, YouTube and Soundcloud; there are diamonds in that there dust.

23 Heather On The Hill

In which Mickey turns seventy and takes stock

Home Sweet Home   courtesy Fans of Mickey Jupp

I just know it in my heart
I can feel it in my bones
The way my life is going
I'm gonna end up in a home

I'm gonna end up in a home by **Mickey Jupp, demo**

In March 2014, Mickey turned seventy. To the surprise of many, he decided not to ignore the event, as one might expect, but rather to throw a party up in the Lakes and play a birthday gig with Mo Witham in their regular Mickey & Mo guise. As this book was well underway at the time its author naturally wanted to be there but was pre-booked elsewhere and so, sadly, could not attend.

Luckily for those of us who weren't able to make it, Swedish fan Hakan Pettersson could and recorded in his blog some of what went on during that weekend of celebration:

"In the Eskdale area lays the small village of Boot, where Mickey Jupp has lived since 1983. On the big birthday on Thursday, Lasse Kärrbäck, (who runs the Mickey Jupp website), me and our wives went to Mickey's home in Boot. We were let in to Mickey's bohemian home, with instruments and recording equipment upstairs. Mickey told us among other things that two new songs he is currently working on are called *Seeking Perfection* and *Fine China*. He also told me that it was a pleasure to write new material, but it was hell to record. 'As soon as the red light shines, I think things will be difficult to achieve, to make the most of the song and it locks me up', he says.

Mickey has always had a kind of performance anxiety both on stage and in the recording studio that often made him change or withdraw. He is of a sensitive nature, a man who prefers to remain anonymous and not be centered in the tough music industry. He is a paradox in other words. In the afternoon of his birthday a large number of friends and fans gathered for a dinner at the Brook House Inn. A cheerful and surprisingly funny Mickey told some memories and episodes from a long so-called "career". He also showed off his special place in the corner at the bar of the Brook House Inn, known as "Grumpy Corner". Mickey is often described by the English word "curmudgeonly" but this night, and the next it was a sociable, friendly and spirited Mickey who wanted to take all people in his arms."

Quite a few fans made the trip to Cumbria to help their musical hero celebrate his landmark birthday. They brought good wishes and gifts: items of memorabilia, specially knitted jumpers, that sort of thing, but there was one present that was a real surprise. Russ Cottee explains:

"Fellow fan and friend Koos de Korte approached me to collaborate on a couple of songs as a tribute to Mickey on his 70th birthday gig at The Woolpack (one of which was a re-write of *Standing At The Crossroads*). I took my Gibson 335 guitar, as it is semi-acoustic, meaning I could have a run-through without the need for an amplifier - it was not an instrument that I played to any great extent.

My Finnish friend Sirkka put the thought in my head of giving it to Mickey as a gift - so only a very few people were in on the idea. Having played the two songs with Koos I simply handed the instrument to Mickey and explained that it was a thank-you for all his music through the years. I knew that he'd sold his Guild and Microfrets semi-acoustic guitars and that he was a fan of hollow-bodied instruments. He was literally speechless – probably for the first time ever!"

While Mickey was evidently happy to celebrate becoming a septuagenarian, he did not intend it to be the end of the road as a writer or performer. In fact, in June 2014, he returned to Club Riga, with Mo and some other old friends, to play his usual hometown gigs. Craig Chaligne reviewed the concert for *Record Collector* magazine:

"Mickey Jupp and his band, featuring long-time musical foil Mo Witham on guitar, Dennis Masterton on bass, and ex-Paramounts drummer Mick Brownlee, opened with *Cheque Book*, from 1971's *Legend*. The set-list also featured a few newer songs from the four albums that Mickey has issued in recent years. Highlights included nice versions of *Trying To Unlike You* and *Song For Holly*, plus a rousing *I Should Be Lovin' This*. The set, divided into three parts, didn't bypass his more famous tunes, all the classics getting an airing, notably *Standing At The Crossroads Again, Switchboard Susan* and *Big Black Cadillac*. Some rarely played numbers were dusted off too, *Don't Talk To Me* being introduced by Mickey as 'the nearest to a hit record I ever got'. He appreciated the crowd participation throughout, especially on the sing-along *One Night With You*, and the band closed with a rocking encore, including *Bye Bye Johnny* and *Rockin' Robin*".

And so, pretty well fifty years on from the time he first did so with the Orioles, on exactly the same spot, Mickey ended his show with the song he always used to – *Rockin' Robin*. But it wouldn't have been a true reflection of those fifty years if there hadn't been a spot of bother between the personnel, as bass player Dennis Masterson himself observed:

"After the first gigs I did with Mickey in 2000 and 2001, it had fizzled out until 2011, when he came back down from the Lakes with Mo and asked me to play bass, with Mick Brownlee back on drums. I was playing with Tony Sumner in Hunt, Runt, Shunt and Cunningham at the time so we did the first half of the gig, me on guitar, and then I switched to bass and did the second half with Mickey, Mo and Mick. In 2012 it was the Legend re-union, so Mick and I weren't involved.

Then 2013 it was me back on bass, with Mick on drums, with the support act being Bob Fish, ex-Darts and ex-Mickey Jupp Big Band. This year, June 2014, we had the rather ill tempered affair".

It was indeed rather a black dog of a gig. It certainly felt that way from the audience perspective on the Friday night. Dennis confirmed it was no better up on stage:

"You never get a set list or a run through, which I find quite hard – especially with stuff he's written recently – so it's always a bit tense. On the Friday gig Mick's old Yamaha acoustic guitar had no sound at the start of the show and that threw him a bit. Even though people had flown in from Europe to see him, he was snarling and swearing and carrying on. The atmosphere was terrible. It was better on the Saturday, thank goodness."

Drummer Mick Brownlee recalls the pair of gigs with a similar shudder:

"He's a very difficult man to work with – he's so far up his own arse sometimes. I get paid to do a job playing with him so that's what I do, but he's getting worse, especially those last ones at the Riga. The Friday night he was terrible, in a foul mood, saying to me and Dennis, 'Have you two ever played together before?' that sort of thing. Then the Saturday night we played probably the best we ever have together. At the end Juppy says to me, 'Thanks, Mick'. Whether that just meant that for the night or whether it meant, 'Thanks for everything because we won't be playing together any more', I'm waiting to find out!"

Not only was Saturday night good for the audience, it appeared to be good for Mickey, too, as old hand John Howard, in the crowd, commented on:

"England were playing in the World Cup that night, and it was on the telly at 11pm. As he's a football fan, we all assumed Mickey would knock the show on the head pretty sharpish. But at 11.05 he comes back on and plays another hour!"

On the other hand, John Denton recalls that before the show that night Mickey was beset by doubt, saying how nervous he felt and "looking like he wanted to run away."

Frank Mead was also there and sought out Mickey before the show to wish him luck. "I saw him before he went on, and Juppy gave me a great big hug, That wrong-footed me because he'd never done anything like that to me in his life before!"

Emotions clearly were running high. As well as owning up to this sort of lack of confidence, Mickey readily, if shamefacedly, also confesses to his inherent shortness of temper, although maintains that it's only the niggly little things that get him going:

"I remember doing a Paris gig, at the Olympia – just for the press so there was nothing much to go wrong. My amp blew up and I broke two strings. I thought someone up there doesn't like me. We came back to England to do a gig that night or the one after at the Half Moon in Putney, there my replacement amp fizzled out. I just wanted to curl up and go home. Sometimes you think, why bother? Little things that go wrong, the things you ought to be able to take for granted, that's what does me in. I'm cool with the big disasters but I dread changing light bulbs or breaking eggs into a frying pan – they're the things that always go wrong."

Several of the Riga audience, that Friday night at least, wondered whether Mickey would see his bleak on-stage experience as a timely nudge to retire, at least from full band performances and the dreaded motorway treks needed to get from Cumbria to Essex and back. (On the morning they set off from Cumbria to play those gigs, Mo had asked Mickey how he was feeling. In reply, Mickey hadn't referred to the upcoming shows, the state of his voice or how well he had slept the previous night. All he said was, "Great – because we'll be back home in 48 hours time").

We shall see if and when the centrifugal pull of Cumbria claims him forever.

What we shall not see, regrettably, is Mickey at the Cricketers/Club Riga ever again, for in September 2014 came the shock announcement that the venue was to close for good. Club Riga may live on in new premises elsewhere in Southend but a fifty-year link has been broken. No more sticky carpets, roaring audiences or echoes of that special sixties musical magic shall dwell in Southend's London Road.

No more Cricketers/Riga gigs, no more studio recordings – no way forward, then.

Except there had been, had Mickey not chosen to change his mind once again: for at seventy he was proving still to be as unpredictable as twenty years earlier. At the time of those very seventieth birthday celebrations, there were secret but advanced plans in hand - plans that had been fifteen years in the making - for a further studio album, according to the man behind the initiative, good-old Lasse Kärrbäck.

The new album, to be recorded in Sweden, had a working title of *Songs for Holly*, two demos already having been dispatched to local backing musicians for them to learn. The team involved in the project involved Mo Witham, Chris East and – especially interesting given his past work with Mickey – Mike Vernon. Micke Finell was lined up as producer. The only person not on board in the end was Mickey himself. As per normal.

So all that his fans seemed to have left now was his writing and the resulting demos. Some of his friends have long suspected that whatever happens regarding playing in bands, there may never be a full stop to Mickey's writing – not while he has breath in his body and a keyboard in his home. Yet early in 2014 he did post a Facebook plea about a dry spell:

"Well folks, I am trying veeeeery hard to work on a new song or two, but I am so fucking bored, bored, bored. And the annoying thing is that that's the way I feel every time now. I wouldn't know a good song if it walked up to me and bought me a beer. I really am beginning to think that I don't have any more music in me."

In April 2014, while the first edition of this book was being written, things worsened: Mickey put his recording equipment up for sale, telling this writer he was "stepping back, maybe retiring, but not giving up." Thankfully, within a month he was back on Facebook celebrating the fact that he had written three songs in a single weekend!

It appears that for Mickey, producing new songs is rather like producing milk must be for a cow: instinctive, unavoidable - rather painful if you stop. To an outsider, the prospect of stopping dead after doing something so fundamental for so long seems an alien concept, particularly as Mickey's motivation, his need to write, has always been so clear. Interviewed by Ron Bijnen in 2009, Mickey said:

"I'm writing songs for myself in the first place. I get a kick that satisfies me when I write a new song. Then it doesn't bother me what someone else thinks of it.

It won't make me rich anyway. And being famous doesn't appeal to me.

When I'm out of money I will play gigs for a while again."

But by late 2014 he had suffered another crisis of confidence, as he explained to me:

"A few weeks ago, in a pretty low way, I left the Facebook Fans of Mickey Jupp Group because I didn't want to be Mickey Jupp any more. He is this character I'm not – I felt I could no longer contribute anything to being him. I wondered what it would be like to be Michael again, so I changed my Facebook name to that. At school and in the Orioles I was Mick, so old friends tend to call me that. Close friends sometimes call me Juppy, which I don't mind. I can't remember for sure who named me Mickey - I suspect it was Dave Watson, my first publisher/sort of manager – so that's the name I associate with this other character. Mick was just a shy little chappie playing with his model railway while his brother was going out to the clubs and stuff. I was not a very outgoing sort of person. When I got in the Orioles and became the singer, I started getting all this hero worship and it turned my head. I was thinking what's going on? And ever since then, it's never been the real me. The guy sitting at home, playing with his model railway – that's the real me. I'm just a bloke who plays a guitar and writes a song from time to time.

It's very embarrassing when people call you a genius, and it's happened quite a few times now. It even feels odd to have fans – it's almost embarrassing, like you writing this book is. No offence," he adds.

In an attempt to get back into the old routine Mickey had tried something radical:

"I bought this brand new 24 track Tascam Portastudio in August to see if it would re-kindle any enthusiasm, but it didn't, just sat in its box. Up until last Sunday, when I was so bored because I'd injured my foot and couldn't walk or do much, that I wired it up and I'm working at a little song at the moment. I'm quite pleased with the song – its called *You Stupid Moon*, a bit Dean Martin, actually. And I've got another called *Cute* that I haven't recorded yet. So I'm back – maybe."

Mickey eventually rejoined the Fans of Mickey Jupp Facebook group, fellow member Marilyn Inman perceptively emailing him "I think you just needed a rest from your split personality: half star, half ordinary person". But for a while he retained the name Michael Jupp.

But whether he is Mick, Michael or Mickey, he is never going to be a wealthy man. To those of us who lack his prodigious talent it seems hard to believe that Mickey's simple life could be sufficient reward for a career that might so easily have ended with big homes, big cars, big swimming pools and a trophy wife, (who would no doubt have looked like Susan George). Yet Mickey is OK about it. He never expected to make much, because he has never really appreciated how exceptional his talents are, or perhaps how close he got to the breakthrough. Anyone who possesses great ability tends to undervalue it. Concert pianists are likely to marvel at the skill of athletes, if that's an attribute they lack. And vice versa. But that might not matter as much as something else.

Music business bigwigs frequently observe that talent alone is not enough to guarantee success. Simon Napier-Bell - who managed real stars of their times, like Marc Bolan and Wham - points this out in his book on the history of show business, *Ta-ra-ra-Boom-de-ay:*

"Being a musician was always poorly paid; being the star was what made you a fortune. And stars were the lucky ones. Not always the most talented; they were the ones who arrived at the right moment, were prepared to let the industry manipulate them, and had just enough talent to build on their moment of good fortune."

And so it is that those who know Mickey well are less surprised about his lack of commercial success than those of us who only know him through his wonderful music. Dougie Sheldrake, the Orioles' guitarist of fifty years ago, doubts Mickey ever wanted to be a success from the start. He points out that Mickey never produced music that his era was naturally inclined to buy, quoting music presenter Bob Harris' view that Legend were a band 'most deserving of success but most unlikely to achieve it'. As Mickey himself put it to *Hot Press* at the time of the Stiff tour "I'm not bitter and twisted about it, I've just missed my chance." And that was before he missed a whole lot more.

Instead, Mickey has managed to have the career elements he most wanted - songwriting and relatively low key performing - without too much of the elements he most hated: the business of the business - like promotional work and the pressures of constantly touring major venues. He calls the shots now - every single, orderly one of them. But the price has been not making it as big as he could have, had he been prepared to give a little more. Will Birch is very clear about Mickey's failure to make this vital trade-off. To him it's part unpreparedness and part unsuitability:

"I wouldn't want this taken out of context because I'm one of his biggest fans. He's a genius: a great singer, great songwriter, but what Mick isn't very good at, and why should he be, is being savvy about self-promotion and how to position himself as an artist. Mick's a little bit embarrassed by that aspect of the business. He thinks it shouldn't matter: like if you're Bobby Bland or BB King or Chuck Berry, the music should speak for itself. Unfortunately, it's the *entertainment* industry and the look of the product is more important than the sound. If it looks better than it sounds, great. If it sounds better than it looks, you are marginalising the chances of success. Some artists accept this, some don't, but the fact is that unfortunately the music does not speak for itself."

Wilko Johnson recently pointed out in a radio interview that he, Wilko, is not so much a musician as a performer – and that he's a man who actually doesn't play his guitar much unless he's on stage. Mickey has always been the opposite: a man who produced songs for fun and is then forced to perform in order to get them recognised - validated, if you like. Tex Comer has seen this occurring and re-occurring down the years:

"He much preferred the low-key kind of thing; he wasn't too keen on big stages, big halls, the adulation, having to do the interviews. Give him a little back room in a pub; then he was as happy as Larry. I talked to him a number of times about it because whenever things got to a high professional level you could see him visibly crumbling a bit. It rattled him, so he wouldn't grasp it with both hands. He had the opportunity to build a career but he missed out on it, maybe ducked it; but he knew what he was doing - he just didn't want to go down that road."

Analysing all this it's suddenly clear that Mickey's greatest curse, ironically, has been that amazing voice. Were he a songwriter with a voice nothing more than OK – think, say, Jimmy Webb - the world would have been perfectly happy to leave him alone to get on with his writing. But that voice of his cannot be ignored, it's just too good. People want to hear it. Coupling it with his ability to play piano and guitar so well created an irresistible demand for performance: no, you may not just write songs, you must play them, too. Keith Reid certainly sees it this way:

"He was too good just to be a songwriter - too good a singer – but he's definitely a person who goes into meltdown, who can't handle the big pressure. Really in a way he should have stuck to writing songs, all on his own. Actually, when he's out of the pressure, he even sings better!"

Or as Will Birch put it in the 1972 Roger Deakin TV documentary *Southend Rock*, "For somebody to be almost burdened with being that good a singer *and* that good a songwriter, well for most people it would be too much for them".

I asked Will if Nick Lowe, about whom he is currently writing a biography, ever talked about Mickey these days:

"We talk about Mick all the time! Nick has nothing but admiration for Mick but thinks that Mick is burdened by talent and embarrassed by it, so when fame comes knocking, Mick is always wanting to be busy doing something else. Nick says 'It's as if he was being chased by fame but he didn't want to know'."

While we may find it hard to believe that a man with so much talent could fail to capitalize upon it, promote it at every turn, scheme at ways to bring it to the widest possible audience - that isn't how Mickey sees it. He knows that you either want to make the music or you want to be a star. It's a choice on which Simon Napier-Bell expressed a further view in another of his books, *Black Vinyl, White Powder*:

"The only thing to look out for as a manager, is that the musicians you represent have a total, obsessed, near-suicidal need to be a star. Nothing else matters. The energy and push that makes them a star comes from them, not you."

Many artists who have made it really big are prepared to recognize this rather unpleasant need to drive themselves forward, even over the bodies of others. Don Henley of the Eagles is a great singer, songwriter and drummer, yet doesn't believe these skills to be responsible for his global success:

"I don't want to discount talent and ability but I still maintain that a lot of it is just sheer desire. You've got to want it more than anything else in the world and be able to do whatever it takes. Most of all you must believe in yourself – believe you can do it".

Contrast that with Mickey on the same subject:

"People have had confidence in me, a confidence that I have never had in myself. In my career I said 'no' more times when I should have said 'yes'."

Seasoned music journalist, respected broadcaster and influential label manager, the late Charlie Gillet, knew a thing or two about quality artists and their priorities, having discovered and developed acts as varied as Dire Straits and Ian Dury, as well as producing Lene Lovich's hits, licensed to Stiff by his own Oval Records.

In the past, Gillett had used his radio shows on BBC and Capital Radio to champion Mickey's cause and, as we have seen, once tried to sign Mickey to his label. Here he is, in an unpublished interview, talking about how some artists take to fame while others don't:

"It was an interesting discovery that neither the artist themselves, nor us as the A&R department, knows what will happen when the spotlight shines on someone – it's really, really difficult to tell. Over the years quite a lot of people look as if they're going to be able to deal with it, and that's what they want, but when it comes, it turns out it isn't."

Wilko Johnson made an interesting point to me, suggesting that even if one didn't set one's cap at stardom in the first place, should success comes towards one, it may be prudent not to struggle against it:

"Just because somebody has got an extraordinary talent doesn't mean they want to exercise it. I didn't intend to do this music thing, it just happened and I got swept along. Nowadays, I've stopped moaning about the downsides. It might have started by accident but it's what I do."

He's right. For should you want to reach the very top and stay there, you will have to stop treating what you do merely as an outlet for your personal musical agenda and start thinking box office instead. Lou Reed's wife once commented on how much Lou hated playing his hits, those numbers the audience demanded, like *Perfect Day*, until as she puts it, "He realised the fine print of the contract he had with the world: if he wanted to be a star he had to give his audiences what they wanted."

Mickey never wanted to be a star or play the rock and roll game or give the public what they wanted. And he never, ever read the small print. Right from the beginning he knew he was never going to play ball, he just didn't let on to anyone in case it caused problems. Just listen to him summing up his fifty-plus years in music:

"I may be peculiar, but I never occupied myself with drugs or religion. I'm pretty proud of that, for they seem to be the big solution for maladjusted rockers. Neither am I self-destructive like everybody says. I just don't care that much what will happen to me. I don't try and upset anybody but that's my way. People say I missed my chance; that it all went wrong, but I don't think it did. Every so often people would say 'come and make an album' and I'd say 'alright then'. To be honest, I'm a bit of a bastard to get on with – I like my own space too much. Now I'm writing songs and doing the odd gig now and again and I'm quite happy. I live in Eskdale and from my back garden I can see mountains and cows grazing in the fields."

It's difficult to argue with that. Mickey had no responsibility to us to become a star, or to ensure his music reached an ever-widening audience. He only had a responsibility to himself to pursue his music making however he thought best. Had Mickey looked back on his career and regretted what he did or didn't do - those occasions when he appeared to sabotage himself just as fame was within his grasp - we might feel we had a point. But he does not. In fact, by taking himself out of the game early he made sure didn't have to cope with any feelings of failure. Best to walk away before you are asked to leave, just as Mickey wrote in his song, *Cheque Book*:

I heard my mama and papa talking
They had some words to say.
They said 'get out!'
I said 'I'm leavin' anyway'

Mickey's ex-manager, Nick Blackburn, believes that Mickey never understood, or bothered to understand, the non-musical qualities necessary to succeed:

"Mickey always had plenty of great material – the problem was he was a really difficult character. He was contrary; he had a chip on his shoulder. He didn't know what he had to do to be successful, outside of writing the actual songs. The successful artists I dealt with - Ian Anderson of Jethro Tull, for example - knew exactly how they were going to run their career. As his management, we were just there to facilitate that vision. To succeed you've got to play the game: sometimes that means saying thank you even if you don't mean it.

You can't go around being rude to people like DJs and then expect to make it. That's why Oasis never made it in the States. Mickey just wrote songs and thought it would happen if other people did things for him. He didn't want to do enough himself. Nor was he ever grateful for the help he was given. He was never happy with anything and he never knew how to say thank you."

I asked Nick if there was an event that he felt summed up this failing. He isolated one particular example:

"At one point we took Mickey and his band to Paris to play a Press gig there, as his reputation was growing... and the show was unbelievably bad. He spent the whole night complaining about the sound. He kept stopping songs and moaning. He only likes playing live if there's no pressure – if it's a pub gig or something like that and he's feeling in the mood – but he screwed up that night. The French record company were there and he was so rude afterwards, asking if they were taking him out to dinner. Of course, they were very polite and took him out, but they had already realised it wasn't worth working with him, which was a complete disaster. It was an awful evening; one of the most embarrassing times of my life with an artist."

So, why? What could have possessed Mickey to behave like that?

"What I couldn't work out that night was whether he knew what he'd done or whether all his rudeness and being difficult had just passed him by. I felt it was possible that he didn't know how badly he was behaving. I've thought about it a lot since but I'll never know the answer."

Hot Press pondered the same question back at the time of the Stiff tour, writing:

"Perhaps Mickey Jupp is a fraud, craving stardom like most but being guided along this devious path by the shrewd Stiff starmakers. But more likely Jupp is an anachronism who only cares about writing a few songs and playing a whole lot of rock and roll, eschewing the fame his talents could readily bring."

Ed Deane has an interesting take on Mickey and what might have been:

466

"I just think that he intensely disliked the bullshit end of the music business. Maybe if there was an English equivalent to working just as a songwriter, like in the Brill building in the USA, then he might have been happy with that and been more successful. It's hard to say. I always enjoyed the edginess of his live gigs. It was an event in itself. I'm proud to have worked with him and I'm also proud of the handful of recordings I did with him."

Perhaps Mickey was simply exceptionally wise and far-sighted, somehow understanding that commercial success would have been his downfall, bringing pressures no honest man could be sure he'd be able to cope with. For Mickey hated everything he was doing other than the writing. However, as a man who avoided conflict, he didn't own up to this, which caused all the misunderstandings. He just carried on sort of doing it while hating it, dodging it, resenting it – limping on, making a kind of a living. He knew he wouldn't make it, maybe even relished the fact that one day it would all go away of its own accord. But he couldn't tell his managers and producers that, not as long as they believed there was an outside chance of success and continued to support him, invest in him. So instead he did it all with bad grace; which his managers worked out in the end, as Keith Reid summed up for me:

"That Stiff line about him - a legend in his lunchtime, or whatever - is very apt. He's the epitome of someone who enjoys being a big fish in a small pond; he's much more comfortable with that. He never wanted the big stage. I think he might secretly quite like to be very famous but he would never do what was needed to achieve it. Less talented people achieve a lot because they've got great ambition. Mickey's super-talented but he totally lacks ambition."

It's worth bearing in mind that while Mickey may seem a grumpy bunny these days, you won't find any period of his life when he has been much more cheerful. As he typically puts it:

"Is the glass half full or half empty? The odds are that sooner or later it will be empty, so expect the worst."

If not riotously happy, he seems at least to have been reasonably content of late, which I guess most of us would settle for in our seventies – although, despite his profound love of the Lakes, settle might not be quite the right term:

"For a long time this is the only place I wanted to be but it's getting to the point where I maybe could leave now – though where I would go I don't know.

Sometimes I think I'll move back to Southend but then I think that's pushing it.

There's a lot of good music down there but it's a bit of a dump. Though I could play a lot of gigs. In comparison, it's a desert island up here. On the other hand, I've moved away from this place twice and I've come back both times…"

Settled but restless, then: frequently packing it in, then taking it up again, having trouble inhabiting his own persona, a tiny part of which still wonders what might have been:

"The turning point was Derek Green saying he couldn't tell me why *He Could Have Been An Army* wasn't on the *Pearls album*. I thought, this sounds familiar, this keeps happening. I've made a lot of records - none of them sold. I've been involved with two recording studios – nothing ever happened. I had the gallery – I had to give up. It's like 'No You Can't, You're Not Going To, You'll Get Nowhere'.

There's maybe no God, but there is a Devil."

When compiling what became *Pot-Washing* - the CD he claimed at the time would be the swansong collection of his *Favourites* unreleased demos - a contender for final track on the final CD held a clue to how he was seeing his life:

"The song I'm thinking of closing with is called *The Right Room*. It goes:

I've never been in the right room at the right time, Not so as I recall, I may have been in the building, That is all."

He was even thinking of naming that - his final CD - after the final line: *That is All*, telling me at the time:

468

"I've had it with songwriting; my renaissance only lasted three weeks. I've run out of older songs – I don't think the quality is there. Maybe I need to crowd source a new bunch of songs with the Facebook fans group. It would help my financial dilemma and give me the impetus to write a new batch of material, knowing I wasn't wasting my time."

In the end Mickey left *The Right Room* off the CD and by early 2015 had actually put in place his earlier idea to crowd-source his next home-produced CD. He mailed his Facebook fans:

"Knowing that the CD would already be paid for, will - I'm sure - give me some impetus to actually apply myself more to the writing/recording process. I'll be honest - any boost to my finances will be very, very welcome at this time. I'm afraid that I am nowhere near being rich - never mind famous!!"

But he was famous.

As recently as the autumn of 2014 two events occurred that proved this.

Firstly, Repertoire Records issued that career retrospective collection, *Kiss Me Quick, Squeeze Me Slow*, comprising some seventy audio tracks and the long-lost *Long Distance Romancer* TV documentary. Packed full of old favourites, rarities, alternative versions and single mixes, it was a treasure trove of Jupp delights for any fan. The music press loved it, showering Mickey and his music with a fresh wave of admiration and respect, which Mickey shyly accepted:

"I do recognise that the box set is a great tribute – even though I gave away my copies. But I get just as much satisfaction from the first *Favourites* collection."

Secondly, also in the autumn of 2014, the highly regarded reissue label, BGO, released a remastered two-CD set of Legend's Vertigo albums, *Red Boot* and *Moonshine*. They both sounded fresh and timeless, something the publication *Shindig!* noted:

"*Red Boot* - with its tales of Greyhound buses, doo-wop backing vocals and New Orleans roll – was an unfashionably backward looking concept at the time but now stands as a peerless piece of Americana. The theme continues across the second disc, *Moonshine*, where the band sound like they're having the time of their lives channeling the spirit of Muscle Shoals via the Thames Delta."

Andy Snipper from the website *Blues Matters,* also reviewed the re-releases, commenting "Mickey Jupp is one of those artists who could have been massive but only if that was the way he wanted to go. His problem, if you can call it that, was that he was uninterested in becoming a star and more interested in having a life – commendable but in many ways a waste. These albums are a fitting reminder of what he could do."

Very well put but, from Mickey's perspective, expressed in the wrong tense. Could do? What about can still do? He told me,

"My problem is the past won't let me go. People keep digging me up."

So to put things right, Mickey now wrote, recorded and issued the sixth demo CD in his *Favourites* series, entitled, as mysteriously as ever, *Body-building*. He posted the following message on Facebook:

"Hi folks. A big thank-you to everybody who bought a copy of *Body-building* and other CDs in the *Favourites* series. Your response was far greater than I could have hoped for, and you really helped me to scramble out of a financial hole. *Favourites 7*? Well, you never know!!"

And lo and behold there was. In August 2015, a new compilation of his older material – entitled *Loose Ends* – was released. Followed in Spring 2016 by a familiar series of contradictory Facebook messages:

"Today - for the first time since January 2015 - I have just finished recording a NEW SONG !! "

Next day came this:

"Sorry, but the song has been binned. I listened to it again today, and decide it was crap. So - maybe in another 15 months or so ...."

A few weeks later:

"Once again, I find myself in dire – albeit temporary – financial straits. So – I ask myself – do I put another CD together? Would anybody be interested? Would anybody care? More to the point – would anybody be willing to pay up front for such a thing?" Followed by:

"Well - that's not a bad response !! Now if you all do that PayPal thing, I'll get the recorder machine out of it's box and get cracking !! I guess it'll be a few weeks before I have a finished 'product'. A few new songs, a few old ones. OK? Many thanks to all you kind people who have really helped me out of a hole - you know who you are. Right - I shall finish this cup of tea and then get the recording machine out of it's box and see if it still works."

And then:

"Up-date: I am trying to cobble together some new ditties to the best of my ability. However, I have come to the conclusion that there will be no guitar parts on any new material. I never did consider myself as any good on the guitar, but now I'm finding it virtually impossible to play, due to ageing wrists and fingernails that just won't grow (and if they do grow, they just splinter and break off). And using a pick is out of the question - it's just a barrier between my feeling for a song and the guitar. You have been warned.......and apart from all that, I can never get a guitar in tune - even though I've got gadgets that me tell that it's in tune, I just know it isn't. Maybe my ears are too good - or maybe they are knackered!!!"

All the same, *Songs From Grumpy Corner*, as the next CD was titled, did eventually see the light of day, with three new songs alongside more vintage material, a most encouraging sign. His fans had rallied round as they always did; always will.

At the time of the second edition of this book going to press, Jupp stalwart Roger Dopson is busy organising a re-release for *As The Yeahs Go By*, while Mickey has released another disc in the 'Favourites' series, by the name of *Tutford*, (featuring a sing about the legendary if fictional Tutford Darnell, his old band's nickname for the Dartford Tunnel!)

Meanwhile, another stalwart, Lasse Kärrbäck, is keen to find an outlet for two as-yet unheard live show recordings. The existence of the rest of the Dublin Castle tapes could prove more release material, as might the Spectrum tapes. Plus, of course, Mickey's vaults still contain scores more great compositions.

And the media haven't entirely given up either. Henry Scott-Irvine recently hosted a *Mickey Jupp Hour* on London's Resonance Radio, while the German station PopStop Music Radio ran a *Portrait of Mickey Jupp* show in December 2015. There was even a Mickey Jupp Fanfest event that took place in Sweden in the summer of 2016, complete with another fine CD of demos entitled *I'm An Old Rock 'n' Roller* and even a single, *Plankton*.

So maybe the musical story of Mickey's life has a few twists left in it yet.

But if it doesn't, who are we to complain? We got great songs, great singing and great playing out of the guy for fifty years. If he finally reckons it's time to duck out of the limelight and stop doing something he never planned or much wanted to do in the first place, what right do we have to moan about it?

After all, he'd warned us what was coming, right from the very beginning:

Now and then I like to leave this town
Go back where I used to run around
When I was young
Go back places that I used to go
See the faces that I used to know
When I was young
I like to leave my car and walk across the fields
Now and then I'd stop and sit and watch those daffodils
Where the wind blows lightly
And the moon shines brightly
And there's always heather on the hill

Heather On The Hill by Mickey Jupp

24 Epilogues

It is 2014, nearly 2015.

The Eskdale Valley is in the iron grip of a November evening truly starless and bible black. A freshening wind whips up the autumn leaves, mixes them into the thin drizzle and hurls them into the twin beams of my car's headlamps.

Up ahead I can just make out something glowing a welcome orange, smudgy through the trees.

The Woolpack Inn is packed with happy souls: drinking, chatting, laughing and waiting for the band to play. Some are locals; some have travelled from far away in the UK; some have even flown in from the continent just to be here for this little show.

Two veterans put down their beers and 'one-two' into their microphones. They are three feet from their audience, there is no stage, there are no lights; it matters not one jot. Mickey and Mo are on top form. We get oldies like *Cheque Book, Down at the Doctor's* and *Switchboard Susan*.

We get newies like *Song for Holly, The Difference* and *Trying to Unlike You* - even the rare,at the time unreleased, *Trees Died*. Perhaps most remarkably we get the song Mickey first sang at his Black Diamonds audition, and went on to feature as his first ever demo recording with the Orioles, Don Gibson's *Sweet Dreams*.

Mickey laughs with Mo, banters with the audience, gets us to sing along with choruses, asks us for prompts to regularly forgotten lyrics and constantly threatens us with "one of our famous breaks".

He looks ten, maybe twenty years younger than when he's not performing. He looks fifty per cent happier than he does when he's not performing. He is clearly in his element: relaxed and at home in his skin, more than fifty years on from his first gig.

As Wilko Johnson once put it, "he's just a geezer (but) he'd pick a guitar up and suddenly be transformed into something completely spine-tingling."

He will surely never stop doing this, not until he's in a wooden box.

And if he keeps playing, writing – even recording – he will stay younger than his chronological age. On which basis he might still be making music when he gets his telegram from the Queen. No doubt he'll write a song about it. Or so I thought at the time.

But in June 2015 – just as the first edition of this book was being checked by the man himself before going to press - Mickey suffered a serious bout of pneumonia. This both hospitalized him and caused a malfunction in one of his heart valves.

As a result, his doctors ordered him to take things easier, which meant curtailing his daily walks for a while and not putting himself through strenuous stage performances. Given this trauma, Mickey announced that his upcoming September 2015 gig with Mo at the Woolpack would be his last ever, bringing down the curtain on more than fifty years of music-making, (metaphorically, that is – there is no actual curtain at the pub).

We decided we had better make it the launch event for this book, too.

That night the Woolpack's big room was bursting with fans and well-wishers from all over the globe. Bob Fish acted as the warm-up act. Mickey then played a sequence of short sets to give himself a more gentle time than usual - signing copies of this book in the breaks while other musicians, including old confederate Chris East, took a turn up on stage.

Mickey was game but there was no doubting he wasn't looking 100%. Fragile and less sure than usual, he was actually looking his age, if not a little more. But the gig bucked him up no end, his confidence returning and his performance strengthening as the evening wore on.

By November, just a few weeks later, he looked a different man: back to his regular walks, talking about taking up painting again, even not ruling out the idea of journeying down south in 2016 for a possible musical get-together in Southend. So far, so good.

On the other hand he had already sold the 32-track recorder he had only just bought for the purposes of continuing his writing, an activity he now claimed to have finally put the lid on, (again). Yet, as Mo Witham pointed out to me, he hadn't yet sold his original 8-track, so there was perhaps still a chink of light.

But with Mickey it pays never to get your hopes up.

Those plans to get Mickey back to Southend for a 'tribute night' (although we were banned by him from using such a phrase to describe it) at which he and Mo would play a little, other local musicians with a connection would play – Russ Cottee and Steve Hooker were lined up - where Mickey could meet his fans 'down south' and have a chance to sat hello, or indeed, if he wished, goodbye, finally foundered. Initially he had agreed but then changed his mind. He would not be persuaded otherwise, firmly informing me that this time he really had reached the end of the road:

"I've decided that I won't be doing the gig at the Railway in May - or any other gig. Musically, I am dried up, empty - call it what you will. I've just left Brook House *(his local pub in Boot)* after only one pint because the background music was in my foreground. I am beginning to acquire an active dislike of music - any music. I find I am in a much better mood each day if I don't sit and try to work at writing and recording any music. I'm sorry, but I can do without it - it's been a long time."

You're right, Mickey, it's been a long time and we thank you for taking us on the ride with you.

But excuse us if we don't take no for an answer just yet. Forgive us if we keep on trying to persuade you back to the microphone. You see we aren't yet ready for the end of your music.

In fact, we can't help noticing that shortly after you were looking for crowdfunding for another new home recorded CD, which, of course, you got; that's how loyal we fans are, Mr. Jupp.

We reckon you've got another chapter in you: another twist in the story of your life.

That's our hope and it won't go away, not until you do....

25 The Final Word

From the man himself

courtesy Mike Wade

"*On the last page please quote me as saying 'If I'd have known that all this information was going to be so important thirty five or more years later, I'd have written a lot more of it down!'*

In fact I'm looking forward to reading this book so I can find out all the stuff I've forgotten."

Mickey also asked that the book should end with his personal summation of why he never made it as big as many of us thought he should:

"**Reasons to be not rich and famous:**
I never felt comfortable with the "being a musician" side of things.

I enjoyed the creation of songs, and I still do. But all the other stuff - gigs, touring, interviews, recording etc - I couldn't throw my heart and soul into, like people have to if they want to be a star.

I guess I'm trying to say that I didn't care for the heat, so I never really stepped into the kitchen."

Mickey Jupp, Boot, November 2014

Acknowledgements, Sources And Further Reading

Many thanks to my dear wife Penny, without whose encouragement, assistance and editing skills, writing this book would have been impossible, and without whose love and support I would never have finished it.

Many thanks to Mickey, without whose permission and co-operation writing this book would have been impossible, and without whose enormous talent and wonderful body of work I would never have started it.

My third thank you must be to Lasse Kärrbäck, keeper of the flame and curator of *mickeyjupp.se* and *mickeyjupp.co.uk*, without whose tireless work in compiling and cataloguing the minutiae of Mickey's career I would have been lost many times more than I anyway was, and for his permission to quote excerpts from his site.

I am hugely indebted to all those folk who gave up their time and passed on their stories by being interviewed for the book – in particular Mo Witham, John Bobin, Bob Clouter, Chris East, Will Birch, Wilko Johnson, Keith Reid and Nick Blackburn.

Also, for their valuable input, Frank Mead, Henry Scott-Irvine, Dougie Sheldrake, Dennis Masterton, John Howard, Kosmo Vinyl, Clive Mulcahy, Robin Slater, Tony Visconti, Anne Brown, Nick Ryan, Dave Stephen, Chris Stevens, Ed Deane, Steve Hooker, Tex Comer, Mick Brownlee, Roger Dopson, Russ Cottee, John Denton, Zoe Howe, Mike Stowers, Lynn Wagstaff, Axel Reisenhofer, Stuart Hopper, Ron Bijnen, Alain Noslier, Dave Vickers, John Garza and probably a few more I have forgotten – if so, please forgive me.

Plus, for the photo references, many thanks to Mickey himself, John Bobin, Dougie Sheldrake, John Howard, Russ Cottee, Chris East, Henry Grecourt, Lasse Kärrbäck, Stuart Hopper, Steve Hooker, Mark Williams, Jo Meijs and several others, whose names are on a scrap of paper I appear to have mislaid. Particular thanks go to Adrian Boot for kindly waving his usual fees for those splendid shots of the Stiff tour.

I am grateful to Mickey for permission to quote his masterful lyrics.

Source Material

Bark Staving Ronkers, a Music Memoir
John Bobin (*Booksurge Publishing* 2006)
Tony Visconti Talks
Grundy & Tobler, 'The Record Producers' (BBC Books 1982)
The Ghosts of a Whiter Shade Of Pale
Henry Scott-Irving (*Omnibus Press* 2012)
A Dysfunctional Success: The Wreckless Eric Manual
Eric Goulden (*The Do-Not Press* 2003)
Yeah Yeah Yeah
Bob Stanley (*Faber* 2013)
Looking Back At Me
Wilko Johnson with Zoe Howe (Cadiz Music 2013)
Rockin' Around Britain
Pete Frame (*Omnibus Press* 1999)
The Restless Generation
Pete Frame (*Rogan House* 2007)
No Sleep till Canvey
Will Birch (*Virgin Books 2003*)
Bowie, Bolan and the Brooklyn Boy
Tony Visconti (*Harper Collins* 2007)
Kill your Friends
John Niven (*Vintage Books 2009*)
The Big Wheel
Bruce Thomas (Helter Skelter 2002)
Ride a White Swan
Lesley Ann Jones (Hodder & Stoughton 2nd edition 2012)
It's Not Only Rock'n'Roll
Jenny Boyd (John Blake Books 2013)
Be Stiff
Richard Balls (Soundcheck Books 2014)
Ta-ra-ra-boom-de-ay
Simon Napier-Bell (Unbound 2015)
Cowboys and Indies
Gareth Murphy (Serpent's Tail 2015)
Lee Brilleaux: Rock'n'roll Gentleman
Zoe Howe (Polygon 2015)
Mickey Jupp: The Lost Legends of Southend Rock
Profile and Interview by Max Bell, *NME*, May 1975
Pub Rock Proms: For Those Who Like Their Rock Hot And Sweaty...
Chas de Whalley, *NME,* November 15th 1975
Review of Mickey Jupp Band in Penzance
David Brown, *Sounds*, April 22nd 1978
The Blues came down from Southend
Dave Brown, *Sounds* April 29th 1978
Love and the Poetry of monosodium glutamate
Giovanni Dadamo, *Sounds* October 7th 1978
Stiff Records: Be A Killer Or Be A Real Stiff...
Max Bell, *NME*, 28 October 1978
Mickey Jupp: Juppanese
Review by Max Bell, *NME*, October 1978

The rock 'n' rail tour
Angie Errige *Observer* magazine 19th November 1978
Southend Rock Family Tree
Pete Frame *Zig Zag* Issue 56
Going Up? Mickey Jupp
Mike Davies *Nugget* c. Oct 1978
Mecca! An article on Canvey and Southend
Will Birch, *Mojo*, November 1993
I am the most normal musician in the world
Muziek Express (Holland) September 1980
Southend Evening Echo article on Kilroy
Howell Llewellyn 1973
In   fact   rock'n'roll   is   very   disorderly   music
Utrechts Nieuwsblad 25-09-1982 (translated by Ron Bijnen)
Mickey Jupp; the best British rocker of all times
Written by: Jip Golsteijn for *De Telegraaf* Saturday 7th June 1980 (translated by Ron Bijnen)
Record Collector Magazine May 2014
Terry Staunton reviews of *Long Distance Romancer* and *Oxford*
Record Collector Magazine June 2014
Craig Chaligne review of Mickey Jupp at Riga
Record Collector Magazine December 2014
Daryl Easlea review of *Kiss Me Quick, Squeeze Me Slow*
Record Collector Magazine January 2015
Henry Scott-Irving article on Dr Feelgood
Uncut Magazine January 2015
Mick Haughton review of *Kiss Me Quick, Squeeze Me Slow*
Shindig! Magazine January 2015
Review of Red Boot/Moonshine re-issue
Mickey Jupp The legend of Legend
Ron Bijnen Platenblad issues 169&170, 2010
(Never) Too Old To Roll
Hot Press 12th November 1978
Mickeyjupp.se/co.uk
Lars Kärrbäck
Mickeyjupp.com
Chris East
Bucketfullofnails.com
Nigel Jones
Wilko Johnson
Rick Webb, bluesinlondon.com, March 2006
Things that go bump in the knight
Barney James blog
Mickey Jupp, 70, younger than yesterday
Hakan's Pop 16.3.14 Hakan Pettersson
Stuart Colman's Echoes BBC Radio London show
Sunday April 11th 1981 (thanks to Roger Dopson for the recording)
Repertoire Records "Kiss me Quick, Squeeze me Slow" box set sleeve notes
Will Birch
Shampoo, Haircut and Shave sleeve notes
Roger Dopson

Printed in Great Britain
by Amazon